SACRED REFUGE

Sacred Refuge

New Histories of the US Sanctuary Movement

Edited by
Lloyd D. Barba *and* Sergio M. González

New York University Press
New York

NEW YORK UNIVERSITY PRESS
New York
www.nyupress.org

Library of Congress Cataloging-in-Publication Data
Names: Barba, Lloyd Daniel editor | González, Sergio M., 1987– editor
Title: Sacred refuge : new histories of the U.S. sanctuary movement /
edited by Lloyd D. Barba and Sergio M. González.
Description: New York : New York University Press, [2026] |
Includes bibliographical references and index.
Identifiers: LCCN 2026002721 (print) | LCCN 2026002722 (ebook) |
ISBN 9781479833689 hardback | ISBN 9781479833702 paperback |
ISBN 9781479833719 ebook | ISBN 9781479833733 ebook other
Subjects: LCSH: Sanctuary movement—History—20th century | Sanctuary movement—History—21st century | Church work with refugees—United States | Church work with immigrants—United States
Classification: LCC BV4466 .S23 2026 (print) | LCC BV4466 (ebook)
LC record available at https://lccn.loc.gov/2026002721
LC ebook record available at https://lccn.loc.gov/2026002722

This book is printed on acid-free paper, and its binding materials are chosen for strength and durability. We strive to use environmentally responsible suppliers and materials to the greatest extent possible in publishing our books.

The manufacturer's authorized representative in the EU for product safety is Mare Nostrum Group B.V., Doelen 72, 4831 GR Breda, The Netherlands. Email: gpsr@mare-nostrum.co.uk.

Manufactured in the United States of America

10 9 8 7 6 5 4 3 2 1

Also available as an ebook

CONTENTS

Introduction

LLOYD D. BARBA AND SERGIO M. GONZÁLEZ

On August 15, 2006, Elvira Arellano entered Chicago's Adalberto United Methodist Church. Arellano had walked into that same storefront church countless times before as a faithful member of the congregation. But her arrival that day was anything but ordinary. She arrived not knowing when she would leave again. A deportation order hung over Arellano, who, while working in the country without legal authorization, had been detained as part of Operation Chicagoland Skies, an immigration raid designed to capture potential terrorists working in airports. By mid-2006, she had expended all legal recourse to stay in the country with her young US-born son, Saul. But Arellano still had one more risky and wildly uncertain option to pursue: to take sanctuary in a house of worship.

Arellano and the congregation at Adalberto United Methodist were not sure whether their strategy would be effective. The recently established and enormously well-funded Department of Homeland Security seemed intent on making an example of undocumented residents, all of whom purportedly lived in the country as potential national security threats. Those who gathered at the church in August 2006, however, sought to draw upon the strategies developed by activists in the 1980s, when houses of worship across the country had effectively organized to ward off immigration authorities and protect Central Americans seeking asylum in the United States. Arellano, like the thousands of migrants who had pursued safe harbor in churches and synagogues just two decades before, sought to test the limits of sacred refuge.

Arellano drew upon the historical precedent of the previous sanctuary movement as she charted a new course for her iteration of religious refuge. In describing her decision to take sanctuary in 2006, she noted that

> yo había escuchado acerca de los santuarios cuando los años ochenta para la comunidad de Centro América de El Salvador. Entonces yo conocía como en California en Boston que habían sido ciudades de santuario. Entonces yo decía "porqué no dar santuario a nuestras familias para no ser deportadas." Pero no había salido por allí un valiente o una valiente que dijera, porque para esto se necesita valor, no cualquiera lo hace. [I had heard about the 1980s sanctuary for Central Americans from El Salvador. I knew about how there were sanctuary cities in California and Boston. So I would say, "Why not give sanctuary for our families so they won't be deported." But there had not emerged a brave man or woman to say that, because that requires bravery, and not just anyone could do it.][1]

In the thick of massive immigrant-rights marches in support of comprehensive immigration reform and coordinated protests cropping up all across the country to contest anti-immigrant legislation in the mid-2000s, Arellano's stay in sanctuary infused the discourse on immigration with a palpable sense of sacred resistance.

Within a year of Arellano's entry into sanctuary, congregations and faith organizations joined together to launch a national movement for migrant justice. Dubbed the New Sanctuary Movement, this faith-centered mobilization sought to highlight the plight of families who found themselves in situations similar to Arellano's. But most of those seeking refuge did not enter quietly. Like Arellano, who on August 15 spoke to a room of reporters and supporters, those entering sanctuary made their cases public, seeking to infuse the brutalizing and statistic-centered narratives of immigration with a human face and tears. Arellano's courage to go public with her moving testimony changed (or at least challenged) hearts and minds across the country. By the end of the year, she had earned a spot in *Time*'s distinguished list of "100 People Who Mattered." Thanks to the leadership of immigrants like Arellano, the ancient practice of sacred refuge had found renewed life in the twenty-first century.

This activism, however, came with a high cost. In August of 2007, Arellano left the safety of Adalberto's sanctuary and traveled to Los Angeles to join national migrant-justice leaders calling for immigration reform for the country's estimated twelve million undocumented residents. As she left the city's historic Our Lady Queen of Angels Church,

Arellano was detained by Immigration and Customs Enforcement officers. The arrest occurred in front of a house of worship that had been an important hub for migrant activism for decades, one that held a particularly hallowed spot in the history of the US Sanctuary Movement. In the 1980s the church, also known as La Placita, had become known for revisioning the scale and scope of movement practices. Under the leadership of Father Luis Olivares, La Placita had expanded sanctuary ministry beyond the traditional aid offered by houses of worship to Salvadoran and Guatemalan asylum seekers, welcoming into their parish the city's growing number of undocumented Mexican residents who also feared deportation.[2] When Arellano chose La Placita as the church where she would take an increasingly more public and vocal stand against the country's increasingly draconian immigration policies, a position that would surely place her in the sights of federal immigration officers, she did so joining herself to a long lineage of sanctuary activism.

Over the last four decades, immigrant-justice leaders like Arellano, parishioners like those at Adalberto and La Placita, and countless congregations have called upon a higher power as they have demanded justice for the millions of undocumented residents who call the United States home. In invoking the practice of sanctuary, people of faith have blurred the lines among faith, politics, and activism, and in doing so have wrestled with fundamental questions about the borders that divide church and state. What obligation, sanctuary movement members have asked, do church people have to aid the newcomers to this nation, especially when those individuals and their families find themselves in the crosshairs of potential detention and deportation? And to what end will houses of worship follow the scriptural injunction to "welcome the stranger," especially if action in support of their undocumented neighbor means potentially breaking the law? In engaging in what sanctuary activists have continually referred to as a radical form of hospitality, movement activists in both the 1980s iterations of the movement and its twenty-first-century rebirth have understood their faith as being inextricably linked with their political priorities, engagements, and, most importantly, actions.

But the first decade of the twenty-first century presented new challenges for those committed to migrant justice. In a post–September 11th world, one marked by increased border security and a rising immigration-enforcement apparatus in the interior of the nation, undocumented immigrants who had long called the United States home found themselves unable to return to their countries of origin without running the real risk of never being able to cross back into their adopted homes. Unlike the Central American refugees arriving at the US-Mexico border in the 1980s, Arellano had lived in the country for many years. In their media appearances, Elvira and Saul described the United States as their home and themselves as Americans. Arellano, and sanctuary seekers who have come after her, have forced a national reckoning to confront questions such as, What is the place in the nation for undocumented residents who have lived here for years and call this land home? Will regimes tear apart families or strive to keep them together? Against this backdrop, there have persisted broader questions about what American traditions still matter in a rapidly changing world of global migration. What obligation does the United States have to offer welcome and belonging to supposed "newcomers"? How does the United States reckon with its complicated and oftentimes paradoxical immigration history, one that has seen the country posit itself as a beacon of refuge and a world melting pot but at the same time bears a long history of nativism, xenophobia, and increased hardening of its borders? Two decades since Arellano's entry into sanctuary, this volume has brought together scholars to reassess the history of the Sanctuary Movement as it has played out both in the more distant past and through the contemporary moment.

Sacred Refuge for Newcomers and Neighbors

Over the past decade, "sanctuary" has become a contentious political and cultural term. Following the election of Donald Trump in 2016, religious congregations, college campuses, and cities across the nation invoked the symbolic power of sanctuary as a way to aid undocumented immigrants at risk of deportation and to publicly rebuke the Trump administration's draconian immigration policies. They drew upon the traditions of the 1980s Sanctuary Movement, which offered safe harbor to thousands of Central American asylum seekers. Conservative politicians and pundits, meanwhile, have invoked the concept of "sanctuary" as a catch-all term to criticize policies that seek to welcome and integrate immigrants, refugees, and asylum seekers. This volume calls upon historians to contextualize what has become one of the most powerful traditions of social-religious contestation to governmental power in the United States over the past half-century. While at times attending to the spillover of sanctuary from the religious into the secular (such as in the case of sanctuary cities), this volume focuses primarily on sanctuary activism grounded in faith communities.

In the spring of 1982, six congregations in Arizona and California declared themselves places of safe harbor for Salvadorans and Guatemalans who had been denied legal proceedings for political asylum in the United States. Alleging that immigration officials had intentionally miscategorized Central Americans as "economic migrants" in order to accelerate their deportation, humanitarian organizations, legal advocates, and religious bodies sought alternatives for aid within their faiths' scriptural teachings and the juridical parameters offered by international and national human rights and refugee law. Known as the Sanctuary Movement, this decade-long interfaith mobilization of lay and clerical activists indicted the US detention and deportation system and the country's foreign policy initiatives in Latin America as morally bankrupt while arguing that human lives, regardless of documentation status, are sacred. In accusing the United States of being a violator of both domestic and international refugee legislation, subsequently exposing hundreds of thousands of people to persecution, torture, and death, the movement tested the idea that the country had always extended welcome to victims of persecution.

A central component of sanctuary mobilizations in the 1980s was the intentional effort to cross borders, be they national, religious, or political. The movement operated as a transnational and interfaith network of protection and resistance. In El Salvador and Guatemala, churches and lay people created the foundations of an "underground railroad," moving asylum seekers out of zones of violence and repression. Mexican churches became way stations along this network, offering both shelter and resources as Central Americans moved northward. In Canada, meanwhile, an "overground railroad" provided legal and public channels for asylum, especially when Central Americans failed to find reprieve in the United States. Together, these cross-border efforts formed a hemispheric web of solidarity, linking local acts of refuge to an international struggle for migrant safety and human rights. Along with a broad network of anti-interventionist and humanitarian aid organizations, sanctuary ultimately galvanized more than sixty thousand participants in five hundred faith communities across the nation. This transnational movement spurred congressional action in support of Central American asylum seekers by the 1990s and served as the model for a renewed movement for sanctuary in support of undocumented Americans in the twenty-first century.

Since the 1980s, sanctuary participants have interwoven their religious identities and political commitments in their drive to make the United States a more welcoming place for undocumented residents. Contrary to the way opponents have often framed sanctuary—as nothing more than radical activists cloaking their political ideology under the veneer of religious language—religious faith as well as centuries of hospitality practices have always been central to the way sanctuary practitioners understand their organizing. These individuals and their organizations have long appealed to "usable sacred histories," longstanding traditions of religious safe harbor that draw from biblical, medieval, and more modern examples.[3] This explains how the shared history of sanctuary that all people (especially Hebraic and European medieval, but all cultures have some culture of hospitality) can draw from should be accountable to modern crises that confront people of faith. The imbrication of the deep, ubiquitous, and religious and scriptural traditions of sanctuary is forceful, compelling people of faith to take up the torch. As William Sloane Coffin Jr., pastor of the historic Riverside Church in New York City, warned in the 1980s, the example of the German church and its inaction during the Holocaust should serve as a reminder to all those contemplating offering sanctuary in the face of potential state persecution that "it is not enough to resist with confession, we must confess with resistance."[4]

Since the initial movement's inception, a diverse set of practitioners, journalists, and scholars have traced the development of sanctuary in the United States. The first chroniclers of sanctuary activism were those directly involved with building the movement and working with asylum seekers. Their publications often focused on spreading sanctuary's message to the nation, serving as movement tools to politically conscientize Americans and bring them into the cause of refugee justice. When the Reagan administration's Department of Justice announced seventy-one indictments against sanctuary workers in 1985, movement insiders, which included academics and legal scholars who served as key mobilizers in places like Chicago and San Francisco, rushed to counter the White House's narrative about Central America and asylum law.[5] As the prosecution of sanctuary activists gained national attention, sympathetic journalists provided important historical context as well as blow-by-blow accounts of courtroom proceedings.[6] These early texts remain key sources for understanding the movement's development and social-movement strategy, as they offer a view from within, reflective of external pressure activists faced.

The 1980s movement also proved generative for scholars who had embedded themselves in the pews of sanctuary congregations. Ethnographers and social scientists who had attended discernment and organizing meetings, interviewed participants, and witnessed firsthand state prosecution published several books in the early 1990s. These texts constituted what we refer to as the first generation of sanctuary scholarship and by and large focused on mobilizations in Tucson, Chicago, and the San Francisco Bay Area.[7]

Research on sanctuary movements remained relatively sparse at the turn of the millennium, but renewed faith-based immigration activism in the early aughts brought a new crop of scholarship. A small cohort of sociologists, anthropologists, and political scientists constituted a second generation of sanctuary scholarship, offering both reappraisals of the 1980s movement and early studies of the burgeoning New Sanctuary Movement as congregations and religious organizations began to revive methods of sacred resistance as part of a broader national immigrant- and refugee-justice social movement.[8] Bracketing this period from 2006 to 2016, historians for the first time also began to analyze sanctuary activism, doing so in the context of broader regional and transnational histories of migration. Studies by Maria Cristina Garcia, which broadly analyzed Central American revolutions and migrations in the latter decades of the twentieth century, and Geraldo Cadava, which examined the development of borderlands communities in Arizona, offer important insights for understanding the origins and development of the 1980s movement.[9]

Donald Trump's election in 2016 and subsequent draconian immigration policies sparked a renewed wave of sanctuary activism while also spurring academic interest in studying these forms of sacred resistance. Over the last decade, a cross-disciplinary stream of scholars has generated a third generation of sanctuary scholarship. Historians have led the charge in offering books reexamining the influences and legacies of the 1980s movement. This reinvigorated Sanctuary Movement of the late 2010s occasioned historians to offer peer-reviewed articles and chapters covering the movement from Reagan to Trump's first term. And, in similar fashion to that of the journalists and academics of the 1980s, who left historians with much to reflect on in later years, several participant-observers (an interdisciplinary bench of theologians and ethnographers) have offered book-length treatments of the movement in real time.[10]

This book joins this third generation of scholarship while charting a new path forward for the historical study of the movement. It maintains attentiveness to the foundational religious and political ties that made the Sanctuary Movement a transnational phenomenon. Though anchored in the discipline of history, it draws upon a broader base of interdisciplinary scholarship on the movement. We have intentionally included in this volume scholars from anthropology and religious studies who write on the historical emergence of sanctuary. One particular motivation for a volume of this sort came as the result of current sanctuary scholarship lacking a deep grounding in the 1980s movement. The editors of this volume draw from our own original published scholarship, both academic and public-facing, that assesses the distinctions and continuities between the 1980s movement and more recent manifestations of sanctuary of the twenty-first century.[11] This book represents the first edited collection designed to provide a comprehensive historical analysis bridging nearly fifty years of Sanctuary Movement history.

This volume argues that the history of the Sanctuary Movement offers a central vantage point from which to assess sacred resistance, one that has developed at the intersections of faith, political activism, and transnational solidarity. Throughout the 1980s, the movement invited a collision between church and state, especially with elected officials and church leaders who professed to be deeply Christian yet established and supported unwelcoming and politically motivated refugee policies. While many members of the Sanctuary Movement may not have considered themselves politically liberal, they did understand their mobilization as a direct rebuke to the influence of the ardently conservative Religious Right that had captured the imagination and power of those affiliated with the administration of Ronald Reagan. Sanctuary activists challenged the government's refugee and foreign policies as well as the country's obligation to protect Central American migrants, doing so by centering Jewish and

Christian traditions of "welcoming the stranger." The movement ultimately sought to provide an ideological force counterhegemonic to the Religious Right's support within the Reagan administration. Their work went beyond merely injecting a sense of morality into the debate on Central America; in the words of the Chicago Religious Task Force on Central America, one of the movement's central organizing bodies, sanctuary's practitioners sought to deny the US government the "moral high ground" it desired as camouflage for its actions in the region.[12]

Central questions about immigration that dominated the last decades of the twentieth and opening decades of the twenty-first century continue to bedevil us today. Even as sanctuary in the United States arose in the 1980s as part of particular justice movements, at its core, it interrogated, and continues to interrogate, broader and more fundamental questions about immigration and human rights. The first movement arose as the number of undocumented residents living in the United States also began to rise; sanctuary, then, is inextricably linked to what has become an era of both unprecedented national and unprecedented international migration. With more than 281 million migrants worldwide, however, the United States only has a small share of this global phenomenon. Conflict, violence, and natural disasters have resulted in over 171 million displaced people globally, far outpacing any figure in modern history.[13] Since 2005, the number of undocumented people in the United States has fluctuated around 11 million, reaching a high of 12.2 million in 2007 and reaching a low of 10.2 million in 2019.[14]

In every decade since the 1980s, presidential administrations have framed the growing number of migrants arriving at the US-Mexico border as a crisis. Accompanying popular news sources have exacerbated this sense of threat and doom in the way they portray immigration.[15] As scholars of immigration have noted, the hardline immigration discourse and restrictionist policies that define the second Trump presidency did not emerge ex nihilo but have been fomented over nearly half a century.[16] Trump placed immigration at the front and center of his winning campaigns. In 2016, he fancied that he would build a "big beautiful wall," to the extent that the wall, though never completed, became something of a monument in the mind of Trump and his supporters, complete with rituals of sacralization.[17] For his 2024 campaign, Trump moved on to "mass deportation" as the panacea to solve the nation's criminal and financial woes. It is in this context of stark disagreements over the purpose of immigration and in times when undocumented immigrants have been most vulnerable that sanctuary leaders have risen to the occasion. It should not surprise us, then, that since the 1980s, the Sanctuary Movement has been activated for more years than not. And even in times when the movement has appeared to be dormant, it still surfaces when it is urgently needed, even absent a broader national movement.[18]

As volume contributor Kristina Shull has noted, decades of nativist rhetoric and restrictionist policies have made the United States the international leader in immigrant detention and deportation.[19] But this ramped-up immigration enforcement, carried out for various reasons, begs, at least, a simple question: What is the purpose of US immigration policy? And do these policies even work towards the end of expelling immigrants? Sanctuary activism serves as a reminder of how "refugees" and "families" are all too often swept into the dragnet of deportation. The United States' record urges immigration scholars and advocates to consider questions such as, Are US immigration policies fundamentally punitive? Do the policies aim to police, to punish, to make life more difficult?

Activists and scholars from the abolitionist tradition have turned to sanctuary to imagine how restorative and better futures are possible.[20] Relatedly, some scholars have examined the dynamics of sanctuary to debate the politics of deservingness and the potential pitfalls of a form of advocacy and allyship that can border on charity, interrogating how congregations decide who merits consideration for sanctuary stays.[21] Such debates also have major bearings on the categories used to define contested identities and political categories like refugee, asylee, and undocumented immigrant. And these categories and the process by which they are created and defined remind us to interrogate what the sociologist Zygmunt Bauman refers to as "the realm of moral obligations" that a country has towards newcomers:[22] What obligations do wealthy nations have to asylum seekers, be they people fleeing violence and war or people fleeing economic deprivation? How have foreign and security concerns guided immigration and refugee policies of a country like the United States? And how do we understand the status and place of those who fall outside of these unstable and mutable categories?[23]

Sanctuary participants have been asking these very questions for decades. In critiquing the nation's immigration and refugee policies, they

Figure I.1. *Basta!*, June 1985.

have forwarded a criticism of what they understand to be a duplicitous form of American welcome to newcomers. In the midst of federal prosecution of sanctuary activists in the mid-1980s, for example, the United States prepared to celebrate the centenary of the Statue of Liberty. Movement members questioned whether the federal government had forgotten the touchstone words emblazoned on the monument's base as they prepared their case against individuals who seemed to be lifting the lamp of safe harbor to those who most needed it. Rabbi Francis Barry Silberg of Milwaukee's Congregation Emanu-El B'ne Jeshurun found it "particularly ironic" that tens of millions of dollars were being committed to refurbish the statue and prepare for a celebration while denying refuge to Central Americans. As he noted sardonically, "Here comes the wretched refuse and we're turning them away at the gate. It's bullshit."[24]

Like Silberg, those offering sanctuary have transformed their consternation with the state's failure to live up to its obligations to asylum seekers and migrants into more than just anger. These perceived structural and moral inadequacies have served as a fundamental challenge to people of faith to enact the biblical mandate to "welcome the stranger," even if doing so brings them into conflict with federal officials. This volume seeks to understand, then, how American religious communities have for decades relied upon their faith teachings as they have responded to the needs of undocumented people, especially when those people find themselves in the crosshairs of potential detention and deportation.

As this book documents, sanctuary organizers have turned to a millennia-old tradition and its multivalent application as they have framed responses to the state's inability to welcome newcomers. "Sanctuary," as understood and practiced by communities of faith, bears something of a double meaning, one that holds in productive tension the tradition of sanctuary as a site that is always both "sacred" and a "refuge." The 1980s East Bay Sanctuary Coalition based in Berkeley, California, explained that "sanctuary" "has a seemingly curious double meaning, one of holiness and refuge." As the unnamed drafter(s) of the document further elaborated, "Churches are called on to bring these two meanings of sanctuary together into a powerful unity. The place of worship is to serve as a place of protection. Love of God and love of neighbor are inseparable. Faithfulness to God by preventing harm to sisters and brothers requires resistance against government practices that would do harm. The sanctuary as a place symbolizing holiness points to the primacy of God's compassion and justice over human authorities."[25]

This book attends to organizers' understanding of sanctuary as a "living tradition" while interrogating the material manifestations of sanctuary as a movement practice. It also takes seriously the East Bay Sanctuary Coalition's call for us to understand the practice of sanctuary as having multiple meanings. Since activists first declared sanctuary in 1982, the practice has transcended immigrant organizing and entered into political spaces that would have perhaps befuddled refugee advocates; over the last decade, for example, proponents of gun ownership and anti-abortion activists have appropriated the concept in their own efforts to build "Second Amendment Sanctuaries" and "Abortion Sanctuaries."[26] To better understand the capaciousness of the concept wrestled with expanding what one member called "'small s' sanctuary" as the movement continued apace and as leaders realized that they also had to help refugees settle in the United States, not just find temporary housing in houses of worship.[40] This wrestling with sanctuary for immigrants has entered its fifth decade now in the mid-2020s. While religious sanctuary does not enjoy any legal protection in the United States and sanctuary jurisdictions have faced legal challenges for over forty years, the movement thrives in a liminal space between church and state.[41]

During Trump's second term, sanctuary organizers still attempted to discern how to prophetically answer the call to provide refuge for the vulnerable. In this volume, we find that the answers are manifold and influenced by various streams of thought and histories. In sanctuary, the religious and the political are inextricably interwoven.

Book Roadmap

This book contends that a historically grounded understanding of the New Sanctuary Movement, which is ongoing, requires a close understanding of its 1980s iteration. Our attempt in this book to juxtapose sanctuary movements separated by no more than a decade (at most) calls us to address overlapping questions for the volume more generally as well as discrete questions. The chapters in this volume offer new historical perspectives on the religious dimensions of the movement's intellectual currents, various leaders and groups, and across sanctuary sites and historical moments. Together, these chapters offer intersecting interpretations of the cultural, social, and intellectual forces giving rise to the movement and help us to understand questions about and responses to immigrant and refugee justice, faith, and politics, and social-movement formation. Contributors to the volume show how the religious and faith-based grounding of the Sanctuary Movement set it apart from other forms of social movements, civil disobedience, and challenges to state power in the late twentieth and early twenty-first century.

The first seven chapters of this volume attempt to answer these questions with respect to the 1980s movement. Contributors address the historical antecedents in which Sanctuary Movement participants based their activism. Their chapters analyze the historical and contemporary domestic and foreign policy issues sanctuary responded to, as well as how the movement engaged with debates about the intersections between religion and politics in the 1980s. Across their chapters, contributors also investigate how the movement was a transnational, national, and local phenomenon.

With linkages between the two sanctuary movements constituting a core feature of the book, chapter 1 draws even deeper connections to historical antecedents. In it, Lloyd D. Barba and Katherine Holding draw out some of the main connections between sanctuary for Vietnam War resisters from the late 1960s to the early 1970s and the 1980s Sanctuary Movement for Central American refugees. In chapter 2, Kristina Shull analyzes the power and complicated nature of *testimonios*, a key organizing tactic of the Sanctuary Movement. Drawing from critical refugee studies, Shull interrogates the implications and pitfalls of testimony practices while recentering the importance of Central American movement leadership. In chapter 3, Adam Waters demonstrates how and why US activists endeavored to root sanctuary in Latin American liberation theology. Waters's chapter points to how important Latin American theological innovations were in making US Christian left internationalism in the late twentieth century. Chapters 4 and 5 describe the inner workings of solidarity built into the Sanctuary Movement. Mary Ward-Bucher takes readers to Philadelphia in chapter 4 to revisit the way we understand sanctuary leadership and activism, as Central Americans urged white Americans to move beyond charitable assistance toward a more collaborative work based on shared political struggle and reciprocity, though this aim proved difficult to fully realize. The New Jewish Agenda, as Rachel Buff demonstrates in chapter 5, mobilized a national platform to signal shared struggles and solidarity with Central American refugees.

The following two contributions take stock of reactions to the Sanctuary Movement. Sergio M. González examines in chapter 6 the conservative political and religious responses to the 1980s Sanctuary Movement. These religious neoconservative critics of sanctuary included the political operatives and intellectuals who fueled the political Right's march into the White House, and that pivoted their think tanks, newsletters, and considerable public outreach against sanctuary. Chapter 7 directs readers to an oft-neglected moment in the historiography of the movement, as scholarship on the 1980s movement seldom examines sanctuary after the Sanctuary Trial. In this chapter, Rady Roldán-Figueroa argues that by 1987 the Sanctuary Movement had reached a climactic point as demonstrated in a robust debate hosted by the Jerome Hall Dialogue that was held that year at Harvard Divinity School.

Contributors in the subsequent chapters of the volume examine the New Sanctuary Movement, both in its connections to its 1980s predecessor and in terms of the movement's distinct goals and characteristics. With varying degrees of emphasis, the authors interrogate how the twenty-first-century manifestation of the movement drew upon the early iteration of sanctuary while crafting new strategies in its organizing. They also ask us to consider what the New Sanctuary Movement can teach us about contemporary efforts to achieve immigrant, refugee, and asylum justice in the United States. In chapter 8, Carl Lindskoog analyzes at a macro level the reemergence of the Sanctuary Movement in 2007 and charts its growth and development in the years of the Obama and Trump presidencies. Lindskoog argues that the New Sanctuary Movement was not only revived but also reimagined as it differed from its predecessor in important ways, particularly in the degree to which it focused on domestic politics as its primary sphere of action rather than understanding sanctuary as an extension of an international solidarity movement for peace and justice. Chapter 9 follows organizations and institutions to trace sanctuary's development in California from the 1980s to the New Sanctuary Movement, as Tatyana Castillo-Ramos explores the contours of forty years of sanctuary organizing in California. She explores how sanctuary activists have expanded the scope of the movement in response to shifting local, national, and transnational politics, while consistently hewing to the tradition of sacred refuge. Following with another place-based study, in chapter 10, Gina Pérez examines how the sacred power of place, as fueled by abolitionist histories and legacies in Ohio, generated a particular ethos of "sanctuary people."

In the volume's last chapter, Susan Bibler Coutin draws from her nearly forty years of studying the Sanctuary Movement to offer a reflective essay on this volume's historical study of the Sanctuary Movement to the present. Coutin examines what immigrant rights mean today in light of the forms of solidarity created during the 1980s, when the 1980 Refugee Act's promise to provide access to asylum regardless of country of origin was still new. Based on interviews conducted with religious activists in the San Francisco Bay Area during the 1980s as well as ethnographic fieldwork within sanctuary congregations at that time, this chapter locates sanctuary practices within faith-based social-justice traditions, including antiwar movements, civil rights work, and refugee resettlement.

In our conclusion of the volume, we situate these histories of sanctuary activism within the broader arc of immigration politics and church-state relations, drawing attention to the unfinished questions that continue to shape both scholarship and activism. Surveying the fruitful field of sanctuary scholarship that still remains to be addressed, we call for future research that continues to trace sanctuary beyond national boundaries, examines the denominational and regional diversities inherent in the movement that have too often been overlooked by scholars, and considers how sanctuary has intersected with other forms of racial and social-justice organizing. At the same time, the conclusion underscores the ongoing challenges sanctuary activists face in an era of heightened border enforcement and polarized debates over immigration, where offering refuge can once again expose churches and faith leaders to prosecution and political backlash. By framing sanctuary as both a historical practice and a living, contested tradition, our intention is to highlight the tension between moral obligation and legal authority, urging scholars and activists alike to grapple with the enduring conflicts between personal conscience and the state.

NOTES

1 Elvira Arellano as quoted in *Elvira*, directed by Javier Solórzano Casarin (Grapevine Documentaries, 2009), www.youtube.com/watch?v=9b2kM8tJK-s. Accessed January 25, 2026.

2 On December 12, 1985, the feast day of our Lady of Guadalupe, La Placita welcomed a Salvadoran couple and a Guatemalan mother with her three young children into sanctuary. Olivares recognized the need to offer similar support to a growing undocumented Mexican Angeleno population, and within two years the parish was offering sanctuary services to Central American and Mexican migrants. See Mario T. García, *Father Luis Olivares, a Biography: Faith Politics and the Origins of the Sanctuary Movement* (University of North Carolina Press, 2018), 307–42.

3 Lloyd D. Barba, "'An Historic and Hallowed Principle in Religious Life': The Usable Sacred Histories of the 1980s Sanctuary Movement," *Journal of the American Academy of Religion* 93, no. 1 (March 2025): 18–44. Doi:org.amherst.idm.oclc.org/10.1093/jaarel/lfaf030.

4 Elizabeth Hull, "The Sanctuary Movement: The Fight of the Cross and the Flag," *Migration Today* 13, no. 5 (November 5, 1985): 6–16, cited on 9, Center for Migration Studies Archives, New York City, New York. William Sloane Coffin Jr. quota-

tion in Declaration of Sanctuary (Riverside Church Institutional Records, Record Group 9. Mission/Social Justice, Series 9.4 Programs and Activities of Mission/ Social Justice Commission, Sub-series 9.4.7 Sanctuary Movement, Folder Title: Social Justice—Disarmament—Declaration of Sanctuary—Oct 1984, Box # 131, Riverside Church, New York, New York).

5 Publications from movement insiders include Gary MacEoin, ed., *Sanctuary: A Resource Guide for Understanding and Participating in the Central American Refugees' Struggle* (Harper and Row, 1985); Ignatius Bau, *This Ground Is Holy: Church Sanctuary and Central American Refugees* (Paulist Press, 1985); Renny Golden and Michael McConnell, *Sanctuary: The New Underground Railroad* (Orbis Books, 1986).

6 Accounts of 1980s sanctuary by journalists include Robert Tomsho, *The American Sanctuary Movement* (Texas Monthly, 1987); Ann Crittenden, *Sanctuary: A Story of American Consciousness and the Law in Collision* (Weidenfeld and Nicolson, 1988); Miriam Davidson, *Convictions of the Heart: Jim Corbett and the Sanctuary Movement* (University of Arizona Press, 1988).

7 Robin Lorentezen, *Women in the Sanctuary Movement* (Temple University Press, 1991); Susan Bibler Coutin, *The Culture of Protest: Religious Activism and the U.S. Sanctuary Movement* (Westview Press, 1993); Hilary Cunningham, *God and Caesar at the Rio Grande: Sanctuary and the Politics of Religion* (University of Minnesota Press, 1995). See also Christian Smith, *Resisting Reagan: The U.S. Central America Peace Movement* (University of Chicago Press, 1996). Smith, a sociologist who was not embedded in the movement, contextualizes sanctuary activism within the broad Central America Peace and Solidarity Movement.

8 On the 1980s movement, see Sharon Erikson Nepstad, *Convictions of the Soul: Religion, Culture, and Agency in the Central America Solidarity Movement* (Oxford University Press, 2016) and Linda Rabben, *Sanctuary and Asylum: A Social and Political History* (University of Washington Press, 2016). The earliest studies of the New Sanctuary Movement include Grace Yukich, *One Family Under God: Immigration Politics and Progressive Religion in America* (Oxford University Press, 2013); Amalia Pallares, *Family Activism: Immigrant Struggles and the Politics of Noncitizenship* (Rutgers University Press, 2015); Randy Lippert and Sean Rehaag, *Sanctuary Practices in International Perspectives: Migration, Citizenship, and Social Movements* (Routledge, 2013).

9 Maria Cristina Garcia, *Seeking Refuge: Central American Migration to Mexico, the United States, and Canada* (University of California Press, 2006), 84–118; Geraldo L. Cadava, *Standing on Common Ground: The Making of a Sunbelt Borderland* (Harvard University Press, 2016), 172–211.

10 The following is certainly not exhaustive, but for important selections in the third generation of sanctuary scholarship, see Garcia, *Father Luis Olivares, a Biography*; A. Naomi Paik, Jason Ruiz, and Rebecca M. Schreiber, eds., "Radical Histories of Sanctuary," Special Issue, *Radical History Review* 9, no. 3 (October 2019): 1–191; A. Naomi Paik, *Bans, Walls, Raids, Sanctuary: Understanding U.S. Immigration*

for the Twenty-First Century (University of California Press, 2020); Carlos Ruiz Martinez, "The Question of Sanctuary: The Adorers of the Blood of Christ and the U.S. Sanctuary Movement, 1983–1996," *U.S. Catholic Historian* 38, no. 4 (Fall 2020): 53–70; Kristina Shull, *Detention Empire: Reagan's War on Immigrants and the Seeds of Resistance* (University of North Carolina Press, 2022); Domenic Vitiello, *The Sanctuary City: Immigrant, Refugee, and Receiving Communities in Postindustrial Philadelphia* (Cornell University Press, 2022); Sean T. Dempsey, *City of Dignity: Christianity, Liberalism, and the Making of Global Los Angeles* (University of Chicago Press, 2022), 107–30; Brad Christerson, Alexia Salvatierra, Robert Chao Romero, and Nancy Wang Yuen, *God's Resistance: Mobilizing Faith to Defend Immigrants* (NYU Press, 2023); Michael Woolf, *Sanctuary and Subjectivity: Thinking Theologically About Whiteness and Sanctuary Movements* (T&T Clark, 2023); Leo Guardado, *Church as Sanctuary: Reconstructing Refuge in an Age of Forced Displacement* (Orbis Books, 2023); Carol Lindskoog, "Sanctuary Is Justice: Resilience and Ingenuity in the Sanctuary Movement Since 1986," in *Whose America?: U.S. Immigration Policy Since 1980*, ed. Maria Cristina Garcia and Maddelena Marinari (University of Illinois Press, 2023), 190–208; Gina M. Pérez, *Sanctuary People: Faith-Based Organizing in a Latina/o Community* (NYU Press, 2024); Barbara Andrea Sostaita, *Sanctuary Everywhere: The Fugitive Sacred in the Sonoran Desert* (Duke University Press, 2024).

11 See Lloyd Barba and Tatyana Castillo-Ramos, "Sacred Resistance: The Sanctuary Movement from Reagan to Trump," *Perspectivas* 16 (2019): 11–36; Sergio M. González, "The Sanctuary Movement," *Oxford Research Encyclopedia of American History* (2020), https://oxfordre.com; Lloyd Barba and Sergio González, hosts, *Sanctuary: On the Border Between Church and State* (podcast), 2024, https://redcircle.com/shows/sanctuary-on-the-border-between-church-and-state. Accessed January 25, 2026.

12 "State of the Movement," January 1987, Box 1, Folder 1, Chicago Religious Task Force on Central American Records, 1982–1992, Wisconsin Historical Society.

13 David Scott FitzGerald, *Refuge Beyond Reach: How Rich Democracies Repel Asylum Seekers* (Oxford University Press, 2022).

14 Jeffrey S. Passel and Jens Manuel Krogstad, "What We Know About Unauthorized Immigrants Living in the U.S." Pew Research Center, July 22, 2024, www.pewresearch.org.

15 Leo Chavez, *Covering Immigration: Popular Images and the Politics of the Nation* (University of California Press, 2001).

16 See, for example, Timothy J. Dunn, *The Militarization of the U.S.-Mexico Border, 1978–1992* (University of Texas Press, 2010); Jenna M. Loyd and Alison Mountz, *Boats, Borders, and Bases: Race, the Cold War, and the Rise of Migrant Detention in the United States* (University of California Press, 2018); Carl Lindskoog, *Detain and Punish: Haitian Refugees and the Rise of the World's Largest Immigration Detention System* (University of Florida Press, 2018); César Cuauhtémoc García Hernández, *Migrating to Prison: America's Obsession with Locking Up Immigrants* (New Press, 2019); Jessica Ordaz, *The Shadow of El Centro* (University of North

Carolina Press, 2021); Elliott Young, *Forever Prisoners: How the United States Made the World's Largest Immigrant Detention System* (Oxford University Press, 2021); Kristina Shull, *Detention Empire: Reagan's War on Immigrants and the Seeds of Resistance* (University of North Carolina Press, 2022).

17 Lloyd D. Barba, "Trump's Wall: A Monument of (Un)Civil Religion?," *MAVCOR Journal* 3, no. 1 (2019), doi:10.22332/mav.med.2019.1.

18 Manuel Rodriguez, "Sanctuary Behavior: On the Eve of the New Sanctuary Movement," *Sanctuary Columns* (December 2020), https://sanctuary.wordpress.amherst.edu/columns/faith_history_theology/manuel-rodriguez/.

19 Shull, *Detention Empire*.

20 Paik, *Bans, Walls, Raids, Sanctuary*; Sostaita, *Sanctuary Everywhere*; Paik, Ruiz, and Schreiber, "Radical Histories of Sanctuary."

21 Woolf, *Sanctuary and Subjectivity*; Grace Yukich, "Constructing the Model Immigrant: Movement Strategy and Immigrant Deservingness in the New Sanctuary Movement," *Social Problems* 60, no. 3 (August 1, 2013): 302–20.

22 Zygmunt Bauman, *Strangers at Our Door* (Polity, 2016), 80.

23 Consider, for example, how the amnesty provision of the Immigration Reform and Control Act of 1986, the last iteration of what could be deemed "comprehensive immigration reform," applied only to those who could furnish proof of residency in the country *before* January 1, 1982, thus excluding many Salvadorans and Guatemalans who sought refuge in sanctuary networks. See Garcia, *Seeking Refuge*.

24 Sandy Tolan, "The Strangers Among Us: Milwaukee Churches Are at the Forefront of the Controversial Sanctuary Movement," *Milwaukee Magazine*, December 4, 1984.

25 "Historical and Theological Basis for Sanctuary" (Gustav Schultz Sanctuary Collection, Box 1, Folder 11, Graduate Theological Union Archives, Berkeley, California).

26 Tracy Garnar, Sione Lynn Pili Lister, and Jennifer Carlson, "Whiteness and Impunity: Examining Virginia's Second Amendment Sanctuary Movement," *Sociological Inquiry* 92, no. 2 (May 2022): 597–622; Nicholas J. Johnson, "Second Amendment Sanctuaries: Defiance, Discretion, and Race," *Pepperdine Law Review* 50 (2023): 1–92; Jennifer L. Brinkley, "Sanctuary Cities and Counties for the Unborn: The Use of Resolutions and Ordinances to Restrict Abortion Access," *Northern Illinois University Law Review* 41 (2020): 63–95.

27 See Barba and Castillo-Ramos, "Sacred Resistance."

28 John Fife, "No Middle Ground Between Collaboration and Resistance," in *Faith and Resistance in the Age of Trump*, ed. Miguel A. De La Torre (Orbis Books, 2017), 20–27.

29 William Sloane Coffin Jr. as quoted in "Sanctuary Press Conference, October 10, 1984," Riverside Church in the City of New York Digital Archive, created October 1, 1984, https://riverside.whirlihost.com. Similarly, Corbett reasoned that the Nuremberg Principle applied to Central American refugees. This post–World War II concept ordered that "everyone is obliged to obey international law mandating the protection of those whose rights are violated." See Jim Corbett, "Sanctuary, Basic Rights, and Humanity's Fault Lines: A Personal Essay," *Contemporary West* 5, no. 1 (Spring 1988), www.weber.edu.

30 See *Basta!*, January 1985.

31 Chicago Religious Task Force to Jim Corbett, February 16, 1984, Gustav Schultz Sanctuary Collection, Box 2, Folder 1, Graduate Theological Union Archives, Berkeley, California. For more on political disagreements within the movement on sanctuary as strategy, see Tucson and Chicago debate in Box 2, Folder 1, Gus Schultz. In early 1984, Tucson seemed to want to double down on a humanitarian route ("evasion services") while Chicago pushed back, arguing for the need to expand political organizing against US intervention, especially at a moment when the United States was expanding its footprint in California ("You reduce the multidimensional process of solidarity to a-political humanitarian band-aids rather than expanding it to include all that comes from choosing the side of the oppressed and truly being 'absorbed by the communities formed to serve the Kingdom' and 'adherence to the prophetic faith they proclaim.'")

32 Minutes of Meeting of Sanctuary Churches, Tucson, Arizona, June 20–21, 1985 (Gustav Schultz Sanctuary Collection, Box 2, Folder 29, Graduate Theological Union Archives, Berkeley, California).

33 Barba, "An Historic and Hallowed Principle."

34 Melvin Delgado, *They Are Rioting in Sanctuary Cities: Countering the Emerging Anti-Sanctuary Movement* (Rowman & Littlefield, 2021).

35 James Hennessey, "Sanctuary, Canon Law, and History" (n.d, n.p.) (Gustav Schultz Sanctuary Collection, Box 1, Folder 7, Graduate Theological Union Archives, Berkeley, California).

36 Tucson Ecumenical Task Force on Central America to the Churches, Organizations and Individuals Involved in the Sanctuary Action for March 24, 1982, March 11, 1982 (Gustav Schultz Sanctuary Collection, Box 1, Folder 11, Graduate Theological Union Archives, Berkeley, California). These private sanctuaries were largely unrecoverable in that they were never meant to be detected in the first place. In the early years, Tucson sanctuary workers estimated that one out of every twenty refugees they worked with decided to go into sanctuary. See also Jim Corbett, John Fife, and Phillip Conger to Chicago Religious Task Force, December 6, 1983, Gustav Schultz Sanctuary Collection, Box 2, Folder 1, Graduate Theological Union Archives, Berkeley, California.

37 Rabben, *Sanctuary and Asylum*, 276.

38 "Screening-Counseling—Orientation Process for Refugees," *Basta!*, July 1984.

39 "Screening-Counseling."

40 Bill Cadbury, "A Short Look at the Long Haul," *Basta!*, August 1986.

41 Lloyd D. Barba and Sergio M. González, "Sanctuary Cities Are Not New," *Time*, March 18, 2025, https://time.com.

1

Another Vietnam?

From Resisters to Refugees, Sanctuary in the Late Twentieth Century

LLOYD D. BARBA AND KATHERINE HOLDING

Introduction

On October 16, 1967, William Sloane Coffin Jr. offered the invocation at Arlington Street Church's Service of Conscience and Acceptance. Rounding out the sermon in which he declared the Boston church a "sanctuary of conscience," Coffin maintained that offering sanctuary was "an effort to make the church really a church."[1] With that assertion, he articulated sanctuary by framing faith-based action as central to the Church's mission. The events of that day embodied such action as hundreds of young men symbolically rejected conscription during the interfaith service. Some turned in their draft cards to clergy members and religious leaders, while others turned to the sanctuary's candles, burning their cards.[2] Coinciding with a national day of resistance, this event inaugurated sanctuary in the antiwar context, cementing the connection between the two efforts. Over the next few years, sanctuaries of conscience cropped up throughout the country.

Seventeen years later, on October 1, 1984, Coffin led the Declaration of Sanctuary service at New York City's historic Riverside Church. He began the formal declaration, "We are not here to say 'No' to the United States government out of a perverse rebellious instinct. Rather, we are here to say 'Yes' to the one we swear by and live for in this place—Jesus Christ; to say 'Yes, we'll join you,' to the 160 churches and synagogues that have already declared sanctuary; and to say 'Yes we will,' to sisters and brothers all over Central America who are asking us to help them stop the carnage."[3] With its declaration, Riverside joined hundreds of congregations across the country as part of a larger grassroots religious movement that offered shelter or support to Central American refugees. Once again, sanctuary manifested as an active ministry that contravened US law in service of a higher divine or moral law.

Coffin was but one of the various activists involved in Vietnam War–era sanctuary who went on to offer refuge to Central Americans in the 1980s. Although the two movements appear ostensibly separate and have largely been treated as such in existing literature, the widespread participation of Vietnam War–era sanctuary veterans in 1980s activism compels students of the Sanctuary Movement to reevaluate that connection. Rather than treating sanctuary for Central American refugees as entirely detached from that provided for conscientious objectors, this chapter elucidates the connections between the two movements, thereby introducing a novel framework to existing scholarship. While this intervention recontextualizes academic representations of twentieth-century sanctuary activism, many of the overlapping dynamics this chapter addresses would have been evident to those on the ground. After all, sanctuary organizers in the 1980s, as well as a broader array of critics of US involvement in Central America, could not help but provocatively query whether the US proxy wars in the region were amounting to "Another Vietnam."[4] And if so, what ethical and religious obligations did faith communities have to act? In response, to help the most vulnerable in the United States during these wars on foreign soil, religious activists summoned the power of sanctuary.

This chapter brings to light the vital links between the two movements as exemplified by key religious leaders and congregations. Considering the legacy that the sanctuary effort for Vietnam War resisters (hereafter referred to as 1960s/70s Sanctuary) left for the 1980s Sanctuary Movement, this chapter explores the parallels between the two iterations of church refuge. It then examines how the two movements approached sanctuary histories and traditions of conscience, drawing evidence primarily from the Northeast and the West Coast. Finally, it takes up the respective violations of sanctuary involving both legal and sacred dimensions. To be sure, this chapter does not seek to overly conflate the two movements, presupposing connections that did not exist. Accordingly, it also notes aspects of divergence. By assaying such continuities and contrasts, this chapter demonstrates how the 1980s movement developed as a distinct movement inspired by sanctuary for Vietnam War resisters. Was this "another Vietnam" moment as it concerned sanctuary? To some extent, yes; and in other strategic ways, no.

Context

Sanctuary and Social Movements

Twentieth-century sanctuary emerged in connection with existing social movements that opposed interventionist US foreign policy. In the late 1960s, antiwar demonstrations led by grassroots-activist movements opposed to US military presence in Vietnam—the Resistance—spurred conversations in progressive Christian churches about the Vietnam War and conscientious objection.[5] Likewise, the 1980s Sanctuary Movement (especially as it developed in the Midwest and the Northeast) arose in response to concerns articulated by the Central American Solidarity Movement and ecumenical task forces. Guided by underlying religious convictions and propelled by increased societal awareness of humanitarian crises engendered by US intervention abroad, congregations opened their doors.

Having been approached by Resistance leaders, Arlington Street Church (ASC) set into motion what would become 1960s/70s Sanctuary with its Service of Conscience and Acceptance following a five-thousand-person rally on the Boston Common.[6] The October 1967 service, which was "planned for the Resistance," provided a morally grounded space for approximately 280 men to relinquish their draft cards.[7] There, religion and resistance merged. One young man explained this by saying that, in handing Coffin his draft card, he "became part of the Resistance."[8] Uniting religious and social activism, the service offered a modern model for an ancient tradition. Sanctuary reemerged within the context of antiwar resistance. In fact, the New England Resistance later went so far as to claim that, given its collaboration with ASC, "the Resistance initiated the sanctuary movement."[9]

Following ASC's model, other religious bodies held sanctuary events in conjunction with major antiwar protests. On August 10, 1969, the Church of the Crossroads in Honolulu held its Celebration of Life, Love, and Revolution ahead of the Hawaii Resistance's GI Walk for Peace, which catalyzed a massive undertaking when seven AWOL soldiers joined a serviceman in sanctuary. Over the next five weeks, sanctuary brought together Resistance members and religious leaders as at least thirty-four individuals sought refuge there and at the Unitarian Church. The Society of Friends meetinghouse later joined the effort on September 11, but its participation was short lived because military police violated all three sanctuaries the following morning.[10] Similarly, the Unitarian Lutheran Chapel (ULC) in Berkeley declared sanctuary on November 7, 1971, in the midst of daily Stop Our Ship (SOS) protests.[11] Three days later, Berkeley became the first municipality in the nation to declare itself a sanctuary, citing in part ULC's position and local congregations' support for church refuge. Although the city council initially anticipated only a "small" number of sanctuary seekers, it severely underestimated the response, and fifty young men sought help at ULC within the first two and a half weeks.[12] In Berkeley, sanctuary brought together congregations, antiwar resistance activists, and local government.

As more religious spaces became sanctuaries for young men refusing to fight in the war, the Resistance's influence became increasingly apparent. Most sanctuary declarations referenced conscientious objection or opposition to the Vietnam War, aligning with general tenets of the antiwar movement.[13] Some declarations further clarified that sanctuary explicitly augmented draft resistance. For example, the Minneapolis Friends Meeting welcomed into sanctuary "all young men who resist the draft," and a congregation in Kalamazoo offered to hold services for those who had "taken a Resistance position."[14] Additionally, members of the Resistance often engaged directly with sanctuary, facilitating and attending services for resisters.[15]

Just as they spoke to the broader antiwar efforts in their declarations, sanctuaries incorporated visual representations of the Resistance by strategically deploying its symbol, the omega (Ω). Church of the Mediator in Providence and Washington Square Church in New York City displayed signs with the word "SANCTUARY" and an omega.[16] Similarly, Natick Wellesley Community Church (outside Boston) included a large omega on the cover of its "Chronicle of Symbolic Sanctuary."[17] Banners, posters, and fliers also frequently incorporated the omega, associating sanctuary with Resistance. Myriad visual cues ensured that, during the Vietnam War, sanctuary was logistically, organizationally, and visually interconnected with and inextricable from the broader Resistance movement.

Less than two decades later, the Sanctuary Movement emerged in response to the Central American refugee crisis. Like its counterpart during the Vietnam War, 1980s sanctuary developed within a context of established social activism. The Central America Peace and Solidarity Movement (CAPSM) was vocal about its opposition to US involvement in the Salvadoran and Guatemalan civil wars, and it expressed concern for the millions of displaced refugees fleeing those wars.[18] Meanwhile, activists in the American Southwest—including Sanctuary Movement cofounder Jim Corbett—were already engaged in humanitarian work with such refugees, helping them cross the border. Inspired by Corbett to build upon that momentum, on March 24, 1982, Rev. John Fife publicly declared Southside Presbyterian Church in Tucson, Arizona, a sanctuary. In the following years, over four hundred religious bodies and faith communities across the United States followed suit, collectively comprising an "overground railroad."[19] Grounded in scripture, the Sanctuary Movement sought to extend solidarity to Central American refugees by providing tangible support in the form of shelter as well as food, legal aid, and accompaniment.

Given its ethos of transnational solidarity, element of public activism, and strong opposition to the civil wars in Central America, the Sanctuary Movement aligned with certain tenets of CAPSM.[20] Such overlap was evident in both movements' emphasis on *testimonios* (refugees' public testimonies about the violence in Central America) and their public protests against US interventionism.[21] Nevertheless, sanctuary's focus on protecting refugees and its starkly religious overtones marked a clear strategic separation between the two movements. In particular, the Sanctuary Movement's tactic of sheltering refugees in houses of worship distinguished it from the constellation of grassroots organizations that comprised CAPSM. Unlike 1960s/70s Sanctuary, which remained closely connected to antiwar resistance organizations, the Sanctuary Movement of the 1980s burgeoned on its own.

Growing into a complex railroad of interconnected congregations uplifted by secular support and even emulated by some local governments (as in the cases of "sanctuary cities"), sanctuary developed into a full-fledged social movement during the 1980s. Although it lacked a single, central governing body, the grassroots movement established national and regional organization, collaboration, and leadership; articulated a relatively consistent religious position; and employed recurrent tactics.[22] Most importantly, it viewed itself as an autonomous movement rather than an arm of CAPSM.

At the local and regional levels, both instances of sanctuary organizing—1960s/70s Sanctuary and the Sanctuary Movement—can be regarded as nonviolent peace endeavors. Grounded in religious conviction, activists turned to spiritual and scriptural antecedents to transform ideological opposition into tangible support.

Church Support for Sanctuary

Whereas the 1980s Sanctuary Movement amassed widespread support and participation across American congregations, 1960s/70s Sanctuary received comparatively less approval, even among progressive churches. After all, the US public was more willing to sympathize with refugees fleeing war-torn countries than with young men resisting conscription.

Ministers who declared sanctuary during the Vietnam War flagrantly broke rank with most established churches and clergy. Up until at least the 1970s, more US Christians supported American intervention in Vietnam than opposed it. Even among those who opposed the war, declaring sanctuary represented a radical stance.[23] Although some liberal Protestant clergy prominently led the effort to condemn the Vietnam War, public perception of the war and draft resisters rendered sanctuary churches outliers even within ecumenical Protestant denominations. Despite the public blowback, these progressive Christians, convicted in their beliefs, continued to advocate and offer sanctuary. By the end of the war, churches that offered sanctuary to war resisters included those from Unitarian Universalist, United Church of Christ, American Baptist, Presbyterian, Quaker, and Catholic traditions.

Although the practice of sanctuary in the 1980s still proved divisive, it enjoyed far better reception within US congregations. Approximately fifteen congregations declared sanctuary by the end of 1982, and as of October 1984, well over one hundred churches had joined the movement. By the end of the decade, there were nearly five hundred public sanctuary congregations in the United States. The movement included Catholic,

Presbyterian, Unitarian, Quaker, Lutheran, Methodist, Episcopalian, Baptist, Mennonite, United Church of Christ, Reform Judaism, and Conservative Judaism congregations.[24] Likewise, Protestant denominations (the United Methodist Church, United Church of Christ, and Presbyterian Church USA, to name a few) drafted resolutions authorizing or endorsing sanctuary at the national level in support of local efforts.[25] The uneven public support for sanctuary across the two iterations of late-twentieth-century sanctuary, however, belies their key commonalities.

Behind Sanctuary: Religion, History, and Conscience

Sanctuary Religion and Conscience

In order to ground their action in religious motivation, churches involved in both 1960s/70s sanctuary efforts and the 1980s Sanctuary Movement framed their endeavors in sacred terms. Critical to any congregation's claim to sanctuary was the practice's moral and conscientious underpinning. Based in liturgical interpretation and religious tradition, sanctuary derived its authority from historical precedents and traditions of conscience. These "usable sanctuary histories" allowed congregations to tap into "historic" and "hallowed" refuge traditions from across human civilizations.[26]

From biblical imperatives to medieval practices to contemporary history, activists identified stories of sanctuary that demonstrated the ritual's lasting presence. Turning to the Hebrew Bible, proponents invoked the historical concept of sanctuary for individuals whose lives came under threat, pointing to protection offered in the six Cities of Refuge of ancient Israel. Advocates also noted that medieval churches had served as sanctuaries, places for those accused of various crimes to flee in order to seek ecclesial mediation. Establishing this collective history enabled leaders to justify sanctuary's contemporary reinvocation, for both movements believed that their declarations stood upon centuries of sacred history. In his October 16 sermon, Coffin questioned, "If in the Middle Ages churches could offer sanctuary to the most common of criminals, could they today not do the same for the most conscientious among us?" By situating themselves and their actions within religious history, sanctuary leaders located their challenge to state power in a continuing legacy of faith traditions.

During the Vietnam War, Canon 1179 of the 1917 Pio-Benedictine Code supported Catholic activists' framing of sanctuary as a legitimate religious practice applicable to contemporary issues. The canon, which stated that "churches enjoy the right of asylum such that pursued ones who take refuge in them shall not be removed," bridged the chronological divide between historical refuge and modern sanctuary by sanctioning its continued practice. This canonical recognition carried more than symbolic religious import. In fact, Marquette University professor of law Thomas Cannon argued that, given the 1917 Code of Canon Law and the practice's documented history, an incursion on church sanctuary could also constitute an intrusion of First Amendment rights.[27] While this line of legal reasoning ultimately failed to deter public raids of churches, Sanctuary Movement advocates nevertheless decried its elision from the 1983 Code of Canon Law.[28] As medieval scholar Rev. Francis Murphy lamented at the January 1985 Inter-American Symposium on Sanctuary, "In effect, though not totally repudiating the ancient claim of the right to immunity, this canon so emasculates the claim as to come close to abrogating its possible use in our court system."[29] As the new movement was gaining momentum in the mid-1980s, the updated code eliminated a key source for sanctuary activists, especially Catholics, who had hoped to argue the basis of longstanding canon law. Thus, while 1960s/70s Catholics were able to turn to canon law to support their cause, the updated code denied 1980s activists that possibility. Although based in the same tradition, the two iterations of twentieth-century sanctuary were unable to adopt identical legal justifications to support their specific forms of sacred resistance.

As the political and social circumstances of offering sanctuary differed between the two movements, the primary moral and faith-based reasonings behind the decision to declare sanctuary also shifted. Whereas 1960s/70s Sanctuary participants defended the primacy of individual conscience and cited the historical precedents of religious opposition to injustice, 1980s Sanctuary Movement leaders tailored their response to the refugee crisis.

During the Vietnam War, sanctuary's sanctity often was derived from the sacredness of individual conscience, and many churches described themselves as "sanctuaries of conscience."[30] The focal point of these sanctuary gatherings was not so much the beliefs of a certain congregation; rather, it was the convictions of the sanctuary seekers themselves. In order to ensure that the focus remained centered on morality, some congregations restricted sanctuary to those avoiding military service for expressly conscientious reasons.[31] By offering "encouragement and warm support," churches "help[ed] young men in their opposition to war."[32] Critically, this framing centered the free conscience of the sanctuary seeker, thereby placing the locus of dissent upon him rather than the congregation. Sanctuaries thus framed their intentions and actions not as supporting violating the law but instead as fulfilling their Christian duty to promote conscience.[33]

With the focus on individual conscience, 1960s/70 Sanctuary congregations justified their support for conscientiousness through their own traditions. Identifying long histories of justice-oriented resistance, congregations explained their opposition to war and support of conscientious objection as matters of religious obligation.[34] As explained by ULC, "We offer sanctuary in order to fulfill our religious heritage . . . [and] because it is our conscientious duty to do so."[35] These articulations of sanctuary as a spiritual and ethical obligation carried over to the Sanctuary Movement of the 1980s.

While the context necessitating refuge shifted in the 1980s, across the board religious and secular sanctuary continued to reference principles of conscience and morality. This was especially true for those congregations that linked their sanctuary work to prior 1960s/70s activism. For example, ULC joined the movement by granting sanctuary to Central American refugees by "revis[ing] and reaffirm[ing]" its 1971 declaration.[36] Rather than crafting an entirely new document, the Berkeley church relied upon the same seeds of religious conscience, reorienting its sanctuary stance to become applicable to the contemporary moment. Such continuity evinces not only the clear thread from the late 1960s to the early 1980s but also the conceptual overlap between the two movements.

Even as the Sanctuary Movement continued to emphasize ethics, conscience, and spiritual morality, its messaging adopted a more scriptural valence. Turning to the robust collection of biblical passages emphasizing hospitality and the injunction to care for the stranger, congregations frequently cited holy texts and "usable sacred histories" as their primary motivators in declaring sanctuary for Central American refugees.[37] Nevertheless, conscience remained important, for sanctuaries argued that Christian conscience dictated their actions. Such interplay between conscience and scripture is evident in the American Lutheran Church's "Human Rights and Conscience Believers" resolution, which "remind[ed] all congregations of the biblical call to care for the sojourner and stranger in our midst."[38] During the 1980s, sanctuary communities viewed it as their conscientious responsibility to follow biblical imperatives. They offered sanctuary to the strangers in a strange land: to those who, like the Holy Family, were refugees. Compared to 1960s/70s Sanctuary's emphasis on individual agency, their appeals to faith-based conscience were more communal, offering sanctuary in fulfillment of collective understandings of scripture. The entire dynamic shifted so that the basis of sanctuary was inherently dependent on the congregation and its beliefs.

Better understanding the differences between these two pathways to declaring sanctuary enables scholars to identify broader questions about the essence of sanctuary. First, what was sacred? While 1960s/70s Sanctuary positioned individual conscience as sacred, the 1980s Sanctuary Movement claimed the church premises as sacred. Recognizing this dynamic helps address a secondary question: Who or what posed the primary threat to government authority? If the heart of sanctuary during the Vietnam War was the individual conscience of draft resisters, then it was those sanctuary *seekers* who truly challenged the government. Conversely, in the 1980s, sanctuary was grounded in faith communities' collective understanding of scripture; it was the church itself as a liminal space that was sacred and therefore posed the threat.

Legacy of Sanctuary

When the Sanctuary Movement began to mobilize, clergy and lay leaders did not have to look far for contemporary examples of sanctuary. The tactics employed in church refuge provided to draft resisters had introduced the concept of sanctuary and brought it into the public discourse. To be sure, in the early 1980s many Americans remained unfamiliar with sanctuary, having either missed or forgotten its contribution to the antiwar movement. Nevertheless, refuge for draft resisters served as a recent touchstone. For movement advocates, this legacy offered a rough blueprint for modern American sanctuary from which they could build and adapt their own versions of refuge.

Many organizations adopted 1960s/70s Sanctuary as a usable sacred history to buttress their 1980s claims. The *Ethics and Action: Sanctuary Handbook—1986*, published by the Pacific Central Division of the Unitarian Universalist Association, explained that, in light of "sanctuary to conscience objectors," "those advocating for Sanctuary for Central Americans today feel their acts follow these historical precedents."[39] Likewise, the Chicago Religious Task Force's *Public Sanctuary for Salvadoran and Guatemalan Refugees: Organizer's Nuts & Bolts* packet referenced 1960s/70s Sanctuary as evidence that "the meaning of sanctuary is a living tradition," extending beyond ancient applications.[40] Considering the centuries-old practice combined with its 1960s/70s counterpart, the Twin Cities Refugee Sanctuary Coalition argued that "the roots of sanctuary are deep and strong," making it "the obvious practice to invoke when large numbers of Central Americans began arriving in the United States seeking shelter from the violence in their war-torn countries."[41] The recency of 1960s/70s Sanctuary meant that the practice was readily available to be reappropriated in the following decade.

Individual congregations carried the legacy of 1960/70s Sanctuary beyond the end of the war and continued their mission. First Congregational Church in Madison, Wisconsin, which had become a sanctuary in 1969, still held its weekly meetings to "focus on the issues" up through 1980.[42] Meanwhile, Old Cambridge Baptist Church continued its "sanctuary" work when it welcomed the Leclerc family from Chile in 1977, five years before Southside Presbyterian officially kicked off the Sanctuary Movement.[43] Additionally, Southampton Friends Meeting in Pennsylvania and Old Cambridge Baptist Church in Massachusetts both invoked their churches' past support for draft resisters when announcing their Sanctuary Movement declarations in the early 1980s.[44]

The sanctuary undertakings in Berkeley, California, effectively illustrate the continuity between the two movements. After ULC declared itself a sanctuary on November 9, 1971, it coordinated support for draft resisters with other local ministries and congregations (initially eight but later over a dozen). A decade later, about half of those congregations became sanctuaries for Central American refugees, establishing the East Bay Sanctuary Covenant, reminiscent of the 1970s Sanctuary

Caucus.[45] The robust experience maintained by the Berkeley sanctuary community and veterans of 1960s/70s Sanctuary—including Bob Fitch and Gustav Schultz, both of whom became key leaders throughout the 1980s—ultimately supported the Sanctuary Movement as it garnered faith-based and secular support. The parallels between these two iterations were further cemented when Berkeley declared itself a City of Refuge for Central Americans in February 1985. In fact, mayor Eugene Newport justified his proposed resolution, in part, by invoking the city's history as a sanctuary "for those who refused to fight in the Vietnam War," citing the 1971 "Berkeley City Council Resolution of Support for Sanctuary."[46] The original 1971 resolution contains striking language for scholars wishing to understand the origins of sanctuary-type policies for secular jurisdictions.

> WHEREAS: The University Lutheran Chapel of Berkeley with the support of ten Bay Area churches has announced its availability as a place of sanctuary for "any person who is unwilling to participate in military action," and has issued a statement indicting [*sic*] the nature of the sanctuary offered.
>
> THEREFORE:
>
> 1. The City of Berkeley supports those men who decide to take sanctuary.
> 2. The City of Berkeley supports the sanctuary already established at the University Lutheran Chapel and will support any congregation in Berkeley which engages in sanctuary.
> 3. The City of Berkeley is also willing to provide a facility for sanctuary. The Nature of that sanctuary will be as defined by the statement of the University Lutheran Chapel and its supporting churches. A committee designated by the University Lutheran Chapel and supporting churches will work with the city to find an appropeate [*sic*] facility and to operate that facility in line with the sanctuary statement.
> 4. The City of Berkeley encourages the People of Berkeley to work with the existing sanctuary to provide the bedding, food, medical aid, legal help and friendship that the men may need.
> 5. No Berkeley City employee will violate the established sanctuaries by assisting in investigation, public or clandestine, of engaging in or assisting arrests for violation of federal laws relating to military service

on the premise of offering sanctuary, or by refusing established public services.

6. These motions are intended as support for the actions of the men on the U.S.S. Coral Sea and not intended to influence them into specific actions such as sanctuary.[47]

The City of Berkeley's trailblazing stance during the Vietnam War reverberated throughout sanctuary activism. By adopting a sanctuary resolution, the city council established an important precedent for government-issued sanctuary declarations. In addition to being the first municipality to articulate support for sanctuary during the Vietnam War movement, this document set the stage for future declarations by debuting tactics and rhetoric later adopted by the Sanctuary Movement. Importantly, point five of the 1971 resolution put into place the most basic function of sanctuary jurisdictions in the 1980s: the limiting of cooperation between city officials and federal law enforcement agents. Unbeknownst to the sanctuary providers of the Vietnam War resistance, they had begun to set the template of offering sanctuary and providing the grounds of history and conscience to make sanctuary a viable option in the 1980s.

These pervasive parallels between 1960s/70s Sanctuary and the Sanctuary Movement speak to the broader influence anti–Vietnam War resistance had on activism and organizing in the second half of the twentieth century. In his book *Beyond Vietnam: The Politics of Protest in Massachusetts*, Robert Surburg traces how the protests that characterized the 1960s and 1970s continued to inform both the political landscape and the social movements reacting to it. By following the evolution of liberal organizing from the anti–Vietnam War focus through the opposition to nuclear energy, then the advocacy for a nuclear freeze up to the CAPSM, Surburg connects the movements.[48] That the development from Resistance to CAPSM mirrored the progression of 1960s/70s Sanctuary to the Sanctuary Movement underscores the extent to which the religious activism, while distinct, developed parallel to civic protestations.

Sanctuary and the Law

As congregations strove to uphold God's "good law" over the US government's "bad laws," they invariably ran up against a dynamic in which they were violating US code.[49] Operating in distinct social-political moments to challenge differing mechanisms of government authority, each iteration of sanctuary tested different laws. Whereas sanctuary activists in the 1980s sought to protect refugees fleeing US proxy wars, 1960s/70s Sanctuary resistance opposed the conscription and deployment of conscientious objectors—oftentimes cast as draft dodgers—in an outright-declared US war. To be sure, the Immigration and Naturalization Service maintained significant authority as a subdivision of the Department of Justice. Yet challenging the United States military and Department of Defense during active war bore comparatively much greater weight, a dynamic exemplified and exacerbated by the fact that the sanctuary activisms violated different sets of laws. Though both movements were still fundamentally antiwar or peace movements, the ramifications of civil disobedience during the Vietnam War seemed to be, and ultimately proved to be, much graver than those of the civil initiative of the 1980s.

Vietnam War–Era Sanctuary

By providing spiritual support and a physical space for young men refusing military service, sanctuaries challenged the United States government and its laws. Given this dynamic, many viewed sanctuary as a form of civil disobedience. As churches contributed to mounting resistance to the Vietnam War, attorney Alex Landon cautioned San Francisco sanctuary activists that "if the government felt threatened by mass sanctuary efforts, it is almost certain that [the law] might be used in new and repressive ways."[50] Sanctuary supporters needed to be particularly cognizant of risks tied to Title 18 of US Code Section 1381, which read,

> Whoever entices or procures, or attempts or endeavors to entice or procure any person in the Armed Forces of the United States, or who has

> been recruited for service therein, to desert therefrom, or aids any such person in deserting or in attempt to desert from such service; or
>
> Whoever harbors, conceals, protects, or assists any such person who may have deserted from such service, knowing him to have deserted therefrom, or refuses to give up and deliver such person on the demand of any officer authorized to receive him—
>
> Shall be fined under this title or imprisoned not more than three years, or both.[51]

The very nature of sanctuary risked legal confrontation. From declaring and offering sanctuary (which could be construed as enticing) to providing sanctuary (which might be understood as harboring) to offering sanctuary's protection (which invited accusations of refusing to give up a fugitive), churches toed the line, provoking a federal reaction. Thus, sanctuary ministry clearly crossed into civil disobedience—a point only exacerbated by congregations' connections to the Resistance and Resistance activities.

Although early sanctuaries—particularly in the Northeast—commended moral civil disobedience, sanctuary providers increasingly recognized the need to choose their language with great caution. In the late 1960s, Boston activists embraced the term, openly advocating for conscientiously grounded civil disobedience in both name and action.[52] Building their claims to sanctuary on a history of American and Christian opposition to unjust laws, leaders portrayed sanctuary as a form of righteous civil disobedience. Yet by the early 1970s, government retribution drove West Coast activists to shy away from the term in the hopes of staving off prosecution. While the essence of sanctuary persisted, as the movement developed, organizers refined their ideas and implementation of the practice so as to sidestep potential legal issues. Even as leaders offered their churches to those engaged in civil disobedience, many took clear steps to attenuate government retaliation. These strategies included (1) moving towards "public sanctuary" to avoid charges of concealment, (2) framing sanctuary in religious terms, (3) clearly articulating that the provision of sanctuary was not meant to "entice desertion," and (4) not interfering with government agents who violated sanctuary.[53]

In their public declarations, congregations frequently acknowledged the limitations of sanctuary and openly stated their religious intentions, placing caveats on the tradition in order to reduce personal and institutional risk. Consider the following joint declaration:

> The Religious Society of Friends from its inception has taken a public stand against all wars. . . .
>
> Our Meetings have decided to offer sanctuary to those draft resisters whose stand is the result of conscience and whose resistance is nonviolent. We realize we cannot physically protect any individual. By sanctuary the meetings mean the offer of shelter and spiritual support. This shall be given publicly and shall consist of opening our meetinghouses and our homes to such young men. If the public authorities feel they must take action, we shall try to arrange that. In the spirit of Friends, no violence shall be offered to any public official in the performance of his work.[54]

Conscience Bay Monthly Meeting and Westbury Monthly Meeting outlined their intentions while discernibly addressing each legal concern. They established a strong religious foundation for their antiwar stance and specified that holy sanctuary was restricted for those with conscientious or ethical concerns. Furthermore, the declaration admitted the possibility of sanctuary violations and agreed to cooperate with government agents. Finally, the announcement was public, alerting officials to their action, thereby attenuating accusations of concealment. Ideally, these concessions would mollify government response while still enabling congregations to challenge what they deemed to be an unjust law and war.

Caution, therefore, ultimately characterized much of the Vietnam War–era sanctuary civil disobedience, a marked contrast with the 1980s Sanctuary Movement.

1980s Sanctuary

As 1980s religious leaders adopted sanctuary activism in a new political context, they likewise threatened state power, albeit in a new form. Whereas Vietnam War–era sanctuary confronted the Selective Service

System, the US military, and the Department of Defense, the 1980s movement's focus on Central American refugees challenged Reagan-era immigration policy, chiefly the Immigration and Naturalization Service (INS) and its power to detain and deport undocumented immigrants. Given that the two iterations of sanctuary objected to distinct policies, their civil disobedience contravened different sets of corresponding laws.

During the Sanctuary Movement, the Reagan administration and INS granted legal primacy to the Immigration and Nationality Act of 1952, which stipulated,

> (a) Any person . . . who–
>
> (1) brings into or lands in the United States . . . or attempts, by himself, or through another, to bring into or land in the United States, by any means of transportation or otherwise;
>
> (2) knowing that he is in the United States in violation of law . . . transports, or moves, or attempts to transport or move, within the United States by means of transportation or otherwise, in furtherance of such violation of law;
>
> (3) willfully or knowingly conceals, harbors, or shields from detection, or attempts to conceal, harbor, or shield from detection, in any place, including any building or any means of transportation; or
>
> (4) willfully or knowingly encourages or induces, or attempts to encourage or induce, either directly or indirectly, the entry into the United States of any alien . . . not lawfully entitled to enter or reside within the United States . . . shall be guilty of a felony, and . . . punished by a fine not exceeding $2,000 or by imprisonment for a term not exceeding five years, or both, for each alien in respect to whom any violation of this subsection occurs. . . .[55]

Sanctuary broke the law. From "transport[ing]" refugees on the underground railroad to "harboring" them in churches, sanctuary activists prioritized their moral imperative to provide shelter over Section 274(a).

Southside Presbyterian Church established something of a template in its declaration of sanctuary. Not only did the congregation hold a sanctuary declaration service and pass a formal resolution, but pastor John Fife sent a letter to Attorney General William French Smith informing him of the church's decision. The opening paragraph clearly acknowledged the civil disobedience at hand, stating, "We are writing to inform you that Southside Presbyterian Church will publicly violate the Immigration and Nationality Act Section 274(a). We have declared our church as a 'sanctuary' for undocumented refugees from Central America. . . . We believe that justice and mercy require that people of conscience actively assert our God-given right to aid anyone fleeing from persecution and murder. The current administration of U.S. law prohibits us from sheltering these refugees from Central America. Therefore, we believe the administration of the law to be immoral as well as illegal."[56] The Chicago Religious Task Force on Central America later doubled down on this line of legal reasoning, explaining that "sanctuary offers a concrete and direct way to challenge the inhumane policy of the U.S. government."[57] From the very beginning, the Sanctuary Movement embraced and advertised civil disobedience, recognizing it as central to its mission.

Although 1980s sanctuary necessitated violating immigration law, activists argued that the entire situation was bred from the US government's failure to comply with the Refugee Act of 1980. Codifying the UN Convention and Protocol on Refugees, the Refugee Act of 1980 outlined criteria for asylum, for which sanctuary leaders and the United Nations High Commissioner for Refugees believed Central Americans fleeing the civil unrest qualified.[58] However, the United States consistently refused to recognize and accordingly protect Central American refugees, leading to Fife's accusation that Reagan's immigration policies were "illegal." In light of mass deportations, "church people have had to invoke the practice of sanctuary to attempt to force the United States government to comply with these existing laws."[59] In other words, sanctuary congregations broke the law to compel the government to follow the law. In this sense, their civil disobedience was backed not only by God's "higher law" but also by the "supreme Law of the Land."[60]

This dialectic of breaking the law to uphold the law ensured that conventional conceptions of civil disobedience did not neatly align with the movement's rhetoric. After all, sanctuary activists viewed the government, more so than churches, as the primary offender. Accordingly, sanctuary functioned as "a different kind of civil disobedience" in that activists strove to uphold existing law, rather than simply contest bad laws. Jim Corbett would later characterize this as "civil initiative."[61] Unlike civil disobedience, which mainly operates in "opposition to unjust laws," civil initiative prioritizes upholding an existing law that the government is currently failing to administer.[62] Per Corbett's interpretation, the Sanctuary Movement's fidelity to the Refugee Act of 1980 would constitute civil initiative as it sought to keep the Reagan administration accountable to the act's definition of and protections for refugees.[63] Regardless of terminology—"civil disobedience" or "civil initiative"—the Sanctuary Movement challenged federal authority, and the government responded in kind.

Sanctuary Violated

In spite of activists' and religious leaders' appeals to the sanctity of specific spaces and assertions of inviolability, the US government repeatedly violated sanctuary throughout the twentieth century. The manner in which federal officials transgressed those liminal bounds invites further discussion of table 1.1.

TABLE 1.1

1960s/70s Sanctuary	1980s Sanctuary
The DoD operated under a more expansive and punitive mandate to enforce law during the time of war, especially for draftees and soldiers refusing to return to Vietnam.	The INS remained especially limited in power compared to the DoD.
The government violated sanctuary by forcibly entering into houses of worship and other declared sanctuary sites, primarily to apprehend the sanctuary seeker. Highly publicized violations (by break-in) into houses of worship.	Covert violations were covert infiltrations. FBI informants wore wires (e.g., Operation Sojourner); the more covert violations included break-ins into sanctuary offices and rummaging through materials.
Confrontations were frequent between the government and sanctuary activists.	Confrontations were infrequent but widespread, occurring across the country in an effort to dismantle the movement's leadership and underground railroad.
Law enforcement resorted to forceful entry, and in some cases, activists scuffled with law enforcement.	Activists maintained a commitment to peace throughout.
Law enforcement primarily targeted sanctuary seekers.	Law enforcement primarily targeted sanctuary providers.
Punishment for those arrested included jail time and hard labor.	Punishments were relatively minor, especially for those indicted in the Sanctuary Trial.

During the Vietnam War, the Department of Defense possessed immense authority, particularly as it pertained to pursuing and arresting draft resisters, dissident servicemembers, and the civilians who aided and abetted them. Sanctuaries of conscience housed suspects who violated not only civilian laws but also military code, which brought with it steep punitive repercussions.

Many draft resisters entered sanctuary for a stated purpose of inviting some form of confrontation with the government. While sanctuary organizers consistently reiterated that their strong principle of nonviolence applied universally—meaning that the same position that led them to oppose overseas military intervention also mandated that they repudiate violence as a method of domestic protest—the Resistance's broad antiwar coalition included members who harbored no such compunction. At times that disconnect strained nonviolent endeavors, as zealous members of the Resistance were willing to go further than congregations were comfortable with. The "discipline" or "house rules" that many sanctuaries issued to outline appropriate behavior only pertained to their spaces and could not influence protesters' actions outside church property. That limitation accounted for the sensationalist stories about sanctuary arrests devolving into violent conflict with the government.

Congregations that chose to engage in sanctuary were well aware that this religious stance brought them into conflict with the state. Collisions between the state power and principled religious action were effectively intrinsic to the 1960s/1970s Sanctuary experience. This reality was exemplified in the Unitarian Universalist Association's "Special Report on Sanctuary," which included a section on recommended "Techniques of Sanctuary." Step four of this seven-step guide advised communities to "prepare for the confrontation," acknowledging that federal violations of sanctuary were all but inevitable.[64] Backed by public animosity for perceived "draft dodgers" and armed—literally and figuratively—by US law, federal officers, military police, and US marshals soon began to arrest conscientious objectors, even when doing so required violating religious sanctity. If the purpose of symbolic sanctuary was to offer "community support in worship at the time of these men's arrest or imprisonment," then sanctuary proceedings necessarily encompassed that violation.[65] During the Vietnam War, congregations tacitly understood that the sanctity that endowed sanctuary with its sacred inviolability was precariously liminal and therefore pragmatically incapable of preventing tangible violations.

The Sanctuary Movement of the 1980s endowed much greater power to sanctuary's sacred liminality. With its declaration "LA MIGRA NO PROFANA EL SANTUARIO" (immigration officers shall not profane the sanctuary), Southside Presbyterian effectively drew a line in the sand.[66] By publicly demarcating their sacred space as inviolable, congregations positioned their activism within religiously protected ground. To be sure, there were no meaningful differences between the practical protective barriers this new form of sanctuary offered as compared to 1960s/1970s Sanctuary. But, when coupled with the public's comparatively greater sympathy for refugees, the Sanctuary Movement's consistent, convicted contention of the inviolability of religious spaces rendered the rampant arrests from the Vietnam War era politically untenable in the 1980s. Thus, sanctuary activists succeeded in converting liminal sanctity into a more powerful deterrent against government intrusion. This dynamic afforded sanctuary seekers more protection, as the government exercised restraint to avoid the inevitable public backlash it would invite if it forcibly removed individuals from sacred spaces.

After INS initially dismissed those in attendance at Southside Presbyterian's 1982 declaration service as "anti–Vietnam war protestors. . . . In other words, political misfits," as the Sanctuary Movement increasingly garnered momentum, INS began to view it as a legitimate threat and acted accordingly.[67] In 1984, INS began Operation Sojourner, infiltrating the movement to build a legal case against sanctuary workers. For ten months, government informants implanted themselves within three Arizona sanctuary churches—Alzona Evangelical Lutheran, Southside Presbyterian, and Camelback Presbyterian—surveilling standard religious gatherings in addition to sanctuary meetings. Based on the evidence collected during Operation Sojourner, a federal grand jury indicted sixteen sanctuary leaders the government accused of harboring and transporting refugees. Ultimately, eleven stood trial and only eight of the defendants were found guilty of violating Section 274(a) of the Nationality Act of 1952. Massive public outcry dissuaded the government from publicly pursuing further charges.

Even as the government refrained from additional high-profile trials, its violations of sanctuary continued. Throughout the 1980s sanctuary activists reported evidence of wire-tapping and mail surveillance as well as unexplained searches and seizures at airports. During that time, dozens of sanctuaries also experienced suspicious break-ins, with the burglars seemingly targeting information rather than valuables.[68] Despite never receiving formal verification, sanctuary organizers suspected foul play and decried government surveillance. To be sure, 1980s religious leaders were justified in their anger over violations of sanctuary. Nevertheless, the government's switch to more covert tactics and its widespread unwillingness to target sanctuary seekers, spoke to the movement's successes. Whereas frequent, combative arrests characterized 1960s/1970s Sanctuary, the relative calm of the 1980s made plain the Sanctuary Movement's ability to leverage religious and social will to defend the sacred in order to mitigate INS's response.

Conclusion

On November 25, 1990, ULC renewed its sanctuary commitment for the fourth time. Returning to the roots of its sanctuary mission, the church once again opened its doors to conscientious objectors, this time offering refuge to those who opposed the Persian Gulf War. The perception that sanctuary became dormant after Ronald Reagan left office belies many congregations' concept of the continuity of their sanctuary ministry, as evidenced by ULC's sustained efforts. When debates over comprehensive immigration reform rose to the forefront of national conversation, ULC once again declared itself a sanctuary—this time for undocumented immigrants—anticipating the renewed effort that would eventually become the New Sanctuary Movement. Then in the summer of 2016, the congregation yet again renewed its sanctuary position, reaffirming its solidarity with undocumented immigrants well ahead of the larger wave of churches and campuses that declared sanctuary shortly after Donald Trump's election. Over the past fifty years, in times of war and immigration crises, ULC has summoned the important protections of sanctuary for resisters and refugees.[69] Many congregations since then have taken part in this form of sacred resistance.

Despite their distinct approaches, the effort for 1960s/70s war resisters and the 1980s Sanctuary Movement each embodied a real and consistent ethos of sanctuary. On the surface, the decision to resurrect sanctuary in the 1980s may appear puzzling given its ostensive "failure" during the Vietnam War era to protect draft resisters from the government. But this interpretation of 1960s/1970s Sanctuary provides an ahistorical reading by inappropriately applying the 1980s definition of "success" retroactively. Whereas the Sanctuary Movement strove to establish inviolable, impermeable protection to shield Central American refugees from deportation, Vietnam War–era sanctuary sought to uphold the primacy of conscience and morality by providing space for conscientious objectors to discern their participation in the war and publicly refuse to participate in the violence on religious grounds. Sanctuary for draft resisters was designed for congregations to "stand with" the young men as they exercised their conscience, not to provide long-term shelter. This dynamic was evident in the various ways the draft resisters left sanctuary: Some departed on their own volition, and others were dragged out, while others still received honorable discharges thanks to the advocacy of sanctuary churches.[70] Regardless, 1960s/1970s Sanctuary provided temporary, liminal, safe, sacred places for young men to enact and articulate their moral positions. In short, 1960s/70s Sanctuary offered a refuge of resistance for conscientious objectors. In the 1980s, the goals were varied, but at the heart of the movement was the protection of refugees as well as raising awareness of the devastation wrought by US intervention in the Central American civil wars. These disparate aspirations demonstrate the myriad ways the concept of sanctuary can be reimagined to resist injustice and offer refuge to those who suffer under it.

NOTES

1 William Sloane Coffin Jr., Untitled sermon at service for draft resisters at Arlington Street Unitarian Church, Boston, October 16, 1967 (William Sloane Coffin Jr. Papers, Box 40, Folder 38, Yale University, New Haven, Connecticut).

2 Peter Simon, photographer, Resistance rally: draft resister burning draft card in the Arlington Street Church, October 16, 1967, photograph. Boston, Massachusetts. From Peter Simon Collection (University of Massachusetts–Amherst): https://credo.library.umass.edu (accessed January 15, 2024).

3 Declaration of Sanctuary (The Riverside Church Institutional Records, Record Group 9. Mission/Social Justice, Series 9.4 Programs and Activities of Mission/Social Justice Commission, Sub-series 9.4.7 Sanctuary Movement, Folder Title: Social Justice—Disarmament—Declaration of Sanctuary—Oct 1984, Box # 131, Riverside Church, New York, New York).

4 *El Salvador: Another Vietnam?*, directed by Glenn Silber and Teté (M, J, and E Productions, 1981).

5 Draft resistance took many forms during the antiwar movement, as grassroots organizations cropped up to support local efforts. Beginning in 1967, activists began to create chapters of the Resistance, a noncentralized, grassroots movement that supported draft dodgers and draft resisters. There was overlap between Resistance programming and other, not affiliated protest activities, but Resistance activists benefited from the power/notoriety derivative of larger collaborations. Many sanctuaries specified their support for the Resistance in particular within the context of broader antiwar opposition.

6 Michael S. Foley, *Confronting the War Machine: Draft Resistance During the Vietnam War* (University of North Carolina Press, 2003), 90–94; Bruce Dancis, *Resister: A Story of Protest and Prison During the Vietnam War* (Cornell University Press, 2014), 128.

7 Arlington Street Church, A Service of Conscience and Acceptance, Michael S. Foley Collected Papers, Box 7, "Reference: Arlington Street Church (Boston, MA): sanctuary given to draft resisters; draft card turn-in on Oct. 16, 1967 (and 30th anniversary commemorating this event); etc.," Swarthmore College Peace Collection, Swarthmore, Pennsylvania—hereafter SCPC); Jack Mendelson, "The Church and Draft Resisters," Foley Papers, Box 7, Folder "Reference: Arlington Street Church (Boston, MA): sanctuary given to draft resisters; draft card turn-in on Oct. 16, 1967 (and 30th anniversary commemorating this event); etc.," SCPC. Other sources estimated that 237 to nearly 300 young men turned in their draft cards; see Dancis, *Resister*, 237, and Hilary Cunningham, *God and Caesar at the Rio Grande: Sanctuary and the Politics of Religion* (University of Minnesota Press, 1995), 84.

8 Rolf Kolden, "Dear Friend and Colleague" (Foley, Box 8, Folder "Reference: statements by draft resisters," SCPC).

9 Statement of Support—The New England Resistance (New York Yearly Meeting Records: Outreach and Witness Committees, Box 10, Folder "Sanctuary for COs, 1968–1969," Quaker Meeting Records and Haverford College Quaker & Special Collections and Friends Historical Library of Swarthmore College, Swarthmore, Pennsylvania—hereafter cited as QMR).

10 Hawaii Resistance Notes, "A Chronology of the Crossroads Sanctuary," Reveal Digital, November 14–15, 1968. JSTOR: www.jstor.org.

11 "Sanctuary: Resolution of the University Lutheran Chapel," 1990 (Gustav Schultz Sanctuary Collection, Box 1, Folder 10, Graduate Theological Union Archives, Berkeley, California—hereafter cited as GSSC); "S.O.S. Sanctuary," *Berkeley Tribe* 6, no. 12, iss. 120, November 12–18, 1971, 3 (GSSC, Box 1, Folder 5); "Coral Sea Trip to Viet Protested," *San Francisco Examiner*, November 8, 1971, 4, www.newspapers.com.

12 "Berkeley City Votes Sanctuary," Press Release, November 9, 1971 (GSSC, Box 1, Folder 5); Martin Marty, "Harboring the Objectors," *Context*, January 15, 1972 (GSSC, Box 1, Folder 5).

13 To be sure, antiwar organizing was not limited to the Resistance movement. The sentiments articulated by sanctuaries and sanctuary activists reflected the grassroots opposition expressed throughout the country.

14 "The Meetinghouse as Resistance 'Sanctuary,'" pamphlet (New York Yearly Meeting Records: Outreach and Witness Committees, Box 10, Folder "Sanctuary for COs, 1968–1969," QMR).

15 The Resistance referred Steve David, Neil Banton, and Timothy Springer to Orange Grove Monthly Meeting; William Chase and Robert Talmanson to Arlington Street Church ("On the Sanctuary for three members of the armed forces at Orange Grove Monthly Meeting, Pasadena, California," New York Yearly Meeting Records: Outreach and Witness Committees, Box 10, Folder "Sanctuary for COs, 1968–1969," QMR); Unitarian Universalist Association Division of Social Responsibility, *Sanctuary: Special Report*, "Sanctuary at Arlington Street Church: A. The First Sanctuary" (Young Friends of North America: Committee on Conscription Records, Box DG 083: 02, Folder "Reference material: conscientious objection—general," SCPC).

16 Negative Number: 680229 (The Daily World/Daily Worker Photographs Collection, Box 13c, Tamiment Library and Robert F. Wagner Labor Archives); Unitarian Universalist Association Division of Social Responsibility, *Sanctuary: Special Report*, front page (Young Friends of North America: Committee on Conscription Records, Box DG 083: 02, Folder "Reference material: conscientious objection—general," SCPC).

17 Committee on Sanctuary: Natick Wellesley Community Church, Chronicle of Symbolic Sanctuary with evaluation and guidelines (Foley Papers, Box 9, Folder "Reference: sanctuary given to draft resisters by churches," SCPC).

18 Sharon Erickson Nepstad, *Convictions of the Soul: Religion, Culture, and Agency in the Central America Solidarity Movement* (Oxford University Press, 2004); Christian Smith, *Resisting Reagan: The U.S.-Central America Peace Movement* (University of Chicago Press, 1996).

19 "Manual for Overground Railroad Hosts" (Chicago Religious Task Force on Central America Collections, Box 5, Folder 10, Wisconsin Historical Society, Madison, Wisconsin—hereafter WHS).

20 Nepstad, *Convictions of the Soul*, 128–35; Smith, *Resisting Reagan*, 113–20.

21 For information on CAPSM's implementation of *testimonios*, see Héctor Perla Jr., "Si Nicaragua Venció, El Salvador Vencenrá: Central American Agency in the Creation of the U.S.-Central American Peace and Solidarity Movement," *Latin American Research Review* 43, no. 2 (2008): 136–58; Smith, *Resisting Reagan*; Nepstad, *Convictions of the Soul*.

22 The Tucson Ecumenical Council and the Chicago Religious Task Force operated as the main organizing institutions, providing materials and advice to local sanctuaries. While this dynamic ensured a level of continuity across the movement, neither group constituted a true governing body. Movement cofounder Jim Corbett eschewed any such characterization; see Jim Corbett, "A View from the Border," September 8, 1984 (GSSC, Box 2, Folder 1).

23 David E. Settje, *Faith and War: How Christians Debated the Cold and Vietnam Wars* (NYU Press, 2011), 10.

24 Denominational Breakdown of Sanctuaries, August 1988 (Chicago Religious Task Force on Central America Collections, Box 4, Folder 66, WHS); National Sanctuary Defense Fund, Sanctuary Media Packet, "Historical Highlights of Sanctuary Movement," 4 (GSSC, Box 3, Folder 3).

25 Inter-religious Task Force on Central America, Peacemaking III, *U.S. Religious Statements on Central America, 1985–1986* (The James and Margaret Goff Papers, Box 41, Folder 768, Yale Divinity Library, Yale Divinity School, New Haven, Connecticut).

26 Lloyd D. Barba, "'An Historic and Hallowed Principle in Religious Life': The Usable Sacred Histories of the 1980s Sanctuary Movement," *Journal of the American Academy of Religion* 93, no. 1 (March 2025): 18–44. Rabbi Balfour Brickner quoted in "Service of Welcome, Celebration, and Dedication: An Affirmation of Public Sanctuary" (William Sloane Coffin Jr. Papers, accession 2004, Box 16, Folder 240, Sterling Memorial Library, Yale University, New Haven, Connecticut—hereafter WSCJP).

27 George Volsky, "U.S. Churches Offer Sanctuary to Aliens Facing Deportation," *The New York Times*, April 8, 1983.

28 While the official 1983 code elided the provision on sanctuary following its exclusion from the 1979 draft, according to Guardado, "canon 1179 became canon 14 in the working draft" during the 1977–1979 consultations. Sanctuary's inclusion in the earlier draft demonstrates that the topic was discussed even though it ultimately was dropped. Theologian and historian Leo Guardado tracked the process of eliminating the sanctuary provision from canon law. For more on sanctuary in the Catholic tradition and its exclusion from the 1983 code, see Leo Guardado, "Sanctuary for Asylum Seekers: Revisiting the Religious Principle and Practice of Refuge in the Church," *Theological Studies* 82, no. 2 (2021): 302.

29 Rev. Francis Murphy, "A Historical View of Sanctuary," in *Sanctuary: A Resource Guide for Understanding and Participating in the Central American Refugee Struggle*, ed. Gary MacEoin (Harper & Row, 1985), 77. The 1983 canon law's silence on sanctuary, however, offered Catholic clergy and theologians much to wonder about and debate—even forty years later, arguments for sanctuary's inclusion into the church's canon code persist in light of continued violence and death in Central America. Recently, Guardado has traced a long and robust history of sanctuary's application in Catholic history, noting, in light of continued violence and death in Central America, the need for the church to reintroduce sanctuary into canon law; see Guardado, "Sanctuary for Asylum Seekers."

30 William Sloane Coffin Jr, Untitled sermon at service for draft resisters at Arlington Street Unitarian Church, Boston, October 16, 1967 (WSCJP, Box 40, Folder 38).

31 "Statement of Friends Meeting at Cambridge" (New York Yearly Meeting Records: Outreach and Witness Committees, Box 10, Folder "Sanctuary for COs, 1968–1969," QMR).

32 "Minute of Scarsdale Friends Meeting" (New York Yearly Meeting Records: Outreach and Witness Committees, Box 10, Folder "Sanctuary for COs, 1968–1969,"

QMR); notably, Scarsdale Friends Meeting did not declare "sanctuary"; rather, it offered "hospitality," which in effect provided the same benefits without taking on the legal burdens associated with the term "sanctuary." In spite of the different title, many still viewed such "hospitality" as a form of sanctuary, as evidenced by Scarsdale's inclusion in the "Meetinghouse as Resistance 'Sanctuary'" pamphlet.

33 Dennis Willigan, "Sanctuary: A Communitarian Form of Counter-Culture," *Union Seminary Quarterly Review* 25, no. 4 (Summer 1970): 517–41.

34 For example, see "Offer of Sanctuary to Draft Resisters," September 1968 (New York Yearly Meeting Records: Outreach and Witness Committees, Box 10, Folder "Sanctuary for COs, 1968–1969," QMR). Stances on pacifism and participation in the Underground Railroad were frequently cited.

35 University Lutheran Chapel, "Statement to the Press from November 9, 1971: Berkeley Church Offers Sanctuary Supported by Eight Bay Area Churches," GSSC Box 1, Folder 10.

36 University Lutheran Chapel, Sanctuary Resolution, Revised and Reaffirmed, November 25, 1990 (GSSC, Box 1, Folder 10).

37 Barba, "'An Historic and Hallowed Principle.'"

38 American Lutheran Church, "Human Law and the Conscience of Believers: A Statement of the American Lutheran Church," *Journal of Law and Religion* 2, no. 1 (1984): 195.

39 "Ethics and Action: Sanctuary Handbook—1986," published by Ad Hoc Task Force on Sanctuary of Pacific Central Division of the Unitarian Universalist Association, 2 (Unitarian Universalist Service Committee, Sanctuary Projects, Box 3 (h) "Sanctuary Handbook," Special Collections, Harvard Divinity School Library, Cambridge, Massachusetts—hereafter UUSC)

40 "Public Sanctuary for Salvadoran and Guatemalan Refugees: Organizer's Nuts & Bolts," Published by the Chicago Religious Task Force on Central America #Addendum to Press Release // Historical and Theological Basis for Sanctuary: (25) UUSC Sanctuary Projects Box 1 (f), "Chicago Unit Packets."

41 Nancy J. Berneking, Twin Cities Refugee Coalition, "Sanctuary: A Safe Place," 3 (Cynthia Anthonsen Foster Papers, MC 653, Box 34, Folder 7, Schlesinger Library, Radcliffe Institute, Harvard University, Cambridge, Massachusetts).

42 Richard L. Kenyon, "Continuing a Tradition: Churches Have Provided Sanctuary for Ages," in Basta! Sanctuary Organizers Nuts and Bolts Supplement No. 1, 6 (UUSC Sanctuary Projects Box 2 (c) "Graphics," 6).

43 Old Cambridge Baptist Church, "Interim Report, Task Force Aiding in Settlement of Familia LeClerc" (Old Cambridge Baptist Church, 1980s Sanctuary Files, Folder "Sanctuary 1977 LeClerk," Cambridge, Massachusetts—hereafter OCBC).

44 Southampton Monthly Meeting of Friends, August 15, 1982 (Darlene Nicgorski Papers on the Sanctuary Movement, Box 2, Folder 19, Special Collections, Honnold/Mudd Library, Claremont, California); Old Cambridge Baptist Church, "Statement on Purpose in Providing Public Sanctuary," January 8, 1983 (OCBC Sanctuary Files).

45 "Berkeley Church Offers Sanctuary to Military Dissenters: Sanctuary Supported by Eight Bay Area Churches," Press Release, November 9, 1971; Berkeley City Council Resolution of Support for Sanctuary, November 10, 1971 (GSSC, Box 1 Folder 5). No fewer than sixteen congregations would eventually join by 1972; see "Sanctuary Churches" (GSSC, Box 1, Folder 4); Bob Fitch and Gustav Schultz letter to "Sanctuary Churches," February 1972 (GSSC, Box 1, Folder 6); East Bay Sanctuary Covenant (UUSC Sanctuary Projects, Box 2, Folder "printed matter").

46 Eugene Newport, Resolution for Council Action Declaring Berkeley a City of Refuge, February 19, 1985 (GSSC, Box 1, Folder 43).

47 Berkeley City Council Resolution of Support for Sanctuary.

48 Robert Surbrug, *Beyond Vietnam: The Politics of Protest in Massachusetts, 1974–1990* (University of Massachusetts Press, 2009).

49 William Sloane Coffin Jr. described the Refugee Act of 1980 as an example of a "good act"; see Sanctuary Press Conference 10/1/84, audio recording (The Riverside Church Digital Archive).

50 Alex Landon, "Sanctuary Law" (GSSC, Box 1, Folder 7).

51 As quoted in Landon, "Sanctuary Law."

52 William Sloane Coffin Jr., "Sanctuaries for Men of Conscience," *Union Seminary Quarterly Review* 23, no. 2 (Winter 1968): 184.

53 Landon, "Sanctuary Law."

54 "A Minute on sanctuary for draft resisters" (New York Yearly Meeting Records: Outreach and Witness Committees, Box 10, Folder "Sanctuary for COs, 1968–1969," QMR).

55 An Act to Revise the Laws Relating to Immigration, Naturalization, and Nationality; and for Other Purposes, Public Law 414, U.S. Statutes at Large 66 (1952): 228–29. www.govinfo.gov.

56 John M. Fife, Letter to William French Smith, March 23, 1982 (GSSC, Box 1, Folder 16).

57 Chicago Religious Task Force on Central America, Introduction to "Sanctuary: A Justice Ministry," 2 (UUSC Sanctuary Projects Box 1 folder F).

58 Chicago Religious Task Force on Central America, Introduction to "Sanctuary." 1.

59 Berneking, Twin Cities Refugee Coalition.

60 Berneking, Twin Cities Refugee Coalition.

61 Jim Corbett, "Sanctuary, Basic Rights, and Humanity's Fault Lines: A Personal Essay," *Weber Studies: The Contemporary West* 5, no. 1 (Spring 1988). Accessed June 11, 2023: www.weber.edu; Adam Waters, "Alternative Internationalisms: The Sanctuary Movement and Jim Corbett's Civil Initiative," *Diplomatic History* 46, no. 5 (2022): 984–1009.

62 Corbett, "Sanctuary, Basic Rights, and Humanity's Fault Lines."

63 Waters suggests that Corbett only began to use the phrase "civil initiative" around 1985; see Waters, "Alternative Internationalisms," 1002–3. For Corbett's most thorough discussion of civil initiative, see Corbett, "Sanctuary, Basic Rights, and Humanity's Fault Lines."

64 Unitarian Universalist Association Division of Social Responsibility, *Sanctuary: Special Report*, "Techniques of Sanctuary" (Young Friends of North America: Committee on Conscription Records, Box DG 083: 02, Folder "Reference material: conscientious objection—general," SCPC).

65 "The Meetinghouse as Resistance 'Sanctuary,'" pamphlet (New York Yearly Meeting Records: Outreach and Witness Committees, Box 10, Folder "Sanctuary for COs, 1968–1969," QMR).

66 Lloyd Barba and Tatyana Castillo-Ramos, "Sacred Resistance: The Sanctuary Movement from Reagan to Trump," *Perspectivas* 16 (2019): 12.

67 Thomas Martin (INS Intelligence Agent) quoted in Ann Crittenden, *Sanctuary: A Story of American Consciousness and the Law in Collision* (Weidenfeld and Nicolson, 1988), 75.

68 Appendix to the Testimony of the Center for Constitutional Rights (CCR) Before the House Committee on the Judiciary Subcommittee on Civil and Constitutional Rights, February 20, 1987, box 1, folder 52, Darlene Nicgorski Papers on the Sanctuary Movement, Honnold/Mudd Library, Claremont University Consortium, Claremont, California. For more on reported surveillance by sanctuary and related groups, see Ross Gelbspan, *Break-Ins, Death Threats and the FBI: The Covert War Against the Central America Movement* (South End Press, 1991).

69 University Lutheran Chapel, Sanctuary Resolution, Revised and Reaffirmed (November 25, 1990), Gustav Schultz Sanctuary Collection, Box 1, Folder 10, Graduate Theological Union Archives, Berkeley, California); *The Public Sanctuary Movement: An Historical Basis of Hope—Oral Histories Book I*, edited by Eileen M. Purcell (San Francisco: Sanctuary Oral History Project, 2007), 6; Lillian Dong, "Local Berkeley Chapel Offers Place of Sanctuary for Immigrants," *Daily Californian*, July 24, 2016. Accessed December 9, 2023: www.dailycal.org.

70 Within a year, the Bay Area sanctuary churches had helped twenty-two men receive honorable discharges and nearly ten times that number with "referral, hospitality, and counseling"; see Bob Fitch and Gustav Schultz letter to "Sanctuary Churches."

2

"I Am More Afraid to Remain Silent"

Speaking Truth to Empire from Sanctuary

KRISTINA SHULL

Introduction

January 15, 1986
The first refugee from Central America took the stand Wednesday to testify in the Sanctuary trial.

Dressed in a dark, three-piece suit, his short, stocky frame pulled up, Rodríguez faced the prosecution with a defiant look.

Asked to give a simple identification, Mr. Rodríguez added his own testimony.

"She was the only person that offered me a roof over my head when I was most in need. People told me she had a very good heart. I remember her with much love."

Prosecutor Reno jumped to his feet, furious at this unsolicited information being presented to the jury, and objected. Judge Carroll upheld the objection and Mrs. Aguilar's heart was stricken from the record.

Michael Altman, counsel for Sister Darlene Nicgorski, said, "You rob us of the opportunity to show the jury the truth here," and later added, "The jury is entitled to have some sense of the words that were used to describe Mr. Rodríguez's predicament."

"I have that discretion under law," Carroll commented, as he denied the request. "For the purposes of this case, we do not need to hear about the experiences of a witness or any members of his family in a foreign country.

"We're not going to get into ears and eyes and individual tortures."

The above scene is pieced together from three accounts of a US government trial charging eleven Sanctuary Movement leaders with "alien smuggling" that began in Tucson, Arizona, in November of 1985. As was noted previously in this volume, earlier that year and at the start of Ronald Reagan's second presidential term, federal officials had brought a seventy-one-count indictment against sixteen Sanctuary Movement leaders. Simultaneously, the Immigration and Naturalization Services (INS) conducted a series of raids, arresting over sixty non–US citizens living in or connected to Sanctuary who were labeled "unindicted co-conspirators" in the case. Lasting seven months and garnering much media coverage, the trial hinged largely upon the testimonies of paid federal informants who had infiltrated the movement, as well as sixteen "co-conspirator" Central American refugees who were compelled to testify as witnesses for the prosecution under the threat of deportation. Silence also played a role, as federal judge Earl Carroll prohibited witnesses from speaking on topics of US or international refugee law, conditions in El Salvador or Guatemala, or their religious faith, even barring their use of the words "death," "kill," "torture," and "refugee." This effectively precluded jurors from receiving important background and context surrounding the defendants' motivations. Even so, the defense rested. Ultimately, eight leaders were convicted on felony charges, but sentenced only with probation.

While the trial meted out little punishment to US-citizen Sanctuary Movement leaders in the end, the way it was conducted reveals more insidious—and long-lasting—forms of the US government's repression of the movement: surveillance, legal manipulation, narrative silencing, and disproportionate traumas levied on Central American refugees displaced by US-funded civil wars. Although the trial sent a chill through the movement, it also did as much to publicize it thanks to the size and coordination of a transnational Sanctuary solidarity network that worked to disseminate the movement's own version of events, in effect presenting a public counternarrative to the US government's prosecution throughout the trial. A recent magazine headline about 1980s Sanctuary says it best: "The Sanctuary movement put U.S. foreign policy on trial."[1]

This recounting of Alejandro Rodríguez's testimony comes from two memoirs written by North American women Sanctuary participants who traveled to Tucson to witness the trial, and a media packet published by the Arizona Sanctuary Defense Fund containing weekly updates on the trial and disseminated widely to participating Sanctuary organizations and journalists.[2] In these accounts, the words of Salvadoran asylum seeker Alejandro Rodríguez, translated from Spanish in court and italicized here for emphasis, appear scant among voluminous pages covering the details of the trial. Despite this, accounts emphasize the transformative power of his and the other refugees' testimonies on those whose ears they reached.

In all, Sanctuary participants produced a vast amount of literature about the movement and their interpretations of its various meanings, be they personal, political, or prophetic. In my own research and piecing together of participant and refugee testimonies across time, I have come to understand Sanctuary as an ongoing, iterative dialogue. These interpretations—many of them duplicated and disseminated throughout member networks, preserved, and traceable in archives across North America—describe Sanctuary as a spiritual and political "journey" or "process" of accompaniment and witnessing. As movement leader and Quaker organizer Jim Corbett wrote in 1983, "For the State, sanctuary is a place of refuge that government agents are reluctant to invade. For a community of faith, sanctuary is the community's protective solidarity with the oppressed, practiced openly in the face of oppression"[3]—practiced openly, in the accompaniment of refugees as they fled US-funded violence in Central America; in aiding them in seeking safety in the United States; in listening to and being moved by their stories; in bearing witness to, and denouncing, the impacts of US state violence. But whose testimony is at the center of the story?

In my book *Detention Empire*, I place the Sanctuary Movement at the heart of what I call a "battle over truth" in the 1980s—an escalating contestation between growing forms of protest against war and mass displacements caused by US foreign policy, and counterinsurgent policies of repression and retaliation adopted by the Reagan administration designed to silence dissent. The 1980s Sanctuary Movement was the largest civil mass disobedience organized against detention and deportation in US history.[4] In retaliatory response to Latin American migrations that US Cold War foreign policy and interventions in civil wars in Central America were exacerbating, the Reagan administration embraced new immigration enforcement policies, including the systematic use of detention to deter asylum seekers, the expansion of border militarization under the War on Drugs, and prison privatization. By decade's end, these policies entrenched what I call "a detention empire"—a supercharged system of criminalized migration, detention, deportation, and logics of border enforcement that resistance movements have yet to effectively slow, reform, or abolish.

The 1980s Sanctuary Movement effectively shielded thousands of Central American asylum seekers from deportation, saving countless lives. Revisiting these histories is an urgently timely and instructional task: Sanctuary formations endure to this day and provide a powerful theory and a model for resisting state-sanctioned violence on local and global levels. However, then and now, sanctuary coalitions and workers have confronted challenges, including divisiveness, political disagreements, patriarchy, and white saviorism within organizing spaces, and missed opportunities in expressing solidarity across efforts and across borders.

Inspired by a subfield of ethnic studies called "critical refugee studies," this chapter focuses on the implications of "storytelling" as a central tactic employed by Sanctuary Movement participants. Similar to the stated aim of 1980s Sanctuary to subvert the narrative of the US government by "welcoming the stranger," critical refugee studies provides helpful methods for approaching new histories of Sanctuary by encouraging us to forge "new humane paradigms, dialogues, visuals, and technologies that replace and reverse the dehumanization of refugees."[5] Reclaiming a concept of "refugee" that originated in the global North to instead return focus on people who are the most impacted, this field prompts us to view experiences of refugeeness from the vantage point of people on the move, rather than the nation state. It critically questions the ways legal categories established by nation states and existing international human rights regimes have historically failed to protect people on the move, such as those fleeing Central American civil wars in the 1980s, and aims to uncover root conditions causing displacement in the first place, such as colonialism, capitalism, war, and environmental destruction. In much scholarship and in public discourse, categories of immigration status—the way "refugee" is defined in international law—are often taken for granted and assumed to be fixed. This has resulted in an ongoing dehumanization of immigrants and refugees, cementing ideas that some displaced people are more "deserving" of rights than others.

Ultimately, a critical refugee studies approach recognizes the need to center refugee voices. I define storytelling as the creation, preservation, and public mobilization of literary, artistic, and personal accounts—firsthand testimonies of migration and state violence. What narrative strategies did Sanctuary adopt to put US foreign policy on trial? In what ways were refugee testimonies mobilized? How did storytelling tactics and anti-imperial messaging shape forms of state retaliation and silencing?

US Intervention and Counterinsurgency

The Sanctuary Movement originated as a set of coordinated acts of civil disobedience in resistance to immigration detention and deportation. In my book, *Detention Empire*, I argue that the heightening immigration detention and enforcement practices that the Sanctuary Movement was responding to in the 1980s became an extension, and reflection, of the counterinsurgent US military interventions in Central America that were also causing the mass displacement of refugees. Acts of witnessing, accompaniment, and testimony became centrally important within the Sanctuary Movement because the truths migrants told of the root causes of violence and displacement in Central America, and their connections to US foreign policy, posed a direct conflict with official US government narratives.

Civil wars in Guatemala, Nicaragua, and El Salvador killed a quarter of a million people between 1974 and 1996. In the 1980s, an estimated one million people fleeing violence sought refuge in the United States, stoking a decade-long debate over US asylum policy.[6] US Cold War ideological commitments led the United States to wage counterinsurgent military interventions throughout the region, exacerbating the violence. In 1979, a revolution led by Frente Sandinista ousted US-backed right-wing dictator Anastasio Somoza in Nicaragua. Fearing that a Soviet-Cuba-Nicaragua alliance would spread Communist influence throughout the region, the United States subsequently aided Nicaraguan "Contra" right-wing rebel groups, using Honduras as a training ground. Similarly, in ongoing civil wars in El Salvador and Guatemala, the United States propped up right-wing authoritarian governments and local oligarchs, and funded and trained right-wing death squads to stave off leftist peasant and Indigenous-led insurgencies. When the Reagan administration entered office, it doubled down on US intervention by ramping up aid and counterinsurgent operations. By 1981, five hundred civilians a month were being killed in El Salvador, and by 1984, five hundred thousand had entered the United States without documents. By 1983, Salvadorans occupied 30–35 percent of detention space in the US Southwest.

Controlling immigration became a central policy piece of the Reagan administration's foreign policy plans to contain communism and maintain economic dominance in Latin America, and to militarize law and border enforcement in its renewed War on Drugs at home. The administration became increasingly preoccupied with mediating the growing visibility of asylum seekers arriving telling stories of the sheer violence and horror resulting from US foreign policy interventions in Central America. Reagan's repression of migrants through the increasing use of detention and deportation originated in US counterinsurgent tactics of "low-intensity warfare," as the administration worked to deny and cover up mounting evidence of genocidal levels of violence against Indigenous, peasant, leftist, and resistance groups in Guatemala and El Salvador at the hands of US-trained and -funded right-wing death squads. Rooted in its support for these countries' right-wing governments, the United States subjected war-displaced Salvadorans and Guatemalans to deportation throughout the decade. Although in theory, the 1980 Refugee Act aligned US law with international law to provide all arriving asylum seekers due process to apply for political asylum, the State Department issued blanket advisory statements that were stapled to every Salvadoran and Guatemalan asylum application stating that these applicants should be seen as "economic migrants." Although immigration judges could use their discretion, a sample of ten thousand Salvadoran asylum cases between 1981 and 1986 found that only one judge disagreed with the State Department's advisory. In this way, the Reagan administration subverted, yet claimed it was upholding, the due process provisions of the 1980 Refugee Act.[7]

Stoking Cold War nationalism and public xenophobia, the Reagan administration also characterized asylum seekers from Central America (and those who aided them) as posing a racialized and subversive threat to US interests. Refusing to acknowledge the role of US-backed, right-wing violence, Reagan instead maintained the lie that communism was the sole cause of migrant displacement. For example, at a 1983 fundraising dinner in Mississippi, he warned audiences that if US intervention failed to stop the spread of communism in Central America, it would result in "a string of anti-American Marxist dictatorships" and "a tidal wave of refugees" coming across the US-Mexico border.[8] Similarly, US Army General Ernest Graves warned that if nations across Central America became Communist dictatorships, there "would be a flood of refugees and illegal immigrants larger than any we have experienced to date."[9] Of note is Graves's collapsing of "refugee" and "illegal," and the administration's use of dehumanizing language characterizing asylum seekers as synonymous with hydrological disaster—language that has become ubiquitous in public discourse surrounding immigration.

US interventions in Central America sparked a broad-based and transnational Central American Peace Movement, led and participated in by refugees, antiwar groups, faith leaders, and students—many of whom had protested against US intervention in Vietnam in the decade prior and likened El Salvador to "another Vietnam." Growing resistance led by Central American asylum seekers in detention, especially at the El Centro facility in southern California, for example, also garnered media attention and public sympathy. US interventions in Central America also sparked a wave of local advocacy and legal efforts to grant Salvadoran and Guatemalan asylum seekers Extended Voluntary Departure (EVD), which Reagan had done for exceptional groups fleeing communism, such as the Polish. It was in this context that the Sanctuary Movement was born.

While Sanctuary histories do not pinpoint an exact date or site of origin of the movement, Tucson-based Quaker Jim Corbett and Reverend John Fife of Southside Presbyterian Church are recognized as two of the 1980s movement's founders. After attempting to assist Central American refugees in detention and witnessing INS officials violating their due process rights, Corbett originated the idea of waging "active resistance" by forming a network of bond and legal aid groups.[10] Deciding to "go public," Southside Presbyterian Church and several others across the United States were the first churches to declare themselves publicly as "sanctuary" congregations on March 24, 1982, the second anniversary of the death of Oscar Romero, an archbishop who had been gunned down by a government assassin while offering Mass at a hospital chapel in San Salvador. At Southside Presbyterian, "Alfredo," a Salvadoran refugee who wore a bandana over his face to conceal his real identity, spoke to a crowd, and the *Tucson Citizen* labeled him "one of the most publicized undocumented aliens here ever."[11] At the movement's height by the middle of the decade, Sanctuary had grown to over five hundred official congregations and sixty thousand participants. Sanctuary declarations pointed to concepts of refuge in scripture, medieval tradition, and peace and slavery abolition movements in US history to justify their sheltering of refugees while charging the United States with violating international law and "the most fundamental standards of human decency."[12] Their calling upon these histories suggests dual and simultaneous interpretations of sanctuary as both a spiritual experience and a political statement.

The Arizona Sanctuary Defense Fund's media packet for dissemination surrounding the Sanctuary trial detailed the history of the movement and featured a series of quotations by indicted movement leaders, including Fife and Corbett. Fife offered, "If the United States planned to escalate its involvement [in Central America], it would have good reason to try and shut off the flow of refugees. They wouldn't want all those witnesses standing up in our churches and telling us about the atrocities."[13] This speaks to what many participants envisioned Sanctuary's purpose to be—to present a direct and moral challenge to US foreign policy.

Speaking Truth to Empire: Storytelling as Movement Strategy

How, then, did Sanctuary put US foreign policy on trial in the court of public opinion? Storytelling—defined here as the public mobilization of firsthand accounts of state violence and migration—became a central movement strategy. What kinds of narrative tactics did the movement adopt, and why? In her analysis of the use of narrative in the Sanctuary Movement, Teresa Godwin Phelps reflects, "Only by presenting a competing narrative that exposed the ideological bias in the implementation of the 1980 Refugee Act and the conditions in Central America could the sanctuary movement hope to change the law. *What* they did was only a small part of the story. *Why* they did it was the crucial part."[14] As the Reagan administration's growing embrace of counterinsurgency in US military interventions in Central America was reflected in repressive new border-enforcement measures targeting Salvadoran and Guatemalan asylum seekers at home, Sanctuary workers diversified their tactics. Beyond appealing to elected representatives and participating in rallies and demonstrations, they became increasingly committed to the idea that elevating the visibility of firsthand migrant testimonies in sacred and public arenas was the best way to expose—and shame—US state-sponsored violence and move North American audiences into awareness and action.

The below discussion of storytelling in Sanctuary is by no means comprehensive, but it includes "speech acts" by refugees, public media campaigns, and other performative displays featuring refugee stories. As the 1980s Sanctuary Movement grew, efforts increasingly focused on illuminating the roots of the migration crisis—the hemispheric reverberations of US foreign policy. Historians have noted that the movement became increasingly political, and its storytelling work more public, into the mid-1980s, especially after central coordination moved from Tucson to Chicago and as violence in Central America and contestations between Sanctuary and the INS escalated. As Nathan Ellstrand concludes, Sanctuary operated both as a "practice of solidarity with those victimized and as a critique of the policies that led to their victimization."[15] As the Milwaukee Sanctuary Coordinating Committee put it, the "radical" approach of public sanctuary was "a way to get at the root of the problem" through intersectional, interracial, and interfaith organizing.[16] Often articulated as solidarity, narratives that also turned inward towards self-reflection or made appeals to US audiences and power brokers may also have had the effect of centering US actors and emotions. Even so, Sanctuary organizers demonstrated self-awareness and wrestled extensively with questions of privilege wielded by white and North American participants, intersectionality, and what true solidarity looked like.

Phelps argues that one critical way Sanctuary workers practiced solidarity and controlled a "narrative of civil disobedience" was by adopting an intentional "renaming" practice of giving the label "refugee" to all asylum seekers from Central America whom the US government would commonly label "undocumented aliens."[17] Indeed, "refugee" appears as a ubiquitous term across movement literature. In this way, Sanctuary used narrative to argue for an expanded application of the term as defined by the 1980 Refugee Act, which aligns with the 1967 United Nations Protocol Relating to the Status of Refugees, which defines refugees as those with a "well-founded fear" of "political persecution." This is akin to the Critical Refugee Studies Collective's (CRSC) more recent offering of a more expansive definition of the term as applying to any person uprooted by war, imperial violence, or environmental violence, with a similar intent to challenge the failures of the state in living up to its promise of protecting vulnerable populations, and to offer narrative dignity to the complexities of displaced persons' lived experiences. Similar to Sanctuary's oft-stated commitments to accompaniment and bearing witness, the CRSC states its central goal of "allowing the worlds of refugees to be evident, on their own terms, as much as possible."[18]

From Sanctuary, Salvadoran and Guatemalan migrants testified publicly to the violence they experienced at the hands of US-backed death squads in their home countries, in transit, in refugee camps, and in US detention. To avoid retaliation or harming their chances of obtaining legal asylum, they often hid their faces and identities by adopting aliases and wearing face coverings while making public appearances or giving media interviews. While movement participants made efforts to center Central American voices, these were mediated by translators and often paired with firsthand accounts of (predominantly) white North Americans who accompanied refugees in Central America or scholarly "experts" also bearing witness to civil wars in Central America and US militarism. As Sergio González explains, "Sanctuary leaders coordinated the sharing of their own experiences with those of arriving asylum seekers, as the movement was by design formulated to bring congregation members into closer contact with those suffering from war and repression."[19] These perspectives, while intended to provide context and amplify testimonies, could at times serve to overshadow refugee voices and garner more media attention, as occurred during the Sanctuary trial.

In public "speech acts" or in printed media, refugee testimonies featured detailed tellings of the horrors of war and displacement. Truth also remained a central theme in migrant stories. For example, Juan, a Salvadoran speaking from sanctuary in San Francisco, related, "I still have plenty of fear. But I am more afraid to remain silent. . . . You have beautiful concepts here. You believe in truth."[20] Other frequent themes included hope, gratitude for sanctuary spaces and participants, and belief in the kindness of US people and the promise of democratic institutions, which stood in sharp contrast to shocking stories of US militarism in Central America.

Consider, for example, excerpts of testimonies prepared by University Baptist Church sanctuary and how they were presented in a University of Washington newspaper in March of 1983: "These stories are first person testimonies told through Sabina Astete who translates for Pilar, Lydia, Carlos and Patricia (not their real names)—Salvadoran refugees who recently arrived in Seattle. Each time the refugees testify and tell their stories, they relive much of the pain and trauma they have experienced, as well as the grief they feel for their friends and family who have died or been left behind." Pilar, who witnessed the murder of Archbishop Romero and worked for a Christian Base Community, shared the following:

> They interrogated and threatened me, asking me to tell them who our "leader" and our "guide" was. I told them we had no leader—except for the priest, and they had already killed him—and that the clinic and school were a community project. Then they began to beat and torture me because I would not give them information. I was beaten, raped, burned and given electric shocks to my head and other parts of my body while still handcuffed to my child. . . . I knew that I had to tell the world about the things that had happened to me and about El Salvador. I knew then that I had to come to the United States. . . . When you hear the helicopters and planes flying overhead and you look up and you see that they are American planes and helicopters you know who is behind much of what is happening to our villages and people. And yet in many ways North Americans are the hope for El Salvador. It is only through your actions that your government will stop funding the military in my country and thereby end the atrocities.

After hearing the testimony of Carlos, a lay minister and Red Cross refugee camp aid worker whose village was destroyed by the military and who was listed as a suspected "terrorist" by the Salvadoran government,

Patricia added, "All this is true. I was in the village when it was bombed and they shot the rockets. The helicopters fly over the houses so low that you can see the men throwing bombs and rockets out the doors of the helicopters. I could see the 'norteamericanos' who flew the helicopters."[21] Similar to the way refugee testimonies were replicated in Sanctuary newsletters and other formats, the testimonies were published in long form, yet also seem edited and curated to have a story arc. US involvement in the war appears as a prominent "punchline" to the story, with appeals to US audiences and recurring themes mentioned above often appearing near the end.

Although refugees often expressed gratitude for North American allies in testimonies given to media and public audiences, those living and working in Sanctuary also expressed frustrations, especially in private settings and internal Sanctuary communications. Perhaps because of these difficulties, individual refugees appeared more frequently in public, with some testimonies replicated across publications and archives, in effect producing a trail that helps trace Sanctuary's shifting dialogues and meanings in various contexts. Pilar, whose story is shared above, also participated in a "Freedom Caravan" speaking tour across the Pacific Northwest, appeared in multiple newspapers and on radio shows, and spoke to a large crowd after she and her children were arrested in an INS raid that led to the Sanctuary trial in which she was named an unindicted co-conspirator. "If they're going to kill me, let them do it here," she challenged. "If they deport us, death is what awaits us, us and our children."[22] In this instance, Pilar's personal politics are clear as she frequently stated her belief that she had been targeted in retaliation for her visibility and for speaking out.

In other instances, North American Sanctuary participants may have infused new meaning in the process of curating and republishing testimonies. Some perspectives vaunted refugee testimony as transformative, liberatory—prophetic, even. For example, a testimony given by the Vargas family in Sanctuary at Wellington Church in Chicago in 1982 appears in one archive as "Personal Witnesses from Sanctuary Participants." When the father, Daniel, is asked if he feels his family is being used for political purposes, he answers, "No. Let me begin by saying that we aren't political. . . . People who ask if we are being used are asking the wrong question. They should be asking, 'Why are they fleeing?' The answer to that would be because of the genocide in my country, that they are terminating the people. . . . The extermination of our people is being made possible by the aid that this government (U.S.) is sending to El Salvador."

The family's story appears again the following year, this time in an article written by Renny Golden, cofounder of the Chicago organizing hub Chicago Religious Task Force on Central America (CRTFCA), an interfaith solidarity organization with a stated mission "to inform, educate and activate people on the conditions in Central America and the plight of refugees." Golden writes, "Daniel insists he isn't political. When asked about his work, however, he talks of taking part in a workers' strike which involved taking over a power plant. When the government moved toward the plant, the workers were prepared to blow up the plant and themselves rather than surrender." Her commentary is followed by two quotations of faith leaders on the politicization of the movement. The first was by Reverend Chevrier, who hosted the Vargas family at Wellington Church and said, "One of the most important things that happened to us is the connection being made between faith and the political situation in Central America." Reverend Sid Mohn then added, "When the church has to break the law in order to provide refuge for homeless people, the struggle for justice has reached a new stage. Now the pastoral has merged with the political, service is prophetic and love a subversive activity."[23] Inspired by liberation theology, Golden has demonstrated a lifelong commitment to Sanctuary and its meanings. In a 1990 piece published in CRTFCA's newsletter, *Basta!*, she wrote, "Refugees are the prophetic word in our day. . . . As a people they have arrived in our land implicitly prepared to be defenders of the truth, to denounce a complicity of silence that roars above the chatter of ordinary, sanitized U.S. cultural life."[24] In a recent conversation I had with her about the evolution of the movement and contestations over the politicization of refugee testimonies, she explained CRTFCA's position: "If you're accusing us of trying to stop US intervention, you're correct. If you're accusing us of using refugees to do that, you're incorrect. It's simply presenting the truth of the suffering."[25]

Silencing Sanctuary

Once in office, Reagan took a slew of actions to facilitate interdepartmental military and law enforcement cooperation—in effect, expanding legalities and capacities for domestic surveillance. This was in large part in response to a perceived immigration crisis and growing public dissent over US Central American foreign policy, which the administration acknowledged (at least privately) its interventionist wars would exacerbate. Early measures taken included supporting the passage of the Department of Defense Authorization Act of 1981, which allowed for the military to assist civilian law enforcement in monitoring and intelligence gathering; and pardoning two agents convicted of crimes relating to the FBI's 1960s COINTELPRO program that surveilled, harassed, and even murdered members of the Black nationalist movement. In December of 1981, Reagan issued Executive Order 12333, which legalized infiltration tactics in domestic security and terrorism investigations for the first time in US history. This privilege extended to the FBI and anyone working on its behalf as a private contractor. It also authorized CIA members to "operate anywhere . . . in support of national foreign policy objectives abroad." This effectively legalized interagency cooperation and the use of military equipment for domestic counterintelligence.[26] These moves facilitated INS and FBI cooperation in US government infiltration and surveillance of the Sanctuary Movement through Operation Sojourner.

Worried about negative publicity, the INS at first did not make Sanctuary-related arrests. In January of 1984, the Sanctuary Coordinating Committee of Milwaukee sent a memo out to the national movement warning of FBI visits to nine solidarity movement members in recent weeks. They questioned links between members of the Committee in Solidarity with the People of El Salvador (CISPES) and recent bombings of federal facilities in Washington, DC, and New York City, describing solidarity groups as possible "fronts for bringing leftist guerillas" into the United States and connections to Sanctuary.[27] At the time, FBI agents denied any collaboration with the INS, but subsequent events would reveal otherwise. At the Inter-American Symposium on Sanctuary in Tucson in April of 1985 and in the wake of the January raids that would lead into the Sanctuary trial, Gil Dawes, pastor of Faith United Methodist Church, joked, "The Reagan Administration and INS are to be credited for their unwitting assistance!" Galvanizing movement organizing, the arrests "set the stage" for thirteen hundred participants to attend. "Clearly it was an opportune moment to broaden the base of the Sanctuary Movement."[28]

One Sanctuary action literally put US empire on trial and took place that fall—with refugee testimonies at the center. A mock "Trial of Truth" organized at the Dirksen Federal Building in Chicago and religious vigil on November 6, 1985, coincided with the start of the Sanctuary Movement trial in Tucson. Newspaper images show that during the action, demonstrators were pushed out of the federal building by police officers.[29] A script found in indicted movement leader Darlene Nicgorski's papers was also disseminated to Sanctuary congregations to be adapted for their use, with instructions for roles that local Sanctuary participants and refugee "unindicted co-conspirators" could play.[30] It invites the "Trial of Truth" to be performed in church services or community spaces, and includes real testimonies of torture, chemical warfare, and Indigenous persecution that could be used if other testimonies were not readily available.

The "Trial of Truth" features three defendants: Religious Freedom, Equal Treatment for Refugees under the Law, and Testimony of Central Americans, who are all silenced by the judge—a direct critique of judge Earl Carroll's gag ruling in the Sanctuary trial. When it is Testimony's turn "to speak for the suffering of Central Americans," the role reads, "We have been raped, mutilated, and imprisoned. Indiscriminate bombing and flesh-searing chemical warfare are used against us. All too often the weapons and training bear the stamp, MADE IN THE USA." The trial ultimately finds the defendants innocent and the "U.S. government guilty of murder in its policy of death and destruction throughout Central America. . . . The blood of more than 100,000 Central American victims is on the U.S. government's hands." One by one, gagged defendants are freed and speakers in unison repeat, "We will not be silenced."

Meanwhile, the Sanctuary trial had begun. The interpretation of Sanctuary as largely an act of witness extended to the trial itself as participants and supporters from around the country traveled to attend and document court proceedings. By many accounts, some of the most moving and dramatic moments of the trial took place when refugees took the witness stand—witnesses that Judge Carroll deemed "hostile." Although Judge Carroll barred refugees from telling their stories of war and displacement, they still exerted agency in the courtroom.

Judith McDaniel, an Albany, New York, Sanctuary participant who was captured by Contra forces in Nicaragua and detained for twenty-nine hours while taking part in a Witness for Peace delegation in 1985, characterized witnessing in her memoir as "a circle." Hearing testimony of a Salvadoran man named Pedro inspired McDaniel to make the journey to Nicaragua in the first place; then, witnessing violence firsthand reaffirmed her commitment to return to the United States and tell her own story to others. She wrote, "I understood that witnessing is especially necessary when the reality of a lived experience is denied by the culture at large, the culture to which the witness is brought." She traveled to Tucson to see the trial against Sanctuary workers and "to hear what kind of a case the government was making against their work, hear how they themselves would explain their work."[31]

Upon McDaniel's arrival, the Arizona Sanctuary Defense Fund media office gave her a press packet, and a sister at a local convent offered up her entire file on the movement, containing news clippings, articles, committee reports and minutes, and her personal notes. McDaniel wrote that she felt overwhelmed by the amount of documentation produced by the movement about the movement—a sentiment I relate to, having spent much time in the archives of Sanctuary leaders. In sum, the trial primarily consisted of evidence and testimony provided by US government informant Jesús Cruz, who had infiltrated the movement, attended meetings, coordinated with leaders, and assisted refugees while wearing a body bug. The defense rested. However, witness accounts paid special attention to the testimony of refugees—stories that were told in the courtroom but could not be considered in the case.

Alejandro Rodríguez was a labor organizer who experienced torture and imprisonment at the hands of US-backed death squads in El Salvador. When indictments were first handed down in January of 1985, he was arrested while outside of sanctuary in Rochester and named an "illegal alien unindicted co-conspirator." It became clear during the trial that Jesús Cruz had been paid a bounty for each refugee family he turned in, after befriending and assisting them into Sanctuary. Rodríguez was then required to testify as a witness for the prosecution, or, as McDaniel put it, "required to give testimony against those who had helped him, those with whom he was in solidarity," or else he was threatened with deportation.[32] Given the restrictions on evidence placed by Judge Carroll, however, Rodríguez was disallowed from speaking of his reasons for leaving El Salvador. Just as US intervention in El Salvador's civil war ultimately compelled Alejandro Rodríguez and his family's presence in the United States, so US asylum policy denied it. And just as the prosecution compelled his speech, the court silenced it.

On the stand, however, refugee witnesses remained undeterred. McDaniel noted that when asked to identify defendant Maria del Socorro Pardo de Aguilar, who had aided him, Alejandro Rodríguez "added his own testimony" by saying, "People told me she had a very good heart. I remember her with much love." Infuriated, INS prosecutor Donald Reno objected, and "Mrs. Aguilar's heart was stricken from the record. And so was every attempt to allow Mr. Rodriguez to explain to the jury why he had fled El Salvador." Although the defense lawyers argued that not allowing the jury to be present while Rodríguez recounted his story would "rob him of his story and rob the jury of the chance to know the truth," Carroll countered, "I have that discretion under law."[33]

Judge Carroll did eventually allow Rodríguez, his wife Leticia, and thirteen other refugees to tell their stories in the courtroom, only for the record and after adjourning the jury each time. Many of the testimonies moved audience members to tears. One jury member later recounted that even though she did not hear all of Alejandro Rodríguez's story, she still went home and cried all night after he testified.[34]

Four months after Mr. and Mrs. Rodríguez testified and returned to Sanctuary in Rochester, he was arrested once again. This time, INS placed a fifty-thousand-dollar bond on him, noting his being a "national security risk" as the reason. A local newspaper speculated that the reason he was arrested was that he had traveled to Cuba and the Soviet Union in the early 1960s. The Rochester Sanctuary Committee raised the money for his bond, and he was released. A month later, by the end of June 1986, the Rodríguez family had fled to Canada. According to Miriam Davidson, "He said he had lost faith in our legal system."[35] Others mused, however, that the community raising bond funds for the Rodríguez family was the most important act of solidarity. After witnessing the Sanctuary trial, Judith McDaniel moved on to the Navajo Nation to witness the injustices facing Indigenous people being relocated from Big Mountain for mineral mining. "Those who are being affected by the potential relocation should be allowed to set the terms of their resistance, but that has not always been the reality of solidarity work when white people have been willing to undertake it," she wrote.[36]

Censored by the US government and hopefully landing safely in Canada, Alejandro Rodríguez left behind a message for his co-conspirators. Speaking candidly from Sanctuary in Rochester in 1985, he described his desire to "deepen the work until the movement becomes more aware of itself and its people, with a real expression of its historic roots. There is little vision of the work directed in solidarity with the people who are truly suffering repression. This manifests itself when you ask for a message without content."[37] Others in Sanctuary also urged allies to see it as a process of political education, and of learning to make way for migrant voices and leadership.

Conclusion: The Limits and Possibilities of Solidarity

A core tension arose within the Sanctuary Movement in its early years: Should participants work within existing frameworks of church-sponsored compassion, international human rights, and US electoral politics, or did the crisis demand pushing imaginatively beyond to question and challenge the foundations of US immigration law—and the global imperialism it rested upon—entirely? Beyond the question of political versus religious fractures within the movement, other fractures arose around the limits of solidarity. Real limits of capacity and the movement's focus on asylum seekers from Central America (and often more narrowly those politically on the left), and on antiwar activism could often lead to unfortunate choices. These included having to select which refugees to help, and whose stories to tell.

In 1986, Jim Corbett reflected on these critiques in a publication of his writings called "Borders and Crossings" with a tongue-in-cheek warning on the cover that reads, "The U.S. Attorney General may consider the acquisition of these papers to constitute participation in a criminal conspiracy." Corbett wrote,

> Most of our refugee services to date have been paternalistically organized, denying the refugees a voice, weakening their community development, and preparing them to serve Anglo America as a highly exploitable underclass. By fusing humanitarian and political concerns and by providing an opportunity for the refugees to be seen and heard, the sanctuary movement opens a way out of the bog of condescension that is created

> when well-meaning sympathizers develop programs modeled on establishment charities. But the sanctuary movement is only an opening; it does not in itself assure the growth of a community that looks beyond exile and is preparing to go free.[38]

It is notable that Corbett recognized Sanctuary as an "opening"—the beginning of a process that may be open-ended. In the same volume, Corbett discussed strategies around making distinctions among "refugees," "illegal" migrants, and those with criminal records. In many other instances, movement participants debated and drew lines of solidarity between aiding Central American refugees and other groups and causes.

Recent scholarly work and self-reflection have rightly identified weaknesses in the modern-day mainstream immigrant-rights movement's focusing more narrowly on narratives of immigrant deservingness, rights claims, or electoral politics. Some Sanctuary scholars have concluded that the movement's curated forms of storytelling have given rise to divisive "good" versus "bad" immigrant narratives and may have served to reproduce the very "exclusions it has sought to dismantle."[39] This recent discourse instead calls for a more effective and inclusive centering of migrant voices and framing of immigrant rights in anticapitalist, anti-imperialist, and/or abolitionist terms to target the root causes of global displacement and forced migration.[40]

Critical refugee studies approaches to new histories of Sanctuary that question the premise of state sovereignty and foreground migrant journeys and lifeworlds as sites of critique, decolonization, and reparation can help build new solidarities across groups and across borders. These visions are not new. As Alejandro Rodríguez concluded in 1985, "The sanctuary movement must take the next step, which is a historic step: to forge an anti-investment solidarity movement."[41] Ultimately, he was asking US audiences to divest from complicity in empire in all its forms.

NOTES

1 Natascha Elena Uhlmann, "The Sanctuary Movement Put U.S. Foreign Policy on Trial," *In These Times*, June 6, 2024. https://inthesetimes.com.

2 "Sanctuary Media Packet," Arizona Sanctuary Defense Fund, p. 3, folder "Sanctuary efforts/sites in Arizona: Arizona Sanctuary Defense Fund," box 5, Carol Cummings and Frank Cummings Papers (hereafter Cummings Papers), Swarthmore Peace Collection, Swarthmore College, Pennsylvania (hereafter SPC); Judith Mc-

Daniel, *Sanctuary: A Journey* (Firebrand Books, 1987), 136–37; Miriam Davidson, *Convictions of the Heart: Jim Corbett and the Sanctuary Movement* (University of Arizona Press, 1988), 122–23.

3 Jim Corbett, "One Year After: Some Thoughts on Sanctuary," box 2, folder 15, Darlene Nicgorski Papers on the Sanctuary Movement, Honnold/Mudd Library, Claremont University Consortium, Claremont, California (hereafter DNP).

4 Kristina Shull, *Detention Empire: Reagan's War on Immigrants and the Seeds of Resistance* (University of North Carolina Press, 2022), 160–61.

5 Yen Le Espiritu et al., *Departures: An Introduction to Critical Refugee Studies* (University of California Press, 2022), 11–13.

6 María Cristina Garcia, *Seeking Refuge: Central American Migration to Mexico, the United States, and Canada* (University of California Press 2006), 1.

7 Robert S. Kahn, *Other People's Blood: U.S. Immigration Prisons in the Reagan Decade* (Westview Press, 1996), 44; Garcia, *Seeking Refuge*, 84–118; Shull, *Detention Empire*, 139–40.

8 *Weekly Compilation of Presidential Documents* 19 (June 27, 1983): 901, Ronald Reagan Presidential Library, Simi Valley, California.

9 Quoted in Shull, *Detention Empire*, 130.

10 Ann Crittenden, *Sanctuary: A Story of American Conscience and the Law in Collision* (Weidenfeld and Nicolson, 1988), 30–31.

11 James R. Wycoff, "Church Goes Public with Sanctuary Offer," *Tucson Citizen*, March 24, 1982.

12 Jim Corbett, *CBS Evening News*, March 24, 1982. Quoted in Shull, *Detention Empire*, 163.

13 "Sanctuary Media Packet," Cummings Papers, SPC.

14 Teresa Godwin Phelps, "No Place to Go, No Story to Tell: The Missing Narratives of the Sanctuary Movement," *Washington and Lee Law Review* 123 (1991): 130. http://scholarlycommons.law.wlu.edu.

15 Nathan Ellstrand, "Politicized Refuge: Chicago and the Transformation of the Sanctuary Movement," *Middle West Review* 9, no. 1 (Fall 2022): 43. doi.org/10.1353/mwr.2022.0022.

16 Quoted in Sergio M. González, *Strangers No Longer: Latino Belonging and Faith in Twentieth-Century Wisconsin* (University of Illinois Press, 2024), 174.

17 Phelps, "No Place to Go, No Story to Tell," 131.

18 Espiritu et al., *Departures*, 20.

19 González, *Strangers No Longer*, 175.

20 Quoted in Robert Tomsho, *The American Sanctuary Movement* (Texas Monthly Press, 1987), 5–6.

21 "Tales of El Salvador," from the Daily of the University of Washington, March 1, 1983, folder 3, "Testimonies—refugee," box 3, University Baptist Church Sanctuary Movement Records, Special Collections, University of Washington, Seattle, Washington (hereafter UBC).

22 Carey Quan Gelerntner, "Salvadorans Vow to Fight Deportation," *Seattle Times*, n.d. [January 1985]; folder 12, Clippings, 1982–1989, box 3, UBC.

23 Renny Golden, "Refugee Sanctuary: Churches Challenge the INS," *WIN*, January 1, 1983, folder 15, box 2, DNP.
24 Renny Golden, "Refugees as Prophetic Word," *Basta!*, February 1990, 23. Wisconsin Historical Society Library–Archives Digital Collection. https://content.wisconsinhistory.org.
25 Author phone interview with Renny Golden, September 18, 2020.
26 Timothy J. Dunn, *The Militarization of the U.S.-Mexico Border, 1978–1992: Low-Intensity Conflict Doctrine Comes Home* (University of Texas Press, 1996), 106–7; Brian Glick, *The War at Home* (South End Press, 1989), 30–31.
27 Memo, Sanctuary Coordinating Committee of Milwaukee, January 1984, folder 8, box 2, DNP.
28 Gil Dawes, "Reflections on Tucson Symposium and Consultation," *Basta!*, April 1985, 29. Wisconsin Historical Society Library–Archives Digital Collection. https://content.wisconsinhistory.org.
29 "Push Comes to Shove," *Chicago Tribune*, November 7, 1985, 3, sec. 2.
30 CRTFCA newsletter, October 1985, folder 12, box 2, DNP.
31 Judith McDaniel, *Sanctuary: A Journey* (Firebrand Books, 1987), 128–29.
32 McDaniel, *Sanctuary: A Journey*, 135.
33 McDaniel, *Sanctuary: A Journey*, 136–37.
34 Miriam Davidson, *Convictions of the Heart: Jim Corbett and the Sanctuary Movement* (University of Arizona Press, 1988), 125.
35 Davidson, *Convictions of the Heart*, 125.
36 McDaniel, *Sanctuary: A Journey*, 166.
37 *Sanctuary Perspectives*, Task Force for Central America, Tucson Ecumenical Council, January 1985, folder 47, box 2, DNP.
38 Jim Corbett, "Borders and Crossings," folder, Miscellaneous; Borders and Crossings by Jim Corbett 1986, box 1, Philadelphia Yearly Meeting of the Religious Society of Friends Papers, Swarthmore College Friends Historical Library, Swarthmore, Pennsylvania.
39 A. Naomi Paik, "Abolitionist Futures and the U.S. Sanctuary Movement," *Race and Class* 59, no. 2 (2017): 3–15; Grace Yukich, "Constructing the Model Immigrant: Movement Strategy and Immigrant Deservingness in the New Sanctuary Movement," *Social Problems* 60, no. 3 (August 2013): 302–20.
40 Walter J. Nicholls and Tara Fiorito, "Dreamers Unbound: Immigrant Youth Mobilizing," *New Labor Forum* 24, no. 1 (Winter 2015): 86–92; Leisy J. Abrego and Genevieve Negrón-Gonzales, eds., *We Are Not Dreamers: Undocumented Scholars Theorize Undocumented Life in the United States* (Duke University Press, 2020); Tina Shull and Jamila Hammami, "Resistance Archiving: Reflections on the IMM Print Detention Stories Project," in *Resistance and Abolition in the Borderlands: Confronting Trump's Reign of Terror* (University of Arizona Press, 2024), 406–38.
41 *Sanctuary Perspectives*, Task Force for Central America, Tucson Ecumenical Council, January 1985, folder 47, box 2, DNP.

3

Hospitality, Liberation, and Covenant

The Theological Roots of Sanctuary

ADAM WATERS

Introduction

In January 1985, Darlene Nicgorski, a forty-one-year-old nun with the School Sisters of St. Francis, was attending a religious retreat outside Detroit when she heard that federal agents were searching her home in Phoenix. She had been a leader in the Sanctuary Movement in Arizona for several years, so she understood that her work entailed some legal risk, but she was shocked by this turn of events. "I didn't expect the tactics," she told a reporter. "I was so engrossed in what I was doing, I didn't think of all the consequences." When she returned home several days later, she was arrested and arraigned on multiple counts related to illegal smuggling of "aliens" into the United States.[1]

Nicgorski's arrest was part of a large-scale government crackdown on the Sanctuary Movement. Over the following year, she and her codefendants proceeded through a highly publicized and intensely scrutinized trial in which they were routinely prevented from speaking openly with the jury about why they had gotten involved in sanctuary work and why they saw that work as necessary. In the end, Nicgorski was convicted of five felonies, including counts of conspiracy to violate US immigration law, transporting undocumented migrants, and aiding and abetting the harboring of undocumented migrants. Together, these counts carried a possible prison sentence of up to twenty-five years.[2]

But despite her conviction, Nicgorski remained firm in her commitment to sanctuary. And during sentencing, she was finally able to share her story. As she told the judge, she joined the Sanctuary Movement because of the missionary work she had done with her order in Latin America in the early 1980s. Nicgorski recounted how she and the other sisters fled Guatemala after a village pastor with whom they collaborated was labeled a Communist for his ministry to the poor and was murdered. From there, she went to Chiapas in southern Mexico, where she provided aid to Guatemalan refugees and recorded testimonies of the abuses they had suffered.

These experiences shaped her personal theology and influenced her understanding of sanctuary work. "The conditions I have seen and heard in which our brothers and sisters from Central America are forced to survive . . . call out to me and all persons of faith and decency," Nicgorski told the judge. "The message of the prophets and martyrs of the Latin American Church has set the stage for my response." For Nicgorski, the message was to join the side of the poor and to reject the forces of political and economic power that oppressed them. Her choice—and the choice before all people of moral conscience—was stark: "Either I believe and serve a God of LIFE AND JUSTICE or I serve the idols of death, power, money, and law." This was not easy work, by any means. "To give Life to the poor, one must give from one's own life. This is what is happening every day in Central America," she explained. "People are giving up their lives that there may be life for their children; they are living their faith. They are living in the real world and experiencing the same consequences as Jesus did for their choices; being threatened, accused, and tortured." This was the meaning of the Sanctuary Movement. And so, Nicgorski requested that, instead of being sentenced to prison time, she be allowed to continue her work assisting Central American refugees, whether in the United States or abroad.[3]

Nicgorski's remarkable sentencing statement reveals how closely intertwined religion and politics were for many activists in the 1980s Sanctuary Movement. Indeed, theology—talking about religion and religious belief—was not an afterthought in the Movement, nor was it merely a cover for churches and synagogues to adopt a particular political line promoted by secular radicals. Rather, theology was at the core of sanctuary in the United States, and disagreements about theology were as much a motivating force in the frictions within the Movement as were other differences. Centering theology and its relationship to politics in our analysis of the Sanctuary Movement can help us to develop a clearer understanding of how the Movement took shape, why it proved so popular, and what it meant to religious activists and communities.

The 1980s Sanctuary Movement was large and heterogenous, drawing in both secular and religious activists. Some came to sanctuary through their involvement in the wider Central America solidarity movement of the 1970s and 1980s, and their experiences with and subject matter expertise on Central American affairs were critical for helping set the direction of the Sanctuary Movement.[4] Many other sanctuary activists, however, would not have been able to point to El Salvador on a map before the early 1980s. They found their way into the work through their membership in religious communities. Indeed, at the core of the Sanctuary Movement were a wide variety of Christian churches, most notably representing the mainline Protestant denominations and Roman Catholicism. But the Movement also involved Jewish and other non-Christian religious communities, and a network of nongovernmental, faith-based organizations. Each of these entities brought its own theological perspective to bear, born from and shaped by the specificities of its history, constituency, and relationships with other groups. Although there is much to be gained from denominational histories of sanctuary, it would be too monumental a task for this chapter to try to document all of the different ways in which faith-based sanctuary activists appealed to theology.

It is possible, however, to discern some broader theological currents that crossed the boundaries of tradition and denomination.[5] In particular, three overarching theological themes appeared repeatedly in Sanctuary Movement spaces, sometimes coexisting and at other times competing for relevance. First, the Movement as a whole was suffused with a general theology of hospitality marked above all by its invocation of commandments in Christian and Jewish scripture to welcome the stranger and provide for the needy.[6] Second, as suggested by Nicgorski's sentencing statement, sections of the Movement reached for a radical interpretation of sanctuary that focused on the idea that God's message to humanity was one of liberation, and thus that heeding God's call meant struggling against the oppression that had given rise to and perpetuated the Central American refugee crisis. Third, some groups and leaders posited sanctuary as an act of covenant that would help to birth a new, universal community of moral peoples. The latter two themes were most closely associated with two geographical centers of gravity in the Movement, Chicago and Tucson, respectively. But across the United States, sanctuary congregations and leaders freely drew on, adapted, and combined these three themes, giving rise to a Movement theology that had some common and some particularistic elements. Exploring each of these themes in turn highlights how theological language acted as a tool both for knitting together the component parts of the 1980s Sanctuary Movement and for accentuating the divisions that would ultimately undermine its power and effectiveness.

Hospitality

Sanctuary activists and religious leaders connected the provision of sanctuary to the commandments in Jewish and Christian scripture to welcome the stranger, love the neighbor, and provide for the downtrodden.[7] This is evident in the written materials created by many of the sanctuary churches, from declarations of sanctuary to prayerbooks and informational pamphlets. For example, an interfaith prayer vigil and candlelight procession hosted at Milwaukee, Wisconsin's St. John's Cathedral in December 1982 spotlighted readings from the Book of Isaiah, in particular chapters 58 and 59, which describe the prophet Isaiah's calls to atone through acts of justice like feeding the hungry and sheltering the wanderer.[8] Likewise, when the College Hill Presbyterian Church in Tulsa, Oklahoma, held an ecumenical worship service as part of its sanctuary program in the fall of 1984, the scripture reading came from Matthew 25: "Then the Ruler will say to those on the right side, 'Come, O blessed of God, inherit the kingdom prepared for you from the foundation of the world: for I was hungry and you gave me food, I was thirsty and you gave me drink, I was a stranger and you welcomed me, I was in prison and you came to see me.'"[9] These teachings from Isaiah and Matthew were mainstays in sanctuary services.

Sanctuary churches both took cues from and helped to shape the theological and political positions of the denominations with which they were affiliated. Many Protestant denominations issued statements of support for the Sanctuary Movement in the 1980s, and these statements often embraced the hospitality theme. In 1985, the Episcopal Church expressed "deep disturbance and regret" at legal targeting of sanctuary activists, whom it identified as "acting out of religious conviction to offer protection and safe haven to Central Americans, based on Judeo-Christian imperatives to offer hospitality to the stranger and love to one's neighbor."[10] The 1988 American Baptist Churches USA resolution on Central American refugees affirmed that support for sanctuary was "rooted in biblical faith which commands hospitality for 'the stranger in our midst' (Exodus 23:9)." The statement went on to connect caring for the stranger with the description in the Bible of cities of sanctuary in Canaan, noting that the "cities of refuge were for the Israelites, 'as well as the stranger and sojourner among you' (Numbers 35:15)."[11] As in this case, the theology of hospitality was frequently joined with reference to the biblical roots of sanctuary practice, presenting the actions of the Sanctuary Movement as clearly and convincingly legitimized by core Christian and Jewish texts.

Related ideas also appeared in the writings of prominent Christian theologians affiliated with the Sanctuary Movement. For these theologians, the theme of sanctuary as welcoming the stranger functioned as a kind of *apologia* aimed at defending the Movement against its doubters and critics. In 1985, the Council on Religion and International Affairs hosted a debate pitting the Reverend William Sloane Coffin Jr., pastor of the interdenominational Riverside Church in New York City and a leading proponent of a number of progressive political causes including sanctuary, against Alan C. Nelson, the commissioner of the Immigration and Naturalization Services (INS) under President Ronald Reagan and one of the chief opponents of the Sanctuary Movement. Nelson focused in his remarks on the legal and constitutional implications of sanctuary, arguing that activists were impeding the proper functioning of the US immigration system. Coffin, meanwhile, called for shifting attention from "the legal questions surrounding sanctuary" to "the moral, political and historical aspects" of the Movement, and in particular to the meaning of sanctuary for American churches. He thus decried the arrest the previous year of two Texas sanctuary workers by suggesting that they were simply trying "to heed the biblical commandment found in the chapter of Leviticus" to love the foreigner as oneself.[12]

Robert McAfee Brown, the Presbyterian theologian, adopted a similar approach when he gave a lecture defending sanctuary work to the prestigious Commonwealth Club in San Francisco in 1986. For Brown, sanctuary was first and foremost a "humanitarian act" that embodied the biblical call to "love the neighbor." To the critics who argued that sanctuary was also or even primarily a political act (and therefore an improper overreach by religious communities into the sphere of government), he conceded that sheltering refugees had "inevitable political consequences." "To 'love the neighbor' involves politics, if the neighbor is hungry or out of work and you have to provide food or a job," Brown argued. "Motivated by love, you work through political structures that are created to extend justice and do away with injustice." For Brown, this combining of "love" and "justice" in the practice of sanctuary placed it squarely at "the heart of both Jewish and Christian agendas."[13] Faith-based sanctuary activists entered into the fray around immigration and asylum in order to live out the values of hospitality enshrined in their traditions.

Indeed, as Brown suggested, the hospitality theme served as a guiding ethic beyond the Christian churches and theologians. One of the first Jewish organizations to embrace the Sanctuary Movement was New Jewish Agenda (NJA), a nondenominational group of progressive and left-wing Jews formed in 1980. NJA was active in a wide variety of domestic and international political causes, attracting particular opprobrium in the American Jewish community for its criticism of Israel's occupation of the West Bank territories and treatment of Palestinians. But it also played an important role in the Central America solidarity movement and in promoting sanctuary among Jewish congregations.[14] In a pamphlet titled "Jews and Central America: The Need to Act," NJA located American Jewish support for sanctuary in the practices of *tzedakah* (acts of righteousness) and *rachamim* (compassion) toward those less fortunate. In the past, NJA noted, the US government had failed to do enough to save Jewish refugees from Nazi persecution. Now, Jewish Americans had the chance to be a part of pushing the government to make a different decision. "We in New Jewish Agenda believe that we can no longer afford to be silent," the pamphlet continued. "Drawing on our experience of homelessness and senseless murder, and our history of resistance to persecution, we have an obligation to know the facts and speak out."[15] Underlining the urgency of the hospitality principle by calling forth historical examples of when others had failed to fulfill it was a common and powerful move for Jewish members of the Sanctuary Movement.

Hospitality also featured prominently in many Jewish congregational and denominational statements on the Sanctuary Movement.[16] The Rabbinical Assembly, representing rabbis in the Conservative Jewish movement, endorsed sanctuary in 1984. Its resolution opened with recognition that "the Torah commands us not to oppress the stranger since we know what it is like to be a stranger (Exodus 23:9)." It then went on to invoke the failed hospitality theme by arguing that "millions of Jews were murdered by the Nazis because the nations of the World, including the United States, did not open their gates to those fleeing the Nazi onslaught."[17] Similarly, the Union of American Hebrew Congregations (now the Union for Reform Judaism) proclaimed in 1985 that Reform Jews were "instructed in the Code of Holiness (Lev. 19:33) to take to heart the lessons of our own history by treating aliens in our midst with justice and compassion." "The history of the Jewish people from Egypt through the Holocaust and continuing today is the story of a group forced time and again to flee the lands in which it resided," the statement continued. "Repelled often in times of greatest need, Jews recognize the necessity for havens for the persecuted."[18] Thus, for American Jews, support for sanctuary was derived from linking the Torah's and the Talmud's instructions to provide shelter and support to the stranger with the experiences of antisemitism and displacement experienced by the modern Jewish diaspora.

The move to posit sanctuary as the carrying out of the obligation to welcome and care for the Other was clearly repeated across a variety of religious contexts. Indeed, the ubiquity of the hospitality language was precisely its purpose. Within the multicreedal Sanctuary Movement, faith-based leaders and activists needed to devise a shared theology that could appeal to diverse audiences and provide a foundation for building solidarity across lines of religious difference. The hospitality theme helped to bridge the divide between Jews, Protestants, and Catholics, in particular, because the source texts for this appeal were plentiful in both the Old and the New Testament—in Leviticus, Isaiah, Matthew, and beyond—and so could offer meaning to all three groups.

In this way, the theology of sanctuary as hospitality resembles other efforts in twentieth-century America to stitch together a supposed "Judeo-Christian" cultural heritage. As the religious historian K. Healan Gaston has shown, the language of a "Judeo-Christian America" brought faith communities together in common effort at a time when Americans perceived themselves to be facing growing internal and external threats, from secularism to totalitarianism to communism. "Judeo-Christian" was always a contested concept, deployed to advance widely varying agendas, and by the 1980s, religious liberals and progressives had largely ceded the terminology to the ascendant New Christian Right.[19] Support for the Sanctuary Movement was not always couched in specific "Judeo-Christian" language, although the Episcopal Church resolution quoted above did use the term. But whether explicitly "Judeo-Christian" or not, the appeal to a biblical imperative on hospitality reflected an impulse similar to other efforts to pull Christians and Jews together. In interfaith prayer services across the country, Jewish and Christian sanctuary activists affirmed their commitment to a collective political project rooted in the shared theological vocabulary of welcoming the stranger, loving the neighbor, and offering charity to the poor.

The hospitality theme served another purpose, as well, reflected in its frequent use in denominational endorsements of the Sanctuary Movement and in defenses against its critics. Arguing that sanctuary was an act of humanitarianism derived from the Bible blunted the power of claims that the Movement was simply using church communities as a cover for leftists and revolutionaries.[20] As Robert McAfee Brown argued, sanctuary was surely political, but that was due above all to the US immigration apparatus having politicized what was in essence charity. And as Reform Jewish leaders formulated their support for sanctuary, how could anyone assail American Jews for acting from a sense of their own history of persecution to offer support for persecuted Central Americans? In both cases, the frame of caring for the stranger not only spoke to biblical injunction but also appealed to familiar narratives about the United States as a nation with a long history of welcoming immigrants and of ministering to the poor.[21] Speaking of sanctuary theology in the language of hospitality therefore helped to bridge divides between theologically and politically more moderate and more radical factions in the Sanctuary Movement, and to explain sanctuary work in a way that would be more legible to journalists, politicians, and nonactivists.

Liberation

If the hospitality frame was intended to hold the various parts of the Sanctuary Movement together, two other theological frames played an inadvertent role in sowing the seeds of Movement division. The first was to cast sanctuary within the theological language of liberation, and in particular to draw on the liberation theology emerging from the Latin American churches. Given that the target of sanctuary work was the ongoing Central American refugee crisis, looking southward for theological inspiration was in some ways a natural choice. But it was also a controversial choice, sparking debate both inside and outside of the Movement because liberation theology advanced a radical, structural critique of class conflict and imperial domination that sounded to its critics like Marxism dressed up as Christianity.

The constellation of theological concepts and arguments that came to be known collectively as liberation theology was first popularized in the writings of various South American Catholic and Protestant theologians, including Gustavo Gutiérrez and Rubem Alves in the late 1960s. They hoped to correct what they saw as a deficiency in their churches' historical ministry in Latin America, especially as it pertained to the poor and racially marginalized. At the core of their liberation theology were two key ideas. The first was a vision of God intervening on the side of the poor and oppressed, including those subjected to US imperialism. The second was the argument that theology should be a reflective exercise coming only after Christian engagement with social, economic, and political reality. Christians, according to the liberation theologians, were called to join struggles for liberation wherever they were being waged. At the same time that this current was growing in significance in Latin America, new theologies of liberation were also being birthed in the United States—among them Black and feminist liberation theology. Importantly, these theological movements were not separate. Through the second half of the 1970s, Latin American and US liberation theologians engaged in regular dialogue and built close working relationships.[22]

Meanwhile, news of Latin American liberation theology was reaching nontheologians in the United States through a variety of means. Missionaries like Darlene Nicgorski, the convicted sanctuary activist, experienced firsthand what it looked like to live out the insights of liberation theology on the ground in Latin America and shared their stories widely once they returned home. Orbis Books, a publishing house operated by the Maryknoll Catholic order, also began to print English-language translations of the major works of Latin American liberation theology. Thus, as the Sanctuary Movement was kicking off in the early 1980s, the US Christian Left had already become quite familiar with liberation theology and, through that, with the liberation theologians' analysis of the economic and political situation in Latin America.

Latin American liberation theology was most closely associated with the Chicago branch of the Sanctuary Movement, headed by the Chicago Religious Task Force on Central America (CRTFCA). The CRTFCA was a coalition of faith-based groups in the Chicago area that had started working together to coordinate actions in solidarity with the liberatory struggle in El Salvador, but quickly expanded their vision and analysis to cover all of Central America. By 1982, the CRTFCA was one of the most prominent leaders of the Sanctuary Movement, particularly important in coordinating sanctuary placements and in facilitating information sharing among the many congregations and organizations involved.[23] Its staff and volunteers were primarily Christian leftists who were strong proponents of liberation theology and close observers of the development of new theological ideas in Latin America. Nicgorski was one of these CRTFCA workers.

Another important figure was Renny Golden, one of the founders of the CRTFCA and a key leader of the Movement. Interested in her young adulthood in joining the Dominican order, Golden had subsequently come to embrace political activism and decided against becoming a nun. She went on to receive a doctorate of ministry from the Chicago Theological Seminary in 1976, focusing on liberation theology.[24] Golden was also a collaborator in the "Theology in the Americas" project, wherein Christian theologians and activists from North America and Latin America thought together about how liberation theologies could respond to the most pressing social and political problems of the late 1970s.[25] The founder of "Theology in the Americas" was the Chilean Catholic Socialist Father Sergio Torres, who had fled his home country in exile after the right-wing military coup there in September 1973. At various moments, groups working with the project would explore how theology could be oriented toward liberation for working-class people, women, indigenous Americans, Asian Americans, Latinx Americans, and others.[26] But "Theology in the Americas" was most significant in its efforts to build a new internationalist consciousness on the North American Christian Left. Participants like Golden, who worked for a time on the Women's Project, gained a deeper understanding of ongoing political struggles in Latin America and of the role of liberation theology in providing a moral and ethical framework for determining how Christians should engage in these struggles.

Golden brought the theological convictions she had solidified in the 1970s into her work in the Sanctuary Movement in the 1980s. In a 1985 letter describing her commitment to sanctuary, she argued that a "fundamental mark of faith is choosing to side unequivocally with the poor." Criticism of sanctuary as scrambling the boundaries between religion and politics, she added, "fail[ed] to understand one of the most basic tenets of liberation theology which insists that faith actions on behalf of the poor and oppressed are inevitably political."[27] These ideas were reflected in the pages of *Basta!*, the sanctuary newsletter that Golden and the CRTFCA published from 1983 to 1992. One article outlining the CRTFCA's theology explained that "God's revelation is discovered amongst the poor and oppressed, and therefore, to make a preferential option for the poor and oppressed is to discover the God of history." While the CRTFCA called this a "theology of solidarity," the invocation of the "preferential option for the poor and oppressed" directly tied the organization's theological approach to liberation theology.[28]

The idea of the preferential option maintained that God was on the side of the poor and therefore that the church had an obligation to direct its energies toward these people. It had first gained prominence in the writings of the Latin American liberation theologians in the 1960s. Then, at the 1968 conference of the Latin American Episcopal Conference (Consejo Episcopal Latinoamericano; CELAM) in Medellín, Colombia, the preferential option had been incorporated into official Catholic doctrine in Latin America. The Medellín final document argued that "the Lord's particular mandate to 'evangelize the poor' should lead us to a distribution of efforts and of apostolic personnel that gives effective preference to the poorest and most needy sectors."[29] The CRTFCA saw the work of the Sanctuary Movement as building on the theological foundations established at Medellín by providing church refuge to poor and marginalized Central American refugees.

While CRTFCA leaders like Golden and Nicgorski led the push in the Sanctuary Movement toward liberation theology, they were not alone. Pro-sanctuary theologians also routinely endorsed the liberation frame. Richard Shaull, the Presbyterian theologian and Latin America expert whose 1955 book, *Encounter with Revolution*, had anticipated many of the themes of liberation theology, wrote that sanctuary was properly understood as the North American correlate of the Christian Base Community movement in Latin America.[30] The base communities were small, often lay-led spaces where poor and indigenous Latin Americans could study the Bible in the context of their material conditions and orient themselves toward liberatory action. They were the primary ecclesial mechanism for doing liberation theology beyond the walls of the seminary. Shaull wrote that many US Christians had started out in sanctuary work out of a sense of obligation to the poor and needy. But as sanctuary activists started to hear the stories of Central American refugees, they began to understand the structural nature of oppression and to "dream of and work for a radically transformed society" where "those who are now powerless will have a chance to shape their own lives and destiny."[31] They found that the Bible provided a road map for and a companion on the journey to liberation. Shaull articulated a vision of the Sanctuary Movement that moved beyond a generalized commitment to hospitality and toward a more radical project of political and economic transformation. His public association with Movement leaders, as when he spoke at the Inter-American Symposium on Sanctuary in Tucson in 1985, also helped to legitimize their work within the mainline Protestant theological circles in which Shaull moved.[32]

And the Latin American liberation theologians themselves often played public roles in supporting sanctuary. In late September 1986, more than one thousand sanctuary activists convened in Washington, DC, to celebrate the progress they had made and recommit themselves to the Movement. One of the opening speakers of the gathering was Father Jon Sobrino, a Jesuit liberation theologian based in El Salvador. "You should see the Sanctuary Movement in its proper context," Sobrino advised the largely North American audience. "As we all know, this context is a system, a set of structures which produces injustice and wars."

Many of these injustices were the result of US intervention in Latin America. "So you should try to work and fight," he said. "I hope the word 'fighting' does not frighten anyone. Jesus of Nazareth was a fighter. That's why he was killed."[33] Like Nicgorski, Sobrino saw sanctuary activists and others engaged in solidarity with Central American refugees as emulating the model of Jesus.

Sobrino subsequently developed his justification of the Sanctuary Movement as a way of living a theology of liberation in a longer piece published in 1988 in the Christian journal *CrossCurrents*. He described sanctuary as an act arising out of the recognition of God's preferential option for the poor, as "a way of defending the lives of the poor and thus of believing and acting out biblical faith."[34] It was not "the most radical" way to address the structural oppression that drove Central Americans to the United States, yet it was "a workable and honest procedure."[35] But if sanctuary was in part about uplifting and protecting the most vulnerable, Sobrino suggested that it was also—and perhaps even more so—about the transformation of the oppressors. "Central American refugees and behind them the crucified peoples of the Third World not only receive but also give; and the people of the United States not only give but also receive," he wrote. What North Americans could receive was "a simple world but one in which there is communion . . . a human way of life in opposition to the Western way, which has very little life."[36] Sobrino linked sanctuary to the revolutionary vision at the heart of liberation theology—the overthrowing of an imperial order that stifled not only economic and political freedom but also spiritual and communal flourishing.

The religious and political insights offered by liberation theology shaped sanctuary not only for top-level activists and theologians but also within many sanctuary congregations. When Community Mennonite Church in Markham, Illinois, outside of Chicago, declared itself a sanctuary church in 1983, parishioners sang a song titled "El Salvador, Live On!" that included the lines, "Too many martyrs / —too many in El Salvador / The hope of the poor / is not lost forever" and "the blood of the people / flowing through El Salvador / There's power in that blood / flowing through El Salvador."[37] At Walker Community United Methodist Church in Minneapolis, congregants declared their church a public sanctuary that same year with a call-and-response lament that asked,

"God of our liberation, who promises to raise up those of us who are oppressed[,] how long must we wait? How long must we watch our people tortured to death? How loud must we cry before we are heard?"[38] Through its many publications, the CRTFCA broadcast how these and other sanctuary churches spoke about their work through the language of liberation theology, and reinforced the connection between sanctuary on the one hand and resistance against poverty, militarism, and imperialism on the other.[39]

The prevalence of concepts and language derived from Latin American liberation theology reveals important dimensions of the Sanctuary Movement that have at times been overlooked or underestimated. Like other Central American solidarity efforts in the 1980s, the Movement was always deeply international and internationa*list*. Golden interfaced with Latin American liberation theologians through the Theology in the Americas project. Nicgorski, meanwhile, recognized that her life as an activist was inextricably connected to her time as a missionary in Guatemala, which she described as a kind of religious conversion.[40] She was just one of many sanctuary activists who went to Latin America in the 1980s; sanctuary archives are replete with brochures for and reflections on group trips to Guatemala, El Salvador, and, especially after the founding of Witness for Peace in 1983, Nicaragua. These trips, often sponsored by church and denominational organizations, gave activists a firsthand look not only at the conflict driving Central American migration but also at the changes taking place in the Latin American Church as it reoriented itself toward empowering the poor and documenting human rights abuses. When a CRTFCA leader traveled with sanctuary activists to El Salvador in 1986, she and her group met with peasants involved in the Christian Base Community movement. They told her that "any reading of the scripture clearly shows that one has to work for the poor, that this is the only right thing to do, and that was what they were doing."[41] Much planning and work went into these trips because sanctuary activists recognized their effectiveness both in raising political consciousness and in bringing liberation theology into the Sanctuary Movement through personal encounters with the situation in Central America.

Indeed, the political and theological radicalization of US religious people and institutions was an explicit goal of many—although certainly not all—leaders of the Sanctuary Movement. When the CRTFCA took stock of its work in a series of internal communications in 1987, it struck a generally pessimistic tone, noting that the Movement had gone "comatose," amid internal and external pressures. However, it also identified several "positives," including that sanctuary work had "provided an opening for talking about U.S. imperialism and the systemic roots to Third World oppression in a way that has gained a 'popular' appeal."[42] In the realm of theology, it was through the Sanctuary Movement, the CRTFCA concluded, that "liberation theology penetrated experientially into the North American religious community."[43] Sanctuary was, of course, about assisting Central American refugees in avoiding deportation. But many in the Movement understood that assistance as part of a much larger project aimed at pushing churches and synagogues leftward, so that they would be able to more effectively combat US imperialism and militarism, support revolutionary movements in the Third World, and revitalize a progressive prophetic tradition in American religion that was losing ground against the New Christian Right.

This facet of the Sanctuary Movement produced discomfort because, at some level, it seemed to validate right-wing critics of sanctuary. As Sergio M. González's chapter in this volume shows, conservatives caught up in the Reagan era's renewed Cold War fervor painted religious participation in Central American solidarity efforts as simply dressing up the infiltration of atheistic communism in God talk. There is no archival evidence, to be clear, that substantiates the accusation that the leaders of the Sanctuary Movement were agents or puppets of an international Communist agenda. And even despite the work of the CRTFCA, the larger part of the Movement remained attached to the hospitality frame that downplayed sanctuary's radical implications. Still, it is undeniable that among the thousands of sanctuary activists—and particularly in positions of Movement leadership—there were Marxists, Socialists, and revolutionaries, many of whom embraced Latin American liberation theology and saw its message of God's liberating power for the poor as implying a left-wing politics. And, for many more people, the Sanctuary Movement was an avenue for spiritual and political evolution toward these positions.

Covenant

While the engagement with liberation theology helped to strengthen sanctuary activists' political vision and internationalism, it also exacerbated conflict within the Sanctuary Movement. The sharpest divide opened between the CRTFCA and the Tucson-based collective led by Jim Corbett and John Fife. The Chicago-Tucson split was complex and multifaceted, encompassing disagreements over goals, politics, logistics, positionality, and many other issues. But it was also a theological conflict, one that saw Jim Corbett in particular trying to develop an alternative understanding of the relationship of sanctuary to Christian (and, to a lesser extent, Jewish) faith.

Corbett is the leader of the 1980s Sanctuary Movement whose actions and ideas have received the largest amount of public and scholarly attention, both at the time and since. Given the extensive bibliography on his life, it will suffice to give a short summary. In the 1960s, Corbett became a Quaker and a vocal objector to the Vietnam War, two decisions that would have profound impacts on the subsequent course of his life. As he recounted it, he happened into sanctuary almost accidentally when he learned about the growing movement of Central American refugees across the Mexico-Arizona border in 1981. He had connected with Pastor John Fife at Southside Presbyterian Church and others in the Tucson religious community, and together they declared Southside a sanctuary church in March 1982, kicking off the public Sanctuary Movement. As the Movement expanded across the country, Corbett was one of its most visible spokespersons. But he also remained a committed activist, working closely with his colleagues in Tucson and Mexico to bring refugees across the border and to place them into sanctuary.[44]

Corbett was, like many others in the Sanctuary Movement, clearly influenced in this thinking by the changes taking place in the Latin American church and the emergence of liberation theology. He traveled throughout Mexico and Central America in the early 1980s, and the conversations he had with migrants, clergy, and aid workers during these trips increased his familiarity with Latin American theological concepts. Like Shaull, Corbett frequently compared sanctuary congregations to base communities. Just as the base communities were helping Latin American Catholics to overcome the church's traditional support for the established political order and "live according to the prophetic faith that they discover in the Bible," so too North American congregations that engaged in sanctuary work were "initiating their conversion from the Constantinian captivity to the prophetic faith," Corbett wrote.[45] He believed sanctuary was a first step toward the bottom-up religious revitalization he saw embodied in the base communities, helping push churches away from collaboration with the state and toward independent action rooted in commitment to God's word.

But Corbett also worried about what he saw as a tendency to twist liberation theology to suit political ends. He argued that there was "a clear temptation for some professed followers and nominal allies to package the dialogical process [of liberation theology] as partisan ideology delineating immutable adversary relationships which can be resolved only by destroying the adversary." In other words, theological appeals could be used to rationalize violence against one's enemies. "Putting it baldly," Corbett concluded, "when liberation theology is reduced to ideology, it becomes the Christian slave morality denounced by Nietzsche," a condemnation and resentment of the powerful that then makes war and death seem necessary for freedom.[46] After just a short time working with the CRTFCA, Corbett started to believe that its leaders were committing this fundamental theological error in the way they talked about sanctuary and connected it to revolutionary movements in Central America.

Thus, while the conflict between the Chicago and Tucson branches of the Sanctuary Movement was partly about political strategy, it was also about theology, and the theological and political disagreements were closely intertwined. Whereas Golden and the CRTFCA argued that sanctuary should function as a form of revolutionary internationalism, Corbett and the Tucson activists conceived of sanctuary primarily as humanitarian assistance to migrants. They therefore opposed the CRTFCA's efforts to limit sanctuary assistance to migrants whom the Chicago activists believed would be best able to help build an anti-imperial analysis in the US public. For the Tucson team, this smacked of ideological exclusionism, allowing sanctuary to become simply a vehicle for left-wing and revolutionary causes.

Golden critiqued the Tucson position by arguing that sanctuary "assumes our accountability is to the God of history revealed in a People's struggle for liberation *rather than an accountability exclusively to refu-*

gees who have been driven to our shores."[47] Golden's point was clear: The purpose of the Sanctuary Movement in her eyes was not simply to use churches to shield Central American refugees from deportation. It was also to build and strengthen a larger religiopolitical vision in which religious people in North America would heed the call of liberation theology's preferential option and join with the oppressed peoples of the Third World fighting for their freedom. This theological imperative also implied needing to screen out sanctuary seekers who would be off the political message.

Corbett, for his part, had already begun to distance his theory of sanctuary from that of the CRTFCA. On the political side, as I have described elsewhere, this involved his positing that sanctuary was civil initiative, the upholding of federal and international immigration law against its violation by the Reagan administration, rather than the civil disobedience or intentional lawbreaking that the CRTFCA was more prone to see in sanctuary work.[48] On the theological side, while he never discarded his attachment to an idea of sanctuary's liberatory potential, Corbett stressed above all that sanctuary was best understood as an embodiment of "Covenant faith."

By "Covenant faith," Corbett meant that the Sanctuary Movement had the potential to bring together diverse peoples and communities—Protestants and Catholics, Jews and gentiles, liberals and conservatives, North Americans and Latin Americans—to do holy work and fulfill a shared commitment to God. The covenanting possibility of sanctuary came particularly from the fact that it was and had to be communal work. Corbett's Quakerism provided him with a deep appreciation for individual religious experience, but he recognized the limits of individualism to overcome the massive power of modern, militarized states. "When the corporate guidance of the gathered meeting leads to corporate rather than individual practice," he wrote, "it can make the difference between socially sterile gestures of individual protest and socially creative community breakthroughs toward a peacemaking way of life."[49] In the Sanctuary Movement, effective refugee placement and protection would demand congregations overcoming internal disagreements to declare themselves sites of sanctuary and setting aside denominational conflict to coordinate with other congregations across the country. "Functionally," as the Corbett-aligned Tucson Ecumenical Council Task

Force on Central America put it, "providing sanctuary is the congregational analogue to the baptism of individual Christians: an initiating act of incorporation into the covenant people."[50]

In calling congregations to assume their covenantal role, Corbett believed that the Sanctuary Movement was at the forefront of building a new, small-c catholic (that is, universal) "church."[51] This did not mean that all sanctuary activists were bound to become Christians, but rather that the Movement itself would come to embody the prophetic message of love and peace that Corbett saw as the original meaning of the early Christian church. For Corbett, sanctuary as covenant entailed restoring the role of religious people as carriers of this message, disruptive in an age of militarism and unbridled capitalism, after centuries of their bending to the whims of states and political and economic elites. This was clearly its own form of theological radicalism, even as it set Corbett and his Tucson followers against the efforts of the CRTFCA and its allies to align the Sanctuary Movement with the aims of Central American revolutionaries.

While Corbett was perhaps the most prominent advocate of the covenant theme in the Sanctuary Movement, he was not the only one who drew on this theological current. In one of the other major hubs of the Movement, the California Bay Area, five Berkeley congregations came together in March 1982 as the East Bay Sanctuary Covenant (EBSC). The choice to use "covenant" in the name reflected the statement of shared principles and commitment that these congregations had signed upon embarking on sanctuary work. And as faith communities joined the ESBC in the following years—twenty-five by the beginning of 1986—they too would be expected to endorse the covenant document. This ritual of entering into the Sanctuary Movement through public solidarity with other EBSC congregations closely tracked Corbett's vision of covenantal sanctuary as a communal project.

Interestingly, the specific faith language used in the EBSC's covenant document drew most directly from the sanctuary-as-hospitality current in the Movement. At the top of the document were quotations from Leviticus 19 and Matthew 25. Likewise, when the EBSC developed a separate "Jewish Covenant of Sanctuary," it included lines from Leviticus 19 and referenced the oppression of Jews in the Holocaust as the basis for Jewish support for Central American refugees. Reform and independent synagogues, as well as the local chapter of New Jewish Agenda, entered into this covenant and joined EBSC.[52]

Corbett saw in the language of covenantal sanctuary the potential for a radical departure from modern church-state relations, but he and the EBSC also recognized a more immediate and practical value in invoking covenant, one that echoed the Movement's use of hospitality. In the Jewish and Christian theology, covenant with God is a central pillar, a core method of understanding individual and communal purpose and relationship with the divine. It could thus act as a theological bridge for sanctuary activists, bringing peoples from different faith traditions and denominations together in collective action rooted in a shared religious vision. Yet, there was an irony here. As Corbett began to talk about covenant as contrasted with the CRTFCA model of sanctuary as liberation, activists and congregations felt more and more pressure to take sides. Covenant theology could help to unify the Sanctuary Movement, but it could also help to divide it.

Conclusion

In January 1985, the Tucson Ecumenical Council Task Force on Central America published results of a survey of twenty-eight Christian sanctuary congregations from across the country. "What is your understanding of sanctuary?" the survey asked. The responses revealed the complexity of nailing down a precise theology of the 1980s Sanctuary Movement. Several congregations straightforwardly invoked hospitality as an explanation for their efforts. For the Lutheran Church of St. John the Baptist in Tucson, sanctuary was about "hospedage," by which they meant "hospitality to those who need it." The San Francisco Friends argued that "Christians have no alternative but to provide sanctuary to those who flee war or persecution in their own land," for such an obligation "is clearly set forth in the Bible and cannot be gainsaid if one is to keep faith with the fundamental idea that our Lord requires us to live as neighbors."

Others, however, gave answers that seemed to cross multiple theological currents. The Baton Rouge Friends wrote that sanctuary was "a loving act of compassion and a public witness on behalf of the politically powerless and needy," as well as "a protest arising from solidarity with the oppressed and from a sense of moral indignation at the injustice of the policies of the U.S. government in Central America," language that would suggest an affinity with the CRTFCA's liberation-theology-centered approach. But the Louisiana Quakers also noted that sanctuary "requires the covenanting of our faith community to stand in support of the refugees and with each other," and echoed Corbett's critique of the CRTFCA in noting that both "rightist" and "leftist" Central Americans should be appropriate candidates for church sanctuary. Meanwhile, St. Michael's Catholic Church in Olympia, Washington, described sanctuary as "the conversion of church people to the true mission of church (feeding the hungry, sheltering the homeless, letting the oppressed go free)"—a statement that in describing a new church coming into existence through acts of liberation would have appealed to both Tucson and Chicago activists.[53]

This theological and ideological hybridity, while defying easy classification, was key to the Sanctuary Movement's strength. Such a diverse coalition could not have come together any other way. As Protestants, Catholics, and Jews from many different denominations and geographies joined the Movement, they looked within their own traditions and beyond to explain why they believed sanctuary was necessary and to facilitate their collaboration with other communities across lines of religious difference. No two congregations would talk about sanctuary in exactly the same way, but through the efforts of national leaders like Golden, Nicgorski, and Corbett, shared themes and discourses emerged. Although Movement participants did not share a single sanctuary theology, they drew on and shaped a series of larger theological currents.

As we have seen, though, built into this strength of the Movement was also its weakness. Without a unifying vision, competing theologies turned, first, into interpersonal conflict and, later, into regional schism. Ultimately, questions about what sanctuary meant for people of faith and how it related to concepts of God, church, justice, and freedom were too thorny to be ignored. These questions were not, and perhaps can never be, fully resolved. But as anti-immigrant and far-right politics gather new energy in our own political moment, it remains imperative to seek their answers.

NOTES

1 Jim Spencer, "Tempo: Law vs. a Nun's Higher Order: Aid to Refugees," *Chicago Tribune*, January 23, 1985, D1.

2 "Obituary: Darlene Ann Nicgorski," *Claremont Courier*, March 24, 2017, https://claremont-courier.com/; Jay Mathews, "Jury Convicts 8 Sanctuary Defendants," *Washington Post*, May 2, 1986, www.washingtonpost.com/; Biography, Guide to the Darlene Nicgorski papers on the Sanctuary Movement (Collection H.Mss.1011). Special Collections, Honnold/Mudd Library, Claremont University Consortium.
3 Darlene Nicgorski, Sentencing Statement, July 1, 1986, MS 362, Box 25, Folder 3, Sanctuary Movement Trial, 1982–1988, University of Arizona Libraries Special Collections, Tucson, Arizona (hereafter Sanctuary Trial Papers).
4 On the Central American Solidarity Movement, see Christian Smith, *Resisting Reagan: The U.S. Central America Peace Movement* (University of Chicago Press, 1996).
5 For the purposes of this chapter, I am adopting a narrow definition of theology, focusing particularly on how sanctuary activists wrote about their work in relation to religious texts, concepts, and images concerned with God's intentions and commandments. But one could also fruitfully analyze sanctuary theology as manifested in a variety of other forms, including rituals and testimonials.
6 In the second half of the twentieth century, the (often forced) migration of people on a large scale and the activist movements like the Sanctuary Movement that emerged to address it spurred new academic interest in the concept of "hospitality," particularly in European philosophy. See, for example, Emmanuel Levinas, *Beyond the Verse: Talmudic Readings and Lectures*, trans. Gary D. Mole (Athlone Press, 1994), 34–52; Jacques Derrida and Anne Dufourmentalle, *Of Hospitality*, trans. Rachel Bowlby (Stanford University Press, 2000); Jacques Derrida, *On Cosmopolitanism and Forgiveness* (Routledge, 2001); Tracy McNulty, *The Hostess: Hospitality, Femininity, and the Expropriation of Identity* (University of Minnesota Press, 2007); *The Conditions of Hospitality: Ethics, Politics, and Aesthetics on the Threshold of the Possible*, ed. Thomas Claviez (Fordham University Press, 2013).
7 For some of the many biblical passages conveying these commandments to hospitality, see Exodus 22:21, Leviticus 19:18, Isaiah 58–61, Mark 12:31, Matthew 25:31–46, and Luke 4:16–21.
8 "Interfaith Prayer Vigil and Candlelight Procession," December 2, 1982, M93–153, Box 6, Folder "Liturgical/Sanctuary Declarations," Chicago Religious Task Force on Central America Records, 1982–1992, Wisconsin Historical Society, Madison, WI (hereafter CRTFCA Records).
9 College Hill Presbyterian Church, "Ecumenical Worship," October 6, 1984, M93–153, Box 6, Folder "Theology of Sanctuary," CRTFCA Records.
10 General Convention, *Journal of the General Convention of . . . the Episcopal Church, Anaheim*, 1985 (General Convention, 1986), 176.
11 American Baptist Churches USA, "Resolution on Church Sanctuary for Central American Refugees," September 1988, www.abc-usa.org/.
12 "A Debate on Sanctuary: Alan C. Nelson and William Sloane Coffin Debate the Legitimacy of a Contemporary Religious Challenge to the Authority of the State,"

Newsletter on Church & State Abroad no. 7, July 1985, M93–153, Box 4, Folder 30, CRTFCA Records. Underlining appears in the original.

13 Robert McAfee Brown, "The Case for Sanctuary," June 20, 1986, GTU 2007-6-01, Box 10, Folder 25, Robert McAfee Brown Collection, Graduate Theological Union Archives, Berkeley, California (hereafter Brown Collection).

14 For a fuller history of New Jewish Agenda, see Ezra Berkley Nepon, *Justice, Justice Shall You Pursue: A History of New Jewish Agenda* (Thread Makes Blanket Press, 2012). For a discussion on the New Jewish Agenda and sanctuary activism, see chapter 5 of this volume.

15 New Jewish Agenda, "Jews and Central America: The Need to Act," Found SF: The San Francisco Digital History Archive, 1983, https://www.foundsf.org/File:ShapingSF3.png, accessed January 28, 2026.

16 Congregation B'nai B'rith, "Covenant of Sanctuary," n.d., M93–153, Box 6, Folder "Liturgical/Sanctuary Declarations," CRTFCA Records.

17 "CENTRAL AMERICAN REFUGEES, Resolution adopted by the Rabbinical Assembly Convention (1984)," T'ruah: The Rabbinic Call for Human Rights, www.truah.org, accessed January 28, 2026.

18 Union for Reform Judaism, "Resolution: Refugees and Sanctuary," 1985, www.truah.org/wp-content/uploads/2017/06/RA_res_Central_American_Refugees_1984.pdf, accessed March 10, 2026.

19 K. Healan Gaston, *Imagining Judeo-Christian America: Religion, Secularism, and the Redefinition of Democracy* (University of Chicago Press, 2019), chap. 9.

20 For more on right-wing attacks on the Sanctuary Movement, see Sergio M. González's chapter in this volume.

21 Sanctuary activists frequently appealed to this narrative of the United States as a nation for immigrants and for the needy, as when they criticized the Reagan administration for refurbishing and rededicating the Statue of Liberty at the same time as it was deporting Central American refugees. See Paul A. Kramer, "Who Does She Stand For?," *Slate*, March 5, 2018, https://slate.com/.

22 For a detailed discussion of liberation theology in Latin America and the United States, see Lilian Calles Barger, *The World Come of Age: An Intellectual History of Liberation Theology* (Oxford University Press, 2018).

23 CRTFCA Proposal for Sanctuary Project, n.d., M93–153, Box 3, Folder 20, CRTFCA Records

24 "Renny Golden Papers," Women and Leadership Archives, Loyola University Chicago, www.luc.edu/media/lucedu/wla/Golden%20Renny.pdf, accessed March 1, 2026.

25 "TIA Staff Meeting—September 21, 1977," MS 369, Box 1, Folder 48, Theology in the Americas Project Records, Schomburg Center for Research in Black Culture, Manuscripts, Archives and Rare Books Division, The New York Public Library (hereafter TIA Records).

26 Summary of Theology in the Americas Projects, n.d., MG 369, Box 1, Folder 48, TIA Records.

27 Renny Golden, Letter to the Editor, October 29, 1985, MS 502, Box 3, Folder 4, Jim Corbett Collection 1960–1965, University of Arizona Libraries Special Collections, Tucson, Arizona (hereafter Corbett Collection).

28 Chicago Religious Task Force on Central America, *Basta!*, January 1985, MS 502, Box 2, Folder 19, Corbett Collection.

29 "El particular mandato del Señor de 'evangelizar a los pobres' debe llevarnos a una distribución de los esfuerzos y del personal apostólico que dé preferencia efectiva a los sectores más pobres y necesitados . . . ," II Conferencia General del Episcopado Latinoamericano, "Documentos Finales de Medellín," El Consejo Episcopal Latinamericano (CELAM), 1968, www.celam.org/documentos/Documento_Conclusivo_Medellin.pdf, accessed January 28, 2026.

30 M. Richard Shaull, *Encounter with Revolution* (Association Press, 1955).

31 Richard Shaull, "Sanctuary: A Faith Journey into Social Responsibility," n.d., M2004–170, Box 2, Folder 5, CRTFCA Records.

32 Shaull's address to the Tucson conference can be found in Gary MacEoin, *Sanctuary: A Resource Guide for Understanding and Participating in the Central American Refugees' Struggle* (Harper & Row, 1985), 62–72.

33 Comité Européen pour la Défense des Réfugiés et Immigrés, "The National Celebration of the American Sanctuary Movement," September 26–28, 1986, M93–153, Box 2, Folder 15, CRTFCA Records.

34 Jon Sobrino, "Sanctuary: A Theological Analysis," trans. Walter Petry, *CrossCurrents* 38, no. 2 (1988): 164.

35 Sobrino, "Sanctuary," 167.

36 Sobrino, "Sanctuary, 170–71.

37 Markham Community Mennonite Church, "A Service of Offering: SANCTUARY," June 5, 1983, M93–153, Box 6, Folder "Liturgical/Sanctuary Declarations," CRTFCA Records

38 "The Order for the Celebration of the Declaration of Public Sanctuary for Refugees from El Salvador and Guatemala at Walker Community United Methodist Church," June 19, 1983, M93–153, Box 6, Folder "Liturgical/Sanctuary Declarations," CRTFCA Records.

39 For another example of the CRTFCA's efforts to connect sanctuary and liberation theology, see Renny Golden and Michael McConnell, *Sanctuary: The New Underground Railroad* (Orbis Books, 1986), 136.

40 Sergio M. González, "Political Fellowship and the Sanctuary Movement: Central American Refugees and Practices of Religiopolitical Accompaniment, 1982–1990," in *Faith and Power: Latino Religious Politics Since 1945*, ed. Felipe Hinojosa, Maggie Elmore, and Sergio M. González (NYU Press, 2022), 222.

41 Robin Semer, Reflections on 1986 El Salvador Trip, M93–153, Box 6, Folder 24, CRTFCA Records.

42 CRTFCA, "State of the Movement," January 1987, M93–153, Box 4, Folder 64, CRTFCA Records.

43 CRTFCA, "An Analysis of the Sanctuary Movement," June 1987, M93–153, Box 4, Folder 64, CRTFCA Records.

44 On Corbett, see Miriam Davidson, *Convictions of the Heart: Jim Corbett and the Sanctuary Movement* (University of Arizona Press, 1988); Hilary Cunningham, *God and Caesar at the Rio Grande: Sanctuary and the Politics of Religion* (University of Minnesota Press, 1995).

45 Jim Corbett, "Some Reflections on Sanctuary, November, 1983," MS 502, Box 1, Folder 19, Corbett Collection.

46 Jim Corbett, "Some Sanctuary Forms and Functions," June 5, 1987, MS 502, Box 1, Folder 19, Corbett Collection.

47 Golden, Letter to the Editor.

48 Adam Waters, "Alternative Internationalisms: The Sanctuary Movement and Jim Corbett's Civil Initiative," *Diplomatic History* 46, no. 5 (November 1, 2022): 984–1009, https://doi.org/10.1093/dh/dhac046.

49 Jim Corbett, "The Sanctuary Church," 1986, MS 502, Box 1, Folder 18, Corbett Collection.

50 Tucson Ecumenical Council Task Force on Central America, Letter to BASTA!, September 25, 1984, MS 502, Box 1, Folder 19, Corbett Collection.

51 Corbett, "Some Reflections on Sanctuary, November, 1983."

52 East Bay Sanctuary Covenant (Unitarian Universalist Service Committee, Sanctuary Projects, Box 2 (p), "Printed Matter" Special Collections, Harvard Divinity School Library, Cambridge, Massachusetts).

53 "Sanctuary Perspectives," January 1985, MS 502, Box 3, Folder 18, Corbett Collection.

4

From Rescue Work to Solidarity

Central American Leadership in Philadelphia's Sanctuary Movement

MARY WARD-BUCHER

At least two schools of thought exist regarding the root of the conflicts in Central America. President Reagan portrays the struggles there as part of one great struggle between East and West, between the Soviet Union and the United States. Under his administration, fear of Communist encroachment has guided U.S. foreign policy and is used to justify intensive intervention in the region. On the other side of the political spectrum, many Central American analysts see the primary issues in Central America as hundred-year-old struggles for land reform, for the right to organize, for the right to political participation and for political freedom.
—Sarah Goldstein and Glenn Stein, *Providing Sanctuary: The Jewish Role*

Introduction

During their sojourn in Mexico in 1984, exiled Salvadoran organizers Ernesto and Linda Fuentes met with Quaker activist Jim Corbett and other Sanctuary Movement leaders, who discussed with them the parallels between the Sanctuary Movement and Harriet Tubman's work with the Underground Railroad.[1] After a period of discernment, they decided to join this "new underground railroad" out of their "commitments and . . . goal to do whatever was needed to seek peace and a better life in El Salvador."[2] Corbett, who would become a minor celebrity for his involvement in the movement, personally accompanied them as they trekked forty miles along the US-Mexico border through the Sonoran Desert.[3] Over the next several months, the itinerant couple would travel over three thousand miles across the United States, eventually arriving in Philadelphia, Pennsylvania, where a crowd of nearly one thousand Christian and Jewish supporters welcomed them to Tabernacle United Church.[4]

Situated at a crossroads in the US mid-Atlantic region, Philadelphia has long been a global nexus of shifting borders—among Lenni Lenape and other Indigenous peoples, Indigenous peoples and settlers, slave and free states, the Confederacy and the United States, racially segregated communities, the fluid boundaries of people moving through seaports and airports, and so on. Drawing endless stories of migration, displacement, and resettlement, Philadelphia's diverse communities have long channeled the power of religion for solace and meaning making, as well as for survival and social reform. In Philadelphia, a place of historic significance for human rights movements like the antislavery Underground Railroad, Central American sanctuary collaborators like Ernesto and Linda encountered deeply engrained social-justice narratives and practices that both meshed and conflicted with their goals and desires. Formed by their experiences with *comunidades eclesiales de base* and other liberationist commitments, Central Americans would influence the trajectory and moral framework of the 1980s Sanctuary Movement in Philadelphia in a variety of ways.[5] As the movement developed, Central Americans urged North American supporters in Philadelphia to broaden their view of sanctuary beyond charity and rescue work. Through political and spiritual leadership, they encouraged their North American allies to seek a more collaborative work based on shared political struggle and reciprocity.

Negotiating Sanctuary

Sanctuary activism in Philadelphia was crucial to the broader 1980s Sanctuary Movement and laid the foundations for transnational development partnerships that continue into the present day. Disproportionate attention to North American sanctuary activists, however, has at times overshadowed the religious experiences, motivations, and labor of Central Americans engaged in transnational sanctuary work.

Sanctuary histories, perhaps drawing from the movement's strategic use of witness testimonies, also tend to focus solely on what happened *to* people. Despite such elisions of agency, it is difficult to overstate the urgency and tragedy of the events that stirred sanctuary activism in the first place. By the 1980s, civil wars in El Salvador (1979–1992) and Guatemala (1960–1996) had displaced about three million people, with nearly three hundred thousand killed and thousands more tortured or disappeared by pro-government forces supported by US military aid.[6] Since this time period, Central American immigrants, exiles, refugees, and asylum seekers have sought temporary and permanent shelter within their own and neighboring Latin American countries, as well as in the United States and Canada, where they have frequently encountered a chilly, if not violent, reception.[7] The United States, in particular, has enacted policies that treat Central Americans as economic migrants "generally undeserving" of state protection, despite US intervention in the region and the passage of the Refugee Act of 1980.[8] As a result of this uneven application of the law, only a small percentage of Salvadoran and Guatemalan applicants over the past several decades have been successful in gaining legally recognized political asylum in the United States.[9]

As described in prior chapters, during the 1980s, Central and North American religious activists adopted the term "sanctuary" to describe their efforts to create enduring safety and visibility for affected communities.[10] As anthropologist Hilary Cunningham notes, religious sanctuaries created in the United States during the 1980s movement were "cultural spaces that drew 'God' and 'Caesar' together into a discourse about power, and, more specifically, into a highly charged discussion about the proper mixture of religion and politics in society."[11] Sanctuary practices, however, are not simply products of power struggles between religion and state, but also include negotiations within and between communities of people.[12] Not limited to religious humanitarianism, sanctuary is embodied within acts of resistance oriented towards community survival and security. Those communities most subject to violence have created powerful networks of mutual aid with varying degrees of engagement with outsiders. Such acts, as anthropologist Aimee Villarreal suggests, make up broader, shifting "sanctuaryscapes" in which affected peoples create physical and intangible spaces of protective "containment" amidst the far-reaching disruptions of colonial and neoliberal violence in the Americas.[13]

Religious institutions in Philadelphia and elsewhere, while deeply implicated in this violence, have also, paradoxically, provided infrastructure for community preservation, survival, and resistance. In this vein, urban studies scholar Dominic Vitiello rightly observes that sanctuary organizing in Philadelphia "grew out of, and then morphed back into, a set of transnational solidarity movements."[14] Foundational among these movements were historical campaigns to end chattel slavery, including the Underground Railroad and other community-generated mutual aid projects linked to religious institutions and liberationist ideologies. Despite criticisms of sanctuary leader Jim Corbett's appropriation of the term "underground railroad," its legacy served as an important motivator and historical signpost for both Central and North American activists.[15] The railroad, intertwined with the development of key religious institutions and movements in Philadelphia, signifies layers of archival and historical memory involving interracial and intercultural responses to American violences and traumas. The railroad and its goal of sanctuary, therefore, were primarily expressions of community-produced mutual support and human rights work with profoundly religiopolitical roots. Although the railroad has been frequently misunderstood as a white-led endeavor,[16] African American leaders, especially women, were primarily responsible for creating and sustaining the network as part of their strategic efforts for self-liberation, with Philadelphia serving as a key border city and operational node.[17] Therefore, African American activists did not regard abolition as the end goal of the railroad, but rather understood it as a means to end racial discrimination and secure full recognition of their human rights, an endeavor that continues into the present day.[18]

Likewise, the 1980s Sanctuary Movement has sometimes been interpreted as an essentially white movement.[19] These critiques, while intended to spotlight the power inequities embedded within the movement, risk oversimplification and may continue to reinforce caricatures of refugees as monolithically constrained, unvariegated groups without creative recourse. Such a view, perhaps too heavily dependent on the perspective of North American humanitarian caretaking efforts, ironically creates a skewed portrait of displacement whereby individuals are, in the words of poet Demetria Martínez, "not so much agents of their own history, but . . . its victims, who function primarily as the objects of knowledge for an alien people."[20] As this chapter argues, however, there is strong evidence that many Guatemalans and Salvadorans who worked within and adjacent to the Sanctuary Movement contributed critical leadership with wide-ranging impacts. As Philadelphia's sanctuary activism demonstrates, this leadership was born not just from personal suffering but also through deeply felt spiritual experiences of *conscientizacíon* that Salvadorans and Guatemalans shared with their North American collaborators and prospective allies.

Public Sanctuary in Philadelphia: Beginnings

On July 5, 1983, a group of Salvadoran activists left New York City for an eighteen-day peace and justice march to Washington, DC.[21] On July 11, the caravan arrived in Philadelphia, where they rallied at City Hall with local leaders and later shared dinner with community members at Tabernacle United Church in West Philadelphia.[22] While Salvadorans elsewhere in the United States had already become highly organized by this time, the march appears to have been their first major public campaign in the northeastern United States, signaling the entrance of Central American activists into the US public sphere, where they hoped to garner North American support to end US military intervention in El Salvador and neighboring countries.[23]

One of the caravan's leaders, nineteen-year-old Saul Solórzano, had been a student organizer of *comunidades eclesiales de base* at the Catedral Metropolitana de San Salvador with Archbishop Oscar Romero, and had engaged in subversive activities drawing attention from Salvadoran counterinsurgency forces.[24] After a harrowing encounter with a pro-government *esquadrón de la muerte*, Solórzano made the difficult decision to depart from El Salvador, leaving behind his parents and four sisters.[25] Solórzano eventually made his way to Los Angeles, California, where he quickly joined together with other Salvadorans organizing solidarity campaigns for those affected by the Salvadoran Civil War.[26] From there, he traveled across the United States, city to city, where he helped grow community leadership and build alliances with religious groups and other human rights supporters.[27]

By the time Solórzano arrived in Philadelphia, several area individuals and religious communities, mostly Quaker and Catholic, were already quietly assisting Latin American and Caribbean refugees and engaging in international solidarity work. Their early involvement led to the formation of Central America Refugee Action (CARA), a religious coalition that would serve as the main organizational vehicle for North American sanctuary and solidarity activists in the Philadelphia region.[28] Although he chose not to enter public sanctuary himself, Solórzano, supported by CARA and other groups, played a major role in helping expand sanctuary and solidarity coalitions in and beyond Philadelphia.[29] Establishing the Interfaith Office on Human Rights and Accompaniment in the offices of the Christian Association of the University of Pennsylvania, Solórzano and other Salvadorans engaged in educational and political outreach to local community organizations.[30] Their involvement with Tabernacle United Church's sanctuary discernment process directly influenced the congregation's decision to join the Sanctuary Movement as Philadelphia's first public sanctuary host congregation on March 4, 1984.[31]

Public Sanctuary and Religious *Conscientizacíon*

Only a few days later, nearing the fourth anniversary of the assassination of the Salvadoran Archbishop Oscar Romero, a Guatemalan refugee family, the Ixcots, and several dozen Catholic activists stopped in Philadelphia during a different caravan trip from Chicago to the Benedictine Monks of Weston Priory in Vermont.[32] While visiting the city, the Ixcots held a news conference, stayed the night at Tabernacle Church, and attended a church dinner with First United Methodist Church of Germantown members, who would declare themselves a sanctuary congregation only a few months later. During public appearances, the Ixcot family masked themselves with bandannas and scarves, a common sanctuary practice intended to protect extended family members and thwart US Immigration and Naturalization Service (INS) detection.[33] At the news conference, Elena Ixcot, a "small, self-possessed" Mayan weaver, expressed herself in the language of biblical metaphor: "We are pilgrims among you. As Joseph and Mary became refugees to protect the life of their child Jesus, who when he grew up worked for the people of his pueblo (village), so now I think of the future of my children, whom I hope will return someday to Guatemala."[34] Elena's *testimonio* provides evidence for the extensive biblical and theological repertoire that many Central Americans brought to the Sanctuary Movement. Her statements are also revealing of the ways that Latin American liberative practices encouraged a profoundly personal understanding of the Bible in which listeners and readers might envision themselves as active participants in an unfolding story. Thus the scriptural references were no doubt carefully selected. Her use of the Holy Family's flight to Egypt and the archetype of the Christian pilgrim demonstrates the legitimacy of their cross-border journey.[35] Like the ancient apostolic texts, Elena also exhorted listeners to abide by traditional religious imperatives to aid refugees and show hospitality to outsiders.

As evidenced by Elena's persuasive approach, many Central Americans who interacted with the Sanctuary Movement were deliberate in continuing their religious consciousness-raising work among North Americans. Like his wife Elena, Felipe relayed the story of their involuntary flight, but also carefully refuted any accusation that he was simply an "economic refugee." Felipe had been a Catholic lay organizer in Guatemala, where he engaged in community literacy outreach with seventeen other Mayan teachers. Local army personnel interpreted these actions as subversive and killed all seventeen men, leaving Felipe as the only survivor. In a written statement published the year following his Philadelphia visit, Felipe shared this socioeconomic analysis:

> When we talk about malnutrition we should not only think about bread and tamales and tortillas but also about malnutrition of the brain, about lack of knowledge—lack of knowledge that comes not because people want to be that way but because they have been forced to be that way. That is why we have the classification of superior and inferior peoples. The monopolizers of power have even gone as far to say that those who are clever or smart were born that way. This is a lie, because God created us equals, endowed us all equally. That is why Guatemala is in the midst of this trouble now, so that we all may have opportunity, so that all of us may indeed be equal. That is what I did in Guatemala, and that is why they wanted to kill me.[36]

Ultimately, Felipe interpreted his own ordeal as an example of the persecution shared by all "Indians" like himself, who by reading the Bible had come to believe that "we are all equal, and . . . no one is born better than another."[37]

Felipe's comments, referencing the sacrificial risks that Indigenous leaders had taken to defend their communities and land, are indicative of the wider, ongoing mission of Central American human rights leaders to educate the public regarding the need to confront US and multinational policies in Latin America.[38] Linda and Ernesto Fuentes, the sanctuary couple mentioned earlier in reference to Jim Corbett, were particularly successful in communicating the urgency of these appeals with both in-person audiences and the media. During their sanctuary stay with Philadelphia's Tabernacle United Church, Ernesto, who had been a humanitarian worker in El Salvador, shared the following frank assessment with *The Philadelphia Inquirer*: "[US policy] is clearly not to protect democracy, but to protect economic interests in the region. Among the corporations in El Salvador are Texas Instruments, General Foods, General Motors, Maidenform, Max Factor, Firestone, John Deere, Goodyear, Coca-Cola and McDonalds. And there are a lot of U.S. coffee companies that depend on the coffee exports. It appears [to be] a total lie that the U.S. government is involved to improve things, because since 1980, when the civil war began, the situation for the people—politically, economically and socially—has gotten worse, not better."[39] Ernesto and Linda met with numerous student, religious, labor, and government audiences, arranged by Tabernacle's sanctuary committee and other solidarity organizations.[40] From Linda's perspective, the flurry of activity demonstrated their desirability as speakers due to their "very fresh" perspective and their ability to directly convey more accurate "alternative news" than that disseminated by mainstream media outlets.[41] Despite the difficult task of recounting traumatic experiences, Linda and Ernesto welcomed such engagements so long as the audiences were receptive; in that environment, according to one Tabernacle volunteer, they found meaning and healing.[42] Linda, who had been a labor organizer in her home community, later shared this sense of resilience in an interview with the press: "We have big hopes. . . . We come from terror, and we are not free from terror here. We have no alternative but to fight. You can't just sit down and be depressed. It's better to live active than die depressed."[43]

Toward Reciprocity and Partnership

On January 14, 1985, as previous chapters have discussed, INS agents arrested nearly eighty Central and North American sanctuary volunteers and participants in Philadelphia, Phoenix, Rochester, Seattle, and Tucson during Operation Sojourner.[44] On the same day, the US Attorney's Office in Phoenix unsealed indictments against several Sanctuary Movement leaders, including clergy members and women religious. These indictments would lead to the second and more prominent of two major Sanctuary Trials,[45] in which eleven US and Mexican citizens would be tried for transporting undocumented individuals into the United States and "harboring" them illegally.[46] Among those arrested during the sweep were Philadelphia-based Guatemalan sanctuary participants Joel and Gabriela Morelos, who were placed in Philadelphia's federal prison along with their four-year-old daughter, Lucy. After their sanctuary congregation, the First United Methodist Church of Germantown, arranged for their release on bail, the family offered gratitude and encouragement to the church: "In you, we have seen manifested the power of God; through you, God has shown us mercy. You, too, have come closer to God in understanding what God really wants from each of us. It is a gift to understand such things, because in many minds there is confusion, doubt, and insecurity. The sacred Scriptures say, 'Look with diligence at the things of God.'[47] We have understood what to do in accord with God's call concerning justice, peace, and liberty, and we must be firm, for God has promised always to be at our side."[48] As the letter continued, however, the family revealed a sense of frustration born from communication struggles with and a lack of trust in North American volunteers, which created a "tremendous number of disadvantages" for them. They felt especially troubled that North Americans did not seem to fully understand their "mission" or their experiences, and at times displayed a "lack of sensitivity" evidenced by the habitual exclusion of the family from sanctuary decision-making and planning processes.[49] To address these concerns, the Morelos family requested greater independence and proposed practical steps that would allow fuller expression of their rights to self-determination and privacy.

Tensions involving sanctuary and independence would also affect other host congregations. Shortly after the Operation Sojourner arrests,

Mauricio Lopez arrived at the newly refurbished sanctuary apartment at Central Baptist Church (CBC), the first suburban Philadelphia congregation to declare itself a public sanctuary host congregation.[50] Unlike other Central Americans who had participated in public sanctuary in the Philadelphia area, Mauricio arrived alone and appeared to be a newcomer to organizing and activism work.[51] After leaving his family behind in El Salvador, he stayed for two years in the "sanctuary apartment" in the CBC chancel—a converted, enclosed area immediately adjacent to the building's physical sanctuary.[52] During his time there, Mauricio engaged in activities similar to those of other Central American sanctuary participants, though, by comparison, he appears to have been less politically engaged, sharing few details regarding his personal circumstances.[53]

Ultimately, Mauricio chose to return to El Salvador in the fall of 1987, despite the still-raging war, and permanently severed all contact with CBC volunteers.[54] Several months after Mauricio's departure, the CBC Sanctuary Task Force renamed itself "Sanctuary Partners" and issued this statement to the congregation:[55] "After a transition period of reevaluation and healing, the Task Force held a congregational dinner to dialogue with the congregation about what our Sanctuary ministry should be in the future. It was recognized that our commitment to our sisters and brothers in Central America is a moral issue, not a fad. It was also recognized [that] the idea of sanctuary as rescue work is shifting toward sanctuary as advocacy and solidarity."[56] As the statement suggests, Mauricio's experience helped inspire a period of reflection on the direction of the CBC Sanctuary Task Force and the quality of its relationships with Central American collaborators, a shared concern among organizations within Philadelphia's sanctuary and solidarity coalition.

Although their presence was not always immediately visible, Central American organizers in Philadelphia remained connected to international solidarity networks and had direct influence on reshaping and broadening Philadelphia's interreligious sanctuary and solidarity coalitions. North American involvement gradually expanded beyond its predominantly Protestant base to include more Jewish and Catholic participation throughout the 1980s and 1990s. Jewish activists, who had been centrally involved in smaller numbers during the earliest years of the Sanctuary Movement, shared considerations that were sometimes distinct from those of their Christian peers. Nationally and in Philadelphia, Jewish peace activists worked particularly hard to persuade other Jews that the political and refugee crises of Central America were a legitimate Jewish concern. While some Jews were open to supporting humanitarian assistance for those who were displaced, many remained averse to the political tenets of the sanctuary and solidarity movement, partly because these aims tended to be promoted by Jewish activist organizations that were openly critical of the State of Israel.[57]

Over time, however, representatives from a few area synagogues did endorse the political goals of the sanctuary and solidarity movement. A member of the mainline Philadelphia synagogue Beth Israel credited the deepening of their community's sanctuary and solidarity work to the Ramos family, who had relocated from El Salvador to the Philadelphia area through the assistance of a suburban Philadelphia religious coalition, the Central American Sanctuary Alliance of Delaware County (CASA): "In the beginning, most people wanted to offer humanitarian kindness to people in trouble. . . . But after having Sonia and Luis with us and meeting other refugees, our mission is now to influence U.S. policy, to stop supplying money to a regime that is killing and torturing Salvadorans."[58] Eventually, thirty families separated from Beth Israel and formed their own synagogue, Mishkan Shalom, or "Sanctuary of Peace."[59] A pledge of support for Central American justice work was written into Mishkan Shalom's founding statement, making the new synagogue a Jewish sanctuary congregation from its inception.[60]

As political and material realities evolved, Philadelphia's Sanctuary Movement gradually moved away from a focus on public, residential sanctuary with North American religious congregations. While peace negotiations progressed in El Salvador and Guatemala, exiles encouraged their North American allies to back community-led repatriation and economic development initiatives in Central America and to continue lobbying for changes in US international and domestic policies. Philadelphia-based community organizers had an integral part in projects such as international sistering relationships between Central and North American religious groups as well as the refugee-led Going Home repatriation campaign.[61] Transnational Salvadoran and Guatemalan leaders would play a crucial role in this shift, as they restructured international ties among organizers and more vocally articulated the need to shift the ethos of North American participation toward a model of intercultural reciprocity and partnership. In doing so, Central American organizers would push North American allies toward a more expansive understanding of sanctuary—one that better recognized the capacity and authority of exiles and refugees in order to achieve a fuller expression of "solidarity" and "accompaniment."

Conclusion: Common Struggle

"Forensic" investigations into Philadelphia and other regionally specific branches of sanctuary activism continue to reveal the extent of Hispanic, Latinx, and Central American contributions to the movement's reach and organizational infrastructure, despite their often hidden nature.[62] As Lloyd Barba and Tatyana Castillo-Ramos argue, it is simply inaccurate to describe the Sanctuary Movement as an "immigrant movement without immigrant leaders."[63] Such misconceptions are reflective of wider colonial and postcolonial social structures that, for centuries, have influenced interpersonal and intergroup dynamics along with the narrative politics of humanitarian activism. For this reason, the underground railroad is again instructive, not only for understanding the symbolic and material links between modern sanctuary activism and abolitionism but also for examining patterns of omission in historicized remembrances.

In the case of the Underground Railroad and antislavery abolitionism, a slowly evolving debate has emerged concerning how best to understand and communicate the role of diverse African American leaders, particularly in relation to white abolitionists. Historian Patrick Rael suggests that three corrective angles have resulted: (1) an approach that continues to treat the Underground Railroad and antislavery abolitionism as a primarily white-led endeavor, with contributions from Black activists, (2) a cooperationist understanding that portrays the movement in terms of equal, interracial collaboration, and (3) a rejection of both cooperationist and collaborative interpretations, instead stressing the independence of African American leadership and organizations.[64] These methodologies are not merely metaphorical or narrative but reflect the stakes of flesh-and-blood realities wherein communities and individuals have, by force or choice, grappled with one another for the sake of survival and a better society.

Given the links between abolitionism and modern sanctuary organizing, in both its secular and its religious forms, as well as its shared embeddedness within the hemispheric landscape, histories of the 1980s Sanctuary Movement must also be held to critical scrutiny with a corrective lens that sharpens our view of Central American leadership in the context of intercultural, interreligious, and interracial activism. Central Americans who interacted with the Sanctuary Movement clearly communicated the need for both collaborative intervention and decolonializing anti-intervention. North Americans sometimes had difficulty parsing this out, especially within the organizational framework of the Sanctuary Movement itself, an ongoing problem manifested in recorded interpretations of the movement as well as structural challenges that continue to affect contemporary human rights work. Be that as it may, one Central American activist, now involved in transnational political advocacy, expressed a "level of clarity" that has evolved in their approach to prospective and current international partners:

> [Displaced people] are not helpless individuals, but people who are actually struggling. [It's important] to really help people identify, "In what way, am I embracing a struggle that is also mine?" It's not just that I am helping somebody, but when I am actually opposing, let's say, the government of Honduras, I'm not just doing it because by doing that I'm helping somebody in Honduras. I'm also helping myself be a more responsible citizen vis-à-vis my own government in the U.S. because that person in Honduras wouldn't be occupying the position he or she occupies because the U.S. has been enabling [that] . . . not because I take pity on them, but in standing with somebody . . . I'm also addressing my own troubles.[65]

Central Americans based in Philadelphia during the 1980s contributed to a significant transformation in approaches to sanctuary and continue to influence international migration policy and grassroots organizing in the present day. In the United States, their work has long outlasted the Sanctuary Movement, as they have helped improve legal access to asylum and expand the infrastructure of immigrant-rights organizations.[66] These organizations have remained unflinching in their advocacy for local immigrant communities and for national immigration reform, even amid the difficult political landscape of the twenty-first century.

NOTES

Epigraph: Sarah Goldstein and Glenn Stein, *Providing Sanctuary: The Jewish Role*, ed. David Saperstein (Union of American Hebrew Congregations, 1987), 107.

1 Ernesto Fuentes in discussion with the author, Zoom, October 14, 2020. Displaced Central Americans often used pseudonyms, a practice some continue several decades later. Only previously published names of Central American sanctuary collaborators will be used here.

2 Linda Fuentes in discussion with the author, Zoom, October 16, 2020.

3 For a representative biography of Corbett, see Linda Witt, "On the Line: Jim Corbett Tilted at the Law on Principle—Now He Has Thousands of Accomplices," *Chicago Tribune*, May 20, 1985, Sports Final, C edition, sec. Magazine.

4 Research contributor in discussion with the author, Zoom, July 30, 2020; research contributor in discussion with the author, Zoom, September 19, 2020; research contributor in discussion with the author, Philadelphia, Pennsylvania, October 27, 2021. Except for those with sanctuary names, the anonymity of all contributors who shared interviews will be maintained for privacy and security reasons.

5 Building from Paulo Freire's theories of *conscientizacíon* ("consciousness raising"), concerned Catholics formed thousands of *comunidades eclesiales de base* throughout Latin America during the latter decades of the twentieth century with the goal of creating lasting social reform through empowering community leadership among the poor. Catholic activists combined *conscientizacíon* with religious education to build action-oriented self-awareness in local communities regarding the causes of poverty and inequity. See "La Segunda Conferencia General del Episcopado Latinoamericano Medellín" (Consejo Episcopal Latinoamericano, 1968), www.celam.org/documentos/Documento_Conclusivo_Medellin.pdf, accessed March 13, 2026; Phillip Berryman, *The Religious Roots of Rebellion: Christians in Central American Revolutions* (Orbis Books, 1984), 27–28, 223; Penny Lernoux, *Cry of the People: United States Involvement in the Rise of Fascism, Torture, and Murder and the Persecution of the Catholic Church in Latin America* (Doubleday, 1980), 40–41; Vanilda Paiva, "Catholic Populism and Education in Brazil," *International Review of Education / Internationale Zeitschrift Für Erziehungswissenschaft / Revue Internationale de l'Education* 41, no. 3/4 (1995): 151–75, doi:10.1007/BF01255551.

6 Susanne Jonas, "Guatemalan Migration in Times of Civil War and Post-War Challenges," Migration Policy Institute, March 27, 2013, www.migrationpolicy.org; Cecilia Menjívar and Andrea Gómez Cervantes, "El Salvador: Civil War, Natural Disasters, and Gang Violence Drive Migration," Migration Policy Institute, August 27, 2018, www.migrationpolicy.org.

7 "Immigrants, exiles, refugees, and asylum seekers" represents a compilation of terms Central American contributors used to describe themselves and others.

8 Susan Bibler Coutin, "Falling Outside: Excavating the History of Central American Asylum Seekers," *Law & Social Inquiry* 36, no. 3 (2011): 569, doi:10.1111/j.1747--4469.2011.01243.x.

9 Coutin, "Falling Outside."
10 Hector Perla Jr. and Susan Bibler Coutin, "Legacies and Origins of the 1980s US–Central American Sanctuary Movement," in *Sanctuary Practices in International Perspective: Migration, Citizenship, and Social Movements*, ed. Sean Rehaag and Randy Lippert (Routledge, 2013), 75–80.
11 Hilary Cunningham, *God and Caesar at the Rio Grande: Sanctuary and the Politics of Religion* (University of Minnesota Press, 1995), 101.
12 Gervase Rosser, "Sanctuary and Social Negotiation in Medieval England," in *The Cloister and the World: Essays in Honour of Barbara Harvey*, ed. John Blair and Brian Golding (Clarendon Press, 1996), 60.
13 Aimee Villarreal, "Sanctuaryscapes in the North American Southwest," *Radical History Review* 2019, no. 135 (2019): 47, doi: 10.1215/01636545-7607821.
14 Domenic Vitiello, "Sanctuary and the City," *The Metropole* (blog), March 6, 2019, https://themetropole.blog.
15 Renny Golden and Michael McConnell, *Sanctuary: The New Underground Railroad* (Orbis Books, 1986), 57–62.
16 Christopher Densmore, "Aim for a Free State and Settle Among Quakers: African-American and Quaker Parallel Communities in Pennsylvania and New Jersey," in *Quakers and Abolition*, ed. Brycchan Carey and Geoffrey Plank (University of Illinois Press, 2014), 130.
17 Ashley Council, "Ringing Liberty's Bell: African American Women, Gender, and the Underground Railroad in Philadelphia," *Pennsylvania History* 87, no. 3 (2020): 517, doi:10.5325/pennhistory.87.3.0494; Golden and McConnell, *Sanctuary*, 61.
18 Megan C. Del Mar, "Convergence of Networks to Freedom: African-American Participation on the Underground Railroad in Kennett, Pennsylvania" (PhD diss., George Washington University, 2016), 7.
19 For example, Cunningham, *God and Caesar at the Rio Grande*; Robin Lorentzen, *Women in the Sanctuary Movement* (Temple University Press, 1991); Michael Woolf, *Sanctuary and Subjectivity: Thinking Theologically About Whiteness and Sanctuary Movements* (T & T Clark, 2023). This misconception is reinforced by the continued lack of sufficient scholarly literature on sanctuary and asylum outside of North Atlantic and Christian societies (See Villarreal, "Sanctuaryscapes," 48).
20 Demetria Martínez, "Solidarity," in *Border Women: Writing from La Frontera*, ed. Debra A. Castillo and María Socorro Tabuenca Córdoba (University of Minnesota Press, 2002), 172.
21 Maida Odom, "Salvadorans Bring Message to Phila.: Refugees, Heading to Washington, Protest Reagan Policies," *Philadelphia Inquirer*, July 12, 1983, sec. B.
22 Caryle Murphy, "Salvadoran Refugees End Walk, Protest U.S. Policies," *Washington Post*, July 23, 1983, www.washingtonpost.com; Research contributor in discussion with the author, Zoom, July 30, 2020. Tabernacle United Church, adjacent to Drexel University and the University of Pennsylvania, is affiliated with both the Presbyterian Church (USA) and the United Church of Christ. The organizers' visit was coordinated by solidarity organizations including CISPES (Committee in

Solidarity with the People of El Salvador) and, probably, AFSC (American Friends Service Committee).

23 Murphy, "Salvadoran Refugees End Walk"; Susan Bibler Coutin, "The Formation and Transformation of Salvadoran Community Organizations in Los Angeles," in *Latino Los Angeles: Transformations, Communities, and Activism*, ed. Enrique Ochoa and Gilda L. Ochoa (University of Arizona Press, 2005), 159–61.

24 Research contributor in discussion with the author, Zoom, July 30, 2020; Sara Solovitch, "Offering Sanctuary to Salvadoran Refugees—Illegally," *Philadelphia Inquirer*, March 5, 1984, sec. Local.

25 Solovitch, "Offering Sanctuary"; María Cristina Garcia, *Seeking Refuge: Central American Migration to Mexico, the United States, and Canada* (University of California Press, 2006), 26. The *esquadrón de la muerte*, or "death squad," was a paramilitary group with ties to the Salvadoran military government. These groups were enabled by a system of government informants, some of whom had support from the CIA and wealthy diaspora living in the United States. As Garcia grimly notes (26), "Those believed to have ties to insurgent groups or who challenged the established order in any way—through labor organizing, sermons and public speaking, classroom instruction, publications, and journalism—were tortured, raped, and killed. Thousands of mutilated corpses appeared in town sewers, garbage dumps, street gutters, and shallow graves, left by their torturers as a warning to others: eyes gouged, tongues and limbs severed, breasts, genitalia, and throats slashed."

26 Pamela Constable, "Saul Solorzano Touched Thousands of Lives in D.C.'s Central American Community," *Washington Post*, September 3, 2011, www.washingtonpost.com; research contributor in discussion with the author, Zoom, July 30, 2020; research contributor in discussion with the author, Zoom, July 16, 2022.

27 After several months in Philadelphia, Solórzano moved to the Long Island town of Hempstead, New York, where he engaged in outreach among the area's growing Salvadoran population. Solórzano eventually settled in Washington, DC, where he continued his advocacy work with CARECEN (Central American Resource Center) until his death in 2011. See Alvin E. Bessent and Paul Marinaccio, "Trial by Calendar," *Newsday* (Suffolk Edition), October 19, 1986; Coutin, "The Formation and Transformation of Salvadoran Community Organizations in Los Angeles," 159–64.

28 Research contributor in discussion with the author, Zoom, October 26, 2020; research contributor in discussion with the author, Zoom, July 16, 2022. Carolina Interfaith Taskforce on Central America, "Meeting Agenda: Central America—In Search of Sanctuary," October 21, 1983, Witness for Peace DG 149, Acc 99A-020, Swarthmore College Peace Collection, Swarthmore College, Swarthmore, Pennsylvania; Solovitch, "Offering Sanctuary." Although the coalition was broadly ecumenical, Quaker groups such as the American Friends Service Committee, headquartered in Philadelphia, would form a core pillar of support for CARA's early educational outreach and funding.

29 Research contributor in discussion with the author, Zoom, July 30, 2020.

30 Research contributor in discussion with the author, Zoom, July 30, 2020; research contributor in discussion with the author, Zoom, July 16, 2022; William Westerman, "Reciprocity and the Fabric of Solidarity: Central Americans, Refugees, and Delegations in the 1980s," in *International Volunteer Tourism: Critical Reflections on Good Works in Central America*, ed. Katherine Borland and Abigail E. Adams (Palgrave Macmillan, 2013), 40. The office was loosely affiliated with the Interfaith Office on Accompaniment founded by José Artiga in Berkeley, California, and may have been initially called the "Office of Information and Solidarity with Salvadoran Refugees."

31 Research contributor in discussion with the author, Zoom, July 30, 2020; research contributor in discussion with the author, Philadelphia, Pennsylvaina, October 27, 2021; Solovitch, "Offering Sanctuary."

32 Associated Press, "Churches Help Illegal Aliens," *Philadelphia Inquirer*, March 20, 1984, sec. National; Vincent Del Giudice, "Refugee Accuses Reagan of Supporting Terror Regime," United Press International (UPI), March 19, 1984, www.upi.com; research contributor in discussion with the author, Zoom, July 30, 2020. Weston Priory, a Benedictine monastery situated near the Canadian border, was slated to become the one hundredth official sanctuary host in the rapidly expanding national sanctuary network.

33 Beth Gillin, "Another Night of Sanctuary—Guatemalan Refugees Rest at a Phila. Church," *Philadelphia Inquirer*, March 23, 1984, sec. Local. Now divided into multiple agencies under the Department of Homeland Security, INS managed immigration and naturalization processes in the United States, including Border Patrol enforcement. While religious sanctuary has never been formally protected by federal law, a Philadelphia INS representative commented at the time of the visit that enforcement priorities did not include individuals such as the Ixcot family but rather "illegal aliens employed in well-paying jobs" and those entering the US unlawfully. Offering a different perspective, a North American representative who accompanied the caravan remarked that INS would not arrest Central Americans in public sanctuary because of the negative political attention it would bring to US policies in Central America.

34 Gillin, "Another Night of Sanctuary."

35 The Gospel of Matthew includes a narration of the flight to Egypt (Matthew 2:13–15). The theme of pilgrimage continues throughout the New Testament epistles. See, for example, 1 Peter, addressed "To the exiles of the Dispersion" (1:1 ESV), and the Epistle to the Hebrews, which recounts familiar stories of Noah, Sarah, Jacob, and Abraham, who were also "strangers and exiles on the earth" (11:13 ESV).

36 Felipe Ixcot Jalben, "The Culture of the Mayan-Quiché People," in *Sanctuary: A Resource Guide for Understanding and Participating in the Central American Refugees' Struggle*, ed. Gary MacEóin (Harper and Row, 1985), 144–45.

37 Gillin, "Another Night of Sanctuary."

38 The most well-known leader is K'iche' Mayan activist Rigoberta Menchú Tum, who won the Nobel Peace Prize in 1992. See Rigoberta Menchú Tum, *Me Llamo*

Rigoberta Menchú y Así Me Nació La Conciencia (Siglo Veintiuno Editores, 2000); Arturo Arias, "Rigoberta Menchú's History Within the Guatemalan Context," in *The Rigoberta Menchú Controversy*, ed. Arturo Arias (University of Minnesota Press, 2001), 3–28.

39 Beth Gillin, "Illegal Aliens Here Plan to Tell Their Tale," *Philadelphia Inquirer*, May 22, 1984, sec. Local.

40 Ernesto Fuentes in discussion with the author, Zoom, October 14, 2020.

41 Linda Fuentes in discussion with the author, Zoom, October 16, 2020.

42 Research contributor in discussion with the author, Philadelphia, Pennsylvania, October 27, 2021.

43 Rotem Bar, "If You Knew the Truth, Then Surely You Would Help Us," *Philadelphia Inquirer*, June 2, 1985, sec. Features, Inquirer Magazine, 24.

44 Ronald J. Ostrow, "Clergy, Nuns Charged with Alien Smuggling: 16 Persons Indicted in Crackdown on Growing Sanctuary Effort for Central American Refugees," *Los Angeles Times*, January 15, 1985, Home Edition, sec. 1.

45 J. Michael Kennedy, "Two Convicted of Smuggling Salvadorans, Vow to Continue Sanctuary Refugee Work," *Los Angeles Times*, February 22, 1985, sec. B. The first trial, decided in Houston in 1985, resulted in convictions for Stacey Lynn Merkt and Jack Elder, two staff members of the Casa Oscar Romero border shelter in San Benito, Texas.

46 J. Michael Kennedy, "Two Convicted of Smuggling Salvadorans, Vow to Continue Sanctuary Refugee Work," *Los Angeles Times*, February 22, 1985, sec. B.; "Alien Tells of Aid in Entering U.S.," *New York Times*, Late Edition (East Coast), February 10, 1986, sec. A; "U.S. Indicts 16 on Alien Aid Charges: Clerics in Group Accused of Illegally Giving Sanctuary," *Los Angeles Times*, January 14, 1985, Late Final Edition, sec. 1. The first trial, decided in Houston in 1985, resulted in convictions for Stacey Lynn Merkt and Jack Elder, Casa Oscar Romero border shelter staff based in San Benito, Texas. In the second trial, federal prosecutors offered political asylum to Central American witnesses and secured restrictions limiting defense efforts to demonstrate a religious imperative for sanctuary work. Joel Morelos, a defense witness for the second trial, offered his *testimonio* to the prosecution nonetheless: "I don't hear with one ear and that's because of the torture I was subjected to in Guatemala." Though ultimately stricken from the record, Joel's comment reached national media audiences.

47 This phrase appears to be a summary of epistolary exhortations rather than an exact quotation. Consider, for example, Romans 12:1–2: "I appeal to you therefore, brothers, by the mercies of God, to present your bodies as a living sacrifice, holy and acceptable to God, which is your spiritual worship. Do not be conformed to this world, but be transformed by the renewal of your mind, that by testing you may discern what is the will of God, what is good and acceptable and perfect" (ESV).

48 Joel Morelos and Gabriela Morelos, "Message from the Refugees," *News of the Ten Twigs: A Sanctuary Letter of the First United Methodist Church of Germantown* 1, no. 1 (Spring 1985): 1.

49 Morelos and Morelos, "Message from the Refugees."

50 "Resolution to Declare This Congregation to Be a Sanctuary Church as Adopted by Vote of the Congregation on October 23, 1984," November 1984, Sanctuary Partners/Salvador Partners 1984–92, Box 1–109, Folder "Sanctuary Project, 1984," Central Baptist Church, Wayne, Pennsylvania.

51 Bar, "If You Knew the Truth," 20; research contributors in conversation with the author, Zoom, November 12, 2020.

52 Research contributors in discussion with the author, Zoom November 12, 2020.

53 Research contributors in discussion with the author, Zoom, November 12, 2020; "Sanctuary Task Force Annual Report 1986–1987," 1987, Sanctuary Partners/Salvador Partners 1984–92, Box 1–108, folder "Sanctuary Task Force, 1985–87," Central Baptist Church, Wayne, Pennsylvania.

54 Research contributor in discussion with the author, Zoom, November 9, 2020.

55 A similar change occurred among Quaker organizers. By the late 1980s, the Philadelphia Yearly Meeting's "Sanctuary Working Group" redesignated itself as "The Central America Working Group" due to the "broadening meaning of Sanctuary" and the "wider range of approaches" Quakers and coalitional partners were using in their solidarity activities. See Michael Crauderueff, "1991 Report to Philadelphia Yearly Meeting's Representative Meeting: The Central American Working Group," 1991, Philadelphia Yearly Meeting of the Religious Society of Friends, RG2/Phy/772, Central America Working Group, Series 1: Minutes, Minutes 1985–1992, Friends Historical Library, Swarthmore College, Swarthmore, Pennsylvania; Anne Richan, "Dear Friend," October 27, 1989, Central America Working Group, Series 1: Minutes, Minutes 1985–1992, Friends Historical Library, Swarthmore College, Swarthmore, Pennsylvania.

56 "Sanctuary Partners Annual Report 1987–1988," 1988, Sanctuary Partners/Salvador Partners 1984–92, Box 1–108, folder "Sanctuary Partners, 1988," Central Baptist Church, Wayne, Pennsylvania.

57 Meeting Minutes, July 24, 1984, Jews Concerned for Central Americans, records, private collection; Meeting Minutes, January 31, 1985, Jews Concerned for Central Americans, records, private collection; Meeting Minutes, March 7, 1985, Jews Concerned for Central Americans, records, private collection, 1; New Jewish Agenda, "Jews and Central America: The Need to Act," 1984, Jews Concerned for Central Americans, records, private collection. These documents are currently in the possession of the Swarthmore Peace Collection, Swarthmore College, Swarthmore, Pennsylvania.

58 Leslie Florio, "Political Refugees Find a Home in Media," *Philadelphia Inquirer*, May 22, 1988, sec. Neighbors Delaware.

59 Research contributor in discussion with the author, Zoom, November 23, 2020; "History," Mishkan Shalom, accessed July 9, 2020, https://mishkan.org.

60 Research contributor in discussion with the author, Zoom, November 23, 2020.

61 "History," SHARE Foundation, 2016, www.share-elsalvador.org; research contributor in discussion with the author, Zoom, July 16, 2022; Vic Compher, Betsy

Morgan, and Laura Jackson, eds., *Going Home—Building Peace in El Salvador: The Story of Repatriation* (Apex Press, 1991).

62 A Salvadoran contributor used the term "forensic" in reference to the fragmentary nature of existing archives, a partially intentional circumstance. This contributor never learned the real names of many Central American coactivists, who used pseudonyms and often committed conversations to memory. They indicated that this deliberate cultivation of forgetfulness "made us all fairly invisible, so to speak." Research contributor in conversation with the author, December 2020.

63 Lloyd D. Barba and Tatyana Castillo-Ramos, "Latinx Leadership and Legacies in the U.S. Sanctuary Movement, 1980–2020," *American Religion* 3, no. 1 (Fall 2021), 1–24. doi:10.2979/amerreli.3.1.01.

64 Patrick Rael, ed., *African-American Activism Before the Civil War: The Freedom Struggle in the Antebellum North* (Routledge, 2008), 4–11.

65 Research contributor in discussion with the author, Zoom, December 9, 2020.

66 Susan Bibler Coutin, "Falling Outside: Excavating the History of Central American Asylum Seekers," *Law & Social Inquiry* 36, no. 3 (2011): 569.

5

New Jewish Agenda

Sanctuary as Diasporic Internationalism

RACHEL IDA BUFF

Introduction: Hemispheric Solidarities

In the spring of 1989, Hedy Epstein, a Jewish survivor of the Shoah, traveled to Central America with a delegation organized by two US-based organizations: Witness for Peace and New Jewish Agenda (NJA).[1] There, she met with Jewish Sandinista poet Michelle Najlis, whose family had found refuge in Nicaragua from the Nazi terror in Europe. In an article she wrote about her experience, Epstein quoted Najlis: "My only sense of Jewishness was my grandmother until your President Reagan who did so many bad things, did something for which I am grateful. He said there is anti-Semitism in Nicaragua and that Jews are persecuted. As a result Jews from North America came to Nicaragua. They found no anti-Semitism but I found Jews with whom I could identify. With them I found some of my Jewish identity."[2]

This remarkable meeting was part of a fluorescence of internationalist political connections between organizers in the United States and organizers in Central America during the 1980s. These networks facilitated rare conversations like the one between Epstein and Najlis, who would not have been aware of one another without the solidarity activism of the period.

Through their travels, North American organizers solidified a broad critique of US policies in the region and came to recognize the urgency of providing refuge to the thousands of migrants compelled to flee it. In concert with Central American refugees, these organizers inaugurated sanctuary communities and organizations to shelter those fleeing the consequences of US counterinsurgency. Consequently, they faced domestic repression and accusations that their solidarity activities were, somehow, "un-American."

Founded in 1983, Witness for Peace brought delegations of organizers from North America to observe and report back on events in Central America. Historian Bradford Martin credits such church-based delegations with bringing the terrible consequences of US backing of counterinsurgencies in the region, particularly Guatemala, El Salvador, and Nicaragua, into popular consciousness in North America. Developing in the wake of revelations of the assassination of Archbishop Oscar Romero at Mass in San Salvador and the murder of four American nuns in 1980, consciousness of the immoral consequences of US foreign policy moved many to act against it. Delegations of travelers returned from Central America to the United States and broadcast what they had seen, adding to the groundswell of protest against US foreign policy in the region as well as the emergence of grassroots efforts to shelter migrants fleeing repression and violence: the Sanctuary Movement.[3]

While many of the faith-based organizations that participated in Witness for Peace and the ensuing mobilizations were Christian, Epstein's arrival in Central America came out of her engagement with progressive Jewish organizing. Active between 1980 and 1992, a period often noted for the rise of neoconservative politicians like Ronald Reagan and the resulting implementation of neoliberal policies bent on destroying the social network constructed during the New Deal and Great Society, New Jewish Agenda (NJA) participated in the flowering of internationalist organizing that also characterized this era. That included the movement to end US intervention in Central America and the Sanctuary Movement providing refuge to the thousands of migrants impacted by it, despite the limits imposed by federal asylum and immigration policy.[4]

To Repair the World: *Tikkun Olam*

Founded in December of 1980, New Jewish Agenda adopted the slogan "a Jewish voice among progressives and a progressive voice among Jews," along with an eighteen-point platform addressing issues of racism, antisemitism, and sexism in the United States as well as self-determination for both Palestinians and Jews living in historic Palestine. The group's founding "Unity Statement" proclaimed the necessity of democratizing the Jewish community and opposing oppressive Israeli policies, particularly the construction of settlements on Palestinian lands in the West Bank. Drawing on the Talmudic value of *tikkun olam*, the necessity to repair the world, the statement proclaimed "the validity and vitality of progressive Jewish values at a time when many have lost faith that the goals of justice and peace are attainable."[5]

Jewish studies scholar Jonathan Krasner locates a resurgence of the term "*tikkun olam*" in social justice discourse during the period when New Jewish Agenda was active. To Krasner, the revival of the term to emphasize human rather than divine agency in repairing the world's ills likely originated in the nineteenth-century Jewish enlightenment, or *haskala*, a period that also saw the rise of political Zionism as a solution to the precarious position of Jews in Europe. In the post–World War II era, as Jewish thinkers wrestled with the theological implications of the Shoah, the notion that human action could be part of a divine plan presented a way to make sense out of unimaginable loss. Subsequently, Jewish American educators responded to the social ferment of the 1960s by affirming the centrality of social change to Jewish thought. By the 1980s, Krasner explains, many of those drawn to progressive organizations like New Jewish Agenda looked to notions of *tikkun olam* to frame their organizing work. Krasner writes, "By the end of the twentieth century, *tikkun olam* was widely acknowledged as a central Jewish tenet and even as a rationale for Jewish survival."[6]

In a 1979 "Call to Action" letter, NJA organizers drew on the resurgence of *tikkun olam* to explain the urgency of founding the new organization. They wrote, "We believe strongly that authentic Jewishness can only be complete with serious and consistent attention to *Tikun Olam*, the just ordering of the physical world and human relationships."[7]

Adopted in 1982, NJA's National Platform emphasized *tikkun olam*. The platform invoked domestic struggles around immigration status, gender, race, sexuality, and class, as well as the question of justice in Israel and the occupied territories.[8] The organization's engagement with the question of Middle East peace focused on the impact of US foreign policy abroad, making organizers aware of the necessity of working for *tikkun olam* internationally. An inherent part of their organizing and analysis, this internationalism ultimately disposed New Jewish Agenda to engage with the Sanctuary Movement and to recognize that questions of migrant justice were inherently international. The level of antagonism that NJA drew from Zionist organizations tempered its advocacy, gave force to its analysis, and made it unafraid to draw the ire of neoconservative organizations, including the federal government itself.

Palestine Advocacy and Repression

NJA's advocacy for Palestinian self-determination and its opposition to the construction of settlements distanced the organization from the Zionism that increasingly characterized congregational and organizational life in American Jewish communities after the Six Day War in 1967. In the wake of the 1973 Yom Kippur War, longtime Jewish neoconservative pundit Norman Podhoretz proclaimed the "complete Zionization" of the American Jewish community.[9] With this "Zionization," any advocacy for peace, let alone public sympathy for Palestinians, drew repression from the mainstream Jewish community.

The conference calling for the founding of NJA in 1979 responded to the demise of another Jewish organization attempting to advocate for a two-state solution and to temper uncritical US support for the Israeli occupation of Palestine. Breira: A Project of Concern in Diaspora-Israeli Relations disbanded after a successful smear campaign alleged that the group was a front for the Palestine Liberation Organization (PLO), widely viewed inside and outside of the Jewish community as a terrorist organization. This campaign was led by Americans for a Safe Israel, which was allied with Gush Emunim, the ultranationalist, pro-settlement Israeli movement led by Rabbi Tzvi Yehuda Kook. As a successor to Briera, NJA was conscious of the necessity of anchoring its advocacy for Middle East peace in a multi-issue, grassroots organization in order to survive such repressive tactics.[10]

New Jewish Agenda was the only US Jewish organization to proclaim its opposition to the Israeli invasion of Lebanon in 1982. In 1983, the Jewish Community Council refused to admit NJA to its ranks. Irwin Stein, president of a local chapter of the Zionist Organization of America, spoke for the council when he asserted that the group was "pro-Arab rather than pro-Israel. . . . They don't fall within the kind of thinking that is current in the Jewish community."[11]

Institutional Judaism in the United States during the 1980s was tethered to a Zionism that brooked no assertion of rights for Palestinians. From this Zionist perspective, Israel was the homeland of the Jews and any critique of it, no matter the author, was antisemitic. This included responses in the diaspora to the founding of Peace Now in Israel in 1978.[12]

At the same time that NJA drew ire from the mainstream Jewish community for its criticism of Israeli actions in Lebanon, the organization began to engage in the burgeoning US Sanctuary Movement. In 1982, the predominantly Christian Sanctuary Movement turned to NJA to help locate a Milwaukee synagogue willing to shelter migrants. As a result, Emanu-El B'nai Jeshurun became the first Jewish sanctuary congregation. The synagogues aided a family of Salvadoran migrants. By the end of 1982, NJA had recruited over twenty congregations to become part of the Sanctuary Movement. Through NJA's advocacy, a wide variety of nonorthodox Jewish organizations endorsed the principles of sanctuary, including the Reform Union of American Hebrew Congregations, the Conservative Rabbinic Assembly of America, the Reconstructionist Rabbinical Association, and the Reform Central Conference of American Rabbis.[13]

Diasporic Currents

As NJA became engaged in Central America solidarity and sanctuary work, its internationalism placed it in a tradition of leftist immigrant-rights organizations like the Popular Front–era American Committee for the Protection of the Foreign Born (ACPFB), a New York–based organization that represented a multiracial cohort of leftists, union leaders, and political organizers targeted for deportation from the mid-1930s through the mid-1980s. Like NJA, the ACPFB incorporated advocacy for civil rights with an internationalist awareness of the forces propelling migration around the world, including US foreign policy. Both organizations had headquarters in New York City as well as substantial Jewish leadership. At the time of the NJA's founding, Ira Gollobin, valiant Jewish attorney for the ACPFB for over half a century, was collaborating with Haitian and Latin American advocates to combat repressive immigration policies, including the increased use of detention and deportation against foreign-born communities. The ACPFB survived decades of

McCarthyist repression to go on to organize in the 1970s and 1980s because it was a grassroots organization, anchored in and responsive to the needs of migrant communities from around the United States.[14]

American studies scholar Benjamin Balthaser documents how Jews comprised a large percentage of popular-front and Communist organizations during the mid-twentieth century. The ACPFB was no exception. Balthaser argues that these organizations can be called Jewish organizations on the basis of their culture and composition. While NJA's immigration and sanctuary work found precedents in prior organizations like the ACPFB, NJA was unique in being a specifically Jewish organization that organized around questions of sanctuary and migrant justice.[15]

NJA's engagement in Central America solidarity and sanctuary work emerged from a specifically Jewish perspective: what we might call a diasporic internationalism. Jewish studies scholar Shaul Magid distinguishes between *galut*, or exile, and *golah*, or diaspora, in Jewish thought. He writes that exile is a theological framing, originating in the destruction of the second temple in 70 CE. Exile can only end with divine intervention in the form of the arrival of the Messiah. Many ultra-orthodox Jews espouse anti-Zionism based on this premise: a Jewish state, to them, should not exist before the advent of the Messiah. In contrast, other orthodox theologies profess that the advent of the Jewish state represents the end of exile: Zionism, to them, is a religious imperative. In 1967, Rabbi Kook of Gush Emunim wrote, "Every Jew living in Israel . . . is observing the Torah and every Jew living outside the land of Israel, religious or not, violates the law and this violation is a sin."[16]

To Magid, *golah*, diaspora, is a more political framing, descriptive of lived, historical experience. Many Jews in the diaspora see Israel as a necessary counterweight in a world in which antisemitism is common and often dangerous, a world in which another Shoah is always possible. The Israeli Law of Return offers the possibility to any diaspora Jew of migrating to Israel—making *Aliyah*—and immediately receiving the full benefits of citizenship unavailable to Palestinians dwelling in the Occupied Territories or those Palestinians officially termed "Israeli Arabs," who are technically Israeli citizens. Secular, diasporic Zionism leans on this opportunity, hedging its bets in a dangerous world.

Ironically, the Israeli Law of Return offers the Jewish diaspora a version of what the 1951 United Nations High Commission on Refugee

Convention determined were to be the rights of all refugees. While the UNHCR was not able to guarantee immediate citizenship to refugees compelled to flee their home countries, the convention prescribed an array of refugee rights, including access to identity documents, work, and education.[17] Since its inception, this UNHCR agenda for refugees has been elusive in practice, with few nations willing to grant refugees the rights deemed necessary for their survival. As New Jewish Agenda became engaged in sanctuary work, it participated in a grassroots realization of refuge consonant with the high-minded ideas of 1951.

NJA's aspiration to be "a progressive voice in the Jewish community" dictated the necessity of engaging with Israel as a Jewish state. The organization was far from the anti-Zionism expressed by contemporary groups like Jewish Voice for Peace. Aware of the global dimension of the issues it took on, NJA also framed them in terms of the Jewish diaspora. This set it apart from the mainstream of Jewish institutional life in the United States, which increasingly leaned on Israel as a central component of Jewish identity in diaspora.[18]

As the organization grew, NJA organized its national campaigns into task forces: the Central American Task Force, the Middle East Task Force Sanctuary Synagogues. While these task forces carried out distinct campaigns, their work was thematically united by the call for *tikkun olam* as well as a distinctly Jewish concern with issues of displacement and home: diasporic internationalism. In 1983, for example, NJA was one of the first US groups to take up the issue of the Israeli construction of settlements in the West Bank, advocating for a "negotiated exchange of territory for peace."[19]

In contrast to the Zionist emphasis on the necessity of an increasingly militarized national homeland, NJA framed the conflict between Israel and Palestine in terms of sanctuary and refuge. The organization's first brochure on the Sanctuary Movement, *Jews and Central America: The Need to Act*, continued this line of analysis, explaining that "the Jewish experience as refugees and victims of historical oppression compels our community to respond with compassion to the plight of Salvadoran and Guatemalan refugees who live in daily fear of being deported and the campesinos in the region who must survive both abject poverty and government sponsored violence."[20]

Histories of Jewish Displacement and Sanctuary Work

Taking a diasporic internationalist perspective on issues of displacement and home in Central America, NJA invoked historical and religious antecedents to explain its increasing engagement in the Sanctuary Movement over the course of the 1980s. Some of its religious explanations of the urgency of Jewish involvement paralleled Christian invocations of the Hebrew Bible, with its thirty-six invocations to welcome the stranger. Others drew on the Torah's commandment to "love your neighbor as yourself," and Talmudic doctrines of *tzedakah*, or charity, and *tikkun olam*.

Justifying their involvement in historical terms, NJA organizers relied on historical examples of oppression and displacement from the Jewish diaspora. Their publications often invoked the 1951 UNHCR Convention in asserting universal rights for refugees and acknowledging that the postwar European crisis of displaced persons had included thousands of Jews who had survived the Shoah. Reporting from the trial of sanctuary worker Jack Elder in Corpus Christi in 1985, Rabbi Charles Feinberg wrote, "I ask everyone to recall the years of 1938, 1939, and 1940. In those years our government refused to accept refugees fleeing oppression and violence. . . . The Sanctuary Movement struggles against indifference to the plight of people fleeing violence. The Sanctuary Movement is for life and against death."[21]

The adoption of some of the principles articulated by the UNHCR in the US Refugee Act of 1980 was almost immediately circumvented by the Reagan administration against Haitian and Central American refugees. But NJA organizers invoked the 1980 law to bolster their sanctuary work, offering an affirmative response to displacement that linked the survivors of the Shoah to refugees from Central America.[22]

NJA organizers often connected Jewish history with other experiences of displacement and terror. "I am the son of an undocumented immigrant," proclaimed "sanctuary rabbi" Joseph Weizenbaum of Temple Emanu-El in Tucson in 1986, proceeding to narrate the story of his father's 1913 flight from Europe as a stowaway and subsequent near-deportation.[23] In its 1985 "Covenant of Sanctuary," Temple Emanu-El, explained that "this is not the first time the people of God have been called to bear witness in providing sanctuary to refugees branded 'illegal' in their flight from persecution. The slaves who fled north in our own country and the Jews who attempted to flee Nazi Germany and found no countries of refuge." Such historical parallels were often reflected in the organization's public statements as well as its ongoing organizing. "From Fences to Friendship: An Inter-American Symposium on Sanctuary," at Temple Emanu-El, featured keynote speaker Eli Wiesel, a writer and survivor of the Shoah.[24]

The notion of Jews as a diasporic people having affinities with others forced to flee their homelands and turned back from safe harbor infused the movement culture of NJA, which included Passover seders and "Purim celebrations for human rights." Its political reinterpretations of Jewish holidays had precedent in Rabbi Arthur Waskow's 1969 *Freedom Seder*, which connected the traditional retelling of Jewish escape from bondage to the African American civil rights movement. In 1984, NJA published *The Shalom Seders: Three Haggadahs for Passover*, incorporating a new version of Waskow's text, a feminist seder written on rice paper, and *The Seder of the Children of Abraham*, which called for peace between Jews and Palestinians.[25]

Perhaps surprisingly, even as it criticized the excesses of the Israeli occupation, NJA framed the founding of the state of Israel as an act of creating sanctuary. In a 1984 grant proposal, the organization explained its turn to sanctuary work: "As a people, Jews have experienced homelessness and exile for centuries. Periods of persecution forced countless generations to live in constant fear, yearning for a safe haven. The establishment of the state of Israel reflects active Jewish concern for sanctuary. Our history creates the potential for understanding the plight of the refugees from Central America as well as their desire for sanctuary."[26]

While certainly Zionist, NJA's diasporic internationalism contained the seeds of a nonnationalist and even non-Zionist approach to issues of Jewish security. Their non-Zionist approach sought to remedy the enduring Jewish problem of displacement without reference to the creation of a state or nation. NJA's approach understood the founding of the ethnonationalist state of Israel, with its built-in apartheid regime discriminating between (and sometimes among) Jewish citizens and everyone else, as on par with sanctuary actions against global militarism and imperialism. While the organization remained Zionist, despite its critique of the occupation, its historical analysis facilitated a non–nation-based solution to the issue of displacement.

Because of its diasporic internationalism, NJA easily recognized the role of international conflict in creating displacement. The organization's analysis of the roots of refugee flows led it into Central America solidarity work. For NJA, the work of providing refuge connected to the work of opposing empire.

Alone among Jewish and even non-Jewish Central America solidarity organizations of the period, NJA also called out the role of Israel as a US proxy and instigator of repression and violence in Central America. Courting support from the United States and Israel, for example, Guatemalan dictator Efraín Ríos Montt characterized the indigenous resistance in the Mayan highlands as "Palestinianization" and received military and financial support from both regimes. For Montt and his American and Israeli advisors, "Palestinianization" referred to suspected indigenous resistance in small hamlets. One response to this was to forcibly resettle indigenous communities in alternative enclaves, like the United States' "strategic hamlet" program in Vietnam. Such forcible resettlements also looked to Israeli *kibbutzim* as positive models, despite the fact that Mayans were coerced into resettlement. Another was the catastrophic targeting of all local indigenous people as potential "insurgents."

Montt's efforts against Mayan communities later earned him a conviction for genocide. In 1986, NJA was a cosponsor, along with the New Reform Congregation and the Latin American Studies Program, for a "Central America: The Israel Connection" forum at UCLA. Such internationalist analysis, connecting Israel with western hemisphere counterinsurgencies, was and remains both essential and quite rare.[27]

"Neither Credible nor Independent"

The diasporic internationalism of the NJA did not go uncontested by powerful Zionist institutions in the United States. Organizations like the Anti-Defamation League (ADL) increasingly viewed Jewish welfare in the diaspora as tied to the security of the state of Israel. Invariably, such organizations dismissed any criticism of Israel as antisemitic, even when it came from Jews. Through a Cold War logic of guilt by association, the ADL also viewed solidarity activism as dangerously complicit with regimes it viewed as antisemitic.

The ADL's priorities corresponded with those of the US security establishment, which had long viewed Israel as essential to their interests in the region. The United States and Guatemala were among the first nations to formally recognize the nation of Israel after its founding in 1948. US financial support was foundational to the nation's domestic and military infrastructure. Since the 1970s, Israel has been the leading recipient of US foreign aid, averaging about $3.2 billion annually. Much of this money returns to US arms manufacturers through massive purchases of munitions and defense technologies.[28]

With its renewal of the Cold War under the Reagan Doctrine, the Reagan administration viewed the "Communist" Sandinista regime in Nicaragua as a particular threat to US hegemony in the region. In 1982, CIA Director William Casey began searching for Latin American partners to foment opposition to the Sandinistas. The Boland Amendments that responded to solidarity activism prevented direct military aid for the purposes of overthrowing the Sandinistas. Instead, the Reagan administration turned to unofficial channels to arm the Contras, eventually resulting in the global intrigue known as the "Iran-Contra Affair," through which the National Security Council "overcharged" Iran for vital military supplies during the Iran-Iraq war, funneling money and war materiel to Contra operatives through private airstrips in Costa Rica.[29]

The Khomeini regime that came to power after the Iranian Revolution of 1979 maintained a formal position of anti-Zionism and did not politically recognize the state of Israel. But Israel had previously provided arms to the Shah Rizah Pahlevi government, partially in exchange for permission for Iranian Jews to emigrate. The Iran-Iraq War drove Iran to return to this formally eschewed alliance and purchase arms from Israel. Consequently, Israel became a conduit for arms dealing during the Iran-Contra Affair.[30]

While the subterfuge of the Iran-Contra Affair did not become public knowledge until November of 1986, the ADL had long amplified Reagan administration charges that the Sandinista regime was not only Communist but antisemitic as well. To the ADL, refusal by the Sandinistas to officially recognize Israel constituted antisemitism. The organization created a "white paper" alleging repression against the small Jewish community in Nicaragua as well as pointing to the Sandinista regime's support from the PLO. Executive Director Nathan Perlmutter published a letter to the editor of *The New York Times* in April, entitled "So Are the Sandinistas Anti-Semitic? Of Course They Are."[31]

In response, NJA began to support delegations to visit Nicaragua like the one with which Hedy Epstein traveled. "We intend to investigate whether anti-Semitism exists in Nicaragua or whether these charges are part of a plan to manipulate Jewish concern about anti-Semitism for partisan political advantage," said NJA Rabbi Gerald Serotta. The organization broadcast its findings as a counterweight to the sway of the ADL over Jewish public opinion in support of opposition to the Sandinistas. In April 1984, Serotta countered the charge of Sandinista antisemitism, asserting that many Jews "deplore the aggressive and dangerous policy of this administration, as well as their means of selling them."[32]

During the spring of 1985, the ADL booked speaking engagements in Jewish communities around the country for a Contra delegation that included Elena and Isaac Gorn, who were described as leaders of the Nicaraguan Jewish community. In response, Rabbi Marshall Meyer, who had recently traveled to Nicaragua with NJA, said, "I'm convinced that the government in Nicaragua is not anti-Semitic nor is it motivated by anti-Semitic forces. I believe that the charge is being used by the present administration to garner favor from the American Jewish community, and I am unalterably opposed to the administration's policies in Central America."[33]

Rabbi Meyer had worked for the release of Jacobo Timerman, a Ukrainian-born, Argentinian Jewish writer and publisher imprisoned by the right-wing regime in his home country in 1977. In his book *Prisoner Without a Name, Cell Without a Number*, Timerman accused the Argentinian regime of repression and antisemitism and criticized the Reagan administration for supporting it. Neoconservative Jews like Podhoretz and Irving Kristol attempted to discredit his reputation and undermine these allegations. While the ADL awarded Timerman its Hubert Humphrey award in 1979, Executive Director Nathan Perlmutter countered his critique of Reagan, noting that "most people just reject out of hand the notion that Israel, Reagan, or Haig are fascists."[34]

During the 1984 election, a group called "Citizens for Reagan" warned congressional assistants about NJA. It alleged that this "tiny group," whose publications were funded by the Inter-Religious Task Force on Central America, was not a "credible or independent" political operation, being allied with both "Sandinistas and Salvadoran guerrillas."

Conclusion: Jewish Internationalism

Recognizing that US intervention in Central America was the main cause of refugee displacement, NJA worked both to support those who had already been forced to leave their homes and to oppose the depredations caused by further interference. The organization's engagement in the Sanctuary Movement brought Jewish practices of justice together with an internationalist analysis. Their international solidarities and commitment to grassroots organizing anticipated contemporary formations that link migrant justice to struggles against empire, including the illegal Israeli occupation of Palestine, continuing resource extraction and the resulting environmental degradation, and the long struggle for indigenous sovereignty.

Organized Jewish engagement in the Sanctuary Movement modeled practices of international solidarity. Citing her family's long history of anti-Zionism, Hedy Epstein founded the St. Louis chapter of Women in Black, an antiwar group originating in Israel, in 2001—after a trip to the West Bank in 2003 and losing part of her hearing from an Israeli sound bomb at a demonstration in Ramallah in 2006. Just as she had in Managua, she dismissed charges that her acts of diasporic political solidarity constituted antisemitism, scoffing at security measures directed against her: "I was strip-searched, internally searched at Israel's David Ben Gurion airport, I was told that 'I was a terrorist, I'm a security risk.' An 80-year-old woman is a terrorist? What, do I have a bomb in my vagina?"[35]

Both Epstein and NJA modeled the idea that immigrant-rights advocacy is always internationalist. Even though the quotidian work of ensuring sanctuary, fighting deportation policy, or advocating for in-state tuition or drivers' licenses for undocumented people takes place in domestic political arenas, the broad struggle for refugee and migrant rights is grounded in urgent global arenas of empire and displacement.

NJA created "a political home," in the words of Daniel Rozsa Lang/Levitsky, for leftist Jews at a time of profound political repression and retrenchment—a sanctuary where organizers could mix local and international campaigns, drawing from Jewish traditions and learning from grassroots movements.[36] In doing so, it anticipated the rise of other radical Jewish organizations, like If Not Now, Never Again Action and Jewish Voice for Peace. NJA provided a frame for a broad, emancipatory Jewish practice of *tikkun olam*, untethered to militarism, imperialism, and apartheid.

NOTES

1 Because there are so many holocausts, many of which bear on questions of sanctuary and refuge, I will refer to the World War II holocaust that so severely impacted Roma, queer, leftist, and Jewish people as "the Shoah" throughout this chapter.

2 "A visit with Michelle Najlis, Nicaragua's Jewish Poet," *St Louis Jewish Light*, April 12, 1989, Box 28, Folder: Hedy Epstein, report from Nicaragua and Guatemala, Tamiment Library, New York University.

3 Shaine Scarminach "Resources in the Archives on the Central American Solidarity Movement of the 1980s," *Archives and Special Collections Blog*, https://blogs.lib.uconn.edu, accessed February 7, 2024; Bradford Martin, *The Other Eighties: A Secret History of America in the Age of Reagan* (Hill and Wang, 2012), 25–45.

4 Ezra Berkley Nepon, *Justice, Justice Shall You Pursue: A History of New Jewish Agenda* (Makes Blanket Press, 2012,) 8.

5 Associated Press, "New Group Formed by U.S. Jews: Militant Feminism Among Progressive Causes Espoused," *Washington Post*, January 2, 1981, B16; Nepon, *Justice*, 9.

6 Jonathan Krasner, "The Place of Tikkun Olam in American Jewish Life," *Jewish Political Studies Review* 25, no. 3/4 (October 1, 2013): 59–98.

7 Quoted in Rachel Mattson, "There Is an Alternative: Historical Storytelling and Political Practice," in Nepon, *Justice*, 86.

8 "New Jewish Agenda National Platform, 1982," Nepon, *Justice*, Appendix II, 113–32.

9 Quoted in Shaul Magid, *The Necessity of Exile: Essays from a Distance* (Ayin Press, 2023), 79; Nepon, *Justice*, 28.

10 Nepon, *Justice*, 10–13; Ian S. Lustick, "The Evolution of Gush Emunim," in *For the Land and for the Lord: Jewish Fundamentalism in Israel* (Council on Foreign Relations, 1988). Available at www.sas.upenn.edu, accessed February 11, 2024.

11 Marjorie Hyer, "Jewish Council Excludes New Group over Views on Rights of Palestinians," *Washington Post*, June 4, 1983, B4.

12 In November 1982, for example, three Boston rabbis convened a *bet din*, a religious court, and, blowing shofars usually reserved for the high holidays, excommunicated NJA members and other progressive Jews, including Noam Chomsky and Nobel laureate Salvador Luria. Their crime? "Collaboration with the enemy and committing a traitorous act," because of their criticism of the Israeli invasion

of Lebanon. Jewish Theological Seminary rabbi Seymour Siegel noted that excommunication had not been practiced by Jewish communities since the Middle Ages. See Joanne Omang, "Three Rabbis Excommunicate Hundreds," *Washington Post*, November 25, 1982, A6.

13 Press release, March 24, 1986, New Jewish Agenda Records TAM 183, Box 23, Folder: Central America Task Force 1984–85, Tamiment Library, New York University; Nepon, *Justice*, 35.

14 On the ACPFB, see Rachel Buff, *Against the Deportation Terror: Organizing for Immigrant Rights in the Twentieth Century* (Temple University Press, 2017).

15 Benjamin Balthaser, "When Anti-Zionism Was Jewish: Jewish Racial Subjectivity and the Anti-Imperialist Literary Left from the Great Depression to the Cold War," *American Quarterly* 72, no. 2 (June 2020): 449–70.

16 Magid, *The Necessity of Exile*, 261–95; Kook quotation on 266.

17 United Nations High Commission on Refugees, "Convention and Protocol Relating to the Status of Refugees," www.unhcr.org, accessed February 12, 2024.

18 "Our Vision," Jewish Voice for Peace, www.jewishvoiceforpeace.org, accessed February 12, 2024.

19 Quoted in Nepon, *Justice*, 35.

20 Press Release, March 24, 1986, in New Jewish Agenda Records TAM 183 Box 23, Folder: Central America Task Force 1984–85, Tamiment Library, New York University.

21 Letter, January 22, 1985, New Jewish Agenda Records TAM 183, Box 23, Folder: Central America Task Force 1984–85, Tamiment Library, New York University.

22 See the excellent work by contributors to this volume Carl Lindskoog, *Detain and Punish: Haitian Refugees and the Rise of the World's Largest Immigration Detention System* (University of Florida Press, 2018) and Kristina Shull, *Detention Empire: Reagan's War on Immigrants and the Seeds of Resistance* (University of North Carolina Press, 2022).

23 "Rabbis Support Sanctuary for Central American Refugees," Press Release, March 24, 1986, New Jewish Agenda Records TAM 183, Box 23, Folder: Central America Task Force 1984–85, Tamiment Library, New York University.

24 "Special Congregational Meeting: Covenant of Sanctuary," November 18, 1984, New Jewish Agenda Records TAM 183, Box 23, Folder: Central America Task Force 1984–85, Tamiment Library, New York University.

25 Memo to Central America Task Force Member/contact from Mark Epstein, RE: Follow-up to national Central America mailing to synagogues, 3/22/85. New Jewish Agenda Records TAM 183, Box 23, Folder: Central America Task Force 1984–85, Tamiment Library, New York University; Nepon, *Justice*, 38–39.

26 "Organizing for Peace in Central America in the Jewish Community," New Jewish Agenda Records TAM 183, Box 23, Folder: Central America Task Force 1984–85, Tamiment Library, New York University.

27 Flyer from the personal papers of Mark Epstein, in author's possession. On Israeli engagement in Central America, see my "Sanctuary Everywhere: Some Key

Words, 1945–Present," *Radical History Review* 135 (October 2019): 14–42; also, Stephen Kinzer, "Efraín Ríos Montt, Guatemalan Dictator Convicted of Genocide, Dies at 91," *New York Times*, April 1, 2018, www.nytimes.com, accessed February 14, 2024.

28 Jonathan Masters and Will Merrow, "US Aid to Israel in Four Charts," Council on Foreign Relations, January 23, 2024, www.cfr.org, accessed February 16, 2024.

29 "Understanding the Iran Contra Affairs," Brown University, www.brown.edu, accessed February 16, 2024.

30 Dalia Dassa Kaye, Alireza Nader, and Parisa Roshan, *Iran and Israel: A Dangerous Rivalry* (Rand Corporation, 2011), 9–18.

31 White paper and copy of op-ed both in New Jewish Agenda Records TAM 183 Box 23, Folder: Central America Task Force 1984–85, Tamiment Library, New York University.

32 "Jewish Leaders Urge Congress to Oppose Reagan on Central America," *Chicago Jewish Sentinel*, April 19, 1984; Marjorie Hyer, "Jewish Group Finds No Anti-Semitism by Sandinista Regime," *Washington Post*, August 24, 1984, both in New Jewish Agenda Records, Box 23, Folder: Central America Task Force 1984–85, Tamiment Library, New York University.

33 "Contra-Versy," *LA Weekly*, March 8–14, 1985.

34 Nepon, *Justice*, 23, Martin Schramm, "Timmerman's Charges Anger Jews in the United States, Argentina," *Washington Post*, June 21, 1981, www.washingtonpost.com/, accessed February 16, 2024; Perlmutter quoted in Colin Campbell, "Timerman's Views Bring Debate on Rights Policy and Argentina," *New York Times*, June 8, 1981, www.nytimes.com/, accessed February 16, 2024.

35 "Israel, Gaza: Holocaust Survivor Explains Why She Became Palestine Rights Activist," *Los Angeles Times*, January 6, 2021, www.latimes.com.

36 "Hidden Agenda: Lessons from NJA, Lost and Learned," in Nepon, *Justice*, 93–107.

6

"Bringing the Revolution Home"

The Sanctuary Movement and Its Conservative Opponents

SERGIO M. GONZÁLEZ

Introduction

In November of 1985, the Catholic philosopher and neoconservative intellectual Michael Novak took to the editorial page of the conservative newspaper *The Washington Times* to denounce a fraud. His target was the Sanctuary Movement, a national effort by religious congregations to offer church-based asylum to hundreds of thousands of Central Americans. According to Novak, author of a theological celebration of American culture and political economy called *The Spirit of Democratic Capitalism*, sanctuary was nothing more than political activism masquerading as Christian charity. He accused sanctuary activists of using "careful screening" and "intensive indoctrination" to usher bands of dissident Salvadorans and Guatemalans before "compassionate [church] audiences," when in reality these people were nothing more than undocumented "economic migrants." The movement, according to Novak, was manipulating American church people and the country's "generous" immigration and refugee system (five years earlier changed with Jimmy Carter's signing of the Refugee Act of 1980) when in fact it had more sinister ends in mind: injecting leftist and Communist political activism into churches and advancing the Religious Left's criticisms of the Reagan administration's Central American foreign policies.[1]

Novak's scathing editorial came at a crucial moment for the Sanctuary Movement. Three years earlier, motivated by a centuries-long tradition of offering sacred refuge to those in need, churches and synagogues across the nation had begun to open their doors to Salvadorans and Guatemalans fleeing political repression and violence in their home countries. Congregations across the country joined the movement not only to offer safe harbor to asylum seekers but also to mobilize alongside Central Americans to reorient, in their telling, the country's moral compass. In a period that historians have often noted as an era of ascendancy of right and far right religiosity—most prominently in the televangelists who supported Ronald Reagan's run to the White House—this relatively small but vocal group of organizers in houses of worship and religious organizations also sought to use their social and political capital to influence US immigration, refugee, and foreign policies. By 1985, when Novak published his editorial, the movement had gone national, working with secular solidarity organizations and growing to include hundreds of congregations and thousands of supporters in nearly every state in the country. Sanctuary leaders, however, by January 1985 were also under federal prosecution, accused by the federal government of running an international smuggling ring out of churches and synagogues. Novak's comments, then, came at a time when the movement had never been more prominent and under more scrutiny.

Novak, like many of the movement's opponents, who will be discussed in this chapter, dismissed sanctuary as political activism merely shrouded in the garb and language of religion. It was, as another critic called it, nothing more than "criminal anarchism" that demonstrated the growing influence of "leftist radicals" in US churches.[2] This type of framing, offered most succinctly and stridently by religious neoconservatives like Novak, served as a rebuke of the Sanctuary Movement's successful publicity efforts. This group included a bevy of political operatives and religious intellectuals who had fueled the political Right's march into the White House. One of their principal objectives became binding a primary foreign policy concern—staunching the spread of communism in the Americas—with more pointed efforts to keep churches clean of leftist infiltrators. Their condemnations of sanctuary activists, not so coincidentally, were in lockstep with the Reagan administration's own views of the movement.

While it was religious neoconservatives, a group that political scientist Damon Linker has referred to as "theocons," who offered the earliest and most complex denunciations of the movement, they were certainly not alone.[3] From the movement's inception, sanctuary activists faced resistance from a variety of actors. Antagonists included religious neoconservatives like Novak; officials in the Reagan administration intent on stamping out any opposition to their foreign policy; immigration restrictionists set on limiting asylum entrants to the country; and theologians who resisted what they believed to be a creeping form of political engagement into matters of the church. Their denunciations, offered through conservative periodicals and public forums, grew more strident in tenor as the Reagan administration accelerated its surveillance and eventual prosecution of sanctuary activists and other leftists affiliated with the broader US Central America peace and solidarity movement.[4]

These debates over the legitimacy of sanctuary reveal that the 1980s was a period of open religious conflict, but not just in the usual framing of an ascendent Moral Majority or Religious Right. Sanctuary showed that the divergences within religious spaces were not just about abortion or school choice or pornography; they also occurred at the intersections of debates surrounding US militarism abroad and immigration and refugee policy at home. The fights over the Sanctuary Movement—whether it represented an honest interplay between faith and politics and the role religious organizations should play in advocating for structural political change—ultimately set the church as a site of struggle for US congregants and Latin Americans alike.

Within the context of the Cold War, the Sanctuary Movement became another site, this one on a religious field, for deep ideological struggles between conservatives and leftist religious organizations. Historians of religion and US politics have investigated in great detail faith organizations' robust engagement in and preoccupation with US foreign policy in Latin America in the postwar years.[5] As Andrew Preston has noted, if it was "true that Christians were among the most passionate of America's cold warriors," it was also the case "that Christians were among the most fervent critics of America's Cold War."[6] It was an ideological struggle that played out in domestic and foreign policy, or to frame it another way, it was a battle waged both in the United States and abroad. Religious conservatives fought against progressive sectors of the US church because of their connections with liberation movements in Latin America and specifically the liberation theology that had spread across the region in the second half of the twentieth century. Religious conservatives often framed this as an axiomatic struggle, positing radical differences between their conception of Christianity and those of sanctuary participants. Thus, if the Cold War was an ideological struggle, it was also a theological one, one that would have, conservative religious activists argued, reverberating moral consequences for the nation's soul.

The Institute on Religion and Democracy, Mainline Churches, and Fears of Communist Subversion

Foremost among the Sanctuary Movement's opponents was a neoconservative think tank called the Institute on Religion and Democracy (IRD). Founded in 1981, the organization was established as a bulwark against what members viewed as a growing commitment to political, and particularly politically leftist, causes within American churches. Mainline churches had succumbed to the excesses of the post–Vietnam War and post–civil rights era, the IRD alleged, as church leaders seemed now more focused on supporting leftist political organizing than serving authentic Christian witness to the world. The organization accused the National Council of Churches (NCC), the World Council of Churches (WCC), and the governing bodies of Presbyterian Church (USA), the United Methodist Church, and other denominations of funneling millions of dollars of church funds into Moscow- and Castro-friendly organizations in Latin America and Africa. These venerable faith institutions, according to the IRD, had been captured by a cadre of bureaucrats and church leaders who had betrayed their congregants by turning away from their obligation to the faith and transforming their churches into nothing more than vehicles for left-wing activist groups at home and totalitarian governments abroad. Expanded scrutiny of and accountability for church spending, the IRD argued, was needed to pull these faith organizations from the ledge of theological and political disorder.[7]

In its own origin story, the IRD had emerged as an organic and lay-led response to mainline churches' troubling drift away from the teachings of the church. The reality was much less grassroots, however. Like other neoconservative organizations of the era, the IRD consisted of a mix of established conservative intellectuals and formerly liberal activists who had become dissatisfied with the political New Left of the 1960s and early 1970s, particularly those troubled with what they viewed as radical anti-Americanism and pacifism among their former comrades. While those who took on the political label of "neoconservative" may have come from a variety of political backgrounds, most shared a defining belief, that of a fervent anticommunism that fueled support for American intervention abroad.[8] The IRD's board of directors consisted of leaders from the burgeoning political and intellectual movement, including religious conservative activists, public intellectuals, and veterans of political fights, many of whom held positions with conservative advocacy groups like the American Enterprise Institute and the Heritage Foundation. Among them were the Catholic journalist and academic Michael Novak; prominent Christian cleric Richard John Neuhaus; preeminent sociologist of religion Peter Berger; and a bevy of conservative theologians. Many of these board members were connected to the Coalition for a Democratic Majority, a leading neoconservative think tank associated with the Reagan administration and with board members including US ambassador to the United Nations Jeane Kirkpatrick. IRD funding, meanwhile, came from conservative mega-donors like the Sarah Scaife Foundation, the Smith Richardson Foundation, and the John M. Olin Foundation.[9]

Well-funded and stacked with intellectual heavyweights, the IRD came to play an important role within the Reagan administration, particularly in its relationship to religious bodies. While much contemporary media attention focused on the tenuous relationship between the White House and the more public faces of what had come to be known as the Religious Right such as televangelists like Jerry Falwell and Pat Robertson, more careful observers noted that the real religious influence in Washington, at least as it pertained to policy, came from the IRD. With so many IRD board members either serving in the White House or informally consulting the president, Jim Wallis, editor at the progressive Christian magazine *Sojourners*, branded the IRD as "the official seminary of the Reagan administration."[10]

Despite those clear political connections, the IRD claimed that its primary objective was to ferret politics of all stripes out of churches, or at a minimum moderate the radicalization of mainline Christian organizations. It accused what they referred to as the "Religious Left" of having infiltrated church bureaucracies and of using their positions to funnel congregational dollars from the NCC, the WCC, and Catholic dioceses into radical causes both domestic and international, money that would go on to support Communist revolutions and the destabilization of capitalist and Christian nations. In exposés published in *Reader's*

Digest and friendly interviews on national television, IRD representatives contended that political activism had supplanted spiritual stewardship. As Richard John Neuhaus told *60 Minutes* correspondent Morley Safer in one 1983 segment, churches' political escapades were "evil" and "wrong." This form of intervention into the secular, he argued, "discredits the Church as social witness, it undermines any elementary notion of justice. We have to turn this around."[11] Edmund Robb, an evangelical Methodist pastor who served as the IRD's first chairman, took this argument even further, positing that church bureaucrats had betrayed their congregations by substituting "political propaganda for God's message of grace and salvation."[12]

While the IRD noted in public statements that its intention was to draw churches away from their growing political escapades and back towards their faith commitments, the organization's leaders consistently offered a moral and theological framework to justify US foreign policy during the Reagan era. Operating at the height of the Cold War, the IRD held a familiar axiomatic view of the world, one that posited a clear division between good and evil, Christianity and totalitarianism, capitalism and communism, and the United States and the Soviet Union. As Neuhaus wrote in the IRD's founding document, the United States was "the primary bearer of the democratic possibility in the world today." The Soviet Union, meanwhile, was "the primary bearer of the totalitarian alternative." In this conflict, Neuhaus proposed, the United States needed to serve as "a force for good in this world," and accordingly, US churches had an obligation to defend the capitalist market economy and freedom of religion against totalitarianism, even if it required military intervention.[13]

Shouting Down the "Red Chorus": Growing Conservative Criticism of the Sanctuary Movement

The IRD argued for this type of religiopolitical engagement most enthusiastically in its support of US military intervention in Central America. The organization joined a network of DC-based think tanks working to neutralize a growing transnational Central American solidarity movement, one that consisted of Central American exiles and US activists focused on opposing American intervention in Nicaragua, El Salvador, and Guatemala. These think tanks were particularly concerned with the effectiveness of the solidarity movement among faith organizations and hoped to serve as a counterweight to what Curtin Winsor Jr., the Reagan administration's former ambassador to Costa Rica, referred to as the "Red Chorus" developing within churches.[14] For the IRD, Central America was of principal concern, so much so that the organization highlighted NCC funding for leftist governments in the region during its very first press conference in 1981.[15] The primary enemy of religious liberty and human rights, and perhaps even democracy itself, according to the group, could be found in the growing Latin American movement of liberation theology that shrouded leftist revolutionary political objectives under the banner of Christianity, or, as they referred to it, "Christian-Marxist revolution."[16] The IRD accused US faith groups of funneling hundreds of thousands of dollars into pro-Marxist causes like the Nicaraguan Sandinistas, all of which sought to stifle Christians, they argued, in the name of a godless communism. These funding decisions, the IRD argued, stood in direct opposition to the way everyday church members expected their donations to be spent. They supported their own counterclaims with the signatures of thousands of American Christians who demanded a reallocation of funding and priorities.[17]

To legitimate their own assertions, the IRD elevated Central American religious leaders they thought best personified the fight for religious liberty. In 1982 the organization conferred its inaugural Religious Freedom Award to the archbishop of Managua, Nicaragua, Miguel Obando y Bravo. Obando, a vocal critic of the Somoza regime that had ruled the country for decades, had initially expressed optimism about the Sandinista National Liberation Front and its 1979 overthrow of the dictatorship. By the early 1980s, however, he had become a vocal opponent of the Sandinistas, criticizing their use of military conscription, restrictions of press freedoms, and purported human rights abuses. He decried the role that adherents of liberation theology played in the new revolutionary government, arguing that Catholic priests like Ernesto Cardenal, Fernando Cardenal, and Miguel d'Escoto Brockman, who served in the Sandinista government in positions of authority, helped conceal human rights abuses under the veil of social justice and Christianity. The IRD feted Obando at a swanky Washington, DC, luncheon in his honor, declaring him a stalwart defender of the freedom of religion and a bulwark against Marxism creeping into Latin America's churches.[18]

While underscoring the dangers of liberation theology abroad, the IRD paid even closer attention to the risk of leftist infiltration at home. According to the IRD, one of the most insidious forms of this subversion into American churches could be found in the Sanctuary Movement. Data gathered through congregational questionnaires showed a troubling trend: Churches were listening to what sanctuary activists had to say and, according to the IRD, were increasingly being pressed into political advocacy on behalf of the movement. Sanctuary served, the IRD warned, as the "most visible expression" of churches' growing opposition to US foreign policy in El Salvador and Guatemala. And unfortunately for supporters of the Reagan administration's growing military involvement in the region, the movement was showing marked success. According to Alan Wisdom, a researcher at the IRD, newspaper reporters and television cameras "couldn't resist the well-staged drama of sanctuary."[19] The melodrama of the movement—bandana-disguised asylum seekers recounting shocking tales of persecution and of flight northward; clergy and nuns proclaiming that their conscience required them to defy the law to shelter these suffering people; and immigration officers threatening to break into churches to seize asylum seekers and their religious protectors—threatened to build support among everyday Americans who might have otherwise remained relatively uneducated about US intervention in Central America. This "ideological theater," as IRD board member Richard John Neuhaus described sanctuary contemptuously, may have been deceptive and even morally reprehensible for the way it used "the alien poor," but it was also effective.[20]

The IRD made countering the movement's efficacious media and political education campaign one of its primary initiatives. Through publications and public forums, it worked to show that sanctuary activists operated under a series of misconceptions, mistruths, or even outright lies. The organization did so by questioning the movement's reliance on historical precedent as justification for its church-based asylum. In an article published in the IRD's monthly newsletter, Richard Feen, an official in the Office for the US Coordinator for Refugee Affairs, accused participants of misappropriating the centuries-long history of religious asylum, a concept that, he offered, in fact had no legal standing in any Western society.[21] Citing evidence provided by the State Department, the IRD also refuted the movement's claim that El Salvador and Guatemala were unsafe locations to which to return deportees. The movement, the IRD argued, was merely ginning up "sympathy for the plight of refugees not merely to build opposition to U.S.-Central American policy" but also to "try to bring radical change to the United States." Sanctuary's movements were thus much darker, the organization alleged—activists were working, as the IRD noted in one 1985 article in its monthly periodical, to "bring the revolution home."[22]

With the federal government's arrest and prosecution of sanctuary activists in 1985, the IRD identified an opening through which to reframe the public narrative surrounding Central American asylum seekers and the politics of faith-infused protest, one that had to date pitched movement members as earnest humanitarians. The group's intervention—a conference held in October 1985 in Washington, DC, entitled "Sanctuary: A Challenge to the Churches"—was styled in promotional materials as an opportunity for policymakers and media outlets in the nation's capital to learn more about US refugee and foreign policy in Central America. While the conference was framed as an open conversation to discuss the "ethical and theological roots" of sanctuary, however, its dais was occupied mainly by movement critics.[23] Among them was one of sanctuary's most vocal opponents, Elliot Abrams, an assistant secretary in the State Department. Abrams's portfolio included asylum as well as human rights issues in Latin America. He was also the administration's most vocal defender of US intervention in Central America, referring to himself as the "Gladiator for the Reagan Doctrine" as he argued forcefully for military aid to Nicaraguan Contras on television, in newspaper editorials, and in the halls of Congress. When news programs like *60 Minutes* and *Frontline* sought comment from the White House on the Sanctuary Movement, Abrams was always prepared to provide an acerbic quotation explaining why activists were sorely misinformed about the country's refugee policies.[24] Taking the stage at the IRD conference as attendees enjoyed their lunch, Abrams unveiled a full litany of charges against sanctuary participants. He accused the movement of skirting the country's asylum process and of not only creating "self-appointed refugees" but also using them as "pawns" to attack the Reagan administration's efforts to promote democracy in the region.[25]

Beware the "Feet People": The Federation for American Immigration Reform's Opposition to Sanctuary

That a prominent Reagan administration official enjoyed such a prominent spot on the program was no coincidence. The day's sessions, according to planning documents prepared by IRD organizer Kerry Ptacek, "should leave no doubt about the essential justice of U.S. law."[26] Ptacek had outlined that objective in a letter to the other organization helping set the agenda for the day, the Federation for American Immigration Reform (FAIR). Roger Conner, FAIR's executive director, was even more explicit in what he hoped the meeting might achieve, which was to "inform individuals who can form the core of a counter-sanctuary movement in the United States." Sanctuary, Conner noted, was part of a larger "illegal immigration issue," a "widespread phenomenon" in the country. If allowed to continue, it would encourage "further illegal immigration from El Salvador and other places similarly situated."[27]

The IRD and FAIR made somewhat strange political bedfellows. Beyond its focus on sanctuary, the IRD had offered no public comments on immigration policy during the 1980s.[28] FAIR, on the other hand, had become the leading national voice on immigration restriction and was a growing political player in Washington, DC. The nonprofit, tax-exempt lobbying group was making its mark at a time when national sentiment towards immigrants was shifting. As the rate of both documented and undocumented migration from Latin America, the Caribbean, and Asia increased in the late 1970s and early 1980s, FAIR drew upon bubbling anti-immigrant sentiment in the United States in its calls for reducing *all* forms of migration to the country. In position papers to members of Congress and pamphlets to the thousands of followers on their mailing list, FAIR readily drew upon racist tropes to stoke fears of a swell of impoverished, nonwhite people flooding the nation, a surge that would bring disease, crime, and political subversion to the United States. As historian Carl Bon Tempo notes, the group "repeatedly questioned the abilities of newcomers to assimilate culturally to the United States," a tactic, he notes, whose "racial and ethnic undertones echoed early twentieth-century restrictionists."[29]

In the 1980s, FAIR joined the IRD as one of the most active critics of the Sanctuary Movement. The DC-based FAIR worked the halls of Congress regularly as part of its larger mission to reduce immigration to the country. FAIR resolved to stymie any legislative resolutions to help Central American migrants seeking asylum in the United States, including lobbying against efforts to provide extended voluntary departure (EVD) to Salvadorans. This legal mechanism, advanced by Maryland Congressman Joseph Moakley and Arizona Senator Dennis DeConcini and supported by sanctuary activists, would have offered temporary relief from deportation to migrants. The Sanctuary Movement's support of EVD, FAIR director Roger Conner argued before the Senate Subcommittee on Immigration and Refugee Policy, was foolhardy and would lead to drastic unintended consequences for the United States. Its passage, he warned, would mean everyday Americans would have to foot the bill to support more than half a million Salvadorans, many of whom, he alleged, were not even political refugees but instead economic migrants who "came for the same reasons as millions of other illegals: to take jobs."[30] Even worse, FAIR warned, it would create a magnet for people all around the world, sending a message to would-be asylum seekers that "anyone who wishes to leave a country with overpopulation, high unemployment, and political violence can come to the United States."[31]

FAIR took these charges beyond the nation's capital, hoping to educate those same everyday Americans about the perils of overpopulation and tax burdens that Central American migrants might bring. FAIR prepared a "Sanctuary Information Packet" in 1985 to motivate citizens to contact their congressional representatives and voice opposition to EVD. It included an assortment of legislative bulletins, political cartoons, and opinion pieces published in national and regional newspapers. Among those articles was an op-ed from Wyoming Senator Alan Simpson, who warned in *The Washington Post* that offering sanctuary to Salvadorans and Guatemalans would only further the nation's "compassion fatigue" and ultimately diminish the "nation's willingness to respond to the millions of truly persecuted humans all over the planet."[32] The fastest way to reach Americans, however, would be through the airwaves. FAIR's founder, John Tanton, and executive director, Roger Connor, debated sanctuary activists on CNN, PBS's *MacNeil/Lehrer NewsHour*, *Donahue*, and even the *Today* show. On national television, Tanton and Connor downplayed their organization's central objective—to restrict all immigration, legal or otherwise, to the United States—and instead emphasized that, while sanctuary activists might be well intentioned, their skirting of the law threatened to subvert the nation's already generous immigration system.[33]

While the IRD warned of Communist subversives guiding the Sanctuary Movement and FAIR rang the alarm of a runaway liberal immigration and asylum system, members of the Moral Majority found a way to thread the needle and combine all of these charges. As Sara Diamond and other scholars have noted, Religious Right groups served as the "vanguard" of supporting anti-Communist efforts in Central America throughout the 1980s.[34] Pat Robertson's *Freedom Report* admonished sanctuary activists for advancing "a fundamental misunderstanding of God's delegation of authority to the individual, to the Church and to the state."[35] In the pages of Jerry Falwell's monthly magazine, *The Fundamentalist*, meanwhile, one contributor melded the antileftist and restrictionist arguments against the movement. While sanctuary's primary goal may have been to pressure the American government to stop backing military governments in Guatemala and El Salvador, journalist and conservative activist Martin Mawyer wrote, it was nefariously most interested in fulfilling a "hidden agenda of smuggling aliens" into the country. Deploying quotations from IRD representatives and FAIR's Roger Connor, Mawyer suggested that sanctuary had a much larger goal than just providing humanitarian aid to those in need. In a multipage spread that was ostensibly about the Sanctuary Movement and Central American asylees, the magazine included images of migrants waiting to slip across the border, with an accompanying caption that read, "Mexicans wait for the 'right moment' to cross the Rio Grande, illegally, compounding the serious problems the U.S. has with illegal aliens." While the article made no explicit connections between the two migrant groups, readers were left to make their own assumptions about the dangers posed by leftist instigators, an unsecured border, and the potential oncoming rush of illegal and radical entrants.[36] Seizing on FAIR's primary anxiety—that Central American migrants represented an existential population threat to the United States— in his fundraising appeals, Falwell was more explicit about the threat of swarms of migrants. In one 1983 letter to supporters following a "fact-finding mission" to El Salvador, Falwell warned readers that the "peace-niks and the freez-niks" who made up the Central American solidarity movement planned to "force millions and millions of 'feet people'" across the border "to weaken our country socially and economically so the Communists can then step in and take over the United States." Opposition to the Sanctuary Movement and any effort to halt the Reagan administration's policies in Central America would be tantamount to national suicide. As Falwell noted, "Central America is a hand grenade waiting to blow up into the soft underside of the U.S. border."[37]

That last point—that the Sanctuary Movement was dangerous not only because it signified a Communist takeover of Christian churches but because it represented a frontal assault on the country's ostensibly generous immigration and asylum system—became one of the most enduring and salient charges against the movement that religious opponents, government officials, and immigration restrictionists would readily make. According to both the IRD and FAIR, what perhaps made sanctuary most disingenuous was the way in which the movement manipulated poor and vulnerable "economic migrants" from Central America for their own political ends. The IRD warned that if the activists were allowed to continue to organize, and if mainline churches continued to offer their verbal and financial support of the movement, it would not only undermine "the moral credibility of our churches" but also make a mockery of the country's asylum system.[38]

Prosecuting a "Sanctimonious Fraud": The Reagan Administration Responds to the Sanctuary Movement

The White House repeated these claims in meetings with Hispanic evangelical pastors, a contingent it courted in efforts to find spokespeople for its domestic and foreign policies. As Geraldo Cadava has shown, Reagan officials regularly sought Hispanic surrogates to help make the administration's case for US military intervention in Central America and its developing immigration policies.[39] When it came to asylum and sanctuary, the administration depicted the potential for a pitched battle between American Hispanics and Central American newcomers. In one meeting with Hispanic faith leaders, the administration appealed to attendees as American citizens and taxpayers who had a place in the economy to protect. An influx of eight million Central American economic migrants would cost the country more than $115 billion, they warned, but the larger price could be to the standing of middle-class and striving Latinos who would have to contend with the racial backlash of so many Latin American migrants arriving at the United States' doorstep. As one official told Hispanic pastors, the "human costs" of this rising tide of asylum seekers would be "incalculable" for Hispanic citizens seeking to fulfill the American Dream and rise into the country's middle class.[40]

The Reagan administration deployed the menace of a growing tide of poor Latin American migrants at the nation's doorstep in its broader appeal to the American public. As Kristina Shull has noted, despite Reagan's passage of the compromise Immigration and Reform Control Act of 1986, the president's policies towards Haitians, Cubans, and Central Americans belied any sort of welcoming impulse to nonwhite migrants.[41] Throughout the 1980s, administration officials regularly warned of the perils of offering asylum to those fleeing revolutions in Latin America and the concurrent necessity for increased military spending in the region to stem their arrival. Secretary of State George Schultz, speaking to a meeting of Dallas businessmen in 1983, cautioned that the "stability of our neighbors" to the south would "prevent unprecedented flows of refugees northward to this country."[42] Alan Nelson, commissioner of the Immigration and Naturalization Services, was even blunter, cautioning that absent stiffer asylum laws, the United States faced "an invasion of 'foot people.'"[43] Elliot Abrams, sanctuary's most vociferous opponent in the administration, regularly invoked the looming specter of hundreds of thousands of "feet people" arriving at the US-Mexico border. One widely circulated 1984 State Department memo prepared by Abrams warned that 10 percent of Latin America's population would swarm northward if El Salvador fell. The alarm over an incoming flood of asylum seekers struck many Central American advocates as disingenuous considering that a tenth of El Salvador's population had already made their way to the United States as a result of the US-arms-fueled violence.[44]

The charge that sanctuary was nothing more than a trafficking operation seeking to accelerate those migrant flows became central to the federal government's eventual prosecution of the movement. The Department of Justice, which had been surveilling sanctuary congregations from nearly the movement's inception, going so far as to place undercover agents in the pews of Bible study groups, had accelerated its policing of sanctuary in 1984 when it first launched Operation Sojourner, resulting in a series of raids of churches and arrests of activists and asylum seekers. The following year, a Tucson federal grand jury issued the seventy-one indictments against sixteen sanctuary leaders that would catapult the movement into the national spotlight. Like the movement's detractors, federal prosecutors accused the sanctuary participants of gross violations of immigration law and having created a network analogous to a drug-smuggling ring, one that moved illegal entrants across national and state borders. Within the courtroom, meanwhile, the presiding judge forbade the defendants from referencing conditions in Central America or US intervention in the region, their own religious justifications for partaking in the movement, or even the United States' own obligations to asylum seekers as outlined in the Refugee Act of 1980. The proceedings amounted to what one legal scholar referred to as a "political trial," one in which the federal government sought to neutralize not only those facing federal indictments but sanctuary as a whole.[45]

Conservative media outlets readily tracked the sanctuary indictments throughout the 1985 trial. Newspapers and magazines published articles and editorials criticizing movement members for hiding their political intentions behind the veil of religious commitments. In the pages of *National Review*, one contributor opined that sanctuary was just a "new folly" for churches that had gone astray, another example of the excesses of the civil rights era in which "liberal guilt's done got religion."[46] In *Human Events*, the conservative journalist and activist M. Stanton Evans referred to sanctuary as a "sanctimonious fraud" that was using Salvadorans and Guatemalans as "political weapons" in their fight against US foreign policy.[47] *The Washington Times*'s editorial board deemed movement members to be nothing more than "hucksters" who were abusing "America's goodness to aid America's enemies."[48] And in *The Wall Street Journal*, the editorial board offered that activists were merely seeking to advance "a familiar far-left agenda." Citing IRD research, the newspaper wrote that despite the allegedly altruistic aims of sanctuary workers, the movement was not "so much a spontaneous outpouring of Christian concern" as it was a movement "led by a politically selective network of activists running an aggressive offensive against U.S. foreign policy in Central America."[49]

Federal prosecutors, while perhaps not invoking the political invective splashed across the pages of *The Wall Street Journal* or *National Review*, argued much the same. And following a contentious year-long trial, they won their case; eight of the sanctuary defendants were ultimately found guilty of multiple felony counts of transporting and harboring migrants. Much to the chagrin of the Reagan administration and conservative opponents alike, however, the convictions did little to abate the growth of the movement. Instead, the publicity generated by the trial allowed activists to add *more* houses of worship to the sanctuary roster. Four years after the end of the trial, meanwhile, congressional lobbying by religious and civic organizations spurred Congress to include provisions in the Immigration Act of 1990 that permitted Salvadorans to receive an eighteen-month-long protection under Temporary Protected Status. That same year, sanctuary activists and a coalition of more than eighty refugee and religious organizations secured a civil suit settlement (ABC Agreement) against the federal government that allowed thousands of Salvadorans and Guatemalans the right to reapply for asylum. The legal victories, coupled with decreasing migration from Central America with the opening of peace processes in El Salvador and Guatemala, brought the Sanctuary Movement to a quiet end in the early 1990s.

Conclusion

Through the 1980s, conservative religious activists spilled considerable ink and expended substantial political capital to discredit the Sanctuary Movement. Given the movement's eventual accomplishments, perhaps they had a reason to ring the alarm. As IRD staffer Alan Wisdom wrote in the think tank's newsletter, "Normal means of church political activism had never spread the message of the religious Left so effectively."[50] The irony of Wisdom's comments, and perhaps purposeful obfuscation of the IRD's own brand of religiopolitical activism, serves as a reminder that in the 1980s, religious spaces served as crucial sites of struggle over the future of immigration, refugee, and foreign policy in the United States.

In the twenty-first century, the term "sanctuary" remains a controversial one. As was the case in the 1980s, when invoked in the negative—"antisanctuary," or "anti-sanctuary city," in its secular variant—it has become a catch-all term, a shibboleth, not only to describe opposition to immigration, both legal and otherwise, but also as a way of setting parameters for the proper role of politics in religious spaces. When immigration activists invoked the practice of sanctuary in the mid-2000s and formed the New Sanctuary Movement, opponents were again prepared to offer an alternative answer to the way people of faith should welcome the stranger, one that was decidedly less inviting than the one being offered by sanctuary proponents.

Such was the case in the spring of 2007, when members of the immigration restrictionist group the Minutemen Project led protests outside churches in San Diego. There, twenty area houses of worship had joined together pledging to offer sanctuary to Marco Castillo, a graphic artist and college graduate who had moved from Mexico to California as a child but who had overstayed his visa and was now facing removal proceedings. Minutemen members paced the sidewalk across from the San Diego Friends Meeting House offering Castillo safe harbor, waving American flags and carrying signs reading "No Amnesty!," "Stop Illegal Immigration," "Terrorists [Heart] Open Borders," and "Let the church pay for the Illegals! Not my tax dollars!" On their website, the Minutemen offered a one-hundred-dollar reward for any information leading to the deportation of undocumented residents living in the United States. For Jeff Schwick, the leader of the protests, their demonstrations were about more than just immigration policy—they were about ridding the church of leftist radicals espousing a minority position among people of faith. As he told the local press, "We're saying that these people don't speak for us. They don't speak for all Christians. They don't speak for the majority of Christians. Christians want secure borders."[51]

Over the next few months, the Minutemen took their antisanctuary protests around the city. They squared off with Mexican and Central American day laborers trying to find work on street corners. With megaphones in hand, Minutemen scared away would-be employers, leading to physical clashes with the young men looking for work.[52] They then took their protests to Fallbrook Church, a congregation that facilitated the hiring of workers while offering day laborers a warm breakfast and a place to wait for a job. There the Minutemen were joined by San Diego Christians for Secure Borders (SDCFB), another organization that had a decidedly different take on how people of faith should approach the intersection of immigration politics and religion. When asked by a reporter, "What would Jesus do?" on the question of sanctuary, Neil Turner, founder of SDCFB responded, "I think Jesus would enforce Biblical law [which says that] all governments are established by God, and we ought to make sure to obey the laws." Together, the two groups escalated their political theater in front of the church, waving signs declaring, "Hire U.S. citizens, let Mexico feed her own" and "Tax the Catholic Church; a political organization." Perhaps most dramatically, they hoisted an effigy of a priest with horns brandishing a name tag that read "Father Satan."[53] These escalations did nothing to stem the growth of sanctuary activism in the city; instead, they earned the rebuke of southern California Latino Catholics and the national Catholic League for Religious and Civil Rights, who accused the Minutemen of "flagrant anti-Catholic bigotry."[54]

The spirit that guided antisanctuary counterprotests in San Diego in the mid-2000s, grounded in a restrictionist impulse that seeks to reduce the number of immigrants and asylum seekers allowed to enter or remain in the United States, has continued well into the twenty-first century. At the forefront of efforts to curb sanctuary practices has been FAIR, a familiar Sanctuary Movement antagonist. The organization has largely shifted its focus from ending sanctuary in houses of worship to campaigning against so-called sanctuary cities and states. FAIR has identified these jurisdictions, which pass legislation that prevents local officials from participating with federal efforts to detain and deport undocumented residents, as the most pressing battlefronts in their war against what they deem to be irresponsible and permissive immigration policies.[55]

FAIR's work, however, has advanced much farther than sending informational fliers to their mailing lists, lobbying in Congress, or appearing on nightly news shows, as was the case in the 1980s. Now, the organization is actually helping pass legislation that would outlaw sanctuary practices altogether. In 2019, FAIR worked with Floridians for Immigration Enforcement to draft Senate Bill 168, a measure that banned sanctuary cities in the state. Passed by the state legislature and signed by Governor Ron DeSantis, the law became the first of its kind in the nation.[56] It served as a model for enacting the type of legislation that 1980s sanctuary opponents could have only dreamed of, and that President Donald Trump had worked to realize in his own antisanctuary city campaigns and executive orders.[57] These contemporary efforts, as this chapter has shown, are part of a long history of opposition to sanctuary activism. FAIR's focus on sanctuary practices, now stretching into its fifth decade, speaks not only to the importance of a movement first born in houses of worship in 1982 but also to the persistence of antagonists' efforts to end it.

NOTES

1 Michael Novak, "Sanctuary Fraud," *Washington Times*, November 1, 1985. Novak reprinted this editorial in his magazine, *Catholicism in Crisis*. See Michael Novak, "Editorial: The Fraud That Failed," *Crisis Magazine*, December 1, 1985, www.crisismagazine.com.

2 Quentin L. Quade, executive vice-president of Marquette University, spoke out strongly against the Milwaukee Archdiocese's support for the Sanctuary Movement. Quade bemoaned the archdiocese's endorsement of measures that were "encouraging parishes to break the law" by offering "illegal sanctuary to illegal refugees." "Writer Sees Anarchism in Sanctuary for Illegal Refugees," *Milwaukee Sentinel*, March 26, 1983.

3 Damon Linker, *The Theocons: Secular America Under Siege* (Anchor Books, 2006).

4 For more on the surveillance, infiltration, and prosecution of these movements, see Christian Smith, *Resisting Reagan: The U.S. Central America Peace Movement* (University of Chicago Press, 1996), 280–324.

5 See Andrew Preston, *Sword of the Spirit, Shield of Faith: Religion in American War and Diplomacy* (Knopf, 2012); Lauren Frances Turek, *To Bring the Good News to All Nations: Evangelical Influence on Human Rights and U.S. Foreign Relations* (Cornell University Press, 2022), 124–50; Greg Grandin, *Empire's Workshop: Latin America, the United States, and the Making of an Imperial Republic*, 2nd ed. (Picador, 2021), 90–226; Charles T. Strauss, "Quest for the Holy Grail: Central American War, Catholic Internationalism, and United States Public Diplomacy in Reagan's America," *U.S. Catholic Historian* 33, no. 1 (2015): 163–97; Theresa Keeley, *Reagan's Gun-Toting Nuns: The Catholic Conflict over Cold War Human Rights Policy in Central America* (Cornell University Press, 2020).

6 Andrew Preston, "Peripheral Visions: American Mainline Protestants and the Global Cold War," *Cold War History* 13, no. 1 (2013): 109–30, quotation on 112.

7 Steven M. Tipton, *Public Pulpits: Methodists and Mainline Churches in the Moral Argument of Public Life* (University of Chicago Press, 2008), 146–87.

8 See Michael Harrington, "The Welfare State and Neoconservative Critics," *Dissent* 20 (Fall 1973): 435–54; Peter Steinfels, *The Neoconservatives* (Simon and Schuster, 1979); Sara Diamond, *Roads to Dominion: Right-Wing Movements and Political Power in the United States* (Guilford Press, 1995), 178–202; Gary J. Dorrien, *The Neoconservative Mind: Politics, Culture, and the War on Ideology* (Temple University Press, 1993); Mark Gerson, *The Neoconservative Vision: From the Cold War to the Culture Wars* (Madison Books, 1996).

9 John Fast, "Political Theology or Ideological Politics? An Analysis of the Institute for Religion and Democracy," *Direction* 14, no. 1 (Spring 1985): 51–57; Peter Steinfels, "Neoconservative Ideology," *Democracy: A Journal of Political Renewal and Radical Change*, April 1982, 18; Leon Howell, "Who Funds IRD?," *Christianity and Crisis*, March 21, 1983.

10 Jim Wallis, "In Defense of CEPAD," *Sojourners* 12, no. 10 (November 1984): 4–5, quotation on 5.

11 Neuhaus quoted in Richard John Neuhaus and Edmund Robb Jr., "The Gospel According to Whom?," *60 Minutes*, CBS, January 23, 1983. See also Joseph A. Harris, "What Master Is the World Council of Churches Serving . . . Karl Marx or Jesus Christ?," *Reader's Digest*, August 1982, 130–34; Rael Jean Isaac, "Do You Know Where Your Church Offerings Go?," *Reader's Digest*, January 1983, 120–25.

12 Edmund W. Robb and Julia Robb, *The Betrayal of the Church: Apostasy and Renewal in the Mainline Denominations* (Crossway Books, 1986), 11.

13 Richard John Neuhaus, *Christianity and Democracy: A Statement of the Institute on Religion and Democracy* (Institute on Religion and Democracy, 1981), 13.

14 Curtin Winsor Jr., *The Washington Battle for Central America: The Unmet Challenge of the "Red Chorus"* (Washington Institute for Values in Public Policy, 1987). A variety of traditional conservative, neoconservative, and New Right think tanks like the Heritage Foundation, the Council for Inter-American Security, the Inter-American Security Educational Institute, and the Council for the Defense of Freedom published multiple reports on the Central American solidarity movement. See Joan Frawley, *The Left's Latin American Lobby* (Heritage Foundation, 1984); S. Steven Powell, *Second Front: Advancing Latin American Revolution in Washington* (Capital Research Center, 1986); "The Sanctuary Movement: Revolution Walking Across Our Border," *West Watch: Council for Inter-American Security* 8, no. 2 (April/May 1985), CRTFCA Records, Box 5, Folder 19, Wisconsin Historical Society (hereafter WHS); Allen C. Brownfeld and J. Michael Waller, *The Revolution Lobby* (Council for Inter-American Security and the Inter-American Security Educational Institute, 1985). James L. Tyson, *Prophets or Useful Idiots? Church Organizations Attacking U.S. Central American Policy* (Center for Public Diplomacy Studies, Council for the Defense of Freedom, 1986).

15 Sara Diamond, *Spiritual Warfare: The Politics of the Christian Right* (South End Press, 1989), 151–52. The IRD scrutinized agencies like the Evangelical Committee for Aid to Development (CEPAD), an ecumenical humanitarian organization formed in 1973 after an earthquake devastated Managua. They alleged that CEPAD, which served as mainline Protestant churches' primary relief and development program in Nicaragua, was in fact a front to pass along church dollars to the socialist Sandinista government.

16 "Sandinista Crackdown Tests U.S. Church Ties," *Religion and Democracy: A Newsletter of the Institute on Religion and Democracy*, January/February 1986. IRD board member Michael Novak took liberation theology to task in a 1986 book, arguing that Latin America's only legitimate path to success lay in capitalism. See

Michael Novak, *Will It Liberate? Questions About Liberation Theology* (Paulist Press, 1986).

17 Edmund W. Robb Jr. to Bishop Philip R. Cousin, November 5, 1984, Box 171, Folder: IRD—Support of Nicaraguan Churches, Records of the Institute on Religion and Democracy and Presidential Papers of Diane Knippers, Asbury Theological Seminary Special Collections and Archives, Wilmore, Kentucky (hereafter Asbury Records); Institute on Religion and Democracy, "A Petition to American Christians: Defend the Churches of Nicaragua," n.d., Box 171, Folder: IRD—Support of Nicaraguan Churches, Asbury Records; William Bole, "Conservative Critics Begin Drive to Halt Church Aid in Nicaragua," *Religious News Service*, July 11, 1984; The Institute on Religion and Democracy, "IRD Report: Church Support for Pro-Sandinista Network," 1984, WHS Pamphlet Collection.

18 Introductory remarks by Archbishop James A. Hickey at IRD luncheon honoring Archbishop Miguel Obando y Bravo, Washington, DC, January 8, 1982, Box 164, Folder: IRD—Religious Freedom Award 1982—Archbishop Miguel Obando y Bravo, Asbury Records; "IRD Honors Archbishop Obando y Bravo of Nicaragua," *Religion & Democracy: A Newsletter of the Institute on Religion and Democracy*, January 1982.

19 Quoted in Alan Wisdom, "Slowed Sanctuary Movement Sidesteps Facts, Hews to Ideological Line," *Religion and Democracy: A Newsletter of the Institute on Religion and Democracy*, January–February 1987. See also "Untitled [Sanctuary]," *Religion and Democracy: A Newsletter of the Institute on Religion and Democracy*, Fall 1983; Presbyterians for Democracy and Religious Freedom, "Press Release: National Survey Suggest [*sic*] 'Massive Rejection' of Sanctuary Movement by Local Churches, Says PDRF," June 1, 1987, Box 163, Folder: News Release Sanctuary 6-1-87, Asbury Records.

20 Richard John Neuhaus, "A 'This World' Symposium: Sanctuary and the Sanctuary Movement," *This World: A Journal of Religion and Public Life* 11 (Spring/Summer 1985): 19–21.

21 Richard H. Feen, "Sanctuary: A Look at Church Tradition," *Religion and Democracy: A Newsletter of the Institute on Religion and Democracy*, March 1985.

22 "Bringing the Revolution Home . . . ," *Religion and Democracy: A Newsletter of the Institute on Religion and Democracy*, March 1985.

23 The Institute on Religion and Democracy, "Registration Form—Sanctuary: Challenge to the Church," October 4, 1985, Box 15, National Council of the Churches of Christ in the United States (72D), Presbyterian Archives, Philadelphia, Pennsylvania.

24 Dorrien, *The Neoconservative Mind*, 181. Abrams discussed the administration's opposition to the Sanctuary Movement on various news outlets in the 1980s. See for example Ed Bradley and Joel Bernstein, "Underground Railroad," *60 Minutes* (CBS), December 12, 1982; and June Massell and Hector Galán, "Episode 23: Sanctuary," *Frontline* (Public Broadcasting Service), July 11, 1983. For a sample of Abrams's public writing on sanctuary, see Paul A. Fisher, "*The Wanderer* Asks Elliot Abrams," *The Wanderer*, February 9, 1984; Elliot Abrams, "A 'This World'

Symposium: Sanctuary and the Sanctuary Movement," *This World: A Journal of Religion and Public Life* 11 (Spring/Summer 1985): 10–12; Elliot Abrams, "U.S. Refugee Policy Is Nothing to Flee," *Los Angeles Times*, January 17, 1985.

25 Elliot Abrams, "Contending Views of the Future of Central America," in Maria H. Thomas, ed., *Sanctuary: Challenge to the Churches* (Institute on Religion and Democracy, 1986), 50.

26 Kerry Ptacek to Roger Conner, May 13, 1985, Box 166, Folder: Sanctuary: FAIR, Asbury Records.

27 Roger Conner to Ken Campbell and Kerry Ptacek, May 8, 1985, Box 166, Folder: Sanctuary: FAIR, Asbury Records.

28 Neoconservatives were more likely to reject anti-immigrant policies in the 1980s, and were sometimes known to do so forcefully. In 1989, for example, IRD board member Richard John Neuhaus and movement intellectual Norman Podhoretz clashed with the Rockford Institute, a leading paleoconservative organization, when the group began to use its journal *Chronicles* to promote restrictionist immigration policies. Neuhaus and Podhoretz condemned the organization as nativist, racist, and antisemitic. Dorrien, *The Neoconservative Mind*, 345–49.

29 Carl J. Bon Tempo, *Americans at the Gates: The United States and Refugees During the Cold War* (Princeton University Press, 2008). See also Carly Goodman, "Unmaking the Nation of Immigrants: How John Tanton's Network of Organizations Transformed Policy and Politics," in *A Field Guide to White Supremacy*, ed. Kathleen Belew and Ramón A. Gutiérrez (University of California Press, 2021), 203–19.

30 Roger Conner, "Extended Voluntary Departure: Statement Before the Senate Subcommittee on Immigration and Refugee Policy," April 22, 1985, Box 166, Folder: Sanctuary: FAIR, Asbury Records.

31 Federation for American Immigration Reform Legislative Bulletin, "Extended Voluntary Departure (EVD) for Salvadorans, S. 377/H.R. 822," n.d., Box 166, Folder: Sanctuary: FAIR, Asbury Records.

32 Alan K. Simpson, "We Can't Allow All Salvadorans to Stay," *Washington Post*, July 7, 1984, included in Federation for American Immigration Reform, *Sanctuary Information Packet*, n.d., Box 166, Folder: Sanctuary: FAIR, Asbury Records.

33 "The MacNeil/Lehrer NewsHour," 1985-01-16, NewsHour Productions, American Archive of Public Broadcasting (GBH and the Library of Congress), Boston, Massachusetts, and Washington, DC, accessed June 11, 2024, http://americanarchive.org; The MacNeil/Lehrer NewsHour, "Problem Banks/Hi-Tech Pollution/Storm over Illegals/Troubles in the Tropics: Transcript #2428," January 16, 1985, Box 166, Folder: Sanctuary: FAIR, Asbury Records; Darlene Nicgorski on Phil Donohue show, circa 1986 Spring, VHS Videocassette, Box 15, Darlene Nicgorski Papers on the Sanctuary Movement, Special Collections, Honnold/Mudd Library, Claremont University Consortium, Claremont, California; Jane Pauley, "The Sanctuary Movement," *Today*, September 16, 1987, accessed June 11, 2024, /www.youtube.com/watch?v=ymZUkKSohQM; Romero Institute, "Sanctuary Movement—

Freeman Reports: Stacy Merkt," YouTube, July 9, 2015, video, www.youtube.com/watch?v=nTzXYrhqtHo&list=PLVza7sesLJh5zhAPZENjM_gTjizpklRSF.

34 Quoted in Sara Diamond, *Spiritual Warfare: The Politics of the Christian Right* (South End Press, 1989), v. See also Grandin, *Empire's Workshop*; Lauren F. Turek, "Ambassadors for the Kingdom of God or for America? Christian Nationalism, the Christian Right, and the Contra War," *Religions* 7, no. 12 (December 2016): 1–16.

35 Paul McConnell, "Sanctuary: Compassion or Crime?," *Freedom Report* 4, no. 2 (September/October 1985): 1–3, CRTFCA Records, Box 5, Folder 19, WHS.

36 Martin Mawyer, "Sanctuary Movement: The Hidden Agenda of Smuggling Aliens," *Fundamentalist* 5, no. 9 (October 1986): 59–62. Mawyer would go on to found the Christian Action Network in 1990, an organization that would protest the National Endowment for the Arts' funding of sexually explicit photography and the creation of an Islamic community center and mosque near the World Trade Center site in Lower Manhattan. It has been classified as a hate group by the Southern Poverty Law Center.

37 Newsletter from Jerry Falwell, October 14, 1983, Group 1 Subgroup 2 Series 4 Folder 35C, The Conservative Caucus Records, The Jerry Falwell Library, Liberty University, Lynchburg, Virginia, https://liberty.contentdm.oclc.org.

38 "The Sanctuary Movement: A Time for Reappraisal," *Religion and Democracy: A Newsletter of the Institute on Religion and Democracy*, March 1985.

39 Geraldo L. Cadava, *The Hispanic Republican: The Shaping of an American Political Identity* (Ecco, 2020), 234–60.

40 Juan Williams, "White House Pitches Latin Policy to Public," *Washington Post*, September 24, 1983; The White House, "Briefing Paper: Meeting with Hispanic Evangelicals, September 14, 1983," Box 57, Blackwell Morton Files, Ronald Reagan Presidential Library, Simi Valley, California, www.reaganlibrary.gov.

41 Kristina Shull, *Detention Empire: Reagan's War on Immigrants and the Seeds of Resistance* (University of North Carolina Press, 2022).

42 KXAS-TV (Television station: Fort Worth, Texas). [News Clip: Schultz], video, April 15, 1983, 5:00 p.m., Fort Worth, Texas (https://texashistory.unt.edu, accessed August 21, 2024), University of North Texas Libraries, The Portal to Texas History, https://texashistory.unt.edu; crediting UNT Libraries Special Collections.

43 Nadine Cohodas, "Salvadoran Refugee Question Debated," *Washington Times*, May 1, 1985.

44 Jonathan Rowe, "Murder by Deportation," *Washington Monthly*, February 1984.

45 Sophie H. Pirie, "The Origins of a Political Trial: The Sanctuary Movement and Political Justice," *Yale Journal of Law & the Humanities* 2, no. 2 (1990): 381–416. See also Ann Crittenden, *Sanctuary: A Story of American Conscience and Law in Collision* (Weidenfeld and Nicholson, 1988).

46 Fred A. Slimp II, "Gimme Sanctuary: The Right of Asylum," *National Review*, May 17, 1985.

47 M. Stanton Evans, "Sanctuary Movement: Sanctimonious Fraud," *Human Events*, July 26, 1986. For more antisanctuary articles in *Human Events*, see Thomas J.

Fleming, "Disturbing Implications of Sanctuary Movement," *Human Events*, December 14, 1985; Smith Hempstone, "Sanctuary Movement: Criminal Acts Must Be Punished," *Human Events*, May 31, 1986.

48 Editorial Board, "Sanctuary Sanctimony," *Washington Times*, October 25, 1985. The *Times* had multiple editorials and cartoons lambasting the movement from 1985 to 1986. See Georgie Anne Geyer, "Sanctuary Movement Masks Political Agenda," *Washington Times*, May 14, 1985; Dorothy Rabinowitz, "Refugees in Service to a Cause," *Washington Times*, July 15, 1985; Steve Benson, "White Collar Crime," *Washington Times*, November 1, 1985; Cal Thomas, "The 'Sanctuary' Convictions,'" *Washington Times*, May 12, 1986; Smith Hempstone, "Marching to a Ragged Beat," *Washington Times*, May 16, 1986.

49 Editorial Board, "Review & Outlook: The 'Sanctuary' Movement," *Wall Street Journal*, April 17, 1985. Later that year, the board referred to sanctuary as "purportedly a religion movement [that] has a highly secular motive behind it." See Editorial Board, "Review and Outlook: The Politics of Religion," *Wall Street Journal*, September 16, 1985.

50 Alan Wisdom, "Slowed Sanctuary Movement Sidesteps Facts, Hews to Ideological Line," *Religion and Democracy: A Newsletter of the Institute on Religion and Democracy*, January–February 1987.

51 Schwick quoted in Edward Sifuentes, "Religious Leaders Offer Sanctuary to Illegal Immigrants," *San Diego Union-Tribune*, May 10, 2007. See also Leslie Berestein, "Self-Made Immigrant to Receive Symbolic Sanctuary," *San Diego Union-Tribune*, May 9, 2007.

52 Kristina Davis, "Keeping the Peace: Protests at Day-Labor Sites," *San Diego Union-Tribune*, July 1, 2007.

53 Edward Sifuentes, "Anti–Illegal Immigration Activists Eye Fallbrook Church," *San Diego Union-Tribune*, July 8, 2007; Elena Gaona, "National Catholic Group Decries 'Bigotry' of Day," *San Diego Union-Tribune*, July 11, 2007.

54 Editorial Board, "Attention Seekers: End the Theatrics in Immigration Discourse," *San Diego Union-Tribune*, July 13, 2007.

55 "Sanctuary Policies," Federation for American Immigration Reform, accessed September 12, 2024, www.fairus.org.

56 Ana Ceballos, "Hard-Line Anti-immigrant Group Works to Sway Florida's Sanctuary City Bill," *Orlando Sentinel*, April 6, 2019; Mitch Perry, "Groups Sue to Stop Florida's New Hardline Anti-immigration Law," *Florida Phoenix*, July 16, 2019, https://floridaphoenix.com; Daniel Wiesner, "Judge Says Florida Ban on 'Sanctuary Cities' Unconstitutional," *Reuters*, September 22, 2021, www.reuters.com.

57 As one of his official acts in office, Trump signed Executive Order 13768, "Enhancing Public Safety in the Interior of the United States," which sought to ban federal grants from jurisdictions that passed sanctuary policies. An immediate legal challenge from the City of San Francisco halted the policy before it could go into effect. See Exec. Order No. 13768, 82 Fed. Reg. 8799 (January 25, 2017), www.federalregister.gov; Maura Dolan, "San Francisco Sues Trump over Executive Order Targeting Sanctuary Cities," *Los Angeles Times*, January 31, 2017.

7

The Sanctuary Movement at the Crossroads

The 1987 Jerome Hall Dialogue at Harvard Divinity School and the Meaning of Sanctuary

RADY ROLDÁN-FIGUEROA

Introduction

Named after the legal scholar Jerome Hall (1901–1992), the Jerome Hall Dialogue was a forum regularly held in the 1980s at Harvard Divinity School for the examination of the intersections of religion and law that shaped and informed issues of interfaith relations.[1] In the words of the 1987 organizers, "The Dialogue seeks extended and rigorous interaction among people holding significantly different positions on important religious issues."[2] The Jerome Hall Dialogue held on May 4–5, 1987, was organized by Clarissa Atkinson, Bernadette Brooten, Nancy Jay, William McLennan, and Margie Thornton. The focus of the event was "The Sanctuary Movement: How Firm the Religious and Legal Foundations?" The organizers framed the dialogue as a debate between two opposing sides, namely, the religious organizations that embraced the practice of sanctuary and the US government. Sanctuary activists, according to the organizers, were "convinced that the refugees" were "fleeing violence and persecution, partially attributable to U.S. policy." In turn, the US government argued that the "sanctuary movement disguises political motives with religious rhetoric." In the end, organizers hoped that "legal advisors and theologians" would "explore the clash of interpretations in an effort to understand the foundations of the sanctuary movement."[3]

This chapter examines the presentations delivered by several participants during the 1987 Jerome Hall Dialogue. The selection is limited to those papers that were preserved in the archives of Community Church of Boston, each of which was neatly labeled "Jerome Hall Forum

Harvard Divinity School, May 4–5, 1987," in a handwritten note by an unknown author. Position papers reveal that in the spring of 1987 the Sanctuary Movement was facing serious existential questions. Among these were questions related to the movement's identity, legal theory, organizational structure (or lack thereof), and ends. In addition to increased and aggressive government pressure, the movement had also been openly fractured since 1984, with James Corbett and Renny Golden representing different poles of the movement. Consequently, position papers reflect a splintered movement with important ideological inconsistencies that were openly disputed and publicly exploited by the government. The Jerome Hall Dialogue provided a forum for debate but not simply between the government and the movement's leadership. Instead, some of the position papers demonstrate the depth of the debate that had unfolded between Corbett and Tucson-area activists, on the one hand, and Golden and activists associated with the Chicago Religious Task Force on Central America, on the other.

Robin Lorentzen described differences between the Tucson and Chicago branches of the movement using humanitarian and political ideal types.[4] Tucson's humanitarian approach prioritized providing protective services, while Chicago focused on political activism and advocacy. Lorentzen concluded that despite the greater participation of women, the Sanctuary Movement was not in itself a feminist movement. Moreover, as Hilary Cunningham approvingly noted in her comments on Lorentzen, gender was an issue that distinguished "two general Sanctuary orientations."[5] Examination of the position papers presented during the Jerome Hall Dialogue will hopefully contribute to a deeper understanding of these differences.

Close reading of these position papers shows that as they sought to elucidate the "foundations of the sanctuary movement," activists drifted into a consideration of the meaning of sanctuary as community, or as communities of solidarity. That is, activists gravitated towards the following question: What does it mean to be a sanctuary community? Because of the decentralized nature of the movement, sanctuary activists felt the need to explain what it meant for local communities of faith to be in solidarity with the stranger. Participating activists were faithful to a Sanctuary Movement organizing principle first stipulated by a group of Tucson activists gathered on June 22–24, 1984, and propagated in the

Tucson Ecumenical Council Task Force for Central America's *Sanctuary: A Resource Guide* (1985). According to this principle, "groups participating in sanctuary—whether religious or secular—must be those for whom sanctuary is deeply rooted in their tradition and heritage."[6] Rootedness in particular traditions was deemed of paramount importance for the authenticity and distinctiveness of the movement. Faced with a changing legal and political landscape, Sanctuary Movement leaders endeavored to respond to the crucible by digging more deeply into their own traditions to find the meaning of solidarity with the stranger.

Organizers of the Jerome Hall Dialogue arranged the program into four sessions. The first session, "Witness and Testimony," covered three main topics related to contemporary conditions and human rights in Guatemala and El Salvador as well as general treatment of US immigration from Central America. The first session included Central American speakers, like Estela Ramírez and Manuel Hernández, who were living in sanctuary at the time at Old Cambridge Baptist Church and Community Church of Boston, respectively. Movement leaders Jim Corbett and Sister Darlene Nicgorski, SSSF, were also scheduled to participate in the opening session. The second session, "The Legal Foundations," examined questions of international and domestic law related to the legal status of refugees, asylum law, and the recent criminal prosecutions of sanctuary activists. Legal scholars and government officials participating in this session included Catherine W. Brown (at the time affiliated with the US Department of State), Deborah Anker (Harvard Law School), and William Joyce (Immigration and Naturalization Service, US Department of Justice). The third session, "Sanctuary Analogies?," sought to examine parallels between the Sanctuary Movement and experiences of civil disobedience and defiance enacted in the Underground Railroad and in response to "anti-semitic laws in Nazi Europe." Historian and Black Church studies scholar James Washington and historian of German Protestantism Leonore Siegele-Wenschkewitz were the main panelists elucidating this topic. Lastly, the fourth session of the conference, "The Religious Foundations of Sanctuary," explored Central American perspectives on sanctuary as well as the "theological basis for the acceptance or rejection of the concept of sanctuary."[7] Panelists included the Guatemalan refugees Felipe Ixcot and Elena Ixcot, living at the time in sanctuary at the Weston Priory in Vermont, as well as the Jesuit theologian Jon Sobrino, sanctuary activist and women's studies scholar Renny Golden, conservative Catholic philosopher George Weigel, and Rabbi Charles Feinberg. The papers preserved in the archives of Community Church of Boston included those by Catherine W. Brown, James Corbett, Charles Feinberg, Renny Golden, William Joyce, Darlene Nicgorski, Leonore Siegele-Wenschkewitz, and Jon Sobrino.

Historical Context of the 1987 Jerome Hall Dialogue

By 1987, the Sanctuary Movement was at the crossroads of a transnational effort of solidarity with the internationally displaced people of Central America. As sociologist Christian Smith noted, at the time there were 371 religious groups and 52 secular groups around the country that were part of the movement.[8] In New England the Sanctuary Movement had become a vibrant and well-organized interfaith protest movement. Historian Robert Surbrug interpreted the New England Sanctuary Movement as a continuation of the culture of protest that flourished in the Cambridge-Boston area in the 1960s and '70s, especially in reaction to the war in Vietnam.[9] Surbrug posited that there was a gradual transition among New England activists from the nuclear-weapons-freeze movement—at its height in 1982—to the Central American solidarity movement, which was gaining momentum in 1983.[10]

Surbrug's proposal is confirmed by the trajectory of some of the New England communities of faith that embraced the cause of Central American refugees in the 1980s. Primary among them were the Benedictine monks of Weston Priory, who mirrored Vermont's political culture of the late 1970s and early 1980s. The Benedictine brothers were deeply enmeshed in the fabric of the region's culture of protest. By the time they declared their monastery a sanctuary in 1984, the monks had already been participating in nuclear-disarmament political action for several years. In the early 1980s, Vermont had a strong nuclear-disarmament movement that channeled its opposition to national policy through local town hall meetings. In 1982, 161 towns passed a resolution calling on the Reagan administration to "propose to the Soviet Union a mutual freeze on the testing, production and deployment of nuclear weapons."[11] The Benedictine brothers collaborated with the Mountain Valley Peace Council in the coordination of events in support of nuclear disarmament. Brothers John, Elias, Robert, and Colombo met with the leadership of the Mountain Valley Peace Council on January 3, 1983, to plan a public gathering on the topic. Their intention was to organize a "Conference on Religion and the Nuclear Arms Race."[12]

By the end of November 1983, the brothers of Weston Priory were already well advanced in their planning to become a public sanctuary. Internal deliberations led the way to active outreach to friends and potential supporters. A meeting with supporters was held on December 3. The priory was coordinating its efforts with sanctuary activists from Boston while drawing on literature and video resources that were already in circulation. In their letter of invitation to join the movement, the brothers were clear about the risks involved: "We would like our friends to know that, given our present Administration's interpretation of U.S. Immigration Laws, the Sanctuary movement involves civil disobedience. Therefore, persons who come to take part in this meeting are taking a certain risk."[13] The Benedictine monks declared the priory a public sanctuary on March 24, 1984, making it the one-hundredth public sanctuary in the country.

While the Benedictine brothers exemplified the crossover of militancy among social movements in New England, their involvement in the Sanctuary Movement occurred within a broader context. In fact, tracing the early trajectory of the movement reveals the complex nature of its beginnings in New England. Activists in Boston and Cambridge were at the forefront of the Sanctuary Movement in the region. In 1983, Community Church of Boston (CCB) became the first community of faith in New England to offer sanctuary to Central American refugees.[14] In September 1983, CCB's leading minister, Rev. William E. Alberts, and members of the church's Sanctuary Planning Committee drafted a "Sanctuary Statement" in which they explained their decision to provide sanctuary "for Central American and other refugees who are pursued by immigration authorities and whose deportation would result in their imprisonment or execution."[15] On November 27, 1983, a few days after Thanksgiving, Community Church of Boston held a joint worship service at Arlington Street Church. Using the pseudonym of Manuel Hernández, Diego Mendoza Lacán spoke during the service, and selected poems by the Guatemalan writer Julia Esquivel were read.[16] At the end of the service, Manuel Hernández and his supporters walked in procession from Arlington Street Church, located at 351 Boylston Street in Boston, to the building of Community Church of Boston, located at 565 Boylston Street.

On January 8, 1984, Old Cambridge Baptist Church (Cambridge, Massachusetts) adopted by a unanimous vote its own "Statement of Purpose in Providing Public Sanctuary for Central American Refugees."[17] Estela Ramírez lived in the facilities of the American Baptist congregation and participated in advocacy efforts throughout the region.[18] By early 1985, the Boston Area Network on Central America, "a coalition of more than 30 organizations working for peace in Central America," was coordinating events such as the Central America Week (March 17–24).[19] Cambridge became an important regional center of advocacy, and the City of Cambridge became a sanctuary city on April 8, 1985.[20]

The reach of the movement extended beyond the Boston-Cambridge area. For instance, the New Hampshire province of the Sisters of Mercy opened its doors to Central American refugees.[21] Sister Angeline Whidden, of the Justice and Peace Office of the Diocese of Manchester, was an active advocate on behalf of the refugees. In 1986, Havurat Shalom of Somerville became the first sanctuary in the Greater Boston Jewish community. The egalitarian Jewish fellowship had already been considering the needs of Salvadoran refugees since the previous year. On October 4, 1986 ("first day of Tishre—Rosh Hashanah, 5747"), Havurat Shalom adopted its own Sanctuary Declaration.[22] A few months later, on March 29, 1987, it held a special ceremony to welcome "Emilio," a refugee from El Salvador. Thus, when the Jerome Hall Dialogue was held in 1987, the Sanctuary Movement was well organized in New England.

Two developments of national scope contributed to the urgency of the questions addressed during the 1987 Jerome Hall Dialogue. One of them was the criminalization and prosecution of sanctuary-related activities by the US government.[23] From February 1984 to July 1986, the legal, philosophical, and theological foundations of the Sanctuary Movement were tested.[24] As Smith observes, after following a policy of publicly downplaying the Sanctuary Movement and avoiding the arrest of sanctuary activists, in 1984 the Immigration and Naturalization Service turned to the aggressive detention and prosecution of key leaders involved in sanctuary activities.[25] In Texas, sanctuary activists were arrested in separate incidents in the months of February and April 1984.[26]

In October 1984, Stacey Lynn Merkt and Jack Elder were indicted, and convicted in February of the next year.[27] In Arizona, the US government issued indictments and arrested sixteen sanctuary activists in January 1985, in what Sophie H. Pirie described as a "political trial" of the movement.[28] These high-profile cases marked a turning point in the criminalization of sanctuary and sanctuary-related practices. On May 1, 1986, eight sanctuary workers were found guilty in Arizona. More importantly, the Fifth Circuit Court of Appeals' decision in *US v. Stacey Lynn Merkt and John B. Elder* (July 17, 1986) was a major setback for the juridical theory of the Sanctuary Movement (see below).

The other development was the uncovering of the Iran-Contra Affair in late 1986.[29] Scholars have varying opinions about the significance of the Iran-Contra Affair for the Sanctuary Movement. Smith advanced the thesis that the Iran-Contra Affair led to the demise of the movement. According to Smith's thesis, public revelations of the Reagan administration's unlawful scheme to finance the Contras in Nicaragua through the sale of arms to Iran ironically robbed the movement of one of its core bases for mobilization. Once the troubled nature of American involvement in Central America became more widely and publicly known, resulting in the discredit of the Reagan administration, the movement fell into a sense of complacency. "This," according to Smith, "had the effect of somewhat relaxing the intensity of the movement's political struggle."[30] Sociologist Sharon Erickson Nepstad has contended, however, that the Iran-Contra Affair did not represent the "closing of political opportunities" for the Sanctuary Movement.[31] Instead, Nepstad has posited that "as the state's vulnerability was exposed, this was an important chance for activists to increase their leverage and push for reform."[32]

At the time of the Jerome Hall Dialogue, sanctuary activists viewed the Iran-Contra Affair as a vindication of the movement. Indeed, as Renny Golden pointed out in her 1987 Jerome Hall Dialogue presentation, the close engagement and solidarity with Central American exiles made sanctuary activists aware of the situation throughout the region and, therefore, contrary to the rest of the American public, they were not "shocked" by Contragate. The Iran-Contra Affair exposed the "moral and political bankruptcy" of the Reagan administration's policies in the region. Nevertheless, she admitted that the Sanctuary Movement had "not stopped the Empire's assault on Central America."[33]

Sister Darlene Nicgorski, SSSF, also used her Jerome Hall presentation to establish a contrast between sanctuary activists like herself who were found guilty of conspiracy to violate immigration law during the Arizona Sanctuary Trial and Colonel Oliver North.[34] Assigned to the National Security Council under Reagan in 1981, North became the focus of congressional hearings on the Iran-Contra Affair due to his role in the illicit scheme used to finance the armed opposition in Nicaragua. Hence, Nicgorski employed North as a foil to accentuate the severity of the repression against sanctuary activists. "We," Nicgorski wrote, "are called criminals, felons, and threats to national security because we fed, clothed, sheltered, and gave voice to those fleeing persecution." Then she added, "Yet Colonel Oliver North who violated the Boland Amendment, the Anti-terrorism Act and other U.S. laws was deemed a 'hero' by the President."[35]

The Demise of Civil Initiative: William Joyce and Catherine Brown

Activists participating in the 1987 Jerome Hall Dialogue grappled with a new context of shifting political and legal realities. William Joyce and Catherine W. Brown's interventions in the Jerome Hall Dialogue represent the official government response to the claims of the Sanctuary Movement. Their effort to circumscribe the debate over the "foundations of the sanctuary movement" within a legal framework is typical of the ways in which "legal discourse" has been used to *delegitimize* other forms and ways of thinking about questions of truth and justice. Sanctuary leaders participating in the Jerome Hall Dialogue, on the other hand, provide an example of how communities of resistance have continued to think beyond and outside the framework of established legal discourse to articulate popular causes. In spite of their divisions, sanctuary leaders coalesced around the idea that their traditions provided alternative ways of thinking about truth and justice that could lead to more humane and transformative outcomes.

One of the most enduring and provocative proposals of the Sanctuary Movement was the idea of "civil initiative." This philosophical, theological, and legal theory of sanctuary is attributed to James Corbett, who insisted that sanctuary events and other acts of solidarity with Central Americans were not acts of civil disobedience because they were not breaking the law but ensuring that refugees received proper protection under the law.[36] According to Adam Waters, Corbett fully conceptualized the theory of "civil initiative" in 1985.[37] In its simplest formulation, Corbett argued that the aim of civil initiative is "to preserve good laws and extend the legal order."[38] The theory was embraced by Tucson-area activists. Thus, in 1985 the Tucson Ecumenical Council Task Force on Central America maintained that "sanctuary is civil initiative in the defense of everyone's legal right to protect refugees from being returned to a country where they face persecution."[39] Corbett actively endeavored to propagate the notion in the days and months leading to the Arizona Sanctuary Trial. In an op-ed piece published in the *Arizona Daily Star* on September 22, 1985, Corbett claimed that "from the Declaration of Independence to the judgment of the Military Tribunal at Nuremberg, our country has recognized that civil initiative in the defense of human rights is a liberty and a duty that is shared by all human beings. As civil initiative to protect undocumented refugees, sanctuary is a practice of responsive faith and responsible citizenship that is independent of refugees' national or political origins."[40]

Theologian Leo Guardado has elaborated on the Sanctuary Movement's concept of "civil initiative." According to Guardado, the notion of "civil initiative" was rooted in the principles of the Nuremberg Trials (1945–1946), and it can be understood as a "practice of civilians taking initiative for upholding international norms . . . norms that theoretically expand beyond codified human rights."[41] Indeed, Corbett made frequent references to the Nuremberg Trials as well as the 1980 Refugee Act.

However, for other sanctuary activists, the US government's resolve to criminalize and prosecute the Sanctuary Movement as displayed in the Arizona Sanctuary Trial signaled the vulnerabilities of the "civil initiative" theory. For activists associated with the Chicago Religious Task Force on Central America (CRTFCA), the aggressive posture of the government also undermined Corbett's contention that sanctuary is for "the persecuted regardless of the political origins of their persecution or of their usefulness in promoting preconceived objectives."[42] Mounting legal difficulties seemed to have confirmed the strategy followed by CRTFCA to link sanctuary events with protest and criticism of US foreign policy in Central America as well as the advancement of revolutionary causes in the region. As the Chicago-based lawyer and sanctuary activist Jeffrey Haas noted in 1986 while commenting on the Arizona indictments, "Although sanctuary members may assert that their actions are legal—both because they do not violate the letter or spirit of U.S. and international law, and because they stem from well-founded and long-held religious beliefs—it is unlikely that such arguments will prevail against the pointed attack by the government."[43] Haas also argued that the Sanctuary Movement should take the offensive by using every sanctuary trial to "expose" US complicity and sponsorship of "genocide in Central America."[44]

Corbett, however, was not ready to abandon the "civil initiative" legal, philosophical, and theological theory of the Sanctuary Movement. Weeks after eight sanctuary workers were found guilty in Arizona in May 1986, he still claimed that "sanctuary is the extension of the legal order that was mandated at Nuremberg."[45] Nevertheless, the legal conviction and sentencing of sanctuary activists represented a major setback. He faced the legal defeat of the "civil initiative" justification of sanctuary with stern determination: "Establishing that the nonviolent protection of human rights is never illegal requires that we continue to try to make the judicial system work."[46]

Divisions over the "civil initiative" theory as well as its legal demise in the judicial system were exploited by the government. In his remarks for the Jerome Hall Dialogue, the associate general counsel of the Immigration and Naturalization Service, William Joyce, proclaimed the "failure" of the Sanctuary Movement.[47] Joyce's was a bullet point memorandum covering the most prominent themes associated with the Sanctuary Movement. He characterized the movement as a network that encouraged "illegal immigration into the United States from El Salvador and Guatemala," harboring "aliens often in violation of the law." He qualified the nature of religious involvement, claiming that the movement lacked broad support among religious institutions in the country and that mainline denominations had "no interest in confronting the federal government on issues relating to illegal immigration."[48] He cited the treatment of undocumented immigrants from Nicaragua and Honduras by sanctuary activists as evidence of the ultimately political character of the movement.

While Joyce covered other important aspects such as the historical precedents of the Sanctuary Movement, the core of his presentation centered around the legality of sanctuary-related practices. For Joyce the Arizona Sanctuary Trial represented a major defeat for the Sanctuary Movement. The trial offered an "opportunity" for sanctuary activists "to put forth all their arguments," and yet eight of the eleven defendants "were found to be guilty of various criminal laws not by the judge but by a jury of peers."[49] He also cited *US v. Stacey Lynn Merkt and John B. Elder* (1986), which he clearly regarded as more detrimental to the civil-initiative theory. Under the theory, sanctuary activists claimed that Salvadorans were refugees under the Refugee Act of 1980 and that failure by the US government to protect them imposed an obligation on citizens to do so. However, by concluding that Salvadorans "were not refugees per se pursuant to the Refugee Act of 1980," the Fifth Circuit Court of Appeals deprived the Sanctuary Movement of one of its central legal claims. Moreover, Joyce noted that "although defendants' [*sic*] contended that they were religiously motivated in conducting the 'sanctuary' activities," the US Court of Appeals concluded that their conviction was in fact "not barred by the First Amendment."[50] Lastly, Joyce pointed out that in *US v. Stacey Lynn Merkt and John B. Elder* the US Court of Appeals resolved that the 1967 United Nations Protocol Relating to the Status of Refugees "did not create for all 'refugees' an entitlement to 'reside' in the United States." Hence, the frequent claim made by sanctuary activists that certain Central Americans were "Protocol refugees" could not be invoked to undermine immigration law.[51] Joyce's conclusions about the legality of sanctuary-related practices underscore how prominent the civil-initiative theory was in his mind as leading legal counsel for the INS: "These cases show that despite all the claims of sanctuary advocates that it is the government that is breaking the law, such is not the case. We are a nation of laws, and when individuals choose to make their own laws, chaos can result. This is true for individuals both within and outside of the government. The sanctuary movement has however demonstrated that despite considerable legal effort, and millions of dollars devoted to this issue, the sanctuary movement's legal theories do not square with reality or United States constitutional law."[52]

Also representing the government's view in the Jerome Hall Dialogue, Catherine W. Brown described the Sanctuary Movement as "schizophrenic."[53] In a highly technical position paper dedicated to discussing international and national refugee and asylum law, Brown decided to emphasize the movement's division in the opening paragraph. The movement was "schizophrenic" because, in Brown's words, "some people involved in sanctuary say that what they're doing is legal, while others are saying it's illegal and that they are engaged in civil disobedience."[54] The movement's "split mind" led to its most important failure, namely, its legal failure. According to Brown, the movement should have focused its efforts on finding ways to reform the law. The critical question facing the movement was about "how the law might be changed to reflect its moral values."[55]

Brown's position paper represented an important counterpoint to the presentations of sanctuary leaders. Brown made a very precise distinction between humanitarian ideals and moral values, on the one hand, and the rule of law, on the other. Brown insisted that there may be a "vast gulf" separating humanitarian conceptions of what the law "should be" and "what it in fact is."[56] The Sanctuary Movement, in Brown's view, did not grasp this distinction and, therefore, was bound to persist in what ultimately amounted to futile efforts. Instead, Brown insisted that focus on the law and its limitations was the "prerequisite" to change it.

The Persistence of Civil Initiative: Jim Corbett

In his position paper, Jim Corbett offered an abridged account of his involvement with the Sanctuary Movement going back to May 1981, nearly a whole year before the first church publicly declared sanctuary. While retelling his story, Corbett reflected on ideas that he considered to be fundamental to the practice of sanctuary. One of them was the idea of community. For him, a crucial inquiry revolved around the type of community that fosters solidarity with strangers. He had reached the conclusion that "almost everyone wants to protect the violated from their oppressors."[57] However, not everyone is willing to assume the risks of protecting the vulnerable. The goat-milking cooperative that he was a part of at the time, and that was known as the "*caballeros andantes*" (a reference to Don Quixote), was an example of the kind of community that contributes to the flourishing of such altruistic efforts.[58] He characterized these communities as associations that resisted "political subjugation and technocratic alienation."[59] Through "meeting, knowing, and caring," quixotic communities like the goat-milking cooperative nurture "symbiotic bonds" that in turn promote "harmony, diversity, and beauty."[60]

By recalling the experience and principles of the goat-milking cooperative, Corbett was indirectly reverberating his criticism of the Chicago Religious Task Force. He believed the CRTFCA was bound to political ends that had nothing to do with the immediacy of the concern for protecting the vulnerable. He voiced this criticism in his essay "Sanctuary and Revolutionary Struggle," based on a talk he gave at Pendle Hill on November 21–23, 1986.[61] Corbett's criticism was scathing, claiming that some forms of sanctuary were out of step with new realities. The assertion that "sanctuary groups have used refugees for predetermined political purposes" was even more blistering.[62] In fact, he even noted that "the 'humanitarians' and 'politicals' who have gone their separate ways since 1984 also appear to be formalizing their split."[63] He was not as direct in his position paper for the Jerome Hall Dialogue. Yet, he reiterated the criticism. "And we are also obliged," he avowed, "to help refugees according to their need for protection rather than their furtherance of partisan purposes, and to expose human rights violations regardless of political considerations."[64]

Corbett used his presentation paper to further elaborate and develop his notion of civil initiative. While commentators have tended to interpret Corbett within a narrow lens that prioritizes the influence of Latin American liberation theology, his notion of civil initiative has a strong libertarian and anti-authoritarian profile. Surely, his ideological position was informed by his Quaker heritage, as Waters argues.[65] Corbett's anti-authoritarian inclination resonates throughout his position paper, especially in the conclusion.

Corbett relied on a form of mutualism to describe the foundations of sanctuary. According to him, sanctuary is based on "end-independent principles of respect for others." These are the principles that hold a pluralistic society together, and they are prior to human rights and humanitarian laws, and are susceptible to government and political abuse. The relationship of mutualist principles or norms to codified laws, in fact, is analogous to the relationship between a living language and "published grammars and dictionaries." He described them as "meta-legal principles" that have the role of restricting the "state's ability to use coercion and power." Interestingly, for Corbett these principles of mutual respect are the ones that provide the measure of government's legitimacy as well as the reference with which "a free society governs its government." Moreover, principles of mutual respect provide the limits of state power and serve as "the structural precondition for human rights" because they constitute "personal and associational liberty." He responded to bureaucrats like Joyce and Brown by noting that they had replaced management for the rule of law and that in doing so they had now created a new form of absolutism. Consequently, the new absolutism of the federal government treats principles of mutual respect as obstacles rather than as the "foundation of governmental legitimacy."[66] Sanctuary as civil initiative, then, institutes a mechanism for the protection of human rights and humanitarian laws when the "government violates them." Furthermore, sanctuary also provides a "public space" by which civil society can "check and counteract the new absolutism of the national security state."[67]

Sanctuary as *Comunidad*: Renny Golden

The views and positions associated with the CRTFCA were represented in the Jerome Hall Dialogue by Darlene Nicgorski and Renny Golden. Nicgorski's chief contribution was to challenge the silencing of women's contributions to the sanctuary movement.[68] On this point, she openly called out Corbett for neglecting to recognize and give due credit to the women who collaborated on sanctuary initiatives on both sides of the border. Women like her experienced the brunt of government prosecution during the Arizona Sanctuary Trial, while he was exonerated. In response, she shared her own journey in the Sanctuary Movement, including her experience in Guatemala, in Mexico, and in the American Southwest. She concluded her presentation by openly rejecting Corbett's decentralized model of the movement and by explicitly connecting the Sanctuary Movement with hopes for the revolutionary transformation of Central American countries.[69] Nicgorski's critique aligned with that of Renny Golden made a year earlier in the *Journal of Feminist Studies in Religion*.[70]

In her own position paper, "Sanctuary and Comunidad," Renny Golden offered a communitarian criticism of the movement. Her assessment has strong, pronounced, and well-formulated theological dimensions. For Golden the act of sanctuary is a synergic event in which God, the displaced, and sanctuary workers and activists interact, and work together to produce a total effect greater than just hospitality. In Golden's view the act of sanctuary is a path of liberation for both displaced and sanctuary activists.

Sanctuary as a path of liberation for US activists took on several dimensions in Golden's view. Sanctuary is primarily religious, anti-institutional liberation. Through sanctuary, God has called activists out of the "safety and sanctuary of our well insulated comfortable religious institutions."[71] Sanctuary is an act of divine revelation or self-disclosure in which activists come to know the "victorious God of our fathers" for what it is, namely, a "dehistoricized" fetish.[72]

Sanctuary is also an act of social liberation. Meeting the stranger through the practice of sanctuary delivers activists from the false sense of safety built upon racist and classist ideas and practices. In Golden's view, exiles and strangers participate in the divine's power of revelatory disclosure. The exiles are the ones who reveal who we are: "In meeting the exiled community of Central Americans we have met the stranger who revealed us ourselves."[73] The Sanctuary Movement is at the heart of Golden's anti-imperialist critique of American neocolonialism. In addition to damaging and harming the poor and oppressed abroad, American neocolonialism also generates a "death culture" at home. Walking with the exiles marks the beginning of a long exodus, an act of renunciation, that contradicts the empire and its "religious ideological support system."[74]

Golden openly addressed internal differences within the Sanctuary Movement.[75] But before doing that, she emphasized the unity of the movement, which remained in accord on at least three different fronts, namely, the movement's criticism of American foreign policy in Central America; its solidarity with the people of Central America in their resistance to the destructive policies of oppressive regimes in the region; and its own experience of political opposition at home. In face of the situation in Central America, she acknowledged the insufficiency of the Sanctuary Movement. The situation in Central America was not going to be solved by opening more sanctuaries in the United States. She shifted attention to José Napoleón Duarte's and Marco Vinicio Cerezo's "National Security" doctrine, counterinsurgency "low-intensity" wars against noncombatants, and their devastating effects. The domestic policies of national security states turned countries like Guatemala into "controlled democracies" and nations of "prisoners."[76]

Golden maintained that the Sanctuary Movement could be evaluated from two perspectives, namely, the perspective of the "world of accumulated power and wealth" and "the perspective of God, of Yahweh, of love's presence in the world."[77] If the question of gains and losses is to be privileged, then, Golden sustained, the Sanctuary Movement had "not stopped the Empire's assault on Central America." However, the advantage of its anti-imperialist critique was that a "journey of accompaniment" had begun and with it a process of what she called "conversion."[78] Golden drew on theologian Elsa Támez and the murdered Roman Catholic archbishop of El Salvador, Oscar Romero, to explain the conversion that she envisioned. With Támez, Golden asserted that conversion is "metanoia," a complete rebirth and transformation with concomitant disposition to engage in action. Referring to Romero, she endorsed his view that in the face of the suffering of the Salvadoran people, neutrality was impossible. The suffering people of El Salvador demanded that a position be taken, that a choice be made. Romero, according to Golden, summarized this choice as one between "believing in a God of life" or serving the "idols of death," "serv[ing] the life of the Salvadoran people" or being "complicit in their death." Golden concluded that "conversion to the life of the poor is the only way we transcend ourselves."[79]

Golden employed idolatry as a political-theological category against American neocolonialism. For instance, she drew on theologian José Miranda's *Communism and the Bible* to assert that "mental idols are more important than the material ones."[80] For Golden, the practice of sanctuary is a journey of mental and spiritual emancipation. For those who live within the bounds of empire, amid American capitalist society—as she did—the spiritual exodus is tantamount to waking up from the "dreams" of empire. Moreover, Babylon as a metaphor for American imperialism looms large in her anti-imperialist criticism.[81] Babylon is an image drawn from biblical narratives, especially those narratives related to the sixth century BCE captivity of the Jewish people in the region of present-day Iraq. The idols of Babylon are in the mind; the mind is a primary location of colonization. Conversion then describes a process of journeying away from the memory of empire, and the affirmation of personal autonomy in relation to the power of empire. Conversion leads to a new history, the beginning of the creation of a new history. She intimated that the new history is written in situations of mutual aid and collaboration. Casting away false gods and idols requires that they be named. Golden named the doctrine of national security as an idol. The denunciation of the doctrine of national security was the "most urgent theological task."[82]

Golden articulated a form of political communitarianism. In the second part of her position paper, she drew connections between the Base Christian Communities (BCCs) and the Sanctuary Movement.[83] She argued that an important aspect of the BCCs was the strong sense of communitarian identity. Communitarianism was in her view subversive as it undermined the ecclesiastical hierarchy, too ready in some cases to lend its unwavering support to the ideology of the national security doctrine. Peasant communities and their bonds of mutual "faithfulness," constitute the building blocks of Golden's communitarian idealism. Indeed, their pain and suffering provide the "fragmented poor" with a sense of peoplehood. The "*comunidad*" so constituted is the "voice for the God of history."[84] According to Golden, the communitarian imperative is to subvert and reorient the social order by making "compassion for the poor" the "first priority."[85] She proposed the "method of community formation," which she understood as a "reflection process that aims at transformation of structures of violence through organized popular resistance," as the way to reorient the social order.[86]

In contrast, counterinsurgency represented the effort of the national security state to "splinter the community" and to "break the people into subservience to the state as God." Efforts to "splinter" the BCC could be subtle, as they were in the case of the United for Reconstruction Plan. The Plan Unidos para Reconstruir (PUR), as it was known in El Salvador, was adopted in 1986. The PUR was characterized by a significant shift in the government's anti-insurgency campaign, prioritizing political solutions over military actions. At the time this was seen by critics as part of the government's psychological warfare against the insurgency.[87] Golden characterized the plan as a combination of efforts to (re)create community cohesion along the lines of subservience and outright militarized intervention.[88]

Golden constructed a communalist lexicon of principles grounded on the Salvadoran experience of the civil war, with concepts like *compromiso*, *adelante*, *entrega*, and *comunidad*.[89] For Golden, personal commitment provided the cement of the Salvadoran struggle for liberation and as such it represented a core virtue to be imitated by the Sanctuary Movement. Personal commitment could only be gleaned from the actual experiences of those who were mobilized for justice in places like El Salvador. Accordingly, she drew on the example of the Salvadoran lay catechist, Laura López, to illustrate some of these principles, but especially that of *compromise*.[90]

For Golden, Laura López's "existence was risk," and her "*compromise* embodied the essence of community." Golden used the account of López's thirteen-year-old daughter to narrate the death of the Salvadoran religious leader, who was known by locals as the "bishop." When in April 1985 their village of Consolación was under attack by army battalions, she decided to give her and her children's place in the shelter to other families. It was then that military operatives shot her in the back and leg in front of her children. Her daughter, who was by her side, embodied her heroism and carried a six-year-old to safety.[91]

Another lesson that Golden credited to the people of El Salvador was the importance of organizing. She viewed organizing as a "fundamental right" and means for the oppressed to take back their lives.[92] She applied this principle to the Sanctuary Movement and used it to rebuke Sanctuary activists for their lack of organizing: "How do we as a sanctuary community, organize ourselves, we who are afraid of organization as if it was antireligious? How do we organize ourselves is a bit like asking how will we become a people; how will we trust each other, how will we consciously form ourselves against the organized forces of death, international structures of control, looming before us like untouchable, impenetrable edifices?"[93]

She also used this as an opportunity to rebuke religious visions of the Sanctuary Movement that were overly spiritualized and even mystical, probably here referring to Corbett's conceptualizations. "The movement toward a *comunidad* of God's justice and compassion," she argued, "is not mystical."[94] *Comunidad* is a "concrete historical choice," in the context of "popular organizations." Again the BCCs offered a paragon of the importance of ground-level organizing for the undoing of the power of the security state. *Comunidad* is not a romantic principle but a theological approach for the reconstruction of the "dominion of love and holiness."[95]

She was relentless in her criticism of views within the Sanctuary Movement that were antithetical to popular organizing. Thus, she claimed that this resistance could be traced back to ways of thinking about solidarity. In her view, the US Sanctuary Movement had not reached sufficient maturity to understand the kind of solidarity that sustains community as experienced by the Salvadoran people. Using the sociologist Emile Durkheim's concept of solidarity, she argued that the US Sanctuary Movement had fallen short of proper levels of organization because it implicitly operated at the level of mechanical solidarity, or the type of social cohesion predicated upon common traditions and norms. Organic solidarity, on the other hand, was based on complex social interdependence instead of shared beliefs.[96] The shortcoming meant that sanctuary activists still associated organizing with the modern state and the impersonal social relations of its institutional apparatus. Indeed, Golden intimated that many sanctuary activists were apprehensive about organizing because of their own individualism, patriotic "collective selfishness," and liberalism. To live into the kind of community-sustaining organic solidarity embodied by the Salvadoran people, the Sanctuary Movement needed to transcend political liberalism, for it "lacks an alternative vision of social life." Golden concluded by acclaiming a vision for the Sanctuary Movement in which sanctuary is "an alternative vision of human relationship and community which is not based on our security interests but on the interests of the disenfranchised."[97]

Sanctuary and Responses to the Jewish Holocaust: Charles Feinberg

Another common thread uniting some of the papers prepared for the Jerome Hall Dialogue addressed a theme that was present in the minds of Jewish and non-Jewish sanctuary activists: Were there parallels or lessons to be learned from the general indifference in 1930s Europe to the Nazi racist policies against the Jews? In contrast to the other Jerome Hall Dialogue papers, Leonore Siegele-Wenschkewitz's (1944–1999) presentation did not deal directly with the Sanctuary Movement or the situation of Central American refugees.[98] Her chief aim was to categorize the response of the German Confessing Church to the implementation of Nazi racist policies in the 1930s. According to Siegele-Wenschkewitz, the Confessing Church protested the racist ideology of National Socialism. Yet, there was "no public action" by the Confessing Church on behalf of persecuted Christians of Jewish background nor of persecuted Jews.[99] "It was only individuals or small groups," she added, "who found themselves in a position to assist their Jewish fellow men and women or indeed to engage in political resistance."[100]

Nevertheless, in the title of her presentation, Siegele-Wenschkewitz pointed to an important question, namely, "Can the Sanctuary Movement appeal to the tradition of the Confessing Church in Nazi Germany?" Implicit in this question lay another matter of vital importance for Jewish Sanctuary activists; that is, Can the plight of Central American refugees be compared to the plight of Jewish refugees escaping the horrors of Nazi concentration camps? Siegele-Wenschkewitz offered an extremely succinct but definite response to this question, a response that unfortunately remained unsatisfactorily underdeveloped in the essay. She acknowledged that the "principal point of comparison" between the situation of persecuted Jews under National Socialism and those persecuted at the time of her writing was the "perilous situation" in which they found themselves.[101] Otherwise, for Siegele-Wenschkewitz there was no parallel between the way Jews were helped "within the National Socialist ruling sphere" and the kind of protections that the Sanctuary Movement sought to extend to Central American refugees "outside the ruling sphere from which they have attempted to flee."[102] In a strict sense, she argued, the only "proper parallel" to the Sanctuary Movement was to be found in the "aid given or refused to Jewish refugees by political organizations, churches and individuals outside the areas under National Socialist control."[103] But that, she pointed out, was not the subject of her investigation.

Rabbi Charles Feinberg offered a different response to the interrogative concerning the parallels between the plight of European Jewry during the Holocaust and that of Central American refugees in the 1980s.[104] He situated the Sanctuary Movement in a long history of nonviolent resistance that he traced back to the stories of Shiprah and Puah—whom he identified as Egyptian midwives—as told in the first chapter of the

Book of Exodus.[105] According to Feinberg, these women defied the orders of the Egyptian pharaoh who, according to the story, had instructed them to kill all the newborn male Hebrew children. Establishing a continuity between that original, "first recorded" act of resistance and the Sanctuary Movement, he turned to identifying other women who inspired his own involvement in the Sanctuary Movement. These were women like Stacey Lynn Merkt and Sister Marian Klosterman. Merkt was at the time serving a federal prison sentence for "conspiring" to transport de facto refugees out of South Texas. Klosterman, on the other hand, provided food and shelter to refugees from Central America.[106]

In characteristic fashion, Feinberg based the nonviolent resistance of the Sanctuary Movement on seminal moral and ethical principles of Judaism. For instance, he referred to Merkt and Klosterman's actions as *Kiddush Hashem*, or a blessing of God's holy name: "The women I mentioned and the stories of refugees have inspired me because through their acts of courage and love, they have sanctified God's Holy Name."[107] Moreover, he interpreted their actions as affirmations that Central American refugees were made "*b'tzelem Elohim*," "in God's image," proclaiming with their actions that Central American refugees shared the fundamental dignity of all humankind.[108]

Feinberg's chief aim was to ground the practice of sanctuary in his understanding of Jewish radical monotheism. He found two sources for his support of Central American refugees in the Jewish notion of "*b'tzelem Elohim*" as well as in what he described as the "mythic-historic event" of the exodus. This Jewish radical monotheism, or "the belief in one God," he stated, "is an important reason why I have become involved in Sanctuary."[109] Belief in one God is more than an abstract idea or an intellectual orientation. Belief in one God imposes an acceptance of God's care for creation, including if "human beings are exceptionally cruel and brutal to each other." For Feinberg, God cares for creation; God is the one who cares. Furthermore, because God created all humanity after God's image, then every human person is responsible for God's creation. "We are," he stressed, "responsible for other human beings, especially, when they are poor, homeless, and fleeing violence and death."[110]

Feinberg continued reflecting on the significance of *b'tzelem Elohim* as a justification of the practice of sanctuary. He drew on the Mishnah, specifically Mishnah Sanhedrin 4:5: "In accordance with that, the human being was created singly to teach you that if anyone destroys one soul from Israel, Scripture accounts it to him as if he destroyed a full world. And if anyone preserves one soul from Israel, Scripture accounts it to him as if he preserved a full world. And for the sake of peace among people, so that a person will not say to another, 'My father is greater than your father.'"[111]

For Feinberg, the rabbis of the Mishnah were asking one question, namely, "Why is it that God created only one man and one woman on the sixth day?" He noted that when God created stars, trees, and grasses, God did it in "multitudes of them at once."[112] However, on the sixth day, "God created only one man and one woman." He again paraphrased the Mishnah to assert that consequently "no one can say that his father or his mother is greater than someone else's."[113] In this way, Feinberg turned the Jewish idea of *b'tzelem Elohim* into the foundation of solidarity with Central American refugees. "Ultimately," he argued, "we are all brothers and sisters, members of one family, responsible for each other."[114]

He found a source of growing inspiration in the Mishnah Sanhedrin, a tractate describing "the courts, cases, procedures, and punishments that comprise the rabbinic justice system."[115] Feinberg wanted to make a connection between the plight of the Central American refugees and the story of Cain and Abel found in the Genesis 4:1–18. He noted that the Hebrew word for "blood" is a plural construct (דְּמֵי). Thus, he asked in unison with the rabbis of the Mishnah, "The rabbis ask why is the word blood in the plural? What is the Torah trying to teach us?"[116] The answer that he drew from the Mishnah Sanhedrin was a rebuke against those who were indifferent towards the plight of the Central American refugees and a word of encouragement for sanctuary activists: "Thus, the phrase, 'your brother's bloods,' teaches us that whoever destroys a human life is like a person who destroys the whole universe. Conversely, whoever preserves or sustains a human life is as if he is creating a whole universe."[117]

In turning to the story of the exodus from Egypt, Feinberg sought to establish a closer affinity between the Jewish experience of the Holocaust and the experience of the Central American refugees. At this point in his argument, he relied on two images derived from the Torah. First, he used Exodus 23:9 as the basis of his argument: "You shall not oppress the stranger, for you know what it means to be a stranger, for you were strangers in the land of Egypt."[118] For him, the Central American refugees were people who had fled "oppression, violence, and persecution."[119] They were strangers and lacked protections other than their faith and the faith of those who sheltered them. Central American refugees were people who left their land for a variety of very specific reasons, including their political ideas, their labor activism, or because they had witnessed the violation of human rights. They had fled because they were "terribly afraid."[120]

Feinberg also used the story of Abraham's pleading on behalf of Sodom and Gomorrah to prevent their destruction (Genesis 18). He claimed that Guatemala and El Salvador were like the "Sodom and Gomorrah of our time."[121] Furthermore, Lot and his family—who in the Hebrew ancestral story escaped from Sodom before its destruction—were like the refugees from Central America. Thus, Feinberg asked, "If Lot and his family showed up on our doorstep, would we send them back to Sodom and Gomorrah?"[122]

As a rabbi, Feinberg wanted to emphasize that care for the stranger was a salient teaching of the Torah. He maintained that the "commandment not to oppress the stranger" was repeated "more often than the commands to observe the Sabbath." But why? Why did the Torah mention this commandment—at least thirty-six times, he observed, commenting on the Talmud tractate Bava Metzia 59b—so often? "The Torah realizes," he replied, "how easy it is to exploit and oppress the stranger."[123] As strangers, Central American refugees were outsiders, beyond the bounds of community. As such they were more likely to be neglected, ignored, and abandoned, contrary to the demands of the Jewish notion of *b'tzelem Elohim*. Thus, the Torah reiterates the commandment not to oppress the stranger:

> For really, who cares what happens to a stranger? Who cares if they are raped, beaten, and left for dead? Who cares if they get sick and die? The stranger is not part of our community. No relative is going to protest. No one in the community will notice the absence of the stranger, if he or she disappears. And so the Torah reminds us over and over again not to exploit or oppress the stranger. The Torah knows how easy and painless it is to overlook or exploit the stranger. The Torah knows how we will be tempted to turn away from the cries of the stranger.[124]

Feinberg's Jewish perspective on sanctuary reached a climactic point when he personalized the plight of the Central American refugees. "As a Jew," he pointed out, "I cannot help but identify with Central Americans in our midst."[125] Central American refugees were people "fleeing persecution and violence," experiences known by the Jewish people.[126] Alluding to the central dictum of Exodus 23:9, "*yedaatem et-nefesh hager*," he concluded, "The Jewish people knows the Nefesh Hager [soul of the stranger]: we know what it means to be a stranger."[127]

Indifference towards the Central American refugees was an abandonment of the Jewish notion of *b'tzelem Elohim* as well as a violation of the Torah's teaching about regard for the stranger. The Jewish people also experienced indifference in the greatest time of need, during the Jewish Holocaust. Because of indifference, approximately six million Jews died during the Holocaust. According to Feinberg, in 1938 "indifference strengthened the hands of the oppressors and murderers." Similarly, in 1987 "our indifference to the plight of Central Americans fleeing persecution, strengthens the hands of their oppressors."[128] Indeed, Feinberg qualified this position by asserting that the "only common element between the death of six million Jews and the oppression of Central Americans is the indifference of the bystanders."[129]

He approached the practice of sanctuary as a challenge to his faith in one God. The Torah "teaches that God doesn't care only for the Jewish people" but for all of creation and "all humankind." Consequently, as a Jew he believed he was tasked with caring for other Jews as well as for the "stranger in our midst, whoever they are and from wherever they come." He viewed this posture as a faithful response to the covenant between God and Israel, which he deemed to be "both the glory and responsibility of the Jewish people."[130]

Feinberg concluded his presentation by telling the story of Aristides de Sousa Mendes (1885–1954), who as Portuguese consul-general in Bordeaux issued thousands of visas to refugees escaping Nazi persecution. Indeed, Sousa Mendes defied his own government's policy of not granting visas to those seeking refuge in Portugal. Once more, Feinberg highlighted the transformative and humanizing power of personal encounters as he traced—following Yehuda Bauer's account—Sousa Mendes's act of defiance to a conversation he had with Rabbi Chaim Krueger, who was seeking a visa to enter Portugal with his family. This personal encounter changed Sousa Mendes's life and opened the door for an estimated ten thousand refugees to escape from persecution. For Feinberg, Sousa Mendes was an example of moral integrity. "Whenever I wonder what it means to sanctify God's name," Feinberg concluded, "I think of de Sousa Mendes."[131]

Conclusion

Sanctuary leaders involved in the Jerome Hall Dialogue exemplify how resistance communities persist in thinking beyond traditional legal frameworks to advocate for popular causes. Despite their differences, sanctuary leaders united around the belief that their traditions offered alternative perspectives on truth and justice, potentially leading to more humane and transformative outcomes. When we think of the "meanings" of sanctuary that were articulated during the Jerome Hall Dialogue from a *longue durée* perspective, we can reach two tentative conclusions. First, the secularizing forces of modernity, represented by the imposition of a "rule of law" mentality at the service of imperialism, rob humanity of the rich ethical and moral possibilities that religious and humanist perspectives offer. Second, these same religious and humanist traditions are empowered with the imaginative capacity to envision a more just world and, accordingly, they will continue to resist.

NOTES

1 Unpublished primary source materials related to the 1980s Sanctuary Movement in New England can be found in the local archives of participating organizations, such as the Community Church of Boston (Boston, Massachusetts) and Old Cambridge Baptist Church (Cambridge, Massachusetts). Some of this material has been digitized and forms part of a small digital collection that has been organized as part of the Sanctuary Project, attached to the Center for Global Christianity and Mission at Boston University School of Theology. References are made to the original archive and the digital image number in the Sanctuary Project as needed; Harvard Divinity School, *The Sanctuary Movement: How Firm the Religious and Legal Foundations? Jerome Hall Dialogue* (Event Program/Bulletin, 1987), archives of Community Church of Boston.

2 Harvard Divinity School, *The Sanctuary Movement*. Other symposia on the Sanctuary Movement were held at different moments throughout the country. The other well-known gathering was the Inter-American Symposium on Sanctuary held on January 23–24, 1985, in Tucson, Arizona, under the auspices of the Tucson

Ecumenical Council's Task Force for Central Americans and Others. The proceedings were published as Tucson Ecumenical Council Task Force for Central America, *Sanctuary: A Resource Guide for Understanding and Participating in the Central American Refugee's Struggle*, ed. Gary MacEoin (Harper & Row, 1985).

3 Harvard Divinity School, *The Sanctuary Movement.*

4 Robin Lorentzen, *Women in the Sanctuary Movement* (Temple University Press, 1991).

5 Hilary Cunningham, *God and Caesar at the Rio Grande: Sanctuary and the Politics of Religion* (University of Minnesota Press, 1995), 129.

6 Tucson Ecumenical Council Task Force for Central America, *Sanctuary: A Resource Guide*, 198.

7 Harvard Divinity School, *The Sanctuary Movement.*

8 Christian Smith, *Resisting Reagan: The U.S. Central America Peace Movement* (University of Chicago Press, 1996), 185.

9 Robert Surbrug Jr., *Beyond Vietnam: The Politics of Protest in Massachusetts, 1974–1990* (University of Massachusetts Press, 2009), 171–208; see also chapter 1 of this volume.

10 Surbrug, *Beyond Vietnam*, 108, 178.

11 "A Vote for Nuclear Freeze," *Newsweek*, March 15, 1982, 23; H. Nicholas Muller III and Marshall M. True, "Grass Roots and Tradition: Hand in Hand for Peace," *Vermont Life*, Winter 1983, 23–26.

12 "Organizing Meeting of Conference on Religion and the Nuclear Arms Race," January 3, 1983, two pages, typed in single space, featuring handwritten note "Brother Elias," on top-right corner. Located in the archive of the Weston Priory. Digital image in the Sanctuary Project, Boston University School of Theology, Weston Priory digital item #E132.

13 Signed, "The Brothers," typed on single page, letterhead of the Benedictine Monks, Weston Priory (November 23, 1983). Located in the archive of the Weston Priory. Digital image in the Sanctuary Project, Boston University School of Theology, Weston Priory digital item #E148.

14 "Death If He Returns, Says Guatemalan," *Boston Globe*, November 28, 1983, 20; Philip Bennett, "Boston Is Home for Illegal Alien, but He Fears Death If Deported," *Boston Globe*, November 20, 1984, 2.

15 Community Church of Boston, "The Community Church of Boston's Sanctuary Statement," c. September 1983, 2 pages. Located in the archive of Community Church of Boston. Digital image in Sanctuary Project, Boston University School of Theology, CCB digital item #5.

16 Service Bulletin dated November 27, 1983, Arlington Street Church. Located in the archive of Community Church of Boston. Digital image in Sanctuary Project, Boston University School of Theology, CCB digital items #12 and #13.

17 Old Cambridge Baptist Church, "Old Cambridge Baptist Church Statement of Purpose in Providing Public Sanctuary for Central American Refugees" (January 8, 1984). Located in the archive of Old Cambridge Baptist Church. Digital image

in Sanctuary Project, Boston University School of Theology, OCBC digital items #1 and #2.

18 Paul Hirshson, "Refugees Won't Jam City, Cambridge Observers Say," *Boston Globe*, April 10, 1985, 19, 23; for more on the sanctuary experience at Old Cambridge Baptist Church see Michael C. W. Woolf, "Sanctuary and Subjectivity: Rethinking Practical Theological Categories in Light of the Sanctuary Movement of the 1980s" (doctoral dissertation, Harvard Divinity School, 2021).

19 William E. Alberts, Kay Hauer, Peggy Smith, and Jane Guise, "Dear Friends," single-page letter in the letterhead of the American Friends Service Committee, New England Regional Office (February 6, 1985). Located in the archive of Old Cambridge Baptist Church. Digital image in Sanctuary Project, Boston University School of Theology, OCBC digital item #18.

20 Paul Hirshson, "Refugees Won't Jam City," 2.

21 "N.H. Order Offers Latin Refugees Sanctuary," *Boston Globe*, December 31, 1984, 43.

22 Havurat Shalom, "Sanctuary Declaration," single page flyer. Located in the archive of Havurat Shalom (Somerville, Massachusetts). Digital image in Sanctuary Project, Boston University School of Theology, Havurat Shalom digital item #1.

23 Jeffrey Haas, "Commentary on the Arizona Indictments," in Renny Golden and Michael McConnell, *Sanctuary: The New Underground Railroad* (Orbis Books, 1986), 206–9.

24 James Corbett, "Toward a Quaker View of Sanctuary: Preliminary Discussion Draft Prepared for the Annual Gathering of the Friends General Conference" (Carleton College, June 28–July 5, 1986), 11. Original copy in Laura Rambikur's collection of documents from the Tucson Ecumenical Council Task Force, located in the Sanctuary Project, Boston University School of Theology, Boston, Massachusetts.

25 Smith, *Resisting Reagan*, 304–6.

26 Smith, *Resisting Reagan*, 306.

27 Smith, *Resisting Reagan*, 70, 306; "Sanctuary Conviction," *Christian Century* 102 (1985): 240.

28 Smith, *Resisting Reagan*, 306; Susan Bibler Coutin, *The Culture of Protest: Religious Activism and the U.S. Sanctuary Movement* (Westview Press, 1993), 132–48 (134); Sophie H. Pirie, "The Origins of a Political Trial: The Sanctuary Movement and Political Justice," *Yale Journal of Law & the Humanities* 2, no. 2 (1990): 381–416.

29 See United States Congress. Senate. Select Committee on Secret Military Assistance to Iran and the Nicaraguan Opposition, *Report of the Congressional Committees Investigating the Iran-Contra Affair: With Supplemental, Minority, and Additional Views* (U.S. Senate Select Committee on Secret Military Assistance to Iran and the Nicaraguan Opposition: U.S. House of Representatives Select Committee to Investigate Covert Arms Transactions with Iran, 1987).

30 Smith, *Resisting Reagan*, 349.

31 Sharon Erickson Nepstad, *Convictions of the Soul: Religion, Culture, and Agency in the Central America Solidarity Movement* (Oxford University Press, 2004), 138n5.

32 Nepstad, *Convictions*, 138n5.
33 Renny Golden, "Sanctuary and Comunidad," paper prepared for the Jerome Hall Dialogue (1987), archives of Community Church of Boston, 2.
34 Darlene Nicgorski, SSSF, "Women, Church, Conspiracy, and Truth Telling," paper prepared for the Jerome Hall Dialogue (1987), archives of Community Church of Boston.
35 Nicgorski, "Women," 10.
36 Susan M. Gleason, "The Sanctuary Movement: Challenging Perspectives on How to Understand the Relation Between Political and Religious Activity" (honors thesis, Colgate University, May 17, 1989), 45.
37 Adam Waters, "Alternative Internationalisms: The Sanctuary Movement and Jim Corbett's Civil Initiative," *Diplomatic History* 46, no. 5 (2022): 984–1009 (1005–6).
38 Corbett, "Toward a Quaker View of Sanctuary," 3.
39 As cited in Corbett, "Toward a Quaker View of Sanctuary," 7.
40 Jim Corbett, "Sanctuary Responds to Faith, Citizenship," *Arizona Daily Star*, September 22, 1985, 50; also cited in Corbett, "Toward a Quaker View of Sanctuary," 8.
41 Leo Guardado, *Church as Sanctuary: Reconstructing Refuge in an Age of Forced Displacement* (Orbis, 2023).
42 James Corbett, "A View from the Border" (September 1984), as cited in Waters, "Alternative," 1001.
43 Haas, "Commentary," 208.
44 Haas, "Commentary," 208.
45 Corbett, "Toward a Quaker View of Sanctuary," 1.
46 Corbett, "Toward a Quaker View of Sanctuary," 11.
47 William Joyce, "The Failure of the Sanctuary Movement," paper prepared for the Jerome Hall Dialogue (1987), archives of Community Church of Boston.
48 Joyce, "The Failure," 1.
49 Joyce, "The Failure," 2. In spite of Joyce's claims, prosecutor Donald M. Reno successfully convinced the presiding judge at pretrial to exclude any evidence related to religious or humanitarian motives as well as evidence concerning human rights abuses in Central America and US foreign policy towards the region; see Maria Cristina Garcia, "'Dangerous Times Call for Risky Responses': Latino Immigration and Sanctuary, 1981–2001," in *Latino Religions and Civic Activism in the United States*, ed. Gastón Espinoza, Virgilio Elizondo, and Jesse Miranda (Oxford University Press, 2005), 159–73 (167).
50 Joyce, "The Failure," 2.
51 Joyce, "The Failure," 2–3.
52 Joyce, "The Failure," 3.
53 Catherine W. Brown, "Refugee and 'Refugees' in International and Domestic Law: The Status of Central Americans in the United States.," paper prepared for the Jerome Hall Dialogue (1987), archives of Community Church of Boston.
54 Brown, "Refugee," 1.
55 Brown, "Refugee," 1.

56 Brown, "Refugee," 15.
57 James Corbett, "Responding to the Knock on the Door," paper prepared for the Jerome Hall Dialogue (1987), archives of Community Church of Boston.
58 Waters, "Alternative Internationalism," 990.
59 James Corbett, "The Goat Cheese Economy of the South Baja Sierras," *Daily Goat Journal*, July–August 1979, n.p., as cited in Corbett, "Responding," 2.
60 Corbett, "The Goat Cheese Economy."
61 Jim Corbett, "Sanctuary and Revolutionary Struggle (abbreviated from a discussion piece used at Pendle Hill, November 21–23, 1986)," located in the archives of Community Church of Boston.
62 Corbett, "Sanctuary and Revolutionary Struggle," 1.
63 Corbett, "Sanctuary and Revolutionary Struggle," 1.
64 Corbett, "Responding to the Knock on the Door," 3.
65 Waters, "Alternative Internationalism," 988–89.
66 Corbett, "Responding to the Knock on the Door," 4.
67 Corbett, "Responding to the Knock on the Door," 4.
68 Nicgorski, "Women," 1–3.
69 Nicgorski, "Women," 11.
70 Renny Golden, "Sanctuary and Women," *Journal of Feminist Studies in Religion* 2, no. 1 (Spring 1986): 131–49.
71 Golden, "Sanctuary and Comunidad," 1.
72 Golden, "Sanctuary and Comunidad," 1.
73 Golden, "Sanctuary and Comunidad," 1.
74 Golden, "Sanctuary and Comunidad," 1.
75 Golden, "Sanctuary and Comunidad," 2.
76 Golden, "Sanctuary and Comunidad," 2.
77 Golden, "Sanctuary and Comunidad," 3.
78 Golden, "Sanctuary and Comunidad," 3.
79 Golden, "Sanctuary and Comunidad," 3.
80 José P. Miranda, *Communism in the Bible* (Orbis Books, 1982).
81 Golden, "Sanctuary and Comunidad," 3.
82 Golden, "Sanctuary and Comunidad," 4.
83 Golden, "Sanctuary and Comunidad," 5. Base Christian Communities, or base ecclesial communities, are, as the name suggests, intentional communities predominantly led by lay people, which promote participation around common religious and/or social concerns. For a classic statement see Leonardo Boff, *Ecclesiogenesis: The Communities Reinvent the Church* (Orbis Books, 1986).
84 Golden, "Sanctuary and Comunidad," 6.
85 Golden, "Sanctuary and Comunidad," 6.
86 Golden, "Sanctuary and Comunidad," 7.
87 Raúl Benítez Manaut, "Guerra civil en El Salvador y esfuerzos para alcanzar la paz," *Revista mexicana de política exterior* no. 28 (1990): 18–32 (26).
88 Golden, "Sanctuary and Comunidad," 6.

89 Golden, "Sanctuary and Comunidad," 8–9.
90 Golden, "Sanctuary and Comunidad," 8–9.
91 Golden, "Sanctuary and Comunidad," 9–10.
92 Golden, "Sanctuary and Comunidad," 9.
93 Golden, "Sanctuary and Comunidad," 10.
94 Golden, "Sanctuary and Comunidad," 10.
95 Golden, "Sanctuary and Comunidad," 10.
96 Lisa Herzog, "Durkheim on Social Justice: The Argument from 'Organic Solidarity,'" *American Political Science Review* 112, no. 1 (2018): 112–24.
97 Golden, "Sanctuary and Comunidad," 11–12.
98 Leonore Siegele-Wenschkewitz, "Can the Sanctuary Movement Appeal to the Traditions of the Confessing Church in Nazi Germany?" Paper prepared for the Jerome Hall Dialogue (1987), archives of Community Church of Boston.
99 Siegele-Wenschkewitz, "Can the Sanctuary Movement," 5–6.
100 Siegele-Wenschkewitz, "Can the Sanctuary Movement," 6.
101 Siegele-Wenschkewitz, "Can the Sanctuary Movement," 8.
102 Siegele-Wenschkewitz, "Can the Sanctuary Movement," 8.
103 Siegele-Wenschkewitz, "Can the Sanctuary Movement," 8.
104 Charles Feinberg, "Sanctuary: A Jewish Perspective," paper prepared for the Jerome Hall Dialogue (1987), archives of Community Church of Boston.
105 There is a long history of speculation about their identity, as the text does not identify them as either Egyptian or Hebrew women. See for example Irene Nowell, *Women in the Old Testament, Part One*, ed. Jaime Waters (Liturgical Press, 2024), 54.
106 Feinberg, "Sanctuary," 1.
107 Feinberg, "Sanctuary," 2.
108 Feinberg, "Sanctuary," 2.
109 Feinberg, "Sanctuary," 2.
110 Feinberg, "Sanctuary," 2.
111 Shaye J. D. Cohen, Robert Goldenberg, and Hayim Lapin, *The Oxford Annotated Mishnah*, vol. 2 (Oxford University Press, 2022), 513. For a more traditional rendering see Hyman E. Goldin, *Hebrew Criminal Law and Procedure: Mishnah: Sanhedrin—Makkot* (Twayne Publishers, 1952), 116: "For this reason a single man only was created, to teach you that if any man destroys the life of one Israelite he is regarded by the Scripture as though he had caused a whole world to perish, and if any man saves the life of one Israelite he is regarded by the Scripture as though he had saved a whole world."
112 Feinberg, "Sanctuary," 2.
113 Feinberg, "Sanctuary," 3.
114 Feinberg, "Sanctuary," 3.
115 Beth Berkowitz, "Tractate Sanhedrin: Introduction," in *The Oxford Annotated Mishnah*, 2: 490.
116 Feinberg, "Sanctuary," 3.

117 Feinberg, "Sanctuary," 3.
118 As quoted inn Feinberg, "Sanctuary," 4.
119 Feinberg, "Sanctuary," 4.
120 Feinberg, "Sanctuary," 4.
121 Feinberg, "Sanctuary," 3–4.
122 Feinberg, "Sanctuary," 4.
123 Feinberg, "Sanctuary," 4.
124 Feinberg, "Sanctuary," 4–5.
125 Feinberg, "Sanctuary," 5.
126 Feinberg, "Sanctuary," 5.
127 Feinberg, "Sanctuary," 5.
128 Feinberg, "Sanctuary," 5.
129 Feinberg, "Sanctuary," 7.
130 Feinberg, "Sanctuary," 6.
131 Feinberg, "Sanctuary," 9.

8

Building Sanctuary Anew

Sanctuary Revived and Reimagined in the Twenty-First Century

CARL LINDSKOOG

Introduction

Hilda Ramirez and Alirio Gamez were free. In April 2021, both were able to walk out of the Austin, Texas, churches at which they had spent years in sanctuary, Ramirez at St. Andrew's Presbyterian Church and Gamez at the First Unitarian Universalist Church. They were protected by a one-year stay of removal. According to a press release by the Austin Sanctuary Network, shielding Ramirez and Gamez from deportation had taken "relentless pressure on members of Congress, Department of Homeland Security Director Alejandro Mayorkas and President Joe Biden." "I'm happy that I can go and see my son play soccer and take him to the park but I know that the fight for us continues. I have fought many years to keep us together and I will keep fighting to make sure our family is not separated," said Ramirez. Carmen Zuvieta, lead organizer for the campaign, attributed the victory to "hard work from our volunteers who followed the leadership of Hilda and Alirio." Through a combination of providing physical sanctuary and mobilizing political pressure on elected officials, members of the Austin Sanctuary Network had succeeded in shielding members of their community from arrest and removal.[1]

Victories like those of Austin Sanctuary Network represent the fruit of a movement that had been forced to adapt to a political and legal terrain that had, in the previous three decades, mounted new threats to foreign-born people in the United States and unleashed new levels of state violence against them in the name of immigration enforcement. The New Sanctuary Movement that emerged in the early twentieth century maintained many of the traditions of the earlier Sanctuary Movement while also evolving and developing new tactics for supporting the most vulnerable members of their communities. This new movement was built on the foundation created by an earlier Sanctuary Movement that was forged out of war and displacement.

The conflicts in El Salvador and Guatemala that had been the source of displacement for the asylum seekers coming to the United States in the 1980s came to an end in the 1990s with peace agreements in El Salvador in 1992 and in Guatemala in 1996. Just prior to that, the US government was also forced to end its policy of excluding Salvadorans and Guatemalans and denying their right to claim asylum when, in response to a lawsuit brought by sanctuary and Central American solidarity activists (*American Baptist Churches v. Thornburgh*, or ABC), the George H. W. Bush administration agreed to halt deportations to these countries and to give Salvadorans and Guatemalans proper asylum hearings.[2]

The Road to the New Sanctuary Movement

With the drawing down of the Central American conflicts and a change to the US government's mistreatment of Salvadoran and Guatemalan asylum seekers, Sanctuary Movement activists broadened their focus from Central America to the many issues and movements arising throughout Latin America and the world. In the early 1990s sanctuary activists and groups threw themselves into drawing attention to a military coup that had overthrown the democratically elected government of Haiti and the US government's denial of Haitians' right to seek asylum in the United States from the violence in their home country. Sanctuary activists contributed to a growing movement opposing the School of the Americas, a US Department of Defense facility that trained Latin America's military leaders and soldiers and had been linked to some of the worst human rights abuses during the Central American conflicts. And sanctuary groups joined with Latin American workers and unions to fight for labor rights and to oppose the imposition of neoliberal policies on the region.[3]

Another area of concern for sanctuary activists in the 1990s was the passage of harsh new anti-immigrant legislation that criminalized foreign-born people and severely limited their ability to seek asylum and other forms of legal protection. The Illegal Immigration Reform and Individual Responsibility Act (IIRIRA) of 1996 established the 287(g) program, which authorized collaboration between federal agents and local police forces in immigration enforcement. The IIRIRA also made it much more difficult for Salvadorans and Guatemalans who had been covered by the ABC legal settlement but whose asylum claims were denied to fight their removal while limiting the number of people eligible for cancellation of removal to four thousand annually. This was just a small fraction of the three hundred thousand seeking asylum under the ABC agreement.[4]

Just as immigrants and asylum seekers were facing threats posed by the IIRIRA and the government's other anti-immigrant measures, they were struggling with new forms of displacement and new obstacles to their movement and survival. The passage of the North American Free Trade Agreement (NAFTA) in 1994 had a devastating impact on Mexico's rural sector, increasing poverty in the country and leading to an enormous number of displaced people seeking survival through migration to the United States. As US-subsidized corn flooded Mexico, crushing the country's small farmers and agricultural sector, migrants fled north, with annual immigration from Mexico to the United States increasing from 370,000 in 1993 to 770,000 by the year 2000. But when migrants tried to cross into the United States at traditional border crossing points like El Paso, Texas, and San Diego, California, they found the crossings closed due to the US government's new migration-restriction programs, Operation Hold the Line and Operation Gatekeeper. Closing the main border-crossing areas had deadly consequences for migrants, who now were forced to cross the US-Mexico border in the much more dangerous and inhospitable Sonoran Desert, leading to the death of many. As the number of migrant deaths in the desert spanning the border separating northern Mexico and southern Arizona climbed, veterans of the Sanctuary Movement of the 1980s responded by placing barrels of water along the desert migration route and searching for and providing other forms of aid for migrants in danger. In this way, new organizations—Humane Borders, Samaritans, and No More Deaths—formed by many of the southern Arizona–based members of the earlier Sanctuary Movement reshaped sanctuary activism and carried it into the twenty-first century.[5]

In 2006 new attacks on foreign-born people triggered an alarm among immigrant communities and spurred immigrant-rights activists into action. The US government had substantially increased immigration enforcement efforts after the terrorist attacks of September 11, 2001, increasingly targeting immigrants as national security threats and thereby causing the number detained and deported to soar into the millions in the first years of the twenty-first century. At the end of 2005 the House of Representatives passed H.R. 4437 (the "Sensenbrenner Bill"), which made it a felony to be in the United States without authorization as well as to aid or assist an undocumented person. Ten years of escalating attacks on immigrants, capped off by this harsh proposed legislation, unleashed an unprecedented mobilization by immigrants and their supporters, featuring millions of protesters taking to the streets in cities across the United States and a national work stoppage activists called "A Day Without an Immigrant." The mobilizations ensured that H.R. 4437 never made it out of the Senate.[6]

Sanctuary Revived

The escalating attacks on immigrants and the focus on immigrant rights that H.R. 4437 brought to the national fore prompted activists with the Los Angeles–based Clergy and Laity United for Economic Justice (CLUE), under the leadership of Rev. Alexia Salvatierra, to launch discussions about reviving the 1980s Sanctuary Movement. Organizers wondered, however, whether the tactics and strategy of the earlier Sanctuary Movement were appropriate for the political and law-enforcement landscape immigrants and activists found themselves in in the early twenty-first century. As sociologist Grace Yukich has documented, not everyone was sure. Immigrants of all sorts were now cast as criminals and, in the post-9/11 world, national security threats, all of whom were being targeted by a vastly expanded immigration enforcement regime. And unlike the many newly arrived Central American asylum seekers fleeing conflict who were the focus of the Sanctuary Movement of the 1980s, the majority of the millions of vulnerable immigrants in the early 2000s had been in the United States for many years (even decades) but lacked legal authorization to live and work in the country.[7]

One sanctuary story proved central to the ultimate decision to revive the Sanctuary Movement. Elvira Arellano, an undocumented mother from Mexico, had led campaigns in Chicago for the Illinois Coalition for Immigrant and Refugee Rights (ICIRR) and Centro Sin Fronteras (CSF), helping to create a new campaign called La Familia Latina Unida (LFLU). Leading LFLU and fighting for immigrant and labor rights drew government attention, making Arellano vulnerable to arrest, detention, and deportation. As we saw earlier in this volume, to seek protection and extend the impact of her immigrant-rights work, Arellano entered sanctuary at Chicago's Adalberto United Methodist Church in 2006. Arellano's activism and leadership, and the very public manner in which she entered sanctuary, soon drew the attention and support of immigrants and activists across the country.[8] According to pastor and fellow activist leader with CSF, Emma Lozano, Arellano was being targeted by the government for deportation as retaliation for all her leadership. Community members, church people, and activists needed to support "our Rosita Parks, and we should all be rallying around her to make sure they don't deport her." That was what the church was doing in extending sanctuary to Arellano, said Rev. Walter Coleman. Elvira was a member of the church who "could have gone and just disappeared like 12 million other people" or "could have accepted the deportation." According to Coleman, "But she has always said that she would fight what she considers to be an unjust law, so that her son will know that he's a child of God and not a piece of junk that can be thrown away. So the option of sanctuary when she requested it seemed like a good option to give her a holy space to continue a campaign of civil disobedience against an unfair law that is separating families throughout this country."[9] What is more, Arellano's eight-year-old son, Saúl, having been born in this country, was a United States citizen. As a result, Arellano framed her struggle to remain in the United States in terms of motherhood. "The only thing that I want is to stay with my son. I would like for this to come out good, because I want to take my son to school," she said. "I have worked for him all my life, and I still want to keep working for him all my life. That's what I want."[10]

The experience and example of Elvira Arellano proved to be an important influence in the debate about whether to create a new sanctuary movement. According to Yukich, Arellano's example allowed activists considering sanctuary for the twenty-first century to begin "conceiving of it as a broader, more abstract idea of sacrificial, potentially risky immigrant-congregation partnerships focusing on mixed-status families" with at least one member a US citizen and another facing deportation. Moving beyond traditional physical sanctuary and now conceiving of sanctuary as "radical accompaniment" allowed those initially skeptical of the proposal to form a New Sanctuary Movement to get on board. In fact, the Sanctuary Movement of the 1980s had also employed a range of tactics beyond physical sanctuary.[11] Nonetheless, embracing the identity of a New Sanctuary Movement as one that adopted a variety of tactics beyond providing physical sanctuary to immigrants or asylum seekers in a sacred space became central to the new movement.[12]

On May 9, 2007, faith leaders in the Protestant and Catholic, Muslim, Jewish, and Sikh traditions held joint press conferences in cities across the country announcing the launch of the New Sanctuary Movement. The movement would "awaken the moral imagination of the country" and "protect immigrant workers and families from unjust deportation."[13] A large part of the new movement's strategy at this launching point was to highlight the harm being done to families with children or spouses who were US citizens. Of signal importance in the case of Elvira Arellano was her status as a mother, and motherhood became an important framing in the first years of the New Sanctuary Movement.[14] "Families are being broken by a broken immigration system," declared Reverend Salvatierra. "Under current policies, detention and deportation are ripping apart parents from children, husbands from wives and sisters from brothers. Through our sanctuaries, we can help change the laws to create policies that are effective and humane."[15]

The emergence of the New Sanctuary Movement caught the attention of nativist media figures like CNN's Lou Dobbs, who warned viewers of *Lou Dobbs Tonight* that by offering sanctuary to "illegal aliens," religious leaders were "ignoring the doctrine of separation of church and state and our laws by interfering in the debate over amnesty." According to Dobbs's report, supporters of the New Sanctuary Movement were "positioning themselves, not only in opposition to immigration law, but also, the sovereignty of the United States." Responding to the idea that churches had no legitimate role in the public discussion about immigration reform, the Reverend Derrick Harkins of Christians for Comprehensive Immigration Reform insisted that "the church has that mandate, as the Bible says, to do justly, to love mercy, and to walk humbly with our God. And in walking humbly, it means we've got to [be] prayerful about how we address a very difficult [immigration] situation." Many people of faith agreed. By the end of 2007, congregations in approximately fifty cities had committed to supporting the New Sanctuary Movement.[16] By 2008 at least thirty-five sanctuary networks were operating in at least ten states, and at least thirteen immigrants had entered physical sanctuary across the country with many thousands more receiving other forms of support from Sanctuary Movement members.[17]

NSM Compared and Examined

While the New Sanctuary Movement (NSM) was inspired by and built on the movement of the 1980s, one important way in which it did not resemble the earlier movement at all was that it did not have an antiwar or anti-imperial focus. The NSM also differed from the earlier movement in its lack of a close connection to an international campaign for peace, as had been the case in the 1980s. This lack of movement focus on issues of war and empire cannot be explained by an absence of US wars or conflicts in the years when the New Sanctuary Movement was emerging. In fact, the operation that ensnared Elvira Arellano, labeled Operation Chicagoland Skies, was implemented, according to immigration officials, to catch potential terrorists. The US wars in Afghanistan and Iraq that started in 2001 and 2003, respectively, raged on, as did an ever-expanding "war on terror" that threatened and displaced more and more people throughout the Middle East and beyond. But many of the people for whom the New Sanctuary Movement were advocating were immigrants, not asylum seekers, and they were not coming directly from a conflict zone as the asylum seekers from Central America had been in the 1980s. Instead, the immigrants with whom the NSM engaged came from all over the world and often had lived in the United States for many years, which was why the movement's next generation did not see ending war and imperial violence as essential movement goals. It was not as clear to the NSM as it had been to the movement of the 1980s that sanctuary required an anti-imperial framework.

Another likely reason for the new movement's failure to incorporate international solidarity and peace work into its identity and movement goals was the overall decline of the US antiwar movement just as the NSM was emerging in 2007. A widespread and vibrant antiwar movement had vigorously opposed Republican President George W. Bush's wars in Iraq and Afghanistan. But this movement virtually disappeared when Democratic President Barack Obama took office in 2008, despite the fact that Obama would escalate the war in Iraq and expand the "war on terror" significantly by increasing the United States' use of drone attacks and launching military raids or airstrikes in Afghanistan, Iraq, Syria, Libya, Yemen, Somalia, and Pakistan. In subsequent years, some movement members and activists would ask what had been the consequence of not partnering with an antiwar movement and what had the new movement lost when imperial violence disappeared as a part of the equation that NSM activists were seeking to solve.[18]

The struggle to defend immigrants intensified in 2010 when lawmakers in Arizona passed Senate Bill 1070, which required police officers to determine the immigration status of individuals whom they had "reasonable suspicion" of being in the United States illegally. The law also targeted sanctuary jurisdictions by forbidding state officials or agencies from adopting policies that limited or restricted the enforcement of federal immigration laws. Leaders in eighteen other states said they intended to follow Arizona's example. In response, immigrant-rights and Sanctuary Movement activists filed legal challenges and launched a campaign of direct action and resistance, including hundreds of arrests, hunger strikes, and the physical resistance of immigration enforcement, as in Chicago, where faith leaders sat down in front of immigration vans transporting individuals for deportation processing.[19]

In 2011 the NSM achieved some victories that gave the movement new tools to defend its community members. In June the director of the United States Citizenship and Immigration Services issued a memo encouraging Immigration and Customs Enforcement agents to exercise "prosecutorial discretion" in determining whether to carry out or to defer action on an individual's deportation proceedings. In the same year, the Obama administration issued a memo indicating that it would not carry out immigration enforcement in "sensitive locations" such as places of worship, schools, hospitals, or public demonstrations. This was a victory, according to Lloyd Barba and Tatyana Castillo-Ramos, that was "due in large part to NSM activism and pressure."[20]

Strategic Shifts in the NSM: 2011–2015

With these new tools at their disposal and in response to increasing local threats to immigrant communities through laws such as Arizona's SB 1070, by 2011 the national New Sanctuary Movement began shifting towards what Yukich refers to as "a very loose network of local coalitions with primarily political targets." New tactics accompanied this shift, Yukich observes, such as the New Sanctuary Coalition's weekly Jericho Walk outside of ICE headquarters in downtown Manhattan and an accompaniment program wherein volunteers accompanied community members facing deportation to their required "check-ins" with immigration officials.[21] As Reverend Donna Schaper, senior minister at Judson Memorial Church in New York City, explained, members of the New Sanctuary Coalition understood sanctuary as "larger than providing housing." Sanctuary was "moral, spiritual, psychological, financial, legal—and sometimes physical—support for people who are about to be detained or deported." Based on this definition of sanctuary, New Sanctuary Coalition's accompaniment program was "as good a supportive strategy as physical sanctuary [because it] helps more immigrants, and can be a gateway to providing physical sanctuary if it becomes necessary."[22]

In 2014 the New Sanctuary Movement was at a turning point. As the Obama administration's mass deportation program continued apace, reaching more than one thousand deportations per day, hopes for congressional action on immigration reform collapsed. President Obama also indicated that he would not take executive action to shield certain immigrants from deportation until after the midterm elections in November. As "deportations reached record numbers, and as we witnessed too many families in our own community torn apart, we again began to whisper, 'sanctuary,'" recalled Pastor Alison Harrington of Southside Presbyterian Church in Tucson, the birthplace of the original Sanctuary Movement of the 1980s.[23] In May, Southside Presbyterian helped launch a nationwide revival of sanctuary activism when it welcomed Daniel Neyoy Ruiz and soon after Rosa Robles Loreto into sanctuary. In September faith leaders announced a new mobilization of sanctuary communities, declaring that twenty-four congregations were prepared to offer sanctuary to immigrants facing deportation and another sixty faith-based organizations were offering support to the movement. Soon churches providing sanctuary could be found in Phoenix, Tucson, Chicago, and Portland, as well as in Philadelphia, where Honduran mother Angela Navarro became the ninth person in sanctuary nationwide when she entered sanctuary in West Kensington Ministry in November. Two days later the Obama administration announced executive actions on immigration, including expanding eligibility for deferred action from deportation and immigration enforcement guidelines targeting "felons not families," steps that immigrant-rights and sanctuary activists framed as a response to the pressure created by their movement.[24]

While the executive actions of the Obama administration offered some hope for protection from deportation, the work of sanctuary activists now included assisting members of their communities in accessing those protections. In October 2014, Arturo Hernández García, a Mexican father of two, entered sanctuary at the First Unitarian Society Church in Denver, Colorado, seeking protection while he fought against the government's effort to deport him. After the issuance of the new executive actions the following month, Hernández García became eligible for deferred action due to the fact that his nine-year-old daughter, Andrea, was a United States citizen and that he had no criminal record, paid taxes, and had lived in the United States for more than the required five years. "The only issue is he has a deportation order that was issued last year, and that means that we'll have to ask the U.S. Citizenship and Immigration Services to grant him discretion and allow him to qualify," explained Jennifer Piper of the Metro Denver Sanctuary Coalition. After nine months in sanctuary, Hernández García was able to leave the church, having received assurance by immigration officials through "prosecutorial discretion" that, for the time being, he would not be targeted for deportation.[25]

In December 2015, *The Washington Post* announced that the Obama administration was preparing to carry out raids to remove hundreds of undocumented Central American families. In response, New Sanctuary Movement leaders announced that they would open up their churches to those fleeing the crackdown. When the roundups began in January 2016, immigration activists mobilized in their defense. New churches like St. Andrew's Presbyterian in Austin, Texas, joined the movement by taking in Hilda Ramirez and her nine-year-old son, Ivan, who fled criminal and domestic violence in their native Guatemala. The church's action brought the number of congregations providing sanctuary at that moment to twelve. However, according to the ecumenical humanitarian organization Church World Service, more than three hundred congregations in thirty states were prepared to join the sanctuary campaign if the roundups and deportations continued. And the tactic seemed to be yielding the intended results. Of the thirteen immigrants who had taken sanctuary in churches since the Obama administration's roundups had begun, eleven had received stays of deportation through the attention and public pressure that sanctuary provided.[26]

By early 2016 the New Sanctuary Movement was a reenergized, growing movement with an evolving identity and growing set of tactics. Amid the presidential campaigning that year, immigration politics and the Sanctuary Movement became a campaign issue, particularly for Republican candidate Donald J. Trump, who launched his campaign for president a year earlier by labeling Mexican migrants "rapists," claiming that they were bringing drugs and crime to the United States, vowing to build a wall on the US-Mexico border, and promising to end the Obama administration's executive action that shielded some immigrants from deportation.[27] In August Trump delivered a speech on immigration in Phoenix, Arizona, in which he decried the secular variant of sanctuary that restricted local law enforcement's collaboration with federal immigration enforcement, known colloquially as "sanctuary cities," as a dangerous practice putting Americans at risk. He invited "the parents who lost their children to Sanctuary Cities" to join him onstage after claiming he would "end" sanctuary cities, triple the number of ICE officers, and create a special new "Deportation Task Force."[28] In contrast, on the campaign trail Democratic presidential candidates Bernie Sanders and Hillary Clinton criticized the Obama administration's immigration raids and deportation of Central Americans. Like Trump, however, Clinton also invoked the concept of sanctuary cities, criticizing San Francisco for failing to deport an immigrant who had committed a murder.[29] While competing candidates staked out their campaign positions on immigration, however, New Sanctuary Movement activists continued their work.

The movement entered yet another new phase in November 2016, when Donald Trump was elected the forty-fifth president of the United States. In the weeks and months following Trump's election, membership in the Sanctuary Movement rose rapidly, with the number of faith communities calling themselves members doubling from four hundred to eight hundred and the number of people publicly taking sanctuary in church spaces rising from five in 2016 to thirty-seven in 2017.[30]

On January 25, 2017, on his fifth day in office, President Trump issued Executive Order 13768, which announced that it would begin denying federal funds to sanctuary jurisdictions and would, "on a weekly basis, make public a comprehensive list of criminal actions committed by aliens" in order to "better inform the public regarding the public safety threats associated with sanctuary jurisdictions."[31] In response to this and other actions by the Trump administration, Marisa Franco, the director and cofounder of Mijente and leader in the #Not1More Deportation campaign, called for a "radical expansion of sanctuary" that would include "undocumented people, but also non-immigrant Muslims, LGBTQ people, Black and Indigenous folks and political dissidents." This "widest idea of sanctuary," urged Franco, needed to work through the established political system but also build "zones of sanctuary that engage hospitals, schools, business owners, faith communities and neighborhoods." It was time to "build sanctuary anew."[32]

Sanctuary Reimagined

In the following months, more activist perspectives helped grow an expanding vision for sanctuary. Sagnicthe Salazar, a community organizer in Oakland, California, explained that their organization, Xicana Moratorium Coalition, Third World Resistance Network, sought to "reimagine sanctuary beyond the migrant rights movement" as a movement that provided "safety in an imperial state where no place or person is safe." Salazar was in conversation with Charandev Singh, an activist with RISE (Refugees, Survivors, and Ex-detainees) in Melbourne, Australia, an organization whose work was "based on an expansive notion of sanctuary that centers aboriginal sovereignty" and that sought to "challenge the forces of power from which people seek sanctuary" and the "contexts from which people flee, so they can stay." Reverend Mike Yoshii, pastor of Buena Vista United Methodist Church in Alameda, California, called for "sanctuary from the manifestation of the military-security-industrial complex" and from "policing and prisons" as well as for "LGBT persons and disabled persons."[33]

Each of these perspectives, scholar Sunaina Maira observed, reflected a position in a debate in the Sanctuary Movement at the time that included activists' "critique of a liberal conception of sanctuary." Perspectives like these also highlighted the importance of connecting more expansive conceptions of sanctuary to what Maira called "the enduring legacy of Western imperial interventions and the impact of disaster capitalism." For the most part, the modern Sanctuary Movement had so far failed to learn the lessons of the Sanctuary Movement of the 1980s, which was an anti-imperial movement, growing out of resistance to the Vietnam War and seeking to defend Salvadoran and Guatemalan asylum seekers and end US intervention in their home countries. As a result, Maira observed, "The experiences of Syrian, Afghan, Yemeni and (doubly displaced) Palestinian refugees remain largely absent in US mainstream discourse," as did "the US role in the catastrophic wars in Syria and Yemen" and "US violence in Central America."[34] This same concern and "hope for creating a merging of movements into one that links the need for sanctuary with the need to end the wars and militarism that drive people out of their homes and to become refugees in the first place" led the Institute for Policy Studies' New Internationalism Project to create an offering to the movement: a toolkit for "organizing for sanctuary through an antiwar lens."[35]

The Trump administration's attack on immigrants and its plan to build a border wall separating Native lands like that of the Tohono O'odham highlighted the need not only to center war and imperial violence in sanctuary activism but to identify and resist the United States' "border imperialism" and the violation of Indigenous sovereignty that the US occupation of Native lands represented. In a spring 2018 roundtable discussion featuring Native activists and scholars in Albuquerque, New Mexico, Jennifer Marley explained what sanctuary work that was more fully integrated into resistance to settler colonialism could yield. Demanding "no ban on stolen land" and the "abolition of border imperialism" was "the assertion of true Indigenous sovereignty within the United States," which would "negate US notions of belonging; therefore, making the US notions of who belongs, who is a citizen and who is not, invalid."[36]

Observing a series of Central American migrant caravans organized by Pueblo Sin Fronteras collective in 2018, historian Rachel Ida Buff saw an expression of a "broad, emancipatory conceptualization of sanctuary that has evolved since 2016," representing "a resurgence of internationalist possibilities." The New Sanctuary Coalition's launching of a "Sanctuary Caravan" to meet the Central American caravan signaled the growing embrace of "a broad practice that some advocates have begun to call 'sanctuary everywhere,'" Buff noted. The Trump administration's attacks on migrants, refugees, asylum seekers, and the Sanctuary Movement allowed "practices of sanctuary [to] proliferate everywhere." Activists' response, according to Buff, was also informed by an understanding of sanctuary that was closely tied to an international #worldwithoutwalls movement that fights back against "a global system of empire" and connects "struggles for indigenous sovereignty and migrant justice to those against state violence."[37]

In the first years of the Trump administration, the size and scope of the Sanctuary Movement was expanding rapidly. By January 2018 the Sanctuary Movement counted more than 1,110 congregations and forty coalitions or networks among its membership. A report on the state of the Sanctuary Movement at the beginning of 2018 also noted that the movement had by then reached into "regions that have only recently seen an influx of immigrants, states such as North Carolina, Ohio, Oklahoma, and Virginia," as well as a shift from urban to rural and suburban spaces.[38] Taking a number of different forms, alongside the broader immigrant-rights movement, sanctuary activism was becoming the largest grassroots resistance movement in the age of Trump.

To stem the growth of this activity and to undercut the immigrant-rights and sanctuary movements, the Trump administration took a page from the government's campaign against the Sanctuary Movement in the 1980s, when it had used federal law enforcement to surveil, infiltrate, and arrest movement activists and leaders. In January 2018, Ravi Ragbir, executive director of the New Sanctuary Coalition in New York City, was detained by Immigration and Customs Enforcement (ICE) and, within hours, transported to the Krome detention facility in Miami, Florida, far from supporters and advocates. Days later, Jean Montrevil, another activist with the New Sanctuary Coalition, was arrested and immediately deported to his native Haiti. In Seattle, Maru Mora Villalpando, leader of the organization Northwest Detention Center Resistance, received a "notice to appear" from ICE. "ICE is really sending us a message to stop our political activity, to stop our activism," said Villalpando.[39]

The crackdown was sweeping across the country. In Jackson, Mississippi, Daniela Vargas was detained by ICE agents as she was leaving a news conference where she had spoken about the Deferred Action for Childhood Arrivals (DACA) program. In Vermont, ICE arrested Zully Victoria Palacios Rodriguez and José Enrique Balcazar Sanchez, organizers with Migrant Justice. Yesenia Hernández-Ramos and Esau Peche-Ventura, also with Migrant Justice, were arrested after marching for labor rights outside of a Ben and Jerry's facility. In Washington state, Baltazar Aburto Gutierrez was arrested after he was quoted in a newspaper talking about a deportation. "You're the one from the newspaper," the ICE agent said before making the arrest. In Colorado, Eliseo Jurado was arrested after his wife, Ingrid Encalada Latorre, publicly took sanctuary in a Boulder church.[40]

In addition to arresting activists and movement leaders, ICE was surveilling immigrant-rights organizations. Documents obtained by *The Nation* revealed that the Homeland Security Investigations (HSI), a branch of ICE, had collected information on activists in New York City, including the New Sanctuary Coalition, and had circulated a document it titled "Anti-Trump Protest Spreadsheet." "The fact that we have an agency as powerful as ICE targeting our communities because we have chosen to speak out against President Trump and his harsh immigration policies should disturb every American who believes this kind of dissent is critical for protecting our democracy," said Alina Das, attorney for the New Sanctuary Coalition.[41]

Rather than let the campaign of surveillance and arrests intimidate them into silence and inaction, however, Sanctuary Movement activists fought back. And now it was the movement's turn to take a page from the 1980s. Just as activists in the earlier Sanctuary Movement had done, the New Sanctuary Coalition and a number of other immigrant-rights organizations sued the government for violating their constitutional rights. The lawsuit, filed on February 9, 2018, charged that the government had "investigated, surveilled, harassed, raided, arrested, detained, and even deported these activists in order to silence them." These activities targeting immigrant activists and leaders were "intended to stifle dissent," which was "unfair, discriminatory, and un-American," the groups charged, "and it violates the First Amendment."[42]

The Trump administration failed in its efforts to destroy the sanctuary and immigrant-rights movements. In fact, the movement was doing more than surviving. Some of its work was leading to important victories. In April 2020, Suyapa Reyes, a Honduran mother of four, left a Philadelphia church where she had been in sanctuary for 554 days. With support from the New Sanctuary Movement of Philadelphia, Reyes won a grant of deferred action, which allowed her to remain and work in the United States. Later that year Philadelphia sanctuary activists won another victory when Clive and Oneita Thompson, a Jamaican couple who had spent more than two years in sanctuary, were able to return to their home in New Jersey and seek permanent residency after the government dropped its deportation case against them. "My whole heart is ready to go," declared Oneita Thompson.[43]

When Joseph Biden defeated Donald Trump in the presidential election of 2020, the political terrain surrounding immigrant justice shifted, but the movement continued. After years of organizing and building a campaign that included thirty members of Congress, sanctuary activists were able to successfully pressure the Biden administration to halt the Trump-era practice of issuing fines to immigrants in sanctuary for "failure to depart." "Knowing that we have won one more victory against the previous government makes us continue with the hope of having the future for which we are fighting," declared Vicky Chavez, a movement leader who had taken sanctuary at First Unitarian Church of Salt Lake City, Utah. Still, immigrant-rights activists had to keep fighting for fair treatment under the new administration. When President Biden continued the Trump administration's practice of using Title 42, a public health law that allowed the federal government to turn away asylum seekers at the US-Mexico border without hearing their asylum claims, the Haitian Bridge Alliance sued the Biden administration for violating the rights of Haitians and other asylum seekers.[44]

Throughout the Biden years and across the country, sanctuary activists maintained physical sanctuary for those who needed it as well as what A. Naomi Paik, Jason Ruiz, and Rebecca Schreiber have called "ongoing practices of solidarity" and "everyday enactments of sanctuary."[45] Because it is an evolving movement, it remains to be seen whether the Sanctuary Movement will develop a more robust sense of internationalism or incorporate into its work a critique of war and imperialism. US support for Israel's campaign in Gaza beginning in October 2023 has reinvigorated antiwar activism in the United States and around the world, potentially highlighting the fact that the sources of state violence, whether against immigrants or against victims of war, are the same.

NOTES

1 "Hilda and Alirio Walk out of Sanctuary into Freedom for One Year," *Austin Sanctuary Network*, April 14, 2021, https://austinsanctuarynetwork.org.

2 Edward T. Brett, "The Attempts of Grassroots Religious Groups to Change U.S. Policy Towards Central America: Their Methods, Successes, and Failures," *Journal of Church & State* 36, no. 4 (Autumn 1994): 62; Hector Perla Jr. and Susan Bibler Coutin, "Legacies and Origins of the 1980s US–Central American Sanctuary Movement," in *Sanctuary Practices in International Perspectives: Migration, Citizenship, and Social Movements*, ed. Randy K. Lippert and Sean Rehaag (Routledge, 2013), 83.

3 Carl Lindskoog, "Sanctuary Is Justice: Resilience and Ingenuity in the Sanctuary Movement Since 1986," in *Whose America? U.S. Immigration Policy Since 1980*, ed. Maria Cristina Garcia and Maddalena Marinari (University of Illinois Press, 2023), 196–200.

4 Rachel Ida Buff; "Sanctuary Everywhere: Some Key Words, 1945–Present," *Radical History Review* 1, no. 135 (October 2019): 31, https://doi.org/10.1215/01636545-7607809; Perla and Coutin, "Legacies and Origins of the 1980s US–Central American Sanctuary Movement," 83.

5 "NAFTA's Legacy for Mexico: Economic Displacement, Lower Wages for Most, Increased Migration," Public Citizen, September 1, 2019, www.citizen.org; John Fife, "From the Sanctuary Movement to No More Deaths: The Challenge to Communities of Faith," in *Religious and Ethical Perspectives on Global Migration*, ed. Elizabeth W. Collier and Charles R. Strain (Lexington Books, 2014), 262–63; Linda Rabben, *Sanctuary and Asylum: A Social and Political History* (University of Washington Press, 2016), 245–46.

6 Lloyd Barba and Tatyana Castillo-Ramos, "Sacred Resistance: The Sanctuary Movement from Reagan to Trump," *Perspectivas* no. 16 (2019): 21.

7 Grace Yukich, "'I Didn't Know If This Was Sanctuary': Strategic Adaptation in the US New Sanctuary Movement," in *Sanctuary Practices in International Perspectives: Migration, Citizenship, and Social Movements*, ed. Randy K. Lippert and Sean Rehaag (Routledge, 2013), 110–12.

8 Amalia Pallares, *Family Activism: Immigrant Struggles and the Politics of Noncitizenship* (Rutgers University Press, 2015), 38–40.

9 Pallares, *Family Activism*, 38–40; "'I Fear God Much More Than I Fear Homeland Security': Chicago Pastor on Why He Is Allowing Mexican Mother to Stay in Church to Avoid Deportation," *Democracy Now!*, August 22, 2006, www.democracynow.org.

10 Pallares, *Family Activism*, 38–40; "'I Fear God Much More Than I Fear Homeland Security.'"

11 The Sanctuary Movement of the 1980s employed many tactics to highlight the reasons asylum seekers were forced to flee to the United States and to partner with the peace movement that was seeking to end the US war making that was displacing them. For example, Sanctuary Movement activists sponsored a sanctuary caravan, allowing sanctuary space to travel from one community to the next, carrying the stories of displaced people across the country.

12 Yukich, "'I Didn't Know If This Was Sanctuary,'" 113–14.

13 Lee Sustar, "The New Sanctuary Movement: The Fight Against Deportations," *Socialist Worker.org*, May 18, 2007, https://socialistworker.org.

14 Pallares, *Family Activism*.

15 "Religious Groups Launch 'New Sanctuary Movement' for Immigrants Facing Deportation," *Democracy Now!*, May 10, 2007, www.democracynow.org/; Sustar, "The New Sanctuary Movement"; Grace Yukich, *One Family Under God: Immigration Politics and Progressive Religion in America* (Oxford University Press, 2013), 14–15.

16 "Churches Offering Sanctuary for Illegals," *Lou Dobbs Tonight*, May 9, 2007, www.cnn.com; Marta Caminero-Santangelo, "The Voice of the Voiceless: Religious Rhetoric, Undocumented Immigrants, and the New Sanctuary Movement in the United States," in *Sanctuary Practices in International Perspectives: Migration, Citizenship, and Social Movements*, ed. Randy K. Lippert and Sean Rehaag (Routledge, 2013), 92.

17 Rabben, *Sanctuary and Asylum*, 244.

18 Christi Parsons and W. J. Hennigan, "President Obama, Who Hoped to Sow Peace, Instead Led the Nation in War," *Los Angeles Times*, January 13, 2017, www.latimes.com; Phyllis Bennis, "Obama Does Have a Strategy in Iraq: Escalation," *Foreign Policy in Focus*, June 10, 2015, https://fpif.org; Brad Plumer, "How Obama Demobilized the Antiwar Movement," *Washington Post*, August 29, 2013, www.washingtonpost.com; Michael T. Heaney and Fabio Rojas, *Party in the Street: The Antiwar Movement and the Democratic Party After 9/11* (Cambridge University Press, 2015).

19 "AZ SB1070 | 2010 | Forty-ninth Legislature 2nd Regular." April 23, 2010, https://legiscan.com; "Dozens of Immigrant Rights Activists Arrested in Arizona," *Democracy Now!*, July 30, 2010, www.democracynow.org; Daniel Schwartz, "Searching for a New Sanctuary Movement," *Dissent*, June 25, 2010, www.dissentmagazine.org.

20 Myrna Orozco and Rev. Noel Andersen, "Sanctuary in the Age of Trump: The Rise of the Movement a Year into the Trump Administration," Church World Service, January 2018, in Lindskoog's possession; Barba and Castillo-Ramos, "Sacred Resistance," 25.

21 Yukich, *One Family Under God*, 207.

22 Donna Schaper, "Sanctuary Movement Sees Post-Election Resurgence: Here's How to Get Involved," *Sojourners*, December 5, 2016.

23 Alison Harrington, "Can Anything Good Come from Nazareth?," in *Faithful Resistance: Gospel Visions for the Church in a Time of Empire*, ed. Rick Ufford-Chase (UnShelved, 2016), 26–27.

24 Melissa Del Bosque, "Inaction Spurs New Immigrant Sanctuary Movement," *Texas Observer*, September 24, 2014, www.texasobserver.org; Rabben, *Sanctuary and Asylum*, 256; "Undocumented Mother Takes Sanctuary from Deportation in Philadelphia Church," *Democracy Now!*, November 18, 2014, accessed January 8, 2024, www.democracynow.org; "Angela Navarro Enters Sanctuary," New Sanctuary Movement of Philadelphia (n.d.), accessed January 8, 2024, www.sanctuary-philadelphia.org; 2014 Executive Actions on Immigration. U.S. Citizenship and Immigration Services, www.uscis.gov.

25 "Undocumented Father Finds Sanctuary in Denver Church to Fight Deportation to Mexico," *Democracy Now!*, February 13, 2015, www.democracynow.org/; Victoria Bekiempis, "Immigrant Claiming Sanctuary Leaves Church After Nine Months," *Newsweek*, July 21, 2015, www.newsweek.com.

26 "Immigration Activists Vow to Give Refuge to Migrants," *Washington Post*, December 26, 2015, https://research.ebsco.com; John Burnett, "U.S. Churches Offer Safe Haven for a New Generation of Immigrants," *All Things Considered*, National Public Radio, February 9, 2016.

27 Sazanne Gamboa, "Donald Trump Announces Presidential Bid by Trashing Mexico, Mexicans," *NBC News*, June 16, 2015, www.nbcnews.com.

28 "Full Text: Donald Trump Immigration Speech in Arizona," *Politico*, August 31, 2016, www.politico.com.

29 Jesse Byrnes, "Sanders, Clinton Slam New Round of Deportation Raids," *The Hill*, May 12, 2016, https://thehill.com; Al Weaver, "Hillary on San Francisco Illegal Immigrant Murder: 'The City Made a Mistake,'" *Daily Caller*, July 7, 2015, https://dailycaller.com.

30 Orozco and Andersen, "Sanctuary in the Age of Trump," 5–6.

31 E.O. 13768 of January 25, 2017, www.federalregister.gov.

32 Marisa Franco, "A Radical Expansion of Sanctuary: Steps in Defiance of Trump's Executive Order," *Truthout*, January 25, 2017, https://truthout.org.

33 Sunaina Maira, "Freedom to Move, Freedom to Stay, Freedom to Return: A Transnational Roundtable on Sanctuary Activism," *Radical History Review* 1, no. 135 (October 2019); 141, 150–52, https://doi.org/10.1215/01636545-7607884.

34 Maira, "Freedom to Move," 154–55.

35 Maha Hilal, Khury Petersen-Smith, Phyllis Bennis, Domenica Ghanem, Dominique Hernandez, and Sarah Gertler, "War Brought Us Here: Organizing for Sanctuary Through an Anti-War Lens: A Toolkit." Institute for Policy Studies, December 6, 2018, www.jstor.org.

36 Rafael A. Martínez and Rebecca M. Schreiber, "Sovereignty and Sanctuary: A Roundtable." *Chiricú Journal: Latina/o Literatures, Arts, and Cultures* 3, no. 1 (2018): 144, https://doi.org/10.2979/chiricu.3.1.09.

37 Buff, "Sanctuary Everywhere," 15–17, 33–34.

38 Orozco and Andersen, "Sanctuary in the Age of Trump," 6.

39 Amy Goodman and Denis Moynihan, "Trump's Roundup of Immigrant Leaders Has Begun," *Democracy Now!*, January 18, 2018, www.democracynow.org.

40 Nick Pinto, "ICE Is Targeting Political Opponents for Deportation, Ravi Ragbir and Rights Groups Say in Court," *The Intercept*, February 9, 2018, https://theintercept.com.

41 Jimmy Tobias, "Exclusive: ICE Has Kept Tabs on 'Anti-Trump' Protesters in New York City," *The Nation*, March 6, 2019, www.thenation.com.

42 Pinto, "ICE Is Targeting Political Opponents for Deportation."

43 "Honduran Mother Celebrates Freedom After 554 Days in Sanctuary at Philadelphia Church," *Democracy Now!*, April 6, 2020, www.democracynow.org; Jeff Gammage, "Jamaican Couple to Leave Philly Church Sanctuary After Two Years as Government Drops Deportation Case," *Philadelphia Inquirer*, December 20, 2020, www.inquirer.com.

44 "Sanctuary Movement Victory: DHS Ends Trump-Era Policy Fining Immigrants Who 'Fail to Depart,'" US Center for Constitutional Rights, April 28, 2021, https://ccrjustice.org; Joaquin Castro, Edward J. Markey, Elizabeth Warren, et al., to Joseph R. Biden, January 26, 2021, www.markey.senate.gov; *Haitian Bridge Alliance et al. v. Joseph R. Biden*, Case 1:21-cv-03317 Document 1, Filed December 20, 2021, https://innovationlawlab.org; Gerren Keith Gaynor, "After More Than Two Years, Lawsuit Against Biden Administration for Treatment of Haitian Migrants Proceeds," *TheGrio*, February 26, 2024, https://thegrio.com.

45 A. Naomi Paik, Jason Ruiz, and Rebecca M. Schreiber, "Sanctuary's Radical Networks," *Radical History Review* 1, no. 135 (October 2019): 2, 7–8, https://doi.org/10.1215/01636545-7607809.

9

Refuge in the Golden State

Sanctuary Organizing from the 1980s to the Present

TATYANA CASTILLO-RAMOS

Introduction

Donald Trump announced his first presidential campaign vowing to crack down on immigration and secure the US-Mexico border. Most might think of his infamous calls to "Build the Wall" or rhetoric about Mexico not "sending their best" when they think about his performances of xenophobic politics, but it was the murder of Kate Steinle that he would use as proof of his claim of the dangers of undocumented immigrants in the country. Steinle, who was unintentionally shot and killed in the back by an accidental discharge of a gun found by an undocumented immigrant who had been deported numerous times previously, became, not of her own volition, a martyr-type figure for Trump and other proponents of anti-immigrant sentiments on his campaign. Where Steinle was killed was crucial for his political performances: The incident occurred in San Francisco, a municipality with a longtime sanctuary-city status dating back to the original Sanctuary Movement of the 1980s. From then until the present day, sanctuary cities, and the concept of sanctuary itself, have fallen into Trump's direct crossfires. As Lloyd Barba and Sergio González have explained, "Sanctuary cities served as Trump's most fertile site to activate his anti-immigrant platform."[1] Over the next decade, Trump would continue to focus his anti-immigrant messaging on San Francisco, as well as Los Angeles and the state of California more broadly, in his ongoing crusade against sanctuary jurisdictions.

As historians, anthropologists, and journalists reflect on the history of the US Sanctuary Movement, certain geographic areas such as Tucson and Chicago stand out as ideological centers of the movement that have gained the majority of scholarly attention. By scholars focusing on the Tucson-Chicago dialectic, however, the role and relationship of California regions such as the San Francisco Bay Area and Los Angeles to the broader movement have been somewhat relegated to the sidelines rather than generally included as main hubs in their own right of the 1980s movement. This oversight is curious given that prior to the influx of Central American refugees in the last two decades of the twentieth century, San Francisco claimed the highest population of Salvadoran refugees, and would soon be surpassed by Los Angeles. Sanctuary Movement scholars have readily noted, meanwhile, that Reverend John Fife and Southside Presbyterian Church in Tucson were not alone in their initial declaration of sanctuary on March 24, 1982, as they had declared sanctuary concurrently with a collective of five churches in the San Francisco Bay Area.[2] While these California churches seldom receive historical analysis beyond this initial declaration, the legacy of their involvement continues to inform Bay Area sanctuary activism and immigrant rights more generally. Likewise, although Los Angeles activists often do not draw explicitly on their sanctuary history to the same extent as in the Bay Area, the city continues to have a strong sanctuary activism scene that remains prepared to fight for the rights of the large number of immigrants in the area who themselves engaged in immigrant-rights activism.

San Francisco, Los Angeles, and other California cities are essential for understanding the development of the Sanctuary Movement as it is known today. California cities such as San Francisco and Los Angeles were among the earliest to become sanctuary cities, with Berkeley being the very first in February 1985. Sanctuary in California and these large metropolitan areas is significant because it often features as talking points in nationwide immigration debates. Sociologist Pierrette Hondangeu-Sotelo explains that starting in the late twentieth century, "Los Angeles—and California more generally—became the hub of the development of anti-immigrant backlash, and finally, coming full circle, this region has emerged as a key site of creative organizing by labor unions and religious groups working for the immigrant rights movement. . . . Looking at what happens in Southern California gives us a preview of what is emerging elsewhere with the immigrant rights movement."[3] This chapter examines how more recent anti-immigrant sentiments have fueled sanctuary activism not just in Southern California but also Northern California and ultimately at the state level.

Monographs such as Susan Bibler Coutin's *Culture of Protest: Religious Activism and the U.S. Sanctuary Movement* and Grace Yukich's *One Family Under God: Immigration Politics and Progressive Religion in America* have outlined the Sanctuary Movement's emergence in California in the 1980s and the 2006 New Sanctuary Movement, respectively. More recent books such as Mario T. Garcia's *Father Luis Olivares, a Biography: Faith Politics and the Origins of the Sanctuary Movement in Los Angeles* and Sean Dempsey's *City of Dignity: Christianity, Liberalism, and the Making of Global Los Angeles*, have provided long-overdue reassessments of key players in the 1980s Sanctuary Movement of Los Angeles. This chapter draws on this literature and archival research to highlight the history of sanctuary in the Golden State with attention to regional contexts, as well as in relation to the broader national movement. To do so, it takes a top-down approach to trace state and local jurisdiction and local networks to highlight broader patterns of activism throughout different eras and regions.[4]

In recent years, California has featured as an ideological battleground in nationwide discussions on sanctuary jurisdictions and approaches to undocumented immigrants more broadly. The history of sanctuary in California since the 1980s, along with the large number of immigrants in cities like San Francisco, Los Angeles, and the state more broadly, continues to shape both modern sanctuary activism and the state of California's purported values.

The 1980s Sanctuary Movement

Los Angeles

As shown throughout this volume, sanctuary activism has taken many forms. This has included creating municipal structures and policies that support undocumented residents, refugees, and asylum seekers under a category often roughly defined as "sanctuary cities." Los Angeles is a pioneer in this regard, as there were unified efforts to support refugees even before the formal founding of the 1980s Sanctuary Movement. Local liberal activists, and the networks they had formed through labor leaders and other social movements like the civil rights and Chicano movements, had begun entering positions in city government and had initiated more progressive local governmental policies.[5] While there were several religiously affiliated groups organizing refugee support in the late 1970s, the Southern California Ecumenical Council (now renamed the Southern California Christian Forum) would emerge as particularly active and would later be critical in 1980s Sanctuary Movement activism in the state.[6]

The history of organized ecumenical relations in the region dates back to 1913 with the founding of the California Church Federation in San Francisco, led by Edwin Ryland, the pastor of Hollywood Methodist Church, who also previously initiated the earlier, smaller Los Angeles Church Federation in 1906. Originally, these ecumenical churches were focused on following the legacy of the Edinburgh World Missionary Conference by acting together for evangelistic efforts and sponsoring chaplains for World War I. This statewide federation then expanded to other social-justice causes such as women's suffrage, prohibition, and labor unions. In the 1920s it started to work alongside the Council of Women for Home Missions to sponsor national park ministries as well as to work alongside the Council of Women for Home Missions to support new Dust Bowl refugees and migrant workers. It grew over the years, and in 1943 the California Church Federation decided to create two additional regional branches: the statewide California Church Federation would continue to exist, but now there was also a Northern and Southern California Council of Churches that would take more specialized approaches to local topics of concern. Concurrently, the councils were active during World War II and were organizing against Japanese internment. After the war, the Southern California Council of Churches served as the platform for churches to develop curricula for Christian educators and would contribute to the National Farm Worker Ministry. By 1982, after the second Vatican Council and the study project of Baptism, Eucharist, and Ministry from the World Council of Churches, the organization would once again change names to reflect broader changes in church relations, now calling themselves the Southern California Ecumenical Council (SCEC).[7]

As historian Sean Dempsey has shown, the SCEC was a cornerstone of the Sanctuary Movement in Los Angeles. In 1978, the SCEC created an Immigration and Refugee Task Force to specifically monitor both local and worldwide refugee-related issues, with the goal of being a model for other efforts around the country. This task force was mobilized to facilitate the creation of a network that would coordinate refugee sponsorship and resettlement efforts among various ecumenical churches, the Catholic Church, and the Church World Service. The SCEC also planned presentations to area churches to encourage their continued financial sponsorship of refugees.[8] While mainline Protestant churches and the Roman Catholic Church had long been concerned with refugee resettlement and other issues related to migration, the 1970s marked a distinct shift in approaches as "refugee resettlement became a local, urban issue as migrants from Asia and Latin America began to reshape Southern California and its myriad Christian congregations." This influx of refugees in the late 1970s brought what had previously been an international concern to their front door and paved the way for many of the churches involved in refugee resettlement to spearhead the Sanctuary Movement in Los Angeles in the 1980s.[9] It also brought together activists from across the state to collectively assist refugees.

One year after the SCEC created its Immigration and Refugee Task Force, mainline Protestants throughout the West Coast gathered at the San Francisco Theological Seminary in San Anselmo to develop their own strategy for serving the region's growing refugee and undocumented population. Their objective was to share information, develop cross-denominational and transregional networks, learn about the United States' role in the refugee crisis through its military intervention in Southeast Asia, and strategize a coordinated approach to help the increasing waves of refugees from Vietnam, Laos, Cambodia, and elsewhere. One of the programs that came out of this coordinated effort was Operation California, a program for airlifting food and medical supplies to the "so-called boat people of Southeast Asia," further asserting their plan to assist these refugees once they made it to US soil.[10] Notably, the name of this effort, "Operation California," demonstrates how efforts to assist refugees were being conceived of as a statewide effort.

Representatives of the Catholic Church's Refugee Resettlement Bureau, social service heads from various liberal Protestant churches, and the American Jewish Committee were among the leaders of Operation California and also enthusiastically endorsed the Carter administration's plan to double the number of Southeast Asian refugees permitted to enter on humanitarian grounds. Religious leaders made moral appeals on behalf of Southeast Asian refugees that were firmly grounded in human rights rhetoric that would also become a staple of sanctuary activism. Furthermore, Los Angeles's religious leaders called on houses of worship, government facilities, and individuals to be involved in refugee resettlement efforts, as their situation was dire. Dempsey asserts that "this represented a rather remarkable broadening and deepening of religious-based human rights politics, which called for a reorientation of the social face of the churches and synagogues of Southern California to pivot towards the defense of human rights in their advocacy and even their everyday practice, calling quite literally for the faithful to bring refugees home with them." As the 1970s came to a close, a notable number of Cuban refugees joined the masses of people fleeing Southeast Asia, and although the SCEC had vowed to assist these refugees, in practice the effort to assist them was marked by a high degree of disorganization.[11] However, various agencies managed to help resettle thousands of refugees in the early 1980s, learning valuable lessons in terms of organization as their attention began to turn to Central American refugees.

With Ronald Reagan's inauguration in 1981, liberal religious leaders in Southern California immediately began to express concerns over his approach to foreign affairs and human rights situations around the world, including Latin America and especially El Salvador. Most of these leaders were already familiar with him from his back-to-back terms as governor of California from 1967 to 1975. Eighteen of these religious leaders, led by Catholic Auxiliary Bishop Juan Arzube, signed a statement on Reagan's inauguration date to formally express their concern and to urge the president-elect to cut off all military and economic aid to the dictatorship in El Salvador and support Salvadoran efforts to form a democratic alternative.[12]

Women, especially women religious, became an increasingly visible part of church-based resistance in Los Angeles against Reagan administration policies regarding Central America through their leadership of public protests as well as leadership of essential sanctuary groups in the 1980s. Catholic women religious were some of the first religious activists to practice civil disobedience in the Central America peace and solidarity movement, even before the formal declaration of the Sanctuary Movement in 1982, with some of these protests occurring on federal property and resulting in arrests.[13] Catholic sisters, such as Catholic Sister of Social Service Paulita Bernuy, went on to form a loose coalition with Protestant women in the Los Angeles area who had become politicized due to the United States' role in El Salvador and the refugee crisis in the city.[14] These protests went on for years and often resulted in arrests, with the Los Angeles Police Department claiming that "the protests, led in large part by churchwomen, were the longest running campaign of civil disobedience in many years, presumably since the height of the civil rights movement in the 1950s and 1960s."[15] Women worked both on the front lines and in organizing assistance to Central Americans. The main coordinator of the Sanctuary Movement in Los Angeles was the SCEC's task force on immigration, called the Southern California Inter-Faith Task Force on Central America (SCITCA). Its Sanctuary Committee was headed by SCITCA founder Sister Jo'Ann De Quattro, a key Los Angeles sanctuary activist and member of the Sisters of the Holy Names of Jesus and Mary, and was comprised of staff of the Peace and Justice Center of Southern California. SCITCA would grow to focus on four issues: protesting US military intervention in Central America, supporting a diplomatic solution to the conflicts in the region, supporting Central American refugees in the United States, and giving congregations resources and encouragement to offer asylum to these refugees.[16]

Sister Jo'Ann appointed Gloria Kinsler, who had spent thirteen years in Guatemala as a missionary, as coordinator of the SCITCA Sanctuary Committee. As coordinator, Kinsler had the primary responsibility of meeting refugees who had arrived from San Diego or other locations. She also assisted those who had been referred by other Central American refugee-assistance groups such as El Rescate, formed in 1981 by Salvadoran immigrants and US religious and humanitarian organizations with the help of the SCEC, and the Central American Refugee Center (CARECEN) of Los Angeles, founded in 1983 by Salvadoran refugees, US church leaders, community activists, and attorneys.[17] From there, she would help get them to churches, to homes, or to the temporary refugee shelter called Casa Rutilio Grande (named after a Salvadoran priest who had been assassinated by death squads). Kinsler also visited churches every weekend to speak about the Sanctuary Movement.[18] This work was essential as Jim Corbett himself had estimated that "more than half of the Central American refugees coming through Tucson went to

Los Angeles," and also, Los Angeles became a major transfer station for refugees who were sent to sanctuary congregations around the nation.[19] The prominent public civil disobedience by women, especially religious women, is an important exception to the traditionally male-clerical charisma that tended to be the face of the 1980s Sanctuary Movement.[20]

Due to the large population of Central American asylum seekers who had begun to arrive in the city in the 1970s, Los Angeles also developed a wide network of Central American–led sanctuary and peace and solidarity organizations. This substantive immigrant population set Los Angeles, and by extension San Francisco, apart from other prominent sanctuary loci. Social scientists Norma Stoltz Chinchilla, Nora Hamilton, and James Loucky explain that because many Central Americans coming to Los Angeles brought their experience of organizing in their home countries to their activism on Central American issues, "Los Angeles differed from cities such as Chicago . . . in which the Central American population was smaller and lacked legal documentation, with the result that most were less directly involved in immigrant-related initiatives."[21] Organizations like El Rescate and CARECEN showed just how important Latinx people, immigrants, and refugees were in organizing refugee assistance and resettlement in California. The year 1983, the same year CARCEN was founded, would prove to be a monumental year for Central American refugee support in Los Angeles. That same year, sponsored by El Rescate, it would open the Clínica Oscar Romero to provide medical care to Central American refugees.[22] Furthermore, 1983 would also mark the first public sanctuary declaration by a Los Angeles congregation.

Los Angeles congregations, while active in asylum organizing for years, formally joined the Sanctuary Movement one year after its birth. On March 24, 1983, the third anniversary of the assassination of Salvadoran Archbishop Oscar Romero, First Unitarian Church in Los Angeles's Westlake neighborhood (not far from the increasingly Salvadoran Pico Union district) publicly declared sanctuary. Reverend Philip Zwerling made the declaration to protect one particular Salvadoran family, the Zelada family, who had entered sanctuary originally in secret.[23] While the March 24 declaration followed a pattern set a year earlier by Tucson and San Francisco Bay Area churches, it also held important local significance as "Romero had become a patron saint of a burgeoning underground sanctuary community in the Los Angeles area, with congregations including the United Methodist Church of Pico Rivera, Los Angeles's Angelica Lutheran Church, and several area Unitarian congregations."[24] Within a year of First Unitarian Church's declaration, dozens of other congregations had joined the Sanctuary Movement in Los Angeles.[25]

In 1985, arguably the most historically prominent among Mexican churches in Los Angeles, Our Lady Queen of Angels Church (commonly known as La Placita Church), joined the now dozens of other Los Angeles churches publicly involved in the Sanctuary Movement. La Placita was a staple of the Mexican and Latinx community as it drew its parishioners from many other parishes in the Los Angeles Archdiocese due to its fostering of and historical significance for Latino, particularly Mexican, Catholicism.[26] Although its sanctuary declaration came three years after the first public declaration of sanctuary, Mario T. García argues that La Placita "would come to represent one of the most important centers and symbols of public sanctuary in the country."[27] La Placita becoming a sanctuary church established that public sanctuary, a practice often associated with white male Protestant clerical leadership to support immigrants, could be practiced by Latinx churches as well.[28]

Like First Unitarian Church, La Placita had already been functioning as a kind of underground sanctuary, and so its public declaration came as a surfacing of its private work.[29] Father Luis Olivares, La Placita's pastor, was no stranger to social activism and had been involved in community organizing well before the Sanctuary Movement, even being involved with the United Farm Workers and serving as a personal faith advisor to Cesar Chavez.[30] Prior to the declaration, he consulted with others involved with Central American support groups, including Sister Jo'Ann De Quattro of the SCEC's Interfaith Task Force on Central America, who offered both her support and the support of her group.[31] And so, Olivares and his allies prepared to offer a public declaration of sanctuary on December 12, 1985. In doing so, the church broke with the trend of declaring on the anniversary of Archbishop Romero's death, instead choosing to inaugurate sanctuary on the feast day of Our Lady of Guadalupe as it was one of the most important rituals at La Placita and because, as García notes, "Our Lady of Guadalupe was the national religious symbol of Mexico and had always symbolized the Virgin Mother's embrace of the poor and oppressed."[32] As part of the program for the service, there was a prayer reading connecting La Placita's sanctuary efforts to the Virgin of Guadalupe's original apparition to and relationship with Juan Diego, and a rendition of the following prayer: "Nuestra Señora de Guadalupe, protege a estos nuevos Juan Diegos entre nosotros. Ayúdanos a acabar con la violencia en Centro América. Trae Justicia a estos países destrosados por la guerra, hasta que la paz finalmente llegue. Ayúdanos a tener amor y compasión hacia estos Juan Diegos Refugiados" (Our Lady of Guadalupe, protect these new Juan Diegos among us. Help us end the violence in Central America. Bring justice to those countries destroyed by the war, until peace finally comes. Help us to have love and compassion for these refugee Juan Diegos).[33] The service was highly publicized and attracted various civic, labor, and religious leaders, including priests from other churches as well as ecumenical and interfaith clergy, who were all instructed to bring their own vestments for the ceremony.[34] It was monumental for a historically Mexican and Latinx church to publicly declare sanctuary in a way meaningful for their congregation, particularly at the height of the national movement, and was a momentous occasion that drew together activists from around Los Angeles, arguably "represent[ing] perhaps the most important part of Luis Olivares's life."[35]

While the Los Angeles religious community was not among the first in the nation to publicly declare sanctuary, it is arguable that they were the first sanctuary city for immigrants in the United States. On November 27, 1979, the Los Angeles Police Department passed Special Order Number 40. Procedure I of the special order specifically stated, "Officers shall not initiate police action with the objective of discovering the alien status of a person. Officers shall not arrest nor book persons for violation of Title 8, section 1325 of the United States Immigration Code (Illegal Entry)."[36] While local activists were greatly invested in assisting refugees that same year, the order was initiated and passed before the formal creation of the Sanctuary Movement. At the time, the policy was introduced with relatively little fanfare. Regardless, it set the legal precedent for sanctuary cities across the United States despite lacking the ideological component that would become a staple in later sanctuary city resolutions. Despite what, especially in hindsight, was a groundbreaking policy for immigrant rights, political scientists Loren

Collingwood and Benjamin Gonzalez O'Brien note that it is "unclear how aware residents of Los Angeles were of Special Order 40" because of the policy's lack of fanfare and ideological commitment.[37] By the time Los Angeles formally became a sanctuary city on November 27, 1985, Special Order 40 had already been established for six years. This 1985 sanctuary-city resolution specifically stated that it was in favor of diversity and tolerance and was created to ease the fear of Central American refugees around law enforcement.[38] Although Special Order 40 was not challenged by the Immigration and Naturalization Service (INS), Harold Ezell, the western regional INS commissioner, aggressively campaigned against Los Angeles's sanctuary resolution's passage and was ultimately successful in his efforts, as the Los Angeles City Council reversed itself less than a year after its declaration. As Collingwood and Gonzalez O'Brien explain, "This case of Special Order 40 highlights the role that ideological aspects of such a declaration have in making them controversial. The sanctuary resolution did not seek to simply facilitate cooperation between police and immigrant communities but was meant as a show of solidarity with the Sanctuary Movement and as a criticism of the Reagan administration's refugee policies." Although Los Angeles did not officially become a sanctuary city for long in the 1980s, its Special Order 40 set a legal precedent for other sanctuary cities and furthermore showed other municipalities the lack of costs associated with INS noncooperation at the time due to the lack of a federal response to the order.[39]

The San Francisco Bay Area

While the Sanctuary Movement in Los Angeles was influenced by the legacy of civil rights movements and organizational responses to earlier waves of refugees, the movement in the San Francisco Bay Area was preceded by another sanctuary effort a decade prior: sanctuary for Vietnam War resisters (see chapter 1 of this volume). As a result, the legacy and concept of sanctuary were already well established in both organizer circles and public consciousness. It should come as no surprise, then, that when another movement was developing in the early 1980s, churches in the Bay Area that were concerned about the Central American refugee crisis would readily call once again on the legacy of sanctuary.

Statewide church alliances thus developed into regional church organizations such as the Southern California Ecumenical Council and the Northern California Ecumenical Council. These cross-regional connections continued to exist, but while the SCEC played a critical role in the Los Angeles Sanctuary Movement, the Northern California Ecumenical Council would be overshadowed by a grassroots East Bay Sanctuary Covenant (EBSC) that drove the movement in the Bay Area and included founding members of the national Sanctuary Movement.

According to the first volume of the EBSC's newsletter, *The Exodus*, the Bay Area had received an influx of refugees fleeing the civil war in El Salvador. In response to these refugees in need, and the US government's lack of acknowledgment of their refugee status and efforts to deport them, a coalition of five Bay Area churches joined forces to form the East Bay Sanctuary Coalition in February 1982. The initial coalition was formed of five churches in Berkeley, from a variety of denominations: Newman Hall–Holy Spirit Parish, St. John's Presbyterian Church, St. Mark's Episcopal Church, Trinity United Methodist Church, and University Lutheran Chapel.[40] These churches were now bound together by their covenant to provide sanctuary, which they defined broadly as "support, protection, and advocacy," to the refugees from El Salvador. They enacted several forms of support, including individual churches sponsoring refugees, gathering food and clothing, raising funds, and seeking out housing and employment for the Central American refugees. Notably, early Catholic involvement in the EBSC also shaped diocese attitudes towards sanctuary in San Francisco.[41] These iterations of sanctuary all provided assistance on an individual level; that said, the covenant's most recognizable act was one of open defiance of the federal government.

On March 24, 1982, EBSC member University Lutheran Chapel (ULC) in Berkeley, alongside Southside Presbyterian Church in Tucson and with the support of the rest of the EBSC, publicly declared sanctuary in the manner most commonly associated with the original sanctuary movement of the 1980s: a house of worship providing shelter to a refugee at risk of being deported. According to a press release from ULC, prior to the declaration it was clear that the congregation and the rest of the EBSC viewed themselves as a collective at the front of a national movement, as they specified that "on Wednesday, March 24, the second anniversary of the death of Archbishop Oscar Romero, Salvadoran refugees will seek sanctuary in churches in California, Arizona, New York, Washington, D.C., Ohio and other places. Several Protestant and Roman Catholic groups will participate from the Bay Area in the event which will center at University Lutheran Chapel . . . in Berkeley." It was clear that ULC had prepared for this to be a big media event as it specified that "a press conference will be held at the chapel on Wednesday, March 24, at 11:00 A.M. Several Salvadoran refugees and representatives from the churches will announce the beginning of the sanctuary and efforts which will be undertaken to stop the deportation of the refugees back to El Salvador." ULC clarified that its actions were in response to a request received from the Session of St. John's Presbyterian Church (fellow EBSC member) in Berkeley, which stated, "We . . . invite you to join us in a covenant to provide sanctuary—support, protection, and advocacy—for the sojourners who have come among us from El Salvador." In the following paragraph it connects its work to the Sanctuary Movement in Tucson (or perhaps connect the Tucson Sanctuary Movement to itself) by sharing a statement issued by the Tucson Ecumenical Council that further explained the importance and relevance of sanctuary: "The tradition of sanctuary in Christian Churches is a living, evolving and transforming story. At different times and places under varied sets of circumstances, the significance of sanctuary has been recovered and taken on new meaning. Today is one of those times. Here is one of those places."[42] This statement of the evolution and continuation of sanctuary would resonate in the Bay Area, which was strongly involved in the Vietnam War sanctuary of the early 1970s, by tying together new and past movements.

In accordance with this declaration, ULC offered safe harbor to three asylum seekers: Luis Rivas, Ronald Sousa, and Jose Cartagena. These refugees resided in the ULC for five days while the EBSC worked on achieving some "short term goals" in accordance with its definition of sanctuary: It raised over twenty-five hundred dollars, secured more than one hundred letters addressed to the Reagan administration protesting the deportations of these refugees, and recruited volunteers to attend deportation hearings in San Francisco as well as volunteers to help refugees seek their legal rights. In the months that followed ULC's public sanctuary declaration, four additional church groups from the Bay Area joined the EBSC: Berkeley Friends Church, Montclair Presbyterian Church, First Baptist Church Task Force, and First Congregational Church Task Force. By September 1983, EBSC grew to have fifteen churches and religiously affiliated groups.

Two months after the declaration of sanctuary on the second anniversary of Archbishop Oscar Romero's assassination, the EBSC's sanctuary efforts began to take on an international dimension. According to its account of events in the first edition of its newsletter, *The Exodus*, in April 1982 local Salvadoran refugees requested that the EBSC's focus be expanded to include refugees still in Central America, as thousands of Salvadoran and Guatemalan refugees fleeing violent repression from their military governments were settled in refugee camps in Honduras. The conditions in these camps were dire and characterized by "extreme hardship." The EBSC claimed that continued persecution and repression, now coming from the Honduran military as well, resulted in many deaths and disappearances and that "only the presence of international volunteer agencies have [*sic*] mitigated these conditions."[43] Scholars frequently have critiqued power dynamics within the Sanctuary Movement that it appears these sanctuary workers were mindful of.[44] *The Exodus* newsletters offered testimonies from EBSC volunteers as to the impacts of their presence in Central America as aid workers and international observers. One volunteer reflected that "none of us is responsible for being born to privilege, but we are responsible for what we do with what we have. It didn't help the refugees for me to feel guilty. It does help them when we do simple things like sending clothing and medicine and observers. And it would help them most of all if we could stop the flow of arms from the U.S. to Central America."[45]

This transnational consciousness reflected in the EBSC was already well established throughout Central American communities in San Francisco. Preceding these sanctuary-affiliated organizations, San Francisco was a locus of transnational grassroots activism organized by Central Americans themselves. As political scientist Héctor Perla Jr. outlines, the Central American Peace and Solidarity Movement (CAPSM), a much larger movement that the Sanctuary Movement ran parallel to in the 1980s, was a "transnational social movement" driven by Nicaraguan and Salvadoran revolutionaries in both Central America and the United States.[46] Perla explains that "Salvadoran and Nicaraguan activists sought support from U.S. transnational substrate actors not to help against their own governments per se but to help against the Reagan administration's policies toward Central America."[47] In doing so, these activists made it a core part of their strategy to rely on symbolic politics such as personal testimonies, religious narratives, and artistic expression to present their struggle in a viscerally tangible way for the North American public. Part of this strategy of encouraging North Americans to take action included encouraging North Americans to visit Central America, such as through volunteer trips with organizations like the SHARE Foundation and EBSC, and to see for themselves the dire situation so that they might utilize their positionality to advocate for an end to US intervention.[48]

Much as in Los Angeles, due to the large Central American immigrant community in San Francisco, revolutionary activists in diaspora were able to mobilize their community, recruit organizers, and form connections with already-established US organizations. The main goal of early grassroots organizing in the 1970s was to draw community attention to the unjust economic conditions and violence that other Central American nationals were suffering from their home governments with US complicity and interventions. San Francisco became home to grassroots organizations such as El Comité Cívico por Nicaragua en los Estados Unidos (Comité Cívico; The Civic Committee for Nicaragua in the United States) and El Comité de Salvadoreños Progresistas (Committee of Progressive Salvadorans), both of which went on to establish newspapers to publicize transnational news, their dissent with the conditions in their home countries, and calls to action. As these groups developed, they participated in direct actions such as protests and were involved in the development of larger solidarity organizations such as the SHARE Foundation, the Committee in Solidarity with the People of El Salvador (CISPES), and the National Network in Solidarity with the Nicaraguan People.[49]

The Salvadoran Humanitarian Aid, Research, and Education (SHARE) Foundation was created in 1981 in Washington, DC, and that same year its sister organization, New El Salvador Today (NEST), was founded in the San Francisco Bay Area.[50] NEST reportedly defined itself as "a tax-exempt non-profit foundation sending humanitarian aid to those whose lives are most affected by the violence of the U.S. supported war," and even featured the mayor of Berkeley as among its board of directors.[51]

The following year SHARE was already providing aid to Salvadoran refugees in a UN-sponsored refugee camp in Honduras, working closely with Catholic Relief Services (CRS) and Mexican Bishop Sergio Mendez Arceo while NEST focused on supporting economic development projects. Notably, NEST facilitated the creation of the first "Sister Community" relationship between the city of Berkeley and San Antonio Los Ranchos in Chalatengo, El Salvador. In 1986, NEST was largely focused on raising funds for humanitarian aid, and did so through events that garnered region-wide attention such as benefit concerts, for instance the "Blues for Salvador" concert in 1988, which featured renowned guitarist Carlos Santana along with other prominent rock musicians, including Tower of Power, Jerry Garcia, and Bonnie Raitt.[52] Perla categorizes the SHARE Foundation as working "directly with the mainstream U.S. religious community," as the foundation "served as an ecumenical hub of information and coordination, linking U.S. parishes with Salvadoran parishes and communities, especially those displaced by the war."[53]

While it was clear that Central Americans were active in grassroots activism and were supporters of solidarity organizations, their involvement with the Sanctuary Movement is more complicated and has received less attention from scholars. Even before the formal formation of the Sanctuary Movement, Central American activists in San Francisco were working in the late 1970s to house the influx of new refugees. According to Perla, among the first of these Central American organizations focusing on the refugee crisis were the Amigos de El Salvador, a spin-off of Salvadoreños Progresistas, and Casa El Salvador Farabundo Martí, which were taking in refugees where their offices were located: the Most Holy Redeemer's Catholic Church in San Francisco. Casa Farabundo Martí then developed into two new organizations that played important roles in the development of the national Sanctuary Movement: the Central American Resource Center (CARECEN) and the Centro de Refugiados Centroamericanos.[54] Despite Central Americans' involvement in, and being at the center of, the Sanctuary Movement, notably paternalistic attitudes toward Central Americans were prominent in the movements, marginalizing and undercutting Central Americans' participation and agency (see chapter 4 of this volume).

Like Los Angeles, Berkeley is also essential to the history of secular sanctuary cities as it is the oldest sanctuary city in the United States. On

February 19, 1985, Berkeley's City Council passed a sanctuary resolution, formally identifying Berkeley as a "city of refuge" and forbidding city employees from assisting investigations or arrests for alleged violations of immigration laws. With the city being the first of its kind nationwide to carry a sanctuary designation, the resolution also encouraged Berkeley residents to work with the sanctuaries in the city to help provide "housing, transportation, food, medical aid, legal assistance and friendship that will be needed."[55] Notably, this sanctuary policy drew directly from an earlier resolution passed by the city council on November 10, 1971, which stated the city's support for congregations in the city that were offering sanctuary to conscientious resistors who refused to fight in the Vietnam War. The parts of the 1985 resolution that called on the city's residents to assist sanctuary sites and prohibiting city employees from assisting or participating in investigations and arrests relating to federal law were drawn "almost verbatim" from the antiwar sanctuary declaration in 1971 and further cemented the importance of the earlier legacy of sanctuary in the city. As Collingwood and Gonzalez O'Brien explain, "Berkeley's 1985 resolution, like most sanctuary city policies, was based on the Sanctuary Movement but it also drew on an older tradition in the city of resistance to federal laws that residents, and the city council, saw as morally problematic."[56] San Francisco's "City and County of Refuge" ordinance, also known as the Sanctuary Ordinance, was first passed the same year as Berkeley's 1985 sanctuary resolution and later expanded more broadly in 1989.[57] This ordinance "generally prohibits City employees from using City funds or resources to assist Immigration and Customs Enforcement (ICE) in the enforcement of Federal immigration law unless such assistance is required by federal or state law," but lacked the rhetoric indicating support for the broader Sanctuary Movement seen in Berkeley's resolution.[58] As we will see, almost thirty years after the San Francisco ordinance passed, San Francisco's sanctuary-city status would feature at the center of nationwide immigration debates, which were in part about public safety concerns, local jurisdictions, and federal enforcement, as part of the New Sanctuary Movement.

The New Sanctuary Movement

Los Angeles

After many Central Americans were able to receive work authorization and protection from deportation in the settlement of the 1991 *American Baptist Churches v. Thornburgh* case, many considered the 1980s Sanctuary Movement successful. However, in the early 2000s and particularly following the terrorist attacks of September 11, 2001, xenophobia arose throughout the country and new legislation, such as the failed Sensenbrenner Bill proposed in 2005, targeted undocumented people who already had put down roots in the country.[59] Sanctuary activists once again opened their doors to fight for immigrant rights—this time, the focus was on undocumented immigrants who already had established lives and families in the United States rather than on newly arrived refugees.[60]

Los Angeles and San Francisco maintained their importance as sites of sanctuary activism in the New Sanctuary Movement. Faith leaders, as in the 1980s, would take pro-immigrant stances in the public sphere, which in Los Angeles notably included Catholics. Los Angeles Cardinal Roger M. Mahony, already familiar with the sanctuary activism of the 1980s, especially from his disagreements with Olivares's staunch advocacy, gained national media attention when he decried as "un-American" the Sensenbrenner Bill, which aimed to increase punishments against undocumented immigrants and to penalize individuals providing aid to them. Although Garcia's biography of Father Olivares alleges that Mahony was hesitant to get behind sanctuary activism in the 1980s, by the early 2000s he had publicly embraced the cause of immigrant justice, sending out informational packets on immigration to all of his district's parishes.[61] Mahony's public embrace of immigrant-rights activism reflects changes within the Catholic Church's approach to immigration on a nationwide level.

Indeed, Catholics on an institutional, international level would be early proponents of sanctuary work and activism and would call for structural changes. On January 22, 2003, the United States Conference of Catholic Bishops (USCCB) and the Conferencia del Episcopado Mexicano (Mexican Episcopate Conference) published a pastoral letter entitled "Strangers No Longer: Together on the Journey of Hope," in which Mexican and American bishops came together to address the topic of migration. The letter outlined the longstanding history and present state of migration in the Americas from a Catholic perspective, highlighted common misconceptions of migrants, and called for a "conscientious revision" of immigration laws to protect the dignity and human rights of migrants.[62] It also boldly and clearly stated that "we, the Catholic bishops of the United States and Mexico, pledge ourselves to defend the migrant" and asserts that they will continue to advocate for fair migration policies.[63] Two years later, in following the call for action from "Strangers No Longer," the USCCB launched the Justice for Immigrants: A Journey of Hope campaign with the primary objectives of educating the public on the Catholic Church's teachings on migration and immigrants, advocating for positive immigration reform on a political level, and organizing Catholic networks to assist immigrants who qualified to benefit from the reforms.[64]

The Archdiocese of Los Angeles was particularly ready to implement the Justice for Immigrants (JFI) campaign. It quickly joined this nationwide effort and formed a steering committee to implement the JFI within the diocese, bringing a distinctly Catholic approach to immigrant-rights advocacy. Its first priority was to reach out to parishes in the hope that large numbers of Catholics would come to embrace and mobilize for immigration reform. While the USCCB's JFI campaign was optional but encouraged for local dioceses and parishes, the campaign provided legitimacy and precedent for the use of the church's structure and influence to engage local community issues.[65] One of the first major actions of the Los Angeles Archdiocese's JFI campaign occurred during Lent in 2006, when Mahony called upon Catholics to "commit their Lenten practices of prayer, fasting, and good works to immigration reform." Sociologist Luisa Heredia argues that this call signaled the clear religious foundation of the campaign's fight for immigrant rights. Furthermore, during the height of the debates around the Sensenbrenner Bill, Cardinal Mahony called for a "special day of prayer and fasting" on April 5, 2006. That day he celebrated mass at the Cathedral of Our Lady of Angels, where he asked Catholics to pray for legislators who were debating immigration reform as well as fast in solidarity with undocumented migrants who would be affected by the bill.[66]

La Placita would continue to be an important place and space for sanctuary activism in post-9/11 Los Angeles. It continued to operate immigrant-support programs and even hosted an immigrant-rights coalition in its name: The La Placita Olvera Working Group, composed of immigrant-rights organizations working in La Placita, would organize the first major march in Los Angeles against H.R. 4437 on March 25, 2006.[67] The site would also continue to be a frequent stage for migrant-rights performances. Sanctuary seeker and activist Elvira Arellano, who became a national symbol in the US immigration debate when she took sanctuary in a Chicago church in 2006, traveled to Our Lady Queen of Angels Church in 2007 and publicly took sanctuary in the church as part of a nationwide sanctuary tour. La Placita would be the last place Arellano would speak in sanctuary, as she would ultimately end up being detained by ICE agents on August 19, 2007, after she left the church with her son and a supporter.[68] Arellano's sanctuary at the site highlighted Los Angeles's significance in the broader sanctuary movement, as well as La Placita's cultural, religious, and historical importance in the movement.

Outside of the Catholic Church, various other interfaith coalitions also formed that would become key fighters for immigrant rights in Los Angeles. Clergy and Laity United for Economic Justice (CLUE) was first formed by progressive faith leaders and their allies in 1996 to advocate for a living-wage law. In 2000, Reverend Alexia Salvatierra, a Lutheran pastor and sanctuary organizer active in the 1980s movement, became the first full-time director of CLUE, and under her guidance, CLUE continued its fight for economic justice but also expanded to other social-justice issues, including the New Sanctuary Movement.[69] Pierrette Hondangeu-Sotelo explains that CLUE became "among the strongest of the sixty religious-based labor support organizations in the country."[70] CLUE joined with the Interfaith Worker Justice (IWJ) in 2006 to coordinate New Sanctuary Movement activism on the grounds that many of the most exploited workers were immigrants. Both their New Sanctuary Movement activism and their union activism were rooted in scripture and ancient religious traditions.[71] CLUE and Salvatierra played a central role in mobilizing the Los Angeles New Sanctuary Coalition. By 2008 between fifteen and twenty religious communities were regularly involved with supporting the four immigrant families who had entered sanctuary in houses of worship in Los Angeles. Most of the religious communities affiliated with CLUE were themselves immigrant congregations, or had a history of social religious activism.[72]

While CLUE would continue to be essential in New Sanctuary Movement activism in the 2010s, Salvatierra would move on to become the *madrina* (godmother) of another sanctuary organization: Matthew 25/Mateo 25. This organization is a bipartisan effort that began during the first Trump presidency and is composed of mainline and evangelical clergy with varying amounts of experience with the Sanctuary Movement, some having been engaged since the 1980s while others were newcomers. What set Matthew 25 apart was its appeal to evangelicals specifically, offering a number of resources for English- and Spanish-speaking congregations that reconceptualize sanctuary and advocacy for immigrants (traditionally perceived as "liberal" actions) as part of an evangelical spiritual praxis. They sought to encourage churches to divorce caring for the migrant from the political axis and to view it as a purely spiritual act, drawing from the Bible, particularly the titular Matthew 25 passage, to do so. Although in recent years the organization has distanced itself from the term "sanctuary," preferring to embrace the term "accompaniment," Matthew 25 continues to be active in the Los Angeles immigrant-rights movement.[73]

Los Angeles, and the broader Southern California region, maintained their status as a hub for immigrant-rights activism during the New Sanctuary Movement. Los Angeles has remained a cradle for religious sanctuary activism well into the twenty-first century, notably for the Catholic Church but also for interfaith and evangelical organizations like CLUE and Matthew 25. La Placita church, in particular, continued its practice of sanctuary harboring for Elvira Arellano, one of the most high-profile sanctuary seekers in the 2000s.

San Francisco Bay Area

San Francisco organizers continued their sanctuary legacy as they joined the New Sanctuary Movement. But they would inadvertently end up under fire in the nationwide immigration-restriction debate in the 2010s because of their sanctuary-city status and the death of Kate Steinle. In light of President Trump's 2016 election and his 2015 campaign, during which the Steinle shooting was a frequent talking point, many congregations that had been involved in sanctuary work since the 1980s reiterated their investment in the movement.[74] While the legacy of Vietnam War and 1980s Central American sanctuary activism was a strong influence in the Bay Area New Sanctuary Movement, it cannot be overstated how important the Kate Steinle shooting was as antisanctuary politicians and pundits made San Francisco their preferred target.

Kathryn "Kate" Steinle, thirty-two, was tragically shot in the back and killed while walking with her father and a friend along Pier 14, a well-trodden section of the Embarcadero district of San Francisco. The shooter, José Inez García Zárate, a Mexican man living in the United States without documentation, said he had found the gun moments before underneath a bench he was sitting on and that it was wrapped in a cloth, and when he picked it up the weapon went off. The shot ricocheted off the concrete pier and struck Steinle. On November 30, 2017, a jury acquitted García Zárate of all murder and manslaughter charges, and then federal manslaughter and assault charges were dropped due to lack of evidence. He was, however, convicted of illegally possessing a firearm. Republican California state Senator Ted Gaines stated in response to the verdict that "when he steals across the border again I'm sure he'll run right back into the lawless, loving arms of San Francisco or someplace else in our Sanctuary State, because he knows he'll get the protection here that Kate Steinle couldn't."[75] President Trump, who spoke frequently of the shooting during his 2015 campaign as a reason why immigration needed to be restricted particularly at the Mexican border, described the 2017 verdict as disgraceful and tweeted, "No wonder the people in our country are so angry with illegal immigration. His exoneration is a complete travesty of justice. BUILD THE WALL!"[76] Gaines also decried the fact that García Zárate's immigration status was not discussed in court and deemed irrelevant by the judge despite his having been deported five times previously. BBC coverage of the trial outcome explained that because Republicans oppose the sanctuary-city movement, in the aftermath of the trial they began popularizing the hashtag "#BoycottSanFrancisco," which trended on Twitter the morning of the acquittal.[77] Anti-immigrant and anti–sanctuary city legislation followed. In 2015 Senator Ted Cruz and Congressman Matt Salmon of Arizona introduced "Kate's Law," formally known as HR 3011, the Establishing Mandatory Minimums for Illegal Reentry Act of 2015, a bill that ultimately failed. But shortly thereafter the House passed the Enforce the Law for Sanctuary Cities Act.[78] Although Kate Steinle's name was widely invoked by those who called to punish sanctuary cities, Steinle's family had expressed more complicated feelings on the matter, saying that while they believed the sanctuary-city law should remain in place, its current implementation was flawed.[79]

Just days after taking office in 2017, President Donald Trump signed Executive Order 13768, which included instructions to withhold federal funding from sanctuary cities such as Los Angeles, San Francisco, New York, and Chicago. This executive order alleged that "sanctuary jurisdictions across the United States willfully violate Federal law in an attempt to shield aliens from removal from the United States. These jurisdictions have caused immeasurable harm to the American people and to the very fabric of our republic." Although in 2017 there were over four hundred sanctuary jurisdictions, it would be California cities that would lead the efforts against this order.[80] San Francisco and Santa Clara County successfully sued the administration in the Ninth US Circuit Court of Appeals, and California US District Judge William Orrick ruled the order "unconstitutional on its face" and permanently blocked the order.[81] However, throughout his first presidency Trump would continue to target sanctuary cities, notably considering releasing migrants detained at the border into left-wing, sanctuary cities.[82] From the beginning of the first Trump presidency, San Francisco would center in public nationwide sanctuary debates. His presidency and national attention on the issue also fueled sanctuary activism within the Bay Area itself.

On July 13, 2016, in anticipation of the Trump administration's anti-immigrant policies, University Lutheran Chapel reaffirmed its commitment to sanctuary, announcing as part of a press conference a new apartment for sanctuary seekers, which it created by converting an office in the basement of the building, and declaring that it would be available to Bay Area residents who needed refuge from deportation back to violence and persecution in Central America. The chapel was particularly concerned about individuals who would be separated from their families by deportation. The press conference highlighted the voices of two migrants facing deportation: Jeremías Martínez Rodríguez, an unaccompanied minor who left Honduras to escape violence, and Julissa Oliva, whose husband was being held in immigration detention.[83]

The press release for the event historicized the significance of this (re) declaration. It explained that "although exactly 30 years ago, the city of

Berkeley declared itself a city of sanctuary and many East Bay Congregations were involved in the Sanctuary movement of the 1980s, the ongoing deportations and failure of federal immigration reform has [*sic*] left many recent and long-term immigrant communities under grave threat."[84] The declaration was accompanied by nationwide calls for a moratorium on deportations while faith communities around the United States were beginning to reignite the tradition of offering sanctuary. University Lutheran Chapel's declaration garnered both secular-civil and religious support, being made in partnership with the East Bay Interfaith Immigration Coalition and with the support of the City of Berkeley. Its pastor, Reverend Jeff Johnson, explained that "as a faith community, we are doing what Congress has refused to do: protect immigrants from an immigration system that is separating families and deporting people who are woven into the fabric of their communities and congregations."[85] As part of the press conference, Johnson led a blessing ritual for the sanctuary apartment, including sprinkling holy water, swinging incense around the door, and having those in attendance sing and pray for the protection of the space, establishing the apartment as a thoroughly sacred space. Outside the doors of the church itself, the congregation hung brightly colored prayer ribbons to display the community's commitment to and solidarity with sanctuary seekers.[86]

Although a second wave of the New Sanctuary Movement most clearly crystallized under the first Trump presidency, the East Bay Sanctuary Covenant continued to fight for immigrant rights well into the Biden presidency, this time taking to the courts. In *East Bay Sanctuary Covenant v. Biden*, the Covenant, represented by the ACLU Immigrant Rights Project, the ACLU of Northern California, the National Immigrant Justice Center, the UC College of the Law, and San Francisco's Center for Gender and Refugee Studies addressed the "asylum ban" at the US-Mexico border issued on May 10, 2023. The Covenant, with the assistance of these additional immigrant-rights law organizations, filed the suit arguing that Biden's ban violated asylum laws and would result in the unlawful return of refugees to countries where their lives were in danger. The legal challenge was filed in the US District Court for the Northern District of California on May 11, 2023, just a few hours before the asylum ban was to take effect. Although the asylum ban was originally found unlawful on July 25, 2023, the Biden administration appealed the decision, and a few weeks later the Ninth Circuit granted the administration's request for a stay of the ruling pending the resolution of its appeal. On February 21, 2024, the Ninth Circuit issued a published decision granting the jointly filed motion by the two parties to hold the case in abeyance so that they could attempt to settle the case. However, on March 7, 2024, the states of Alabama, Georgia, Kansas, Louisiana, and West Virginia filed a motion to intervene in the litigation by claiming they would be harmed if the ban was lifted. By the spring of 2026, a federal district court reaffirmed an earlier ruling and vacated the ban, arguing that it violated the country's asylum laws.[87]

This nationally important case replays the past while leading critical fights for nationwide immigrant rights. The East Bay Sanctuary Covenant, frequently cast to the sidelines in histories of the 1980s Sanctuary Movement, features as a key plaintiff in an immigrant-rights case, much like the 1980s Sanctuary Trials and the 1991 *American Baptist Churches v. Thornburgh* case that successfully advocated for fair asylum proceedings for Central American refugees. In doing so, the case affirms how California sanctuary activists, and sanctuary activism more broadly, continue to be key players in the fight for immigrant rights on local, state, and national levels.

Conclusion

From the 1980s to the present, Los Angeles and the San Francisco Bay Area have been essential sites for sanctuary activism. Their local Sanctuary Movement networks are essential for understanding both religious and secular sanctuary activism in and of their own right. But beyond these cities, the state of California itself has also followed suit in paving new roads for sanctuary activism.

California has long been and will continue to be an epicenter of sanctuary debate. On October 5, 2017, California passed SB-54, the California Values Act, also commonly referred to as the "Sanctuary State" law.[88] This act ensures that no state or local resources can be used to assist federal immigration enforcement. Thus, police and sheriffs cannot ask about an individual's immigration status or cooperate with immigration agents such as Immigration and Customs Enforcement (ICE) or

Border Patrol even for the purposes of language interpretation.[89] While many celebrated this act, which, by its own name, enshrined sanctuary values in the state, there are still those who denounce it. For example, California Congressman Kevin Kiley put forward his No Sanctuary for Criminals Act of 2023, which seeks to end sanctuary policies around the nation, calling out California by name and claiming that its sanctuary-state status allows for violent individuals to be released back into the community.[90] The result of this bill remains to be seen. Meanwhile, the state of California, with sanctuary provisions in place, to some degree prepared itself for Trump's second presidency, as Trump vowed to launch the largest militarized mass deportation in US history. Communities closest to the border seemed to be at greater risk due to the higher number of ICE and Border Patrol agents. State support would matter more than ever in the face of an extreme federal crackdown. Naureen Shah, deputy director of government affairs at the American Civil Liberties Union, explained that Trump "doesn't own our states. And our states will be the frontline in the defense of our civil liberties and our civil rights."[91] Immediately following Trump's election, former mayor of San Francisco and current California Governor Gavin Newsom summoned the legislature to a special session that began on December 2, 2024. He vowed to "protect California values" as the state began to brace for renewed clashes with the incoming administration.[92] Beyond the state level, cities once again affirmed their sanctuary status. Less than two weeks after the November 2024 election, Los Angeles's city council unanimously voted to formally establish Los Angeles as a sanctuary city.[93] San Francisco's current mayor, Daniel Lurie, along with other city leaders, reaffirmed San Francisco's sanctuary-city status a week after Trump's inauguration.[94] The notable and ongoing public exchange between Newsom, sanctuary-city leaders, and Trump to a large extent stems from fundamental disagreements about sanctuary.

California has established itself as an important state in the history of sanctuary activism both for itself, being an important sanctuary state, and for two historically essential nodes in the movement—Los Angeles and the San Francisco Bay Area. These sites have established themselves as key players for both religious and secular sanctuary. Both cities have large immigrant populations that were and remain actively involved in sanctuary activism. Sanctuary organizing there has defined itself as a bulwark against the federal government with the support of local and state governments. There is no doubt that California activists and the state itself will continue to play a critical role in nationwide immigration debates and immigrant-rights activism going forward.

NOTES

1 Lloyd Barba and Sergio González, "Ep. 6 Part 1: Sanctuary in the Pews and in the Streets," *Sanctuary: On the Border Between Church and State*, produced by Axis Mundi Media, podcast, MP3 audio, 22:00–22:06, https://redcircle.com.

2 See chapter 1 of this volume.

3 Pierrette Hondagneu-Sotelo, *God's Heart Has No Borders: How Religious Activists Are Working for Immigrant Rights* (University of California Press, 2008), 2–3.

4 This chapter's "top down" approach consists of analyzing organizational and civic histories of sanctuary organizing rather than focusing on individual sanctuary seekers and activists. Individuals' experiences and motivations are critical in this history; however, the purpose of this chapter is to trace the development of organizational and jurisdictional approaches to the concept of sanctuary in order to better understand the lasting effects of these networks on local and statewide immigrant-rights activism.

5 Norma Stoltz Chinchilla, Nora Hamilton, and James Loucky, "The Sanctuary Movement and Central American Activism in Los Angeles," *Latin American Perspectives* 36, no. 6 (2009): 101–26.

6 For more on Latinx groups working in and alongside churches to support refugees, see Mario T. García, *Father Luis Olivares, a Biography: Faith Politics and the Origins of the Sanctuary Movement in Los Angeles* (University of North Carolina Press, 2018) and Felipe Hinojosa, *Apostles of Change: Latino Radical Politics, Church Occupations, and the Fight to Save the Barrio* (University of Texas Press, 2021).

7 Southern California Christian Forum, "SCEC History," last accessed February 3, 2025. www.scec1.org.

8 Sean Dempsey, *City of Dignity: Christianity, Liberalism, and the Making of Global Los Angeles* (University of Chicago Press, 2023), 107.

9 Dempsey, *City of Dignity*, 108.

10 Dempsey, *City of Dignity*, 108.

11 See Dempsey, *City of Dignity*, 109–10, quotation on 109.

12 Dempsey, *City of Dignity*, 111. A version of this statement would be personally delivered to the president-elect's Southern California home in December 1980 by Father Wayne King of the Catholic Maryknoll House in Los Angeles and Toni Stuart, regional coordinator of Clergy and Laity Concerned.

13 Dempsey, *City of Dignity*, 111.

14 See Dempsey, *City of Dignity*, 112–14, for more.

15 Dempsey, *City of Dignity*, 114.

16 García, *Father Luis Olivares, a Biography*, 371.
17 Chinchilla, Hamilton, and Loucky, "The Sanctuary Movement and Central American Activism in Los Angeles," 108.
18 Chinchilla, Hamilton, and Loucky, "The Sanctuary Movement and Central American Activism in Los Angeles," 109.
19 Larry Stammer, "Churches Become Part of Illegal Alien Chain," *Los Angeles Times*, February 7, 1983. Cited in Chinchilla, Hamilton, and Loucky, "The Sanctuary Movement and Central American Activism in Los Angeles," 109.
20 For more on the work of women in the 1980s Sanctuary Movement, see Robin Lorentzen, *Women in the Sanctuary Movement* (Temple University Press, 1991).
21 Chinchilla, Hamilton, and Loucky, "The Sanctuary Movement and Central American Activism in Los Angeles," 121.
22 Chinchilla, Hamilton, and Loucky, "The Sanctuary Movement and Central American Activism in Los Angeles," 109.
23 See Dempsey, *City of Dignity*, 119, for more.
24 Dempsey, *City of Dignity*, 119.
25 Dempsey, *City of Dignity*, 120.
26 García, *Father Luis Olivares, a Biography*, 248.
27 García, *Father Luis Olivares, a Biography*, 308.
28 For more on Latinx leadership in the Sanctuary Movement, see Robert Chao Romero, *Brown Church: Five Centuries of Latina/o Social Justice, Theology, and Identity* (Intervarsity Press Academic, 2020); Lloyd Barba and Tatyana Castillo-Ramos, "Latinx Legacies and Leadership in the U.S. Sanctuary Movement, 1980–2020," *American Religion* 3, no. 1 (Fall 2021): 1–24; and Brad Christerson, Alexia Salvatierra, Robert Chao Romero, and Nancy Wang Yuen, *God's Resistance: Mobilizing Faith to Defend Immigrants* (NYU Press, 2023).
29 García, *Father Luis Olivares, a Biography*, 312.
30 García, *Father Luis Olivares, a Biography*, 161.
31 García, *Father Luis Olivares, a Biography*, 317.
32 García, *Father Luis Olivares, a Biography*, 319.
33 Iglesia La Placita Nuestra Señora La Reina de Los Angeles Santuario Público Para Refugiados Centroamericanos (12 Diciembre 1985), Box 6, Folder 22, Darlene Nicgorski Papers on the Sanctuary Movement, Special Collections, Honnold/Mudd Library, The Claremont Colleges Library, Claremont, California (translation mine).
34 García, *Father Luis Olivares, a Biography*, 321.
35 García, *Father Luis Olivares, a Biography*, 342.
36 Loren Collingwood and Benjamin Gonzalez O'Brien, *Sanctuary Cities: The Politics of Refuge* (Oxford University Press, 2019), 17. Collingwood and Gonzalez O'Brien argue that the policy was initiated to increase cooperation between the large Latinx and undocumented communities in Los Angeles and law enforcement and not as part of a larger immigrant-rights organizing effort.
37 Collingwood and Gonzalez O'Brien, *Sanctuary Cities*, 18.

38 Collingwood and Gonzalez O'Brien, *Sanctuary Cities*, 18.
39 Collingwood and Gonzalez O'Brien, *Sanctuary Cities*, 19.
40 *The Exodus: East Bay Sanctuary Coalition Newsletter* 1, no. 1, August 1982, Graduate Theological Union Archives Manuscript Collection, East Bay Sanctuary Covenant Collection, Box 1, Folder: *Exodus* 1982–1984, 1–2.
41 See Sergio M. González, "Catholics and the 1980s U.S. Sanctuary Movement," *U.S. Catholic Historian* 42, no. 2 (Spring 2024): 96–97.
42 "Salvadorans to Seek Sanctuary in U.S. Churches" (Gustav Schultz Sanctuary Collection, Box 1, Folder 13, Graduate Theological Union Archives, Berkeley, California). Emphasis preserved from source material.
43 *The Exodus*, 2.
44 See Chinchilla, Hamilton, and Loucky, "The Sanctuary Movement and Central American Activism in Los Angeles"; Héctor Perla Jr., "Si Nicaragua Venció, El Salvador Vencerá: Central American Agency in the Creation of the U.S.–Central American Peace and Solidarity Movement," *Latin American Research Review* 43, no. 2 (2008): 136–58; and Barba and Castillo Ramos, "Latinx Legacies and Leadership in the U.S. Sanctuary Movement, 1980–2020."
45 *The Exodus: East Bay Sanctuary Coalition Newsletter* 1, no. 3, October 1982, Graduate Theological Union Archives Manuscript Collection, East Bay Sanctuary Covenant Collection, Box 1, Folder: *Exodus* 1982–1984, 4.
46 Perla, "Si Nicaragua Venció, El Salvador Vencerá," 138.
47 Perla, "Si Nicaragua Venció, El Salvador Vencerá," 142.
48 Perla, "Si Nicaragua Venció, El Salvador Vencerá," 143.
49 Perla, "Si Nicaragua Venció, El Salvador Vencerá," 144–48.
50 "History," SHARE Foundation, last accessed January 17, 2025. www.share-elsalvador.org.
51 "Subject: Third/Fourth US-Based FMLN/FDR Support Activities Underway," Declassified CIA Document: CIA-RDP90M00005R000800050048-2, December 3, 1986, Declassified and Approved for Release May 3, 2013, www.cia.gov/; pg. 0007.
52 Jos. Sances, Artist, and Publisher Mission Gráfica, *"Blues for Salvador"—Building a New El Salvador Today: El Salvador Oakland California, 1988* (Mission Gráfica). Photograph. Library of Congress item 201564550, last accessed February 3, 2026. www.loc.gov.
53 Perla, "Si Nicaragua Venció, El Salvador Vencerá," 150.
54 Perla, "Si Nicaragua Venció, El Salvador Vencerá," 153.
55 Berkeley City Council, 1985, cited in Collingwood and Gonzalez O'Brien, *Sanctuary Cities*, 31.
56 Collingwood and Gonzalez O'Brien, *Sanctuary Cities*, 31; see also chapter 1 of this volume.
57 "San Francisco Approves Bill to Designate It as a Sanctuary," *The New York Times*, December 24, 1985; Chapter 12H: Immigration Status, San Francisco Administrative Code, www.sf.gov/information--sanctuary-city-ordinance.
58 Chapter 12H.

59 Grace Yukich, *One Family Under God: Immigration Politics and Religion in America* (Oxford University Press, 2013), 24–29.
60 See Amalia Pallares, *Family Activism: Immigrant Struggles and the Politics of Noncitizenship* (Rutgers University Press, 2014).
61 Hondangeu-Sotelo, *God's Heart Has No Borders*, 2.
62 United States Conference of Catholic Bishops, Inc. and Conferencia del Episcopado Mexicano, "Strangers No Longer: Together on the Journey of Hope," January 22, 2003. www.usccb.org; line 104.
63 United States Conference of Catholic Bishops, Inc. and Conferencia del Episcopado Mexicano, "Strangers No Longer: Together on the Journey of Hope," lines 105–6.
64 United States Conference of Catholic Bishops, "Justice for Immigrants: The Catholic Campaign for Immigration Reform," last accessed January 17, 2025, www.usccb.org.
65 Luisa Heredia, "From Prayer to Protest: The Immigrant Rights Movement and the Catholic Church," in *Rallying for Immigrant Rights: The Fight for Inclusion in 21st-Century America*, ed. Kim Voss and Irene Bloemraad (University of California Press, 2011), 94–111, 98–99.
66 Heredia, "From Prayer to Protest," 101.
67 Heredia, "From Prayer to Protest," 105.
68 Sonia Nazario and David Pierson, "Agents Arrest Immigrant Activist," *Los Angeles Times*, August 20, 2007.
69 CLUE: Clergy and Laity United for Economic Justice, "Our Story," last accessed January 17, 2025, www.cluejustice.org.
70 Hondangeu-Sotelo, *God's Heart Has No Borders*, 76.
71 Hondangeu-Sotelo, *God's Heart Has No Borders*, 105.
72 Yukich, *One Family Under God*, 17.
73 See Christerson, Salvatierra, Chao Romero, and Wang Yuen, *God's Resistance*, for more on the Matthew 25 Movement. Salvatierra and Chao Romero served as founders of the organization.
74 Barba and González, "Ep. 6 Part 1: Sanctuary in the Pews and in the Streets," 20:44–21:22.
75 Ted Gaines quoted in "Sanctuary Policy Killed Kate Steinle," *Gaines Gazette*, January 2, 2018, https://lcmspubcontact.lc.ca.gov.
76 "Kate Steinle: Trump Outrage over Murder Case Acquittal," *BBC News*, December 1, 2017, www.bbc.com.
77 "Kate Steinle: Trump Outrage over Murder Case Acquittal."
78 Barba and González, "Ep. 6 Part 1: Sanctuary in the Pews and in the Streets," 19:49–20:44.
79 John Diaz, "Kate Steinle's Relatives—in Their Own Words," *San Francisco Chronicle*, September 11, 2015. www.sfchronicle.com.
80 Anthony Zurcher, "Trump Starts a 'Sanctuary City' War with Liberal America," *BBC News*, January 26, 2017. www.bbc.com.

81 "Trump Transgender and Immigration Policies Meet Legal Defeat," *BBC News*, November 21, 2017. www.bbc.com.
82 Eileen Sullivan, "Trump Says He Is Considering Releasing Migrants in 'Sanctuary Cities,'" *New York Times*, April 12, 2019, www.nytimes.com.
83 Tracey Taylor, "Local Church Offers Sanctuary to Those Facing Deportation," *Berkeleyside*, July 14, 2016, www.berkeleyside.org.
84 Robyn Gee, "Media Advisory: Religious Communities Pledge Protection from Deportations; Chapel Ready to Provide Sanctuary," University Lutheran Chapel of Berkeley, July 12, 2016, www.ulcberkeley.org.
85 Gee, "Media Advisory," 2.
86 Gee, "Media Advisory," 2; Taylor, "Local Church Offers Sanctuary to Those Facing Deportation."
87 "East Bay Sanctuary Covenant v. Biden," Center for Gender and Refugee Studies at UC College of the Law, San Francisco, California, last accessed January 17, 2025, https://cgrs.uclawsf.edu; "EBSC v. Trump: An Explainer for Advocates on Vacatur of the Circumvention of Lawful Pathways Rule," National Immigrant Justice Center, May 18, 2026, https://immigrantjustice.org.
88 "The California Values Act–SB 54 (de León)," California Immigrant Policy Center, December 1, 2021. https://caimmigrant.org.
89 "California Values Act (SB 54)," ACLU Southern California, last accessed January 17, 2025, www.aclusocal.org.
90 "Kiley Introduces Nationwide Ban on Sanctuary Policies," Congressman Kevin Kiley, California's 3rd District, July 19, 2023. https://kiley.house.gov.
91 Wendy Fry, "'What's Going to Happen to My Kids?': California Prepares to Resist Trump Deportations," *CalMatters*, November 25, 2024, https://calmatters.org.
92 Fry, "'What's Going to Happen to My Kids?'"
93 Nithya Raman, "District 4 Press Releases: City Council Votes to Establish Los Angeles as a 'Sanctuary City,'" November 19, 2024, https://cd4.lacity.gov.
94 Dave Pehling, "San Francisco Officials Reaffirm Sanctuary City Status amid Ramped-Up Immigration Enforcement," *CBS News*, January 28, 2025, www.cbsnews.com.

10

The Sacred Power of Place

Local Histories, Activist Legacies, and the Making of Sanctuary People in Northeast Ohio

GINA M. PÉREZ

Introduction

On February 21, 2017, the city of Oberlin, Ohio, passed a resolution to "reaffirm and extend Oberlin's welcoming commitments to persons and families of all backgrounds and nationalities, including those who have entered the United States as refugees fleeing war and terror in other countries."[1] Like other municipalities, counties, and jurisdictions across the nation following President Donald Trump's inauguration the previous month, Oberlin's sanctuary resolution was clearly a response to the vitriolic anti-immigrant sentiment that defined his campaign. These sanctuary resolutions further responded to the three executive orders he signed within his first week in office. These included Executive Order 13780, which authorized the so-called Muslim travel ban; Executive Order 13779, which directed federal funding for new construction of the border wall along the US-Mexico border; and Executive Order 13768, "Enhancing Public Safety in the Interior of the United States," which strengthened immigration-enforcement priorities to focus on the interior United States, reinstated federal and state agreements such as 287(g) that had been abandoned during the Obama administration, and penalized sanctuary cities.[2] Oberlin's resolution was an affirmation of the city's 2009 public declaration to support immigrants in the wake of a local workplace raid in 2008 that resulted in the detention and deportation of several restaurant workers in the city. The response was also grounded in more than a century's worth of activism, organizing, and resistance by residents of the city and members of Oberlin College.

The community's activist legacy includes challenging the 1850 Fugitive Slave Act, welcoming Japanese American students during the period of Japanese internment during World War II, embracing students, faculty, and staff from Kent State University following the killing of four students protesting the Vietnam War in May 1970, and supporting the 1980s Sanctuary Movement involving Central American migrants. In short, Oberlin's sanctuary resolution in 2017 was swift, was public, and reflected longstanding political commitments that define the city.

In the nearby city of Lorain, less than ten miles from Oberlin, there was no formal sanctuary resolution at the municipal level following President Trump's election. As a city with a large Latina/o population (primarily Puerto Rican and Mexican, and increasingly Central Americans), a growing number of im/migrant families, and a distinguished history of Latina/o leadership and community organizing, Lorain has not been immune to the immigration-enforcement policies that have led to fear, family separation, and immigrant detention and deportation beginning in the mid-2000s.[3] But it is also a place where residents proudly embrace its identity as "the International City," and that has nurtured and benefited from robust immigrant-led organizing and faith-based networks of support, as well as community leaders and elected officials who have been unwavering in their support of immigrant residents. In 2013, for example, Lorain's police chief, Celestino Rivera, put in place specific practices that are often regarded as sanctuary policies.[4] This decision was deeply influenced by immigrant organizers working with Catholic faith leaders from Sacred Heart Chapel to draw Rivera's attention to the ways practices such as routine traffic stops had resulted in immigrant detention and deportation proceedings for many Lorain residents. These changes fostered trust among immigrant-rights organizers, undocumented migrants, and local police over the years, which, in turn, helped create networks of communication, support, and reassurance during the first Trump administration, a time marked by fear, precarity, and profound uncertainty. In essence, faith communities, service organizations, community leaders, and elected officials in Lorain acted in ways that very much resembled the efforts in sanctuary cities like Oberlin, even while Lorain did not declare itself a sanctuary city.

This chapter brings into focus the sacred power of place in shaping sanctuary practices during Trump's first term. Cities like Lorain and

Oberlin have long histories of resistance struggles that communities of faith drew on to ground, fortify, and sustain their contemporary actions, including the distinctive ways the Sanctuary Movement and the wars in Central America in the 1980s informed their approaches. But their understandings were also deeply informed by a broader set of freedom movements—the history of nineteenth-century abolitionist struggle, the civil rights and Chicano movements of the 1960s, and the antiwar, feminist, and anti–nuclear arms movements of the 1970s and 1980s. By focusing on the distinctive experiences of faith-based activists in Lorain and Oberlin, I draw attention to the ways local histories inform the responses, resistance, and possibilities of faith-based organizing and the meanings these histories infuse into contemporary efforts to create sacred refuge. In doing so, I build on the important work of scholars who have documented different coalitions and strategies of the New Sanctuary Movement (NSM) to challenge deportation and family separation, including family activism and other diverse practices that exceeded earlier understandings of sanctuary.[5] In what follows, I focus on the power of local history to ground contemporary immigrant, refugee, and asylum justice and the distinctive role that faith-based organizing plays in efforts to create spaces of refuge and safety for Latinas/os in a time of precarity and great uncertainty. History, place, and faith-based organizing play a crucial role in not only creating spaces of refuge and safety for Latinas/os in a time of precarity and great uncertainty but also in nurturing the efforts of sanctuary people in this collective work.

Sanctuary in Ohio

Between 2016 and 2020, Ohio was home to five people who publicly sought sanctuary in a church, making the state home to one of the largest numbers of public sanctuary cases in the country. According to a Church World Service report from 2018, thirty-seven people entered into public sanctuary in 2017, a 65 percent increase from the previous year, defining this time as one when "more people [were] taking Sanctuary in congregations than at any time since the 1980's."[6] The dramatic rise in public sanctuary cases was concomitant with the proliferation of faith communities developing or joining existing sanctuary coalitions, declaring themselves sanctuaries for immigrants, and organizing with other groups to "prophetically confront the administration's immoral and unjust deportation policies."[7] By January 2018, more than eleven hundred houses of worship and forty coalitions were engaged in actions that demonstrated the enduring ways that "faith resistance continues to grow against harsh and inhumane immigration policies."[8]

In addition to public sanctuary, Ohio is home to cities and counties that have long histories of formal and informal sanctuary policies and practices. By mid-November 2016, local news reports identified at least eight "sanctuary locations" in the state and various efforts to expand and challenge them.[9] As in other cities across the country, these efforts were rarely seamless or uncontested and reflected longer struggles about sacred resistance. Faith traditions were not immune to the divisions that sanctuary practices engendered. Indeed, while some mainline Protestant churches in Ohio mirrored national trends in declaring themselves sanctuaries, many did not. For example, Presbyterian, Mennonite, and Lutheran congregations welcomed people like Leonor Garcia, Edith Espinal, and Miriam Vargas, respectively, and relied on a robust ecumenical network of volunteers from across faith traditions, including Roman Catholics who often questioned and debated what their local parish and diocesan responses should be. These debates were informed by histories of struggle that defined particular places and organizations. More specifically, the Diocese of Cleveland's longstanding relationship with El Salvador, particularly throughout the country's US-backed civil war, offered a model of accompaniment in the face of state-sanctioned power and violence that many Catholics admired. The brutal deaths of four women from the diocese in 1980 were both a sober reminder and a source of admiration of the kind of moral courage many hoped would define the church's responses in the face of the devastating impact of migrant detention, deportation, and inhumane family separation.

Legacies of Accompaniment and Welcoming the Stranger

The Jesuit Retreat Center is a quiet, bucolic space in the bustling city of Parma, just south of Cleveland. In addition to its more than fifty acres of meadow, woodlands, and walking trails, the retreat center is also home to four beautiful chapels, including the small Martyr's Chapel dedicated to nuns, priests, and laypeople who were murdered during the civil war in El Salvador. Inside the sparsely decorated chapel are two comfortable chairs and a simple wooden altar. Natural light filters in from the south-facing window that looks out onto a garden courtyard. Along the walls are framed lithographs, drawings, and watercolor portraits that together tell a story about martyred men and women serving God through their dedication to the poor. The watercolor painting features the faces of the six Jesuit priests, the caretaker, and her daughter, who were brutally assassinated in their residence at the Universidad Centroamericana on November 16, 1989. Words like "truth" and "history" appear around some of the faces, as well as carefully handwritten reflections about service, community, and social justice. Along another wall are two drawings of four women—Ita Ford, Maura Clarke, Dorothy Kazel, and Jean Donovan. One of the drawings features the faceless profile of each of the women done in soft dark charcoal with the title "Martyrs for Justice" appearing below. The other pencil drawing features their smiling faces, a drawing quite familiar to those who mourned their vicious murder on December 2, 1980, nine months after the assassination of Archbishop Oscar Romero on March 24, 1980. On a small wooden table, there is a typed narrative protected in plastic that provides a brief description about these women's lives in El Salvador as well as excerpts from letters and journal entries they wrote during their time working with the poor and war-displaced. Below the heading "Martyrs for Justice" is the following text:

> These four North American churchwomen, Ita, Dorothy, Maura and Jean, responded to God's call to be one with the poor of El Salvador. Aware that the depth of their compassion and commitment could cost them their lives, they freely chose not only to live with them and for the people of El Salvador but also to die with them.
>
> On December 2, 1980, they were brutally tortured and murdered by members of El Salvador's National Guard. Through the memory and witness of the life and death of Ita, Dorothy, Maura and Jean, may we too respond to God's continuing call to solidarity with the poor.[10]

Sister Dorothy Kazel, OSU, was one of many nuns, priests, and laypeople from the Cleveland diocese who had served in El Salvador beginning in the mid-1960s and had been part of the Cleveland Diocesan Latin

American Mission Team in El Salvador since 1974. Jean Donovan joined the Cleveland mission in 1979 and worked with Dorothy, as well as Sister Ita, MM, and Sister Maura, MM, who had arrived in El Salvador earlier that year after years of working in Chile and Nicaragua, respectively.[11]

Like thousands of others who were inspired by liberation theology's call to serve and embrace a life dedicated to a preferential option for the poor, Dorothy, Jean, Ita, and Maura remained in El Salvador, even when it became clear that their work was increasingly dangerous and as priests, nuns, laypeople, and thousands of Salvadorans were detained, tortured, and killed during the brutal civil war. Dorothy explained her decision to remain in a letter to fellow Ursuline Sister Martha Owen:

> We talked quite a bit today about what happens if something begins. And most of us feel like we would want to stay here . . . if there is a way we can help, like run a refugee center or something. We wouldn't want to just run out on the people. . . . I thought I should say this to you because I don't want to say it to anyone else because I don't think they would understand. Anyway, my beloved friend, just know how I feel and "treasure it in your heart." If a day comes when others will have to understand, please explain it for me.[12]

This fierce commitment to remain in El Salvador was echoed by Maura Clarke, who wrote,

> I am beginning to see death in a new way. We have been meditating a lot on death and the accepting of it, as in the Good Shepherd reading. There are so many deaths everywhere that it is incredible. It is an atmosphere of death. The work is really what Archbishop Romero calls "acompañamiento," accompanying the people, as well as searching for ways to help. This seems what the Lord is asking of me, I think, at this moment. We are on the road continually, bringing women and children to refugee centers. Keep us in your heart and prayers, especially the poor forsaken people.

Ita Ford also wrote about her commitment to accompaniment, explaining, "I have no solutions to this situation, but I will walk with you, search with you, be with you." Jean Donovan reflected on how this process had forever transformed her, leaving her with little choice but to remain in

El Salvador: "I love life and I love living. . . . Several times I decided to leave. I almost could, except for the children—the poor, bruised victims of this adult lunacy. Who would care for them? Whose heart could be so staunch as to favor the reasonable thing in a sea of their tears and loneliness? Not mine, dear friend, not mine."

In an article commemorating the fortieth anniversary of Dorothy, Ita, Jean, and Maura's death, Margaret Swedish, a leading figure in the Central American solidarity movement in the 1980s and director of the Religious Task Force on Central America and Mexico from 1981 to 2004, explicitly connects the violence, trauma, and unrest of the 1980s in El Salvador with the injustice, violence, and unrest in the United States in 2020:

> In any historical moment, we are called to enter the reality in which we live and together to read the signs of the times. The violence and injustice experienced by the people of El Salvador was the foundation from which the four US churchwomen discerned what it would mean to accompany the poor and to follow Jesus in their time.
>
> So what of our time? How do we understand this moment in the human journey as we come to the end of this traumatic year? The list of the year's sufferings is long: the pandemic, the collapsing economy and increase in poverty and hunger, the police killings of Black men and women that sparked angry protests around the nation, the resurgence of white nationalism, the raging wildfires in the West and a record Atlantic hurricane season fueled by our warming planet.
>
> We have seen the collapse of good governance and furious political polarization that threatens our democracy. Fear of change, fear of things getting out of control, extreme individualism—these are all signs of a society in crisis, fragmenting as our problems appear increasingly insurmountable.
>
> We must ask ourselves: Where will we take our stand in the midst of such uncertainty?[13]

Swedish continues by reflecting on the importance of discernment—a process, she argues, that should be done in community rather than in isolation and that she describes as a "lost skill in a culture where we never seem able to take the time to just stop and think about what we are doing and why. But it requires some radical shifts in our vantage points, not least of which is stepping into the reality of the suffering ones of our world and seeing the world through their eyes." A crucial feature of this discernment process is understanding history and hearing stories like these so we understand the "historical thread that runs through our history to this day." These sentiments echo those of sanctuary people, individuals whose work is grounded in their understanding of the relationship between faith and social-justice activism, the importance of the history of particular places, and how those histories and the "historical thread" connect their actions in the present with those of the past.[14]

The Cleveland diocese's decades of work in El Salvador is an example of how history, place, and faith ground contemporary faith-based activism. Every person involved in sanctuary work in Lorain and connected to Sacred Heart Chapel, for instance, made reference to this history, even if they had varying degrees of understanding of the details of the relationship to El Salvador. Sister Cathy from Sacred Heart Chapel, for example, described the many ways the parish was unique and distinct as a specifically Hispanic/Latina/o parish that emerged as a result of community organizing in the 1960s and whose mission has always been guided by a commitment to working in Latin America. "This is a unique parish," she explained. "And I think the parishes that have the missionaries from El Salvador from the diocese are the parishes that are the most socially conscious and who have a heart for the immigrant." While Sister Cathy's religious community, Sisters of the Humility of Mary, sent community members to Chile, she reflected on the impact of the Cleveland diocese's enduring relationship with El Salvador:

> The Cleveland Diocese responded by opening up a mission in El Salvador and offering priests and sisters and laity of the diocese to parishes. This enabled other communities to send sisters there instead of opening their own missions. . . . The Sisters of St. Joseph were a part of it. . . . Akron Dominican sisters were a part of it. And the Ursulines . . . made a commitment to always send sisters. . . . There were about ten years where the missionaries would watch the temperature increase in El Salvador before the war. Then there was the war and then there was the postwar. We never

> left. Other dioceses opened up missions, then when there was a revolution, they took their missionaries back. Cleveland never did. And even when Dorothy and Jean were killed, the team met with the bishop and said, "They can't leave." And the bishop let them stay.[15]

This history not only inspired and instructed; it also shaped the priorities and set the expectations of people responding to the rising anti-immigrant sentiment and policies that had a devastating impact on the communities in Lorain. José Mendiola, for example, explained his involvement in programs like Welcoming the Stranger and Compañeros (the Parish Companion Program) that were designed to "accompany parishioners who are in the final stage of immigration removal proceedings, or who are at risk of removal."[16] He also participated in a delegation sponsored by the Cleveland Diocese to the US-Mexico border in 2019 and worked with Sister Rita Mary Harwood from the diocesan office to collect items for the families affected by the workplace raid on Corso's Garden Center in June 2018. This raid resulted in the detention of 114 people and led to a large number of deportations and family separations that devastated Northeast Ohio Latina/o communities. José also worked with immigrant families at Sacred Heart Chapel and participated in the parish's prison visitation program.[17] All of this work, according to José, is grounded in his understanding of Catholic social teaching that includes welcoming immigrants and the stranger and has been a guiding feature of his faith-based activism.[18] It is probably for this reason that he expressed disappointment when the Cleveland diocese stated its decision not to be involved in offering physical sanctuary to immigrants seeking to avoid deportation. José described attending meetings throughout the diocese beginning in 2017 where this question was repeatedly raised, debated, and ultimately rejected by the Catholic Church hierarchy in Cleveland. In one meeting with Bishop Pérez, it became very clear that the diocese's position would be to continue to support its important work with valuable programs like Welcome the Stranger, develop new ones like Compañeros, and continue to train and offer legal resources to those who needed them. But sanctuary was not an option. José explained, "The Diocese of Cleveland said, no, we will not do sanctuary. . . . I was very disappointed. There were a lot of other people that were disappointed." And although he praised the diocese for its other interventions and support, he also expressed admiration for Protestant churches that, despite the legal concerns that were raised about offering physical sanctuary, chose to do so anyway:

> I really have to hand it to the other denominations. They didn't care [about repercussions]. They went ahead and did what they thought was right. Not that we did the wrong thing. We just went about it in a different way. I truly believe that what we're doing at the diocese level with the Welcome the Stranger Committee has had a real impact on our community. They go to different churches and talk to people who are not informed about immigration. I'm talking about Anglo people who don't know anything about immigration. I talk to them and tell them, "These are the facts. Now you decide what you want to do and believe."[19]

José was, of course, not the only one disappointed with the diocese's response. Celestino Rivera, for example, described tense meetings where he was told not to pursue this issue. This was particularly painful since Celestino knew that there were priests who believed that the church was being called to offer sanctuary as a way to challenge an unjust legal system and state power as well as to be a fearless witness. He explained,

> We were having a meeting about sanctuary about the same time [people in Oberlin] were having meetings. And they were talking about the reality of churches being sanctuary and whether that's a good move. . . . If I had to judge the mood, I would say that most of them felt like it's not the right thing to do because at some point they have to leave sanctuary. Where do they go from there? And that's the kind of pragmatic conversations we were having.
>
> When Bishop Pérez came, he cut the conversation off almost immediately and said, "We're not doing it. Period." . . . Well, [one Franciscan priest] said to the bishop, "Bishop, I have to differ with you. How can we teach the Word on Sunday and then not live it Monday through Saturday? . . . Respectfully, I want to tell you that in my parish, they understand what you do unto others—they understand. They understand welcoming the stranger. They want to do something to live that. And if somebody comes to our church and asks for our help, I believe they're going to offer that help." And the bishop says, "I'm telling you, we're not doing it." And

> so I say, "I'm sorry for this, Bishop, but you know what? If you've ever dealt with these people, and I am sure you have, they are so humble. They are so full of faith. If their church doesn't speak up for them, then what chance do they have?" That's all I said to him. Now he turned his anger to me and said, "You should know better, because it's the law." And I said, "Bishop, you know and I know and everybody knows that sometimes they make bad laws. And it's people of faith, it's people of goodwill who make those sacrifices to get those laws changed. There was a time when . . . people had to ride in the back of the bus. There was a time when [African Americans] couldn't drink out of the same fountains [as whites]. . . . But good people came forward and sacrificed and it changed."[20]

Celestino's frustration during this meeting was exacerbated by what he knew about the history of the diocese and a visit to El Salvador he had made years before with one of the priests whom he deeply admired. He recognized the courage of people who, in the past, challenged the status quo in order to remain faithful to their beliefs, even at great cost to themselves. This is what animated people like Celestino, José, Anabel, Sister Cathy, and Father Bill. And it is an important point of reference for the work they continue to do, even when there might be disagreement about the strategies, tactics, and decisions they make. But what guides them is this history of resistance, offering refuge, and bravely challenging state and even clerical power when necessary. As Anabel observed when she reflected on her own experiences, "I never thought that the Lorain chief of police would be on my side, that he would be taking the day off to go with me to my check-ins. For me, that was awesome. Undocumented immigrants are afraid of police officers. Having now the chief of police coming with me and standing by my side saying, 'She's not a criminal.' That was just God's grace."[21] Anabel's comfort in having Celestino, the chief of police, on her side also points to another example of the importance of place. Lorain, for example, never declared itself a sanctuary city. This was a deliberate decision that reflected a keen understanding of the local political culture of Lorain, a city with a long and proud history as the International City, but one that, like other formerly progressive spaces in Ohio, became increasingly conservative politically in ways that shaped conversations and approaches around immigration. As we saw earlier, Celestino Rivera navigated these dynamics carefully by putting in place clear policies governing when the Lorain Police Department would or would not collaborate with federal immigration officials, policies that ultimately protected undocumented residents and largely resembled those of a sanctuary city. In doing so, he demonstrated admirable courage but was also acutely aware of the ways local political, economic, and cultural forces shape what is possible and what is not.

Oberlin, however, has a completely different history. And this history not only enabled it to be public in its sanctuary-city declaration in 2018 but also facilitated religious congregations and local activists taking bold actions following the 2016 presidential election. In fact, many of the faith-based activists I interviewed and talked with over the years explained that it was living in Oberlin and being inspired by the city and college's history that, in many ways, facilitated, supported, and even compelled them to take public and decisive action. As historians Gary Kornblith and Carol Lasser have meticulously documented in their book *Elusive Utopia: The Struggle for Racial Equality in Oberlin, Ohio*, both the city and the college were founded as "an experiment dedicated to radical racial egalitarianism," as the residents believed "that they followed the teachings of Christianity in their embrace of racial equality and that, by ridding the world of the sins of slavery and color prejudice, they would bring about the redemption of humankind." While Kornblith and Lasser also note that this utopian vision was both short-lived and elusive, Oberlin's history of standing "at the vanguard of the abolition and black freedom movements" is frequently invoked as activists justify and persuade others of the need to support contemporary social-justice movements.[22] Indeed, many have shared that it is precisely this history that draws people to live in Oberlin. Others point either to the ways this legacy led them to faith-based activism or to the way it was further cultivated by living in a city with a long history of sacred resistance.

As Steve Hammond shared his experiences in seminary and his search for a church that he could be a part of once he was done with his studies, he described the challenge of finding a place that shared his "vision of the church":

> I realized when I left seminary that I was not going to be able to go to your typical Baptist church. . . . My vision of the church was more social justice–oriented, more community building, trying to give people—the big phrase that came to me in seminary that I should have heard long before seminary was "the Kingdom of the Realm of God." And I was trying to piece that together, because that's what Jesus talks about so much—the realm of God, this world being the realm of God. So I talked about that [in my interviews with executive ministers in seminary helping graduating students find a job]. And one not only shooed me out of his office, but he wrote a letter to me afterwards, despairing about the state of the church that they were turning out graduates like me [laughs]. That the church was going to have absolutely no future. . . . But one of those meetings was with a guy named John Sundquist, who was the executive minister in Ohio. And our fifteen minutes turned into an hour and a half, and we had a great conversation. He understood, and we understood each other. And then he said, "I'd love to have you in Ohio, but there's no place for you in Ohio." So I got up to leave and was on my way out the door when he said, "Wait a minute, wait a minute." And he got his briefcase and said, "Have you ever heard of a place called Oberlin? . . . There's a church there. . . . I think you ought to give it a try."[23]

Steve and his wife did, indeed, give Oberlin a try, even though the job had an uncertain future. There had been talks about closing the church, but they decided to hire Steve for two years to see whether the church would grow, which it did, providing a spiritual home and community that shared Steve and Mary's vision of social justice. Later in my interview with Steve, he returned to this prescient conversation with John Sundquist that led him to take a job with an uncertain future in Oberlin. "That professor said, 'Oberlin's where you want to be.' He knew the history of Oberlin. He knew me and he knew that this is where I should go. He said, 'Go there. Whatever it takes to go there, because that's the place for you.' That heritage sure inspired me. . . . You walk through Tappan Square and you think about all the people who have walked through there. It's pretty crazy to think about."[24]

Oberlin's heritage includes its residents' involvement with nineteenth-century abolitionist movements and its prominent role in the Underground Railroad, challenging the Fugitive Slave Act of 1850, welcoming

Japanese American students in the wake of the passage of Executive Order 9066 in 1942, and welcoming students and faculty following the Kent State tragedy in May 1970.[25] Steve and others invoked this history when explaining why they supported sanctuary and grounded this commitment in their religious beliefs as well:

> I think Jesus would offer people sanctuary. If Jesus is head of the church, shouldn't the church be a place of safety? Not just the building itself, but our church communities. Shouldn't they be sanctuary? And again, if you live in the empire, you're going to have to choose now and then. The empire may not like it if you're harboring people. But you know, that is what this town's about. From the slavery abolitionist days, the government didn't like what they were doing [in Oberlin]. But they did it anyway. And they understood it as what it meant to be Christians. . . . That's the heritage of the church in this town. And we need to keep it going.[26]

Part of the way they kept this work going is through the peace vigil that a small, committed group of protestors participate in every Saturday morning on the corner of Main and College Streets, which began following the September 11 attacks in 2001. They have also kept this work going by participating in activism that does not only emerge from faith-based organizing but also benefits from ecumenical collaborations, like SANE Freeze in the 1980s and, more recently, Black Lives Matter organizing.

John Gates also described how living in Oberlin and Oberlin's history played a pivotal role in nurturing his social-justice activism and inspiring him to be involved in faith-based work. He described how when he and Linda first arrived in Oberlin in the early 1970s, they did not have a church community, but that soon changed when he learned about First Church:

> Oberlin's history played a role in it too. . . . The first college to admit women and people of color. I really think it played an important role for me, you know, this is the kind of society I wanted to be a part of. So I tried to emulate the people that were here and that I thought were speaking out for justice. . . . Oberlin played a very important role in my wanting to become more involved in political action that would bring justice to the United States. . . . What First Church was trying to do and what the his-

> tory of Oberlin [shows us] is to do what is right. That's what we all should be working for. For a common understanding of brotherhood, sisterhood and [against] the unequal distribution of wealth.[27]

Being inspired by a history of social justice led John and Linda to decades of faith-based activism, including housing and working with Central American migrants fleeing US-fueled wars in the 1980s, solidarity with returning communities in Guatemala beginning in the 1990s, and the New Sanctuary Movement beginning in the mid-2000s. These efforts, John explains, are part of the way he both honors the history of Oberlin and contributes to a vision of community he seeks to help create. "A lot of it has to do with the community that I want to live in. I think the community in Oberlin is really rich in that regard. . . . I owe it to the community to do better and to give back. To strengthen areas of compassion and justice and love wherever I can."[28]

Like John, David Hill also shared how Oberlin's history shapes the work he and others do around sanctuary and how the kind of activism that seemed exceptional and life-changing when he was younger is a regular part of people's lives in Oberlin. When he worked as a pastor in Jefferson, Ohio, the county seat of Ashtabula County, he described attending vigils to protest the US invasion of Iraq and how it would be

> me, the Lutheran pastor, and two United Methodists. And that was the whole crowd. . . . I discovered [something] through that. I started going to protests because I wanted to change things and discovered pretty quickly that it didn't matter how many thousands of people showed up in Washington, it wasn't going to change policy. But I kept going because it changed me. It had an effect on me. . . . It gave me a chance to hang out with other people and listen to how they expressed their concerns, how they connected it with their faith life. And that was instructive to me so I could better lift that out of people. And then I came to Oberlin where we have protests and vigils all the time.[29]

These protests and vigils, of course, included antiwar demonstrations and the regular Saturday noon protest for peace on Main Street, and they also included immigration issues. On July 23, 2008, ICE agents raided the restaurant Casa Fiesta in Oberlin and detained five employees. This was one of eight workplace ICE raids that summer that included seven other Casa Fiesta restaurants in Northeast Ohio and resulted in a total of fifty-eight immigrants being arrested and some ultimately deported.[30] Activists and community members in Oberlin mobilized protests and offered support. For some, including David Hill, this was their first experience feeling the outrage of losing valued community members and confronting the consequences of immigration enforcement and the deportation regime that ripped apart families and communities. David described the challenge of wanting to be a pastor who could speak to people as they struggled to make sense of the impact immigration detention had on their community, particularly on the family members of detained migrants who resided in Oberlin and were devastated by the raid. As a faith leader, he also had conversations with the Oberlin police chief and attended community meetings and sessions of the Oberlin City Council where it was clear that there was a divide between what the police chief believed was his job, to enforce laws, and broader community outrage at immigration-enforcement policies that were ripping families and the community apart. David observed, "My sense was that [the Oberlin police chief] had a good sense of what Oberlin was all about and was trying to walk this very challenging line between Oberlin's values and what the law calls him to do and the values of his colleagues in the broader Lorain County that were different than Oberlin's."[31]

David's observation about the ways Oberlin's progressive values come into conflict with more conservative ones—and in this case, anti-immigrant sentiment—was on display in Oberlin City Council meetings where largely non-Oberlin residents angrily decried attempts to pass a sanctuary-city ordinance. David recalls, "It was really, really ugly. A lot of shouting and . . . repetitive [bashing of immigrants]. I remember at one point the chair of city council—I think it was Ronnie Rimbert at the time, saying, 'No. We've heard that argument. . . . We're not going to have any more repetitive [immigrant bashing].'" Indeed, African American elected leaders like Ronnie Rimbert and African American faith leaders and community activists played an important role in challenging anti-immigrant sentiment and enacting the city's 2009 public declaration to support immigrants. This statement was an important foundation for the passage of Oberlin's sanctuary-city statement in 2017. These actions demonstrate how immigration issues in Oberlin are "a natural flow in

Oberlin's history." Yet the resistance also confirms Kornblith and Lasser's prescient observations about the elusive quality of Oberlin's quest for racial equality. The utopian vision that defined Oberlin's founding was similarly challenged by racist resistance. But perhaps more importantly, it was undermined by "well-meaning actions that can have unintended consequences." They write, "Amid today's continuing struggle for the conscience and soul of America, we need the courage to envision a future of racial justice, an inclusive and productive multicultural politics, an economy of abundance widely shared, and a society of mutual respect, generosity, and dignity. Dreams are dangerous, imperfect, and powerful. They are also elusive, as are the utopias we imagine."[32]

The elusive power of dreaming into being egalitarian and inclusive places of safety clearly animates the work of sanctuary people. It requires constant vigilance and the labor of dedicated people who are willing to reach out across difference, to see ways to connect people who are often structurally and socially distant, and to illuminate the ways one's well-being is intimately bound up with that of others. This is not easy work. Sarah Johnson, for example, spoke quite poignantly about how challenging it was to bridge often vast divides and how emotionally difficult it felt "being the only link in the chain" that connected people who clearly needed, depended on, and relied on one another. These chains form bridges that span linguistic, cultural, educational, race, class, and religious communities and are rooted in the unglamorous work of sanctuary people. As an Oberlin College graduate who worked for NISGUA in Guatemala before returning to Northeast Ohio to work in immigrant-rights organizing and as a staff member at El Centro de Servicios Sociales (El Centro) in Lorain, Johnson was quite familiar with the challenges and need to build bridges link by link.[33] Like Sarah, Victor Leandry also frequently reflects on the important work of bringing different communities together. And although his role as the director of a social service agency like El Centro seems to fall beyond the realm of faith-based organizing, he is also a vital bridge between different communities—secular and religious; white, upper-middle-class and Latina/o working-class; long-term African American and Latina/o residents of Lorain; community foundations, philanthropists, and service providers and those receiving services. These differences map onto geographies of opportunity and disinvestment that have a profound impact on the way people respond in moments of crisis. But they are also spaces of opportunity to bring people together in surprising and mutually beneficial ways.

Conclusion: Overcoming Evil with *Valor y Dignidad*

Nancy Finke described how after years of living in Chicago and then back in Missouri where she grew up, she and her husband, David, wanted to return to live in Oberlin, something they had been "thinking about" and "planning for a long time." Although she and David had been involved in faith-based work as students at Oberlin College in the 1960s, she said that once they returned to Oberlin in 2016, they originally planned to not get involved in anything "for a year, although we knew that was kind of impossible." They did not intend to join anything but rather to "just kind of live here and get to know everybody and get to know people at Kendall and at the Quaker meeting and the college. I expected we would be doing more with the college . . . because we were here [as students]. But then two months [after we arrived], Trump was elected. And we just got sucked up into the political work. So we have been pretty active with Lorain County Rising and Community Peace Builders and the Quaker Community." While working with immigrants and sanctuary work were new experiences for Nancy, she sees a connection between that work and the range of activism she has done in Oberlin, Chicago, Missouri, and now in Oberlin once more. As she reflected on the sanctuary work she has been involved in, she elaborated on how her own personal history also influenced her:

> Just wanting to live, wanting to help. To help fill a need. . . . I think maybe for me—my dad was killed when I was two, and so I think about how my mom and I were separated from him and I think that's part of the strong feeling [I have] about this. The notion that children would be deliberately taken away from their parents and . . . that parents put their children on a train and say, "Leave." I just can't imagine that. . . . And somehow to alleviate that would be a good thing. [Long pause.] I guess one thing that gives sanctuary its power is that we're defying evil. Quakers don't talk about evil very much. They [chuckles]—we laugh sometimes because in the Quaker hymnal, some of the hymns have been revised to take out words like "sin." We see God in everyone, which is a good thing. But still,

> there is evil. There are enemies. One of our Quaker friends gave a lecture and said, "Jesus said, 'Love your enemy.' But he never said there is no enemy" [nods approvingly at that statement]. That's good. I'll write that one down.[34]

Acknowledging that there is evil in the world was not something that people like Nancy did very often. In fact, it is rather remarkable how little faith-based organizers talked about evil. "Injustice," "racism," "xenophobia," "white supremacy," "homophobia," "fascism," and "anti-immigrant sentiment" were the terms they used to describe the problems they sought to ameliorate in their modest ways.

Doing so, however, was no easy feat and required sustained efforts across time and space. And it also required organizations, institutions, churches, faith communities, and, above all, personal commitment. Celestino Rivera poignantly referred to this as "*valor y dignidad*"—courage and dignity, the name that he hoped to give his own nonprofit one day. As he spoke about his disappointment with the Catholic Church hierarchy's position on public sanctuary, his disillusionment with what he perceived to be a lack of broader outrage about the political climate, and his plans after his retirement, Celestino reflected on the trajectory of his career in law enforcement and how to build something different, meaningful, and enduring through his dream organization, Valor y Dignidad:

CR: I guess the way I look at it is, I've got limited time. And I want to make an impact while I can. Do you know what my biggest goal is? [Pauses and smiles.]

GP: What?

CR: I already know what my obituary is going to say. [Pauses again.] "Former police chief dies." [Laughs.] If I could somehow change that to "Community activist dies," I'd be a happy person. I don't want that to be my [only] legacy anymore. I know that doesn't sound right.

GP: No, no. It doesn't sound bad.

CR: I'm trying to figure that out. How can I best impact the world? I thought maybe writing would do it. But I don't know how to do that. And I don't know anything about a blog. And I don't know anything about starting one. I just thought maybe if I [started] an organization like Courage and Dignity, then maybe I would just do that work

> under that organization. And then reach out to certain people who I know. . . . I love working with people who actually do things. Who just really care. You can tell right here [points to his heart].[35]

Celestino was absolutely right when he predicted what his obituary would say. Sadly, on June 22, 2022, Celestino Rivera died unexpectedly of heart failure. His obituary did, indeed, pay homage to his many years as Lorain's police chief. But it also detailed the extensive contributions Celestino made to Lorain, his family, Ohio, and beyond. And it also included the dozens of organizations he belonged to and helped create, and the surprising number of awards and recognitions he received. Celestino humbly served so many in so many ways. And his reflections on the importance of *valor y dignidad* capture what was at the core of his vision of what it means to be sanctuary people. For José, Anabel, Sister Cathy, John, Sarah, David, Nancy, and thousands of others in Ohio and beyond, being sanctuary people is about a fierce commitment to community, to justice, and to accompanying others along journeys that are not easy, but are made lighter when done in communion. It is also about having courage in the face of state power to fight and preserve the dignity of others. *Valor y dignidad*—courage and dignity—are at the heart of being sanctuary people.

NOTES

1 Oberlin City memo from Jon D. Clark, law director, to Ronnie Rimbert and Oberlin City Council members, February 17, 2017. For the city of Oberlin's sanctuary resolution, see City of Oberlin Resolution No. R17–04 CMS, https://cityofoberlin.com. This chapter is based on chapter 4 of Gina M. Pérez, *Sanctuary People: Faith-Based Organizing in Latina/o Communities* (NYU Press, 2024).

2 Executive Order 13758, "Enhancing Public Safety in the Interior of the United States," January 25, 2017, www.federalregister.gov.

3 I use "im/migrant" here to capture the fact that as US citizens, Puerto Ricans moving to cities like Lorain are free to move (migrate) across geopolitical borders and boundaries and do not face the specter of illegality and transnational border crossing that immigrants arriving in the United States do.

4 Loren Collingwood and Benjamin Gonzalez O'Brien observe, "There is no concrete definition of just how exactly a sanctuary city should be defined," although broadly speaking sanctuary policies are ones that "limit local cooperation in federal enforcement to varying degrees." Loren Collingwood and Benjamin Gonzalez O'Brien, *Sanctuary Cities: The Politics of Refuge* (Oxford University Press, 2019), 6,

3. Rivera, who led the Lorain Police Department for twenty-five years, implemented policies instructing his officers neither to inquire about the immigration status of people reporting crimes, who are stopped due to minor traffic violations, or who have other minor offenses, nor to notify ICE when Lorain police detained someone who was undocumented.

5 For a discussion of family activism, see Amalia Pallares, *Family Activism: Immigrant Struggles and the Politics of Noncitizenship* (Rutgers University Press, 2015). Grace Yukich's book *One Family Under God: Immigration Politics and Progressive Religion in America* (Oxford University Press, 2013) provides a careful discussion of the changing practices, meaning, and coalitions in the New Sanctuary Movement.

6 Myrna Orozco and Noel Andersen, "Sanctuary in the Age of Trump: The Rise of the Movement a Year into the Trump Administration," Church World Service, January 2018, 5. The numbers of people living in public sanctuary shifted between 2016 and 2020 as some were able to leave and others entered for various legal reasons. Noel Andersen from the Church World Service noted that by 2019 the organization was aware of forty-four people living in sanctuary throughout at least fifteen states, see Yonat Shimron, "Sanctuary Churches Say Fines Against Immigrants Meant to Sow Fear," *Religion News Service*, July 3, 2019, https://religionnews.com.

7 Orozco and Andersen, "Sanctuary," 6. In Ohio and throughout the United States, sanctuary coalitions sometimes emerged organically in response to the immediate needs of migrants. They also developed through ongoing social-movement work to address issues such as police violence in communities of color, criminal justice reform, and LGBTQ rights.

8 Orozco and Andersen, "Sanctuary."

9 Cleveland 19 News identified eight sanctuary locations: Columbus, Dayton, Lima, Lorain, Oberlin, and Painesville, as well as Lake and Lucas Counties. On January 30, 2017, Cincinnati formally declared itself a sanctuary city, with other cities like Cleveland Heights passing welcoming-city resolutions. See Amanda Horncz, "Ohio's 8 Sanctuary Locations and What It Means for Immigration Matters," *Cleveland 19 News*, November 16, 2016, www.cleveland19.com; Jason Williams and Dan Horn, "Cincinnati a 'Sanctuary City': What's That Mean?," *Cincinnati Enquirer*, January 30, 2017, www.cincinnati.com; Thomas Jewell, "Cleveland Heights Opts for 'Welcoming City,' as Opposed to Sanctuary Status on Immigration," *Cleveland Plain Dealer*, February 7, 2017, www.cleveland.com.

10 "Martyrs for Justice," n.d., informational paper in Martyr's Chapel, Jesuit Retreat Center, Parma, Ohio. In author's files.

11 Dorothy Kazel was an Ursuline Sister, while Ita Ford and Maura Clarke were Maryknoll Sisters.

12 "Martyrs for Justice."

13 Margaret Swedish, "Ita, Maura, Dorothy, Jean: The Legacy of 4 Missionaries Murdered in El Salvador 40 Years Ago," *America*, December 2, 2020. Swedish's

powerful article is notable for a number of reasons. As an admired leader in the Central American sanctuary movement in the 1980s and in solidarity work with Central and Latin Americans more broadly, her focus on these women's lives in the esteemed Jesuit monthly *America* reminds readers of the central role women religious and laypersons have played in progressive faith-based social movements in the United States and globally that are sometimes overlooked and/or forgotten. Her reflections are also an invitation to consider how Swedish's own life and commitment to solidarity struggles are deeply grounded in local histories. In a 2007 *StoryCorps* oral history interview, Swedish poignantly describes how growing up in Milwaukee nurtured her lifelong commitment to progressive, faith-based activism. "I feel this incredible love for my city . . . I love it, all its warts are there . . . I feel a real gift having grown up in a town like this. . . . It's part of who I am that I will never let go. And now I realize it's maybe some of the best that I have." "Margaret Swedish and Janet Frey," *StoryCorps*, August 11, 2007, https://archive.storycorps.org.

14 Swedish, "Ita, Maura, Dorothy, Jean." See Pérez, *Sanctuary People*. My use of "sanctuary people" draws on the term used by the late community activist Ruben Castilla Herrera to refer to those whose activism is grounded in an understanding of shared struggle and a commitment to create places of safety and refuge for all.

15 McConnell, interview by author, January 21, 2019. McConnell's observations of the undeterred commitment of Catholic religious from the Diocese of Cleveland as well as the Dominican and Ursuline Sisters to remain in El Salvador points to the important role Catholic religious orders played in Central and Latin America and the United States in the face of significant political persecution.

16 Parish Companion Program Handbook, Catholic Diocese of Cleveland, updated December 5, 2018. In author's files.

17 See Pérez, *Sanctuary People*.

18 In a joint pastoral letter from the United States Conference of Catholic Bishops and the Conferencia Episcopado Mexicano, the Catholic Bishops of the United States and Mexico reaffirmed the church's steadfast commitment to immigrants, stating the following: "We seek to measure the interests of all parties in the migration phenomenon against the guidelines of Catholic social teaching and to offer a moral framework for embracing, not rejecting, the reality of migration between our two nations. We invite Catholics and persons of good will in both nations to exercise their faith and to use their resources and gifts to truly welcome the stranger among us (cf. Mt 25:35)." United States Conference of Catholic Bishops, "Strangers No Longer: Together on the Journey of Hope," January 22, 2003, www.usccb.org. The reference to Matthew 25:35 and the exhortation to "welcome the stranger" is the biblical basis for Catholic social teaching and ecumenical responses to immigrants. This position by the USCCB, however, did not foster widespread diocesan support for physical sanctuary or the New Sanctuary Movement (NSM) in the United States; see Sharon Erickson Nepstad, *Catholic Social Activism: Progressive Movements in the United States* (NYU Press, 2019); Mario T.

García, *Fr. Luis Olivares, a Biography: Faith, Politics, and the Origin of the Sanctuary Movement in Los Angeles* (University of North Carolina Press, 2022). The USCCB's position on immigrants and welcoming the stranger, however, did not foster majority support for physical sanctuary or the NSM in the United States. Sergio M. González, "Catholics and the 1980s U.S. Sanctuary Movement," *U.S. Catholic Historian* 42, no. 2 (2024): 87–115.

19 Mendiola, interview by author, Amherst, Ohio, October 31, 2019.

20 Celestino Rivera, interview by author, Oberlin, Ohio, August 1, 2019.

21 Anabel Barrón Sánchez, interview by author, Lorain, Ohio, August 14, 2019.

22 Gary Kornblith and Carol Lasser, *Elusive Utopia: The Struggle for Racial Equality in Oberlin, Ohio* (Louisiana State University Press, 2018), 2.

23 Steve Hammond, interview by author, Oberlin, Ohio, August 13, 2019.

24 Hammond interview.

25 In the spring of 2018, Oberlin College faculty, staff, and alumni, as well as city residents, collaborated to develop a traveling interactive exhibit titled "Courage and Compassion," which documented the role of Oberlin City and the college in enrolling Japanese American students and providing them refuge and safety in the town and on campus during Japanese internment. This exhibit was supported by the Go For Broke National Education Center and the National Park Service. See *Courage and Compassion: Our Shared Story of the Japanese American World War II Experience*, February 16, 2018, www.oberlin.edu.

26 Hammond interview.

27 John Gates, interview by author, Oberlin, Ohio, July 31, 2019.

28 Gates interview.

29 David Hill, interview by author, Oberlin, Ohio, September 4, 2019.

30 See "Immigration Raids Ohio Restaurants, Arrest 58," *Reuters*, July 23, 2008, www.reuters.com; Martha Grevatt, "Ohioans Demand: Stop the Raids," *Workers World*, August 8, 2008, www.workers.org; Richard Payerchin, "Restaurant Owner Charged with Immigration Offenses," *Lorain Morning Journal*, January 22, 2010, www.morningjournal.com.

31 Hill interview.

32 Kornblith and Lasser, *Elusive Utopia*, 252.

33 Founded in 1974, El Centro de Servicios Sociales "is a Latino non-profit advocacy organization whose mission is to enhance the socio-economic status of the Greater Lorain County community by providing essential social, educational, cultural, and community development services." For the past two decades, it has played a leading role supporting immigrants throughout Northeast Ohio, www.lorainelcentro.com.

34 Nancy Finke, interview by author, Oberlin, Ohio, July 30, 2019.

35 Rivera interview.

11

Solidaridad

Faith-Based Responses to Central American Asylum Seekers in the San Francisco Bay Area in the 1980s and Lessons for Current Practices

SUSAN BIBLER COUTIN

Introduction

As I prepared to write this chapter, I opened up a dusty box of interview transcripts, fieldnotes, newsletters, pamphlets, reports, fundraising letters, church service bulletins, and other documents from the 1980s when I was doing my dissertation research about the US Sanctuary Movement in the San Francisco East Bay and Tucson, Arizona. The first thing that caught my eye was a newsletter that the Comite de Refugiados Centroamericanos (CRECE, the Central American Refugee Committee) published in March 1987, with the headline, "New Immigration Law Multiplies the Hardships of Salvadoran and Guatemalan Refugees," a headline that could just as easily have been written in any of the decades since that time. The newsletter discussed the 1986 Immigration Reform and Control Act (IRCA); caravans in support of Central American refugees; the repopulation of San Jose Las Flores, a Salvadoran town in Chalatenango, after residents had been forced out due to military activity; presentations that the theologians Jon Sobrino and Jon Cortina gave to a national sanctuary gathering in Washington, DC, in 1986; and the Salvadoran government's failure to aid victims of the 1986 earthquake in El Salvador. These themes of violence, forced movement, injustice, and determination are prominent in immigration-rights activism today as well. The newsletter was illustrated with an iconic image of Salvadoran Archbishop Oscar Romero and Central American–style art work evoking flight and liberation. It also featured photos of the theologians

Sobrino and Cortina, a family who participated in the repopulation, and North Americans celebrating with repopulators. The article about IRCA noted, "To disguise its stringent anti-immigrant aspects the law puts on a benevolent façade," something that has also been true of more recent policies, such as the Trump administration's "Migrant Protection Protocols," which, despite their benign-sounding name, forced asylum seekers to remain at squalid camps in Mexico while waiting for their asylum hearings.[1] A blurb about CRECE, the group that published this newsletter, described the organization's objectives, which were to gain recognition as political refugees, to provide material and other support for Central Americans in the United States and in Central America, and to end US military intervention in Central America.[2]

This example from the newsletter highlights three features of US sanctuary activism during the 1980s. First, this work was transnational, as shown by participation in repopulations in El Salvador and CRECE's goal of supporting Central Americans in Central America and opposing US intervention there.[3] Second, sanctuary was deeply collaborative, as Central American refugee organizations such as CRECE worked closely with religious communities and other groups to promote more just policies. Solidarity workers referred to the relationships that they formed with Central Americans who were impacted by political violence as "accompaniment," that is, entering into situations of risk faced by asylum seekers and communities in Central America in order to share risks, witness atrocities, and provide support.[4] Third, the 1980s US sanctuary work combined faith and justice to produce potent interventions, such as critiques of immigration law, caravans protesting US asylum and foreign policies, and denunciations of human rights abuses perpetrated in Central America. In fact, sanctuary itself was one such potent intervention.

In this chapter, I explore how these dynamics of transnational activism, collaboration, and faith-based justice work played out in the San Francisco East Bay, a region with a deep history of social activism and home to some of the original congregations that declared themselves sanctuaries on March 24, 1982. My analysis is based on fieldwork that I carried out in the San Francisco East Bay during 1986 and 1987, when I was a doctoral student at Stanford University. I participated in sanctuary gatherings, attended services and sanctuary-related meetings at two congregations, volunteered in the EBSC office, interviewed approximately fifty local movement participants, and collected reports, bulletins, flyers, newsletters, and other documents. This material formed the basis for my first book, *The Culture of Protest: Religious Activism and the U.S. Sanctuary Movement*, which also discusses sanctuary in Tucson, Arizona. I revisit my fieldnotes, interview transcripts, and other documentation to reflect on the ways that sanctuary activity in the San Francisco East Bay grew out of other social-justice struggles, and the lessons that sanctuary activism of the 1980s may hold for immigrant rights today. These lessons are grounded in the transnational nature of the movement, connections between sanctuary and other issues, leadership provided by impacted community members, an emphasis on community building, attention to narratives, varied tactics, and long-term engagement. For activists today, even when prospects for social change appear bleak, reflecting on accomplishments at earlier moments can be inspiring.

Roots of Faith-Based Justice Work

One Tuesday evening in April 1987, I joined twenty sanctuary volunteers and two representatives from CRECE at the East Bay Sanctuary Covenant office to watch recent videotapes of conditions in El Salvador. One of the videos had been filmed by a human rights commission in El Salvador in collaboration with a Bay Area interfaith task force, and included secretly recorded footage of the Mariona prison in El Salvador, as well as of a Salvadoran town that had been bombed in January 1987. The other video was made by North Americans who were accompanying Salvadorans who were repopulating their village in El Salvador. It included anonymous interviews with displaced people living in camps, accounts of a busload of people trying to avoid land mines while traveling back to their villages, and a discussion of ways that US people who traveled to El Salvador helped to ensure Central Americans' safety. When the videos ended, there was a moment of silence, then one of the CRECE representatives commented, "The message of this video . . . is to not give up, to continue, to provide material aid, and to remember the call of the religious community in El Salvador." Viewers were so moved by the second video that they requested a copy to use when speaking about accompaniment. This video, which depicted harrowing, life-and-death circumstances, was shown in an office where by day, volunteers—including me—performed such mundane tasks as making phone calls, sorting clothing donations, and putting price stickers on crafts made in Central America. This office was supported by approximately twenty-five local congregations that had declared themselves sanctuaries for Salvadoran and Guatemalan refugees. The covenant adopted by the first East Bay congregations five years earlier, in 1982, defined sanctuary as "support, protection, and advocacy," and concluded, "We acknowledge that legal consequences may result from our actions. We enter this covenant as an act of religious commitment."[5] How did these congregations come together to declare themselves sanctuaries? And how did "sanctuary," which prototypically consisted of sheltering a refugee family in the church or home of congregations, come to include accompanying repopulations in El Salvador?

In the San Francisco East Bay, sanctuary was rooted in local organizational structures, earlier social-justice struggles, participants' faith traditions, and movement members' understandings of US and international law. When the movement was officially launched on March 24, 1982, the second anniversary of the assassination of Salvadoran Archbishop Oscar Romero at the hands of the Salvadoran military,[6] a group of ministers from the Sather Gate churches on the south side of the UC–Berkeley campus had been meeting regularly to discuss the prophetic tradition.[7] According to the prophetic tradition, the church was responsible for supporting orphans, widows, and strangers. A study packet published on the movement's tenth anniversary relates that, as they learned about atrocities in Central America and the plight of refugees in the United States, "the pastors discussed the Judeo-Christian concept of 'sanctuary' in which a sanctuary is defined not just as a holy place of worship, but also a place of refuge and protection."[8] During a 1987 interview, a congregation member who joined this effort as his church's representative recalled,

> [The minister] made an announcement during the coffee hour after church one Sunday back in '82 that there was a meeting of Sather Gate churches . . . where they were going to make a proposal having to do with sanctuary. . . . Even though churches had been involved in helping refugees resettle from Cambodia and Africa, and all over the place, this

> was the first time they had done it with a couple that was here illegally. So they wanted a support network of other Southside churches. . . . We were also in touch with Tucson.[9]

Out of such traditional church activities as a liturgical study group, Sunday coffee hours, support for newly arrived refugees, and ties to congregations locally and in other regions, the East Bay Sanctuary Covenant was born.

Congregation members' and volunteers' commitment to sanctuary work often drew on their or their families' prior involvement in social-justice movements, particularly the civil rights movement, which generated strong commitments to human rights and opposition to discrimination, and the anti–Vietnam War movement, which made them critical of Cold War politics and US military interventions.[10] A congregation member who participated despite being an attorney and who could have lost the ability to practice law if convicted for sanctuary work commented, "You can't start your sensitization process with the death of John Kennedy, and grow up in a period when there is the death of Martin Luther King and the civil rights movement, and the death of Robert Kennedy, and then move into Vietnam and the Watergate era, and not have some powerful impact on you."[11] Participants described marching in anti–Vietnam War protests, supporting farm workers, opposing racial discrimination, and boycotting Dow Chemical. During the 1970s, Bay Area congregations had offered sanctuary to conscientious objectors, and individual congregation members had supported refugees from Hungary and Vietnam. As one congregation member noted, "I think that the sanctuary movement locally dates back to the Vietnam War . . . these terrible things that were going on and the kind of doublethink that our government's been dealing with. All of our high ideals and our principles, and then what we do in practice is horrendous."[12] Such critiques of political violence and suspicion of US government "doublethink" made participants sympathetic to Central Americans' need for refuge. A congregation member summarized this perspective: "The need to prevent people from being deported back—and this was during the time when the death squad killings were at their height—was very great and compelling. So I guess the central concern was in trying to stop deportation and help people to hide and avoid deportation."[13]

East Bay sanctuary practices were also grounded in participants' religious traditions.[14] The original sanctuary covenant cited Leviticus 19:33 ("The stranger who sojourns with you shall be to you as the native among you") and Matthew 25:35 ("I was a stranger and you welcomed me"). While sanctuary groups were ecumenical, there were also distinct faith traditions. The Jewish Covenant of Sanctuary grounded its practices in the history of the Jewish people, stating, "The plight of these refugees powerfully reminds us of our own history. . . . Our historical experience of the Diaspora has given us a profound appreciation for the exiled and the homeless among all people." In the East Bay, sanctuary congregations included Buddhists. The Covenant of the Buddhist Peace Fellowship emphasized that "it is within the Buddhist tradition to help prevent suffering in all lives—to see all of life as being integrally connected, interwoven like a vast net."[15] Sanctuary workers were also inspired by liberation theology, as practiced in Central America, which drew connections between biblical accounts and current social-justice struggles, and especially by Salvadoran Archbishop Oscar Romero, who was assassinated after calling for an end to US military assistance to El Salvador.[16] During interviews, movement participants cited the work of the Maryknoll sisters, the four church women who worked with the poor in El Salvador and who were assassinated during the civil war, and how acting in solidarity with Central Americans gave North Americans a perspective that they would not otherwise have had, enabling them to live their faith in new ways.[17] A Jewish participant told me, "I feel that this [sanctuary] *makes* the religious feeling come alive, and you live it, or *try* to live it out, even if it's in a *small* way."[18] Some participants also cited the social gospel tradition, a US religious tradition that interprets theology in light of social problems such as poverty and racism, as an inspiration for their work. A member of one of the original East Bay sanctuary congregations explained, "That was very big in the [19]30s. I . . . went to graduate school along with Harry Emerson Fosdick.[19] Our church was two blocks away. And so, we both started going there, and he was tremendously compelling. In effect, he was enunciating all the time the social gospel. The idea is that we're here to try to make the world a better place. And take care [of] others."[20]

For East Bay participants, these faith traditions aligned with US and international refugee law. East Bay movement members were divided on whether offering sanctuary to undocumented Central Americans was a form of civil disobedience—disobeying unjust laws for a higher cause—or civil initiative, something that should be considered legal in that it carried out laws that the US government was violating.[21] As legal justifications for granting refuge to Central Americans, participants argued that the US government was not following the 1980 Refugee Act, which created asylum procedures and adopted the UN definition of a refugee: "Someone who is unable or unwilling to return to their country of origin owing to a well-founded fear of being persecuted for reasons of race, religion, nationality, membership of a particular social group, or political opinion." They also cited the Geneva Conventions, which prohibit returning individuals to a war zone, and the 1951 Refugee Convention, which established the internationally accepted definition of "refugee" as well as guidelines for refugees' protection. To some participants, anyone from El Salvador or Guatemala, which were active war zones throughout the 1980s, could be considered a refugee, whereas to others, it was important that the movement restrict its assistance to those who clearly met legal definitions of a refugee. One congregation member who adopted the latter stance explained, "One of the first things we did was to meet with various of the refugees, and learn about them and their stories, and some of the things that I was concerned with was to make sure that these people were *truly* refugees in the sense that they would qualify under the terms of what I consider [an] appropriate legal background, that they would suffer persecution and real danger if they went back."[22] While individual sanctuary members may have sympathized with immigrants in general, East Bay sanctuary workers argued that, as a student participant explained, "There is a clear distinction between Central American refugees here, and Mexicans who have come to the United States looking for work."[23] This distinction was important to participants' argument that their work was legal.

These activist, faith, and legal traditions informed the ways that East Bay sanctuary activities have evolved since the movement's founding in 1982. Sanctuary was launched with a focus on housing undocumented refugees in congregation buildings in defiance of US policy. At the time of the original sanctuary declaration, three Salvadoran men took sanctuary in Berkeley's University Lutheran Chapel. They planned to remain there until participants raised five thousand dollars, wrote five hundred letters to president Ronald Reagan, recruited one hundred volunteers to attend deportation hearings, and registered twenty people to be trained as paralegals so that they could assist with asylum declarations. These goals were quickly met, so four days later, a procession of participating congregations accompanied the three men from University Lutheran to another congregation, which would move them into other housing. Only two months after the initial declarations, a program to provide an international presence in UN refugee camps in Honduras was launched, giving the movement a transnational character from the outset. In the coming years, more congregations joined the movement, founding the EBSC office and establishing an urgent action network through which movement members could send telegrams to Central American officials urging the release of individuals who had been detained. Movement members spoke out about issues in Central America, opposed US intervention, aided refugees in the East Bay, and provided legal assistance and bond funding for Central Americans who were in detention. These activities generated opposition from the US government. Local sanctuary offices across the country experienced mysterious break-ins,[24] and, as prior chapters have noted, sanctuary communities in Tucson were infiltrated by an undercover government informer, and in 1986, movement members there were convicted on conspiracy and alien-smuggling charges. At the time of my research, East Bay participants faced cross-cutting pressures. They were defiant in the face of government opposition, and some sought to establish national sanctuary organizations. The need for a continued international presence in Central America had only grown. But my interviews with participants suggested that some felt distant from the very people whom the movement was designed to help. One participant expressed her disappointment with the fact that few Central Americans actually wanted to live with congregations: "I frankly, had visions that there would be a couple living here, or that there would be children. . . . But I don't feel quite as close to it as I originally thought I would be."[25] As the movement matured, what, then, did sanctuary consist of?

Collaboration, Accompaniment, and Social-Justice Struggles

When I was volunteering in the EBSC office one morning in March of 1987, I was given the task of translating a church's written offer of sanctuary into Spanish.[26] Such offers of sanctuary were the hallmark of the movement. I was surprised to learn that this particular offer had been open for nine months, yet no refugee had been found to fill it. When I asked why, a more experienced volunteer who worked closely with refugees in detention explained that it was isolating for a refugee to live away from their community and that it was emotionally challenging to give public testimonies about their experiences in Central America.[27] As I began translating the offer, I saw that it was written much like a job ad, with a set time limit, responsibilities for the church and the refugees, and a statement about what sanctuary meant. The goal of sanctuary in this church seemed to be the consciousness raising that it was hoped would result from personal contact with Central Americans. The church specified the number of refugees that it would house, requesting a family with children. The responsibilities of the refugees included fifteen hours of church work per week, being in charge of household tasks, and ensuring that the children went to school. The offer advised that the family was expected to move toward independence and to learn English. The responsibilities of the church included physical shelter, food, clothing, and a support group to see to the refugees' needs. Sanctuary, I observed, was envisioned as an exchange. To quote the offer, "While the Church works to meet the physical needs of a small Salvadoran or Guatemalan family, the refugees teach us about their faith, their story, their struggles and their culture." Sanctuary, the church noted, was "a step on the road to freedom," but not something that could provide "real freedom," which presumably could only come with social justice in Central America and respect for refugees' rights in the United States.

It is important to note that within the East Bay sanctuary movement, "housing refugees" was not necessarily a paternalistic practice and in fact took many forms, including sponsoring a shelter, helping with rent, supporting other congregations, and providing funds for Central American community organizations to distribute as needed. And agreements between congregations and refugees likely varied considerably. Nonetheless, this offer of sanctuary reveals a tension that characterized sanctuary work more broadly: On the one hand, US participants sought to act in solidarity by taking direction from Central Americans, building close and collegial relationships, and sharing in their risks and struggles, while on the other hand, the movement needed contact with Central Americans in order to fuel its own sense of purpose. This tension sometimes established asymmetrical relationships. In the offer described above, the church presumed to instruct its future refugee family on what would be good for them—independence, learning English, schooling—even as it assumed that the family would be religious and hoped that the family would deepen the church's faith, a tall order. While the participants who were most heavily involved in sanctuary work tended to have more complex understandings, the movement also contended with individuals who idealized Central Americans as innocent victims and consequently sought to forge paternalistic relationships.

In the East Bay, this tension was linked to competing understandings of sanctuary as an antiwar and Central American solidarity movement on the one hand, or as a refugee-rights movement on the other. Clearly, these two understandings were linked, since war created refugees, and since recognizing Salvadorans and Guatemalans as refugees would make it more difficult for the United States to continue to send military aid to El Salvador and Guatemala. Yet the two emphases had different political implications. Central American organizations in the Bay Area challenged congregations not only to address the needs of Salvadorans and Guatemalans in the United States but also to provide support for those who were still in Central America. This was a more oppositional stance, and was more clearly linked to the message that Central Americans conveyed during testimonies. As a volunteer commented during an interview, "These people [Americans] need to know to what use their tax money is being put. How are they personally affecting the lives of Salvadorans who are also human beings? That's why I think the testimonies are so effective. Because they make it so that the violence and repression is no longer just an abstract term, but something that has profoundly affected someone's life, has killed someone's child, has made someone have nightmares every night for ten years, and wake up screaming in the night."[28] In contrast, when I asked another volunteer if he agreed with those who wanted sanctuary to assert strong opposition to US military aid to El Salvador, he responded with surprise, asking me, "It's part of the sanctuary movement?" He then explained his own position: "I certainly do support in any way I can the withdrawing of support [and] military involvement there, but no, I didn't realize that there was that [view.] The sanctuary movement should let *that* aspect of it be handled by a lot of nonreligious people."[29] At the time of my research, a proposal for sanctuary congregations to support a moratorium on US aid was circulating, but due to disagreement between EBSC congregations, it was not adopted until 1989, after six Jesuits, their housekeeper, and her daughter were killed by the Salvadoran Armed Forces, provoking widespread outrage. In fact, tensions over whether sanctuary was dedicated primarily to aiding refugees or to opposing US intervention in Central America existed nationally as well, and, as chapters in this book have shown, have often been characterized as a split between Chicago (allegedly more politicized) and Tucson (allegedly more humanitarian).[30]

Whether they opposed US military aid or supported refugee rights or both, sanctuary activists' commitment to acting in *solidarity* with Central Americans led them to share in the risks that these communities faced in both the United States and Central America. They did so in three primary ways. First, sanctuary workers publicly offered sanctuary in defiance of US immigration authorities, thereby taking on some of the legal risks faced by undocumented Central Americans. Of course, the consequences for sanctuary workers were quite different, in that they did not face deportation to a place where there were death squads. Nonetheless, the risks were not insignificant, as the US government had infiltrated the Tucson segment of the sanctuary movement, leading to indictments and convictions,[31] and East Bay sanctuary workers feared that their phones were bugged and that they were under government surveillance.[32] Although not all agreed that sanctuary was legal, many movement members considered sanctuary to be enforcing US laws that the government had failed to follow. A May 1986 article in *Exodus: The Newsletter of the East Bay Sanctuary Covenant Congregations* quoted Jim Corbett, one of the defendants in the Tucson sanctuary trial, explaining this legal strategy: "We will continue to provide Sanctuary services openly and go to trial as often as is necessary to establish the legality, or more directly, to actualize the Nuremberg mandate that the protection of human rights is never illegal." Providing sanctuary was an act of solidarity that exposed sanctuary workers to the risk of trials, enabling them to join undocumented Central Americans as potential targets of US enforcement strategies.

Second, sanctuary workers practiced solidarity by traveling to Central America, where they accompanied Central Americans who were in communities that were at risk of military incursions. In doing so, they exposed themselves to possible human rights violations, though their risk, as international visitors from the United States, was temporary and was much lower than the risk faced by Central Americans living in communities affected by war. Indeed, maintaining an international presence in communities at risk was seen as a way to provide safety, even though sanctuary workers sometimes had harrowing experiences. A volunteer who had accompanied the repopulations shared this story:

> The second night when we came back from cutting wood, it was quite tense because it was getting dark. . . . What they did was they made a list of all the names of the people on the truck, and then the soldier would call out names, and the people would identify themselves and show their papers. And somehow in the dark, they had gotten to the end of the list and there were still five people standing there. So they asked the people their names, and looked at the list to try to find where the name was crossed off. And there was this real young guy, who looked like he was about fifteen, who either he was too frightened, or he was deaf, because he couldn't talk when they asked him his name. He was just kind of choking. So the other people were saying, "Oh, he's just too frightened." But it was just a real, for me, frightening experience, and the feeling I had was like, this is bizarre, this is like being in a movie. What am I doing here seeing this? It can't really be happening to be around these perfectly mature adult men who moments before seemed real calm and relatively happy and concerned about cutting wood, and now were totally frightened.[33]

This story shows how, through accompaniment, sanctuary workers temporarily became part of the social realities of war-torn communities. The terror of being part of a group of men who clearly feared being apprehended and perhaps tortured or killed by soldiers who were questioning them was so far from the volunteer's experiences that he described it as being unreal, like being in a movie. Such forms of accompaniment exposed sanctuary workers to physical danger.

Third, sanctuary workers practiced solidarity by giving their own time, money, and material goods to the movement. The movement generated enormous amounts of activity. Volunteers participated in vigils and marches, sponsored fundraising concerts and walkathons, commemorated important dates such as the anniversary of Archbishop Romero's assassination, attended organizing meetings, raised funds to bond Central Americans out of detention, drove Central Americans to medical appointments, collected donations of clothing and food, incorporated reflections on sanctuary into their religious services, wrote letters to undocumented Central Americans who were in detention, and sent telegrams to Central American authorities pleading for the release of detained activists there. Some of these activities addressed dire situations, such as one morning when I was awakened by a nun asking me to deliver a check for bail bond to an INS office in San Francisco so that an individual could be released from detention. Other activities were more mundane. My notes about a day that I spent volunteering at the EBSC office in January 1987 read, "What was going on in the office today: shellacking crafts, preparing fundraising grants, preparing for a meeting, and jobs work, and legal rights work. Someone brought donations, a new volunteer came, and there were lots of phone calls." While shellacking crafts and making phone calls seemed a far cry from the policy defiance for which the movement was known, all of these tasks were interconnected.[34]

It is important to note that, despite the image of sanctuary as being outside the law, the work that movement members performed also included legal efforts. In addition to assisting Central American detainees in the asylum process, sanctuary workers advocated for passage of the Moakley-Deconcini bill, which would have granted Salvadorans and possibly also Nicaraguans (depending on which version of the bill passed) Extended Voluntary Departure (EVD) status, enabling them to remain in the United States with work authorization, at least temporarily. To promote this bill, congregation members were urged to contact their congressional representatives to express support. The first page of the March 1988 issue of *Exodus* informed readers,

> Moakley-DeConcini Vote Soon
> The Moakley-Deconcini Bill (S.332), which will grant a two-year stay of deportation to Salvadoran refugees, is coming up for a vote in the Senate

> the first part of March. We urge you to make phone calls encouraging Senator Alan Cranston to take strong action in lobbying the other Senators for its passage. Senator Pete Wilson is presently a swing vote, so it is important to pressure him also. Senator Cranston can be reached locally at 556-8440, and Senator wilson [*sic*] at 556-4307. Please, call. The vote is scheduled soon, and grassroots pressure will make a big difference.

In the long run, these legislative efforts bore fruit through the 1990 Immigration Act, which created Temporary Protected Status (TPS) and designated Salvadorans as the first recipients.[35]

Whether through lobbying Congress to pass legislation, volunteering in the EBSC office, joining a congregation's sanctuary committee, or traveling to Central America as part of a delegation, participating in sanctuary work forged relationships that were characterized by an ethic of care. In interviews, participants stressed that the religious basis of the sanctuary movement created a sense of mutual support and respect, in contrast to what they saw as the more acrimonious nature of secular political organizations. A member of a sanctuary synagogue commented, "I believe in the faith-based nature of it [sanctuary]. Because political action is sometimes very abrasive, and you feel sort of alone out there. There's a quality of camaraderie and togetherness that's somehow missing in many occasions from political action."[36] Similarly, a member of a Protestant congregation told me that in sanctuary meetings, she did not see "the normal biting that goes on." She explained, "We know each other, at least in this work. I think we trust each other's integrity. And while we may not always agree in our preciseness, we agree in overall goals. . . . Where we tend to see sharper divisions, again, are when we begin to act regionally or interregionally. As we spread out, then we see much sharper divisions."[37] It is striking that these participants felt a sense of community despite being from different faith traditions. By contrasting sanctuary with politics—though, in fact, political action might also generate "camaraderie and togetherness"—these participants emphasized the religious nature of the movement. Furthermore, as the second quotation indicates, personal connections and shared goals were key to these relationships, something that was more difficult to achieve nationally, as each region that was involved in the movement had its own localized understandings and practices. Yet, despite being deeply local, sanctuary was also a transnational movement.

Transnational Activism

The transnational nature of sanctuary as practiced in the San Francisco East Bay was fundamental to the movement. Current immigrant-rights activism also has transnational components, as there are groups that provide legal assistance to asylum seekers who are in Mexico, accompany migrant caravans, or volunteer at immigrant shelters outside of the United States.[38] But many immigrant-rights activists today focus on the United States, by targeting US laws for excluding asylum seekers and longtime residents, and denouncing border policies as inhumane.[39] It is less common for immigrant-rights activists to try to change US foreign policies, even if they note ways that the United States has contributed to the conditions that lead people to immigrate. In East Bay sanctuary work, transnationalism took multiple forms. Congregation members traveled to Central America on delegations, tried to stay informed about events in Central America, supported Central Americans who had come to the United States, opposed human rights violations perpetrated by Salvadoran and Guatemalan military and paramilitary forces, sought to prevent US intervention, and established "sister city" and "sister parish" relationships with Central American communities. Of course, not all movement members engaged in all of these practices, and I have already pointed out that some participants thought that sanctuary should only address the needs of refugees, not US foreign policy, which some saw as a political matter. But movement members saw themselves as engaged not only with their own local communities and the refugees who had arrived from Central America but also with religious workers and community leaders in Central America.

The April 1987 issue of a *Human Rights Bulletin* published by the Central American Refugee Center in Los Angeles circulated in the San Francisco East Bay and provides an example of the ways in which the movement was transnational. The bulletin features a photo of protesters holding a sign in Spanish that reads, "No to deportation until achieving peace in El Salvador and Guatemala." This sign immediately couples the goals of halting deportations in the United States and achieving peace in Central America (while also, in contrast to many current sanctuary practices, implying that if there were peace, deportation could be appropriate). Articles in this issue describe the detention and deportation of a grandmother and grandson in Los Angeles, a talk that a victim of atrocities in El Salvador gave in Los Angeles, and the outcome of a Guatemalan asylum case. Such articles linked local communities with those in Central America, as people who experienced atrocities there had come to the United States, and as the United States was unjustly sending these victims back to places of persecution. The newsletter also discussed concerns about the 1986 Immigration Reform and Control Act, which established a legalization program for individuals who had entered the United States before January 1, 1982, an eligibility date that excluded many Central Americans, who came later. Movement members adopted a transnational lens in assessing US laws for their relevance to Central Americans in need of refuge. Lastly, a section on "updates from Central America" described bombings, human rights abuses, the activities of popular organizations, the experiences of displaced people who had returned to their homes, the situation of political prisoners, and government censorship. Such reporting served to overcome distances between California and Central America.

Other documents that circulated in the East Bay positioned the sanctuary movement as a response to a call from religious workers in Central America. For example, movement members copied and distributed a February 17, 1980, letter from Salvadoran Archbishop Oscar Romero to US president Jimmy Carter, opposing US military aid and intervention in El Salvador. Likewise, in 1987, a self-described faith-based campaign for a Moratorium on All Aid to the War in El Salvador circulated a January 1987 call from "the religious community in El Salvador,"[40] an excerpt of which reads, "Accompany us in our journey to peace with justice: Lend us your moral, spiritual and material support to rebuild our lives. Be our voice and give us your active presence to stop the repression against our communities and families. GRANT US YOUR COMMITMENT TO STOP ALL AID TO THE WAR."[41] As I noted above, at the time, EBSC declined to endorse this goal, as not all congregations agreed, but these sorts of documents position movement members as participants in transnational conversations. Other documents that circulated within the movement included a letter from the Office on Human Rights in El Salvador about conditions in the country, requests for delegations to provide an international presence in communities at risk, expressions of moral support from Central American organizations, and information about sponsoring a family in Central America.

My interviews with sanctuary workers suggested that many participants saw the movement as transnational. A Protestant congregation member told me that she was going on a delegation to accompany displaced Salvadorans who were repopulating their village because "it is a major statement to the rest of the world."[42] When I asked this participant to describe the ultimate goals of sanctuary, she talked about ending death squads, refugees being able to return home, a negotiated peace to civil wars, a moratorium on US military aid to Central America, and land reform in Central America. While locally this participant devoted her time and energies to EBSC and a refugee house that her church was establishing, her gaze was also very much on Central America. This perspective was echoed by other participants. A Jewish sanctuary worker told me that her synagogue was organizing a sister-parish or sister-city relationship in Central America, a secular student activist described the goal of sanctuary as "trying to influence national politics so that they [refugees] don't have to leave their homes,"[43] and another Protestant participant stressed that sending delegations to the UN refugee camps in Honduras was "one of the strongest programs that we had at EBSC. There must have been over a hundred delegations down. We were having a delegation go down regularly—every two weeks."[44] Clearly, EBSC was a transnational movement from the outset, a focus that may have implications for immigrant- and refugee-rights movements today.

Conclusion: Lessons of 1980s Sanctuary Activism

Current US asylum policy is riddled with barriers such as the so-called Migrant Protection Protocols, and a Biden administration rule that makes it harder for asylum seekers who have traveled through third countries to apply.[45] Moreover, anti-immigrant sentiment across the country is so high that, during the first Republican presidential debate in 2023, candidates suggested that immigration posed such a great risk to US security that the military should be deployed along the US-Mexico border.[46] Immigration emerged as a central issue in the 2024 US presidential campaign, as border states such as Texas accused the Biden administration of having an "open border," mobilized the

National Guard to police the border, and bused immigrants to other states.[47] Meanwhile, approximately eleven million long-term undocumented immigrant residents were still waiting for the comprehensive immigration reform that has been repeatedly promised by Democratic politicians, but not delivered. A vibrant immigrant-rights movement made up of immigrant residents, lawyers, allies, and faith-based groups has continued to advocate on behalf of immigrants and refugees by providing legal services, material support, and advocacy for policy change. What insights might forms of solidarity created during the 1980s, when the 1980 Refugee Act's promise to provide access to asylum regardless of country of origin was still new, provide for understandings of immigrant rights today, especially when carried out from a faith perspective? To conclude, I detail seven potential lessons of sanctuary activism in the 1980s in the East Bay:

1. Build transnational relationships and coalitions: Immigration is a transnational phenomenon, linking countries of origin, transit, and arrival. In the 1980s, sanctuary activists sought to address both the root causes of immigration from Central America and the needs of refugees in the United States. A key movement goal was to minimize geographic and social distances, so that people in the United States understood the realities of war and persecution and sympathized with Central Americans' need for refuge. Likewise, it is important today for the general public to understand the social conditions that lead individuals to leave their countries of origin, the histories through which these conditions were created, and the role the United States played within these histories. Transnational relationships and coalitions are key to sharing such knowledge.
2. Connect advocacy on immigration to other issues: In the San Francisco East Bay, 1980s sanctuary activism was linked to earlier opposition to the Vietnam War and to the civil rights movement. In creating sanctuary, participants drew on their experiences as organizers, as well as their opposition to political violence and discrimination. Sanctuary was therefore part of a broader movement for peace and justice, which supported coalition building and sharing of information. Likewise, the current immigrant-rights movement has ties with the Black Lives Matter (BLM) movement, in that both oppose racism, police

abuse, and the criminalization of communities of color, and in that both address circumstances of racialized immigrants, including those who identify as Black.[48] Likewise, as "climate refugees" become more prevalent, there are clear connections between immigrant and refugee rights and environmental justice.[49] Further developing these linkages can give rise to new forms of allyship and solidarity.

3. Ensure that impacted communities have a leadership role: For 1980s East Bay sanctuary workers, it was important to take direction from Central Americans. The East Bay Sanctuary Covenant worked closely with refugee organizations, such as CRECE, and when these groups asked sanctuary workers to provide an international presence in Central America, movement members responded. Accompaniment became an important principle within sanctuary work. Likewise, the current immigrant-rights movement is made up to a large degree of people with immigrant backgrounds, whose voices play an important role in decisions about whether to support piecemeal immigration reforms or to hold out for comprehensive changes in policy.[50] Those who are directly impacted are most likely to have the deepest understandings of policies.
4. Process and community matter: East Bay sanctuary activists of the 1980s stressed that their faith made them attentive to process and to each other as well as to assisting refugees and promoting policy change. One participant told me, "I've never heard any two people within the sanctuary movement that I know have sharp words." For example, when congregations disagreed about whether to support a moratorium on US military aid to Central America, EBSC's steering committee did not endorse this call. Current immigrant- and refugee-rights activists, especially those who are motivated by their faith, likewise may prioritize care and support in their work, both for those they seek to aid and for each other. In the broader immigrant- and refugee-rights movement, community agreements and mutual aid have also become important mechanisms of care and community building.[51]
5. Consider the implications of narratives and frames: Sanctuary activists of the 1980s distinguished between Central American refugees and other immigrants, who might have come to the United States for economic reasons. A shortcoming of this narrative was the implication that the United States was justified in deporting immigrants from

Mexico or other countries that were not at war. Likewise, some sanctuary workers in the East Bay unwittingly reproduced narratives of victimization, depicting Central Americans as innocent, suffering, and in need. The current immigrant- and refugee-rights movement includes segments that oppose distinctions between "economic" and "political" immigrants, and that advocate abolishing immigration enforcement altogether.[52] Current activists have been attentive to problematic framings, such as the "Dreamer" narrative, which depicted immigrant students as high achievers, suggesting that those who were not high achieving or who had criminal records were undeserving of status.[53] Further, undocumented student activists adopted the slogan "unapologetic and unafraid" in order to push back against framings depicting them as innocent and blaming their parents for the decision to bring them to the United States without status.[54] The New Sanctuary Movement also leveraged ideas of family to challenge policies that separated relatives.[55] These examples show the importance of thinking carefully about who is blamed or left out in narratives of deservingness, rather than focusing only on political expediency.

6. Adopt multiple strategies: Sanctuary workers adopted a variety of approaches, including housing refugees within congregations, visiting Central Americans in detention, raising money for bond, traveling to Central America to accompany displaced people who were returning to their villages, holding vigils, going on caravans, collecting donations, and performing day-to-day mundane work. The varied nature of these tasks gave participants many different ways to get involved, according to their capacity and the level of their commitment. Likewise, immigrant- and refugee-rights work today takes many forms, ranging from supporting asylum seekers on the Mexican side of the border with the United States, leaving water in remote areas where border crossers may travel, hosting "know your rights" sessions, tracking the location of enforcement efforts, providing legal representation and assistance, lobbying representatives for policy changes, and more.[56] These varied tactics are a strength and demonstrate the imagination and creativity of movement members.
7. Actions taken today may bear fruit tomorrow: At May Day marches in Los Angeles, I have noticed protest signs that read, "When you buried us, you didn't realize that we were seeds." Sanctuary work in the 1980s planted

the seeds for future immigration opportunities. A decade of activism on behalf of asylum seekers during the 1980s led to the creation of Temporary Protected Status (TPS) in the 1990 Immigration Act. As of January 2023, some 355,000 nationals from sixteen countries had TPS.[57] The 1997 Nicaraguan Adjustment and Central American Relief Act enabled more than 184,000 asylum seekers from El Salvador and Guatemala to gain lawful permanent residency.[58] Moreover, TPS served as a model for Deferred Action for Childhood Arrivals (DACA), which has now benefited more than 630,000 DACA requestors.[59] DACA in turn was a model for the announced Deferred Actions for Parents of Americans (DAPA) Program, which was enjoined by the courts and never implemented, but which would potentially have benefited almost half of the undocumented residents in the United States. During the 1980s, sanctuary workers could not have anticipated these outcomes, just as today, immigrant-rights activists may not be able to see the developments that they are setting in motion. Yet, over time, the seeds that are planted by working for refugee and immigrant rights may grow into new forms of justice.

NOTES

1 On the deleterious effects of the Migrant Protection Protocols, see Austin Kocher, "Migrant Protection Protocols and the Death of Asylum," *Journal of Latin American Geography* 20, no. 1 (2021): 249–58.

2 On Central Americans' involvement in the US sanctuary movement, see Hector Perla and Susan Bibler Coutin, "Legacies and Origins of the 1980s US–Central American Sanctuary Movement," in *Sanctuary Practices in International Perspectives*, ed. Randy K. Lippert and Sean Rehaag (Routledge, 2012), 73–91.

3 For an account of repopulation efforts, see Peter Solis, "Displaced Persons and Human Rights: The Crisis in El Salvador," *Bulletin of Latin American Research* 11, no. 1 (1992): 49–67.

4 On accompaniment, see Norma Stoltz Chinchilla, Nora Hamilton, and James Loucky, "The Sanctuary Movement and Central American Activism in Los Angeles," *Latin American Perspectives* 36, no. 6 (2009): 101–26.

5 "Original Covenant of Sanctuary," available in EBSC Steering Committee, East Bay Sanctuary Covenant Study Packet, Section C, "EBSC Covenants," Berkeley, California, September 8, 1991. Available from the author upon request.

6 Lisa Falgiano and Kerstin LeMaire, "El Salvador's Decade of Terror: Human Rights Since the Assassination of Archbishop Romero," *Human Rights Quarterly* 14, no. 4 (1992): 628–37.

7 The East Bay congregations that declared themselves sanctuaries on March 24, 1982, were Newman Hall–Holy Spirit Parish, St. John's Presbyterian Church,

St. Mark's Episcopal Church, Trinity United Methodist Church, and University Lutheran Chapel. See "A History of East Bay Sanctuary Covenant," in *EBSC Study and Reflection Packet for the Tenth Anniversary of Sanctuary* (September 8, 1991), available from author by request. There was likely some overlap between these congregations and the Sather Gate churches.

8 "A History of East Bay Sanctuary Covenant," in *EBSC Study and Reflection Packet for the Tenth Anniversary of Sanctuary*.

9 For a history of religious involvement in refugee settlement, see Lane Van Ham, "Sanctuary Revisited: Central American Refugee Assistance in the History of Church-Based Immigrant Advocacy," *Political Theology* 10, no. 4 (2009): 621–45.

10 For a discussion of the historiography of the civil rights movement, see Steven F. Lawson, "Freedom Then, Freedom Now: The Historiography of the Civil Rights Movement," *American Historical Review* 96, no. 2 (1991): 456–71. On post–Vietnam War attitudes toward US intervention, see Van Gosse, "Vietnam and 'The War at Home,'" in *Rethinking the New Left: An Interpretive History* (Palgrave Macmillan, 2005), 85–109.

11 Interview conducted by author on June 14, 1987, in Berkeley, California. In the author's files.

12 Interview conducted by author on January 21, 1987, in Berkeley, California. In the author's files.

13 Interview conducted by author on March 1, 1987, in Berkeley, California. In the author's files.

14 For a comparative perspective, see Randy K. Lippert and Sean Rehaag, "Introduction: Sanctuary Across Countries, Institutions, and Disciplines," in *Sanctuary Practices in International Perspectives*, ed. Randy K. Lippert and Sean Rehaag (Routledge, 2012), 1–12.

15 The Original Covenant of Sanctuary, Jewish Covenant of Sanctuary, and Covenant of the Buddhist Peace Fellowship are reproduced in a study packet distributed to participating congregations on the tenth anniversary of the March 24, 1982, sanctuary declaration. Available from the author by request.

16 On liberation theology, see Jon Sobrino and Ignacio Ellacuría, eds., *Systematic Theology: Perspectives from Liberation Theology (Readings from Mysterium Liberationis)* (Orbis Books, 2015).

17 The church women were Maryknoll Sisters Ita Ford and Maura Clarke, Ursuline Sister Dorothy Kazel, and Lay Missioner Jean Donovan. See Bernice Kita, "Maryknoll Sisters in Latin America, 1943–1993," *Missiology* 26, no. 4 (1998): 419–30; Amanda L. Izzo, *Liberal Christianity and Women's Global Activism: The YWCA of the USA and the Maryknoll Sisters* (Rutgers University Press, 2018).

18 Interview conducted by author on May 20, 1987, in Berkeley, California. In author's files.

19 Harry Emerson Fosdick was a pastor and a leader within the social gospel tradition. See Robert Moats Miller, *Harry Emerson Fosdick: Preacher, Pastor, Prophet* (Oxford University Press, 1985).

20 Interview conducted by author on April 5, 1987, in Berkeley, California. In author's files.

21 For a discussion of sanctuary as a form of civil initiative, rather than civil disobedience, see Adam Waters, "Alternative Internationalisms: The Sanctuary Movement and Jim Corbett's Civil Initiative," *Diplomatic History* 46, no. 5 (2022): 984–1009.

22 Interview conducted by author on April 5, 1987, in Berkeley, California. In author's files.

23 Interview conducted by author on June 17, 1987, in Berkeley, California. In author's files.

24 See Ross Gelbspan, *Break-ins, Death Threats, and the FBI: The Covert War Against the Central America Movement* (South End Press, 1991).

25 Interview conducted by author on May 20, 1987, in Berkeley, California. In author's files.

26 For a discussion of sanctuary as a form of pastoral power, see Randy Lippert, *Sanctuary, Sovereignty, Sacrifice: Canadian Sanctuary Incidents, Power, and Law* (University of British Columbia Press, 2011).

27 For further details about the complex relationships forged between US congregations and Central American asylum seekers during the 1980s, see Susan Coutin, *The Culture of Protest: Religious Activism and the U.S. Sanctuary Movement* (Westview Press, 1993).

28 Interview conducted by author on March 5, 1987, in Berkeley, California. In author's files.

29 Interview conducted by author on April 5, 1987, in Berkeley, California. In author's files.

30 See, e.g., Nathan Ellstrand, "Politicized Refuge: Chicago and the Transformation of the Sanctuary Movement," *Middle West Review* 9, no. 1 (2022): 25–48.

31 On the Tucson sanctuary trial, see Susan Bibler Coutin, "Smugglers or Samaritans in Tucson, Arizona: Producing and Contesting Legal Truth," *American Ethnologist* 22, no. 3 (1995): 549–71.

32 On government infiltration of sanctuary and its aftermath, see Kristina M. Campbell, "Operation Sojourner: The Government Infiltration of the Sanctuary Movement in the 1980s and Its Legacy on the Modern Central American Refugee Crisis," *University of St. Thomas Law Journal* 13 (2016): 474.

33 Interview conducted by the author on March 1, 1987, in Berkeley, California. In author's files.

34 On the role of women who often provided this sort of day-to-day work within sanctuary activities, see Robin Lorentzen, *Women in the Sanctuary Movement* (Temple University Press, 1991).

35 For an overview of the 1990 Immigration Act, see Warren R. Leiden and David L. Neal, "Highlights of the U.S. Immigration Act of 1990," *Fordham International Law Journal* 14, no. 1 (1900–1991): 328–39.

36 Interview conducted by author on March 3, 1987, in Berkeley, California. In author's files.

37 Interview conducted on May 14, 1987, in Berkeley, California. In author's files.

38 See Veronica Montes, "Fleeing Home: Notes on the Central American Caravan in Its Transit to Reach the US-Mexico Border," *Latino Studies* 17, no. 4 (2019): 532–39; Amelia Frank-Vitale, "Coyotes, Caravans, and the Central American Migrant Smuggling Continuum," *Trends in Organized Crime* 26, no. 1 (2023): 64–79; Heather M. Wurtz, "A Movement in Motion: Collective Mobility and Embodied Practice in the Central American Migrant Caravan," *Mobilities* 15, no. 6 (2020): 930–44; John Doering-White, "Shelter Vision: Compassion, Fear, and Learning to (Not) See Trauma Along the Migrant Trail Through Mexico," *Medicine Anthropology Theory* 9, no. 1 (2022): 1–27.

39 Kevin R. Johnson and Bill Ong Hing, "The Immigrant Rights Marches of 2006 and the Prospects for a New Civil Rights Movement," *Harvard Civil Rights–Civil Liberties Law Review* 42 (2007): 99.

40 The proposal for this moratorium cites the letter from Archbishop Romero as well as the January 1987 call from "the religious community in El Salvador" (first page of "Proposal for a Faith-Based Campaign for a Moratorium on Aid to the War in El Salvador so That Peace Can be Achieved Among Salvadorans," in author's files).

41 Letter from representatives of Salvadoran Catholic, Lutheran, and Baptist churches, January 1987. In author's files.

42 Interview conducted by author on June 14, 1987, in Berkeley, California. In author's files.

43 Interview conducted by author on June 17, 1987, in Berkeley, California. In author's files.

44 Interview conducted by author on March 1, 1987, in Berkeley, California. In author's files.

45 Terence M. Garrett and Arthur J. Sementelli, "Revisiting the Policy Implications of COVID-19, Asylum Seekers, and Migrants on the Mexico-US Border: Creating (and Maintaining) States of Exception in the Trump and Biden Administrations," *Politics & Policy* 51, no. 3 (2023): 458–75.

46 Miriam Jordan and Jennifer Medina, "On Immigration, Republican Candidates Show Little Disagreement at Debate," *New York Times*, August 24, 2023, www.nytimes.com.

47 Ellen Mitchell, "What to Know About Texas's Militarization of the Southern Border," *The Hill*, February 28, 2024, https://thehill.com.

48 Veronica Terriquez and Ruth Milkman, "Immigrant and Refugee Youth Organizing in Solidarity with the Movement for Black Lives," *Gender & Society* 35, no. 4 (2021): 577–87.

49 For a discussion of such connections, see David Pellow and Jasmine Vazin, "The Intersection of Race, Immigration Status, and Environmental Justice," *Sustainability* 11, no. 14 (2019): 3942.

50 Walter J. Nicholls, *The DREAMers: How the Undocumented Youth Movement Transformed the Immigrant Rights Debate* (Stanford University Press, 2013).

51 See Frances R. Morales et al., "An Exploratory Study of Healing Circles as a Strategy to Facilitate Resilience in an Undocumented Community," *Journal of Latinx Psychology* (2023); Dean Spade, "Solidarity Not Charity: Mutual Aid for Mobilization and Survival," *Social Text* 38, no. 1 (2020): 131–51.

52 César Cuauhtémoc García Hernández, "Abolishing Immigration Prisons," *Boston University Law Review* 97 (2017): 245.

53 Leisy J. Abrego and Genevieve Negrón-Gonzales, eds., *We Are Not Dreamers: Undocumented Scholars Theorize Undocumented Life in the United States* (Duke University Press, 2020).

54 Hinda Seif, "'Unapologetic and Unafraid': Immigrant Youth Come Out from the Shadows," *New Directions for Child and Adolescent Development* no. 134 (2011): 59–75.

55 Amalia Pallares, *Family Activism: Immigrant Struggles and the Politics of Noncitizenship* (Rutgers University Press, 2014).

56 For a discussion of such tactics, see Austin Kocher, "The New Resistance: Immigrant Rights Mobilization in an Era of Trump," *Journal of Latin American Geography* 16, no. 2 (2017): 165–71.

57 Diana Roy and Claire Klobucista, "What Is Temporary Protected Status?" Council on Foreign Relations (last updated September 23, 2023), www.cfr.org.

58 U.S. Citizenship and Immigration Services, "NACARA Cumulative Report, 6-21-99 through 8-31-2017," October 15, 2020, www.uscis.gov.

59 U.S. Citizenship and Immigration Services, "Approximate Active DACA Recipients as of March 31, 2020," www.uscis.gov. Accessed July 13, 2023.

Conclusion

LLOYD D. BARBA AND SERGIO M. GONZÁLEZ

Four decades after churches first declared sanctuary for Central American refugees in the US–Mexico borderlands, the movement continues to demand scholarly attention. What began in the early 1980s as a faith-based response to war and displacement quickly grew into a hemispheric struggle that redefined the relationship among religious communities, migrants, and the state. Historical studies of this movement have illuminated not only how churches challenge federal immigration policy but also how grassroots networks of believers, lay leaders, and migrants themselves can create alternative visions of justice, refuge, and solidarity. Revisiting this history is essential for understanding how sanctuary became both a practical tool of protection and safe harbor in the United States and a moral language that has reshaped debates over human rights, citizenship, and the role of faith in public life.

Equally important, the Sanctuary Movement's history remains deeply relevant today. President Donald Trump's third presidential campaign and early days in office during his second term were marked by a resolute focus on attacking sanctuary activism in both its sacred and its secular variants. In his first week back in office in January 2025, Trump revoked the so-called sensitive locations memo, a policy that had long limited immigration enforcement in schools, hospitals, and places of worship. The decision effectively erased protections that immigrant communities had relied on to access essential services without fear. By subjecting these spaces to potential surveillance and raids, the move not only heightened anxiety among undocumented residents but also raised broader concerns about civil liberties and the erosion of long-recognized sanctuaries. As immigrant communities, migration-justice activists, and religious allies once again faced the prospect of criminalization for extending protection to migrants, the lessons of the past iterations of sanctuary mobilizations continued to provide critical perspective on contemporary struggles.

As this volume has made clear, a robust and expanding historical scholarship underscores how sanctuary has never been static but has adapted to new contexts, from Cold War Central America to today's global migration crises. By tracing this forty-year tradition, historians not only preserve the memory of past activism but also equip contemporary communities to grapple with ongoing conflicts at the intersection of faith, law, and human dignity. As the subtitle of this volume notes, the chapters in this book offer "new histories of the Sanctuary Movement." As new histories, the contributions to this book have also pointed to the potential of future directions for sanctuary scholarship. Some of the contributions herein are indeed parts of larger projects, but this book's fullest potential will materialize, we hope, by inspiring future studies. In this conclusion, the editors join with our contributors to offer pathways for that future scholarship.

The evocation of "sanctuary" in the name of migrant justice beyond houses of worship has become nearly ubiquitous in the twenty-first century, but historians have much to learn about how activists carried the concept from sacred to secular spaces. Scholars have begun to study the influence of sanctuary congregations on "sanctuary city" policies, but historians must offer a longer lens to understand the malleable and diffuse nature of the concept of sanctuary as it moves from religious settings to profane ones. In the 1980s, for example, the San Francisco Bay Area sanctuary congregations played no small role in pushing forward sanctuary-city initiatives, with clergy serving on fact-finding committees and reapplying the concept of sanctuary to fit a secular mold.[1] For many religious activists, the very idea of sanctuary in the Hebrew Bible was, after all, anchored in the tradition of cities of refuge, an ancient, albeit jurisdictional, origin of sanctuary. As more municipal governments grapple with the implications of taking on the mantle of "sanctuary city" or "sanctuary state," historians must interrogate the roots of these forms of mobilization.

Scholars writing about the history of sanctuary activism outside the United States have also developed a rich literature that treats sanctuary not as a single, transplantable model but as a set of practices shaped by distinctive local politics, religious traditions, and legal regimes. Comparative studies from Latin America, Canada, and Europe emphasize how sanctuary has been articulated differently in these areas, sometimes as shelter and pastoral care within church compounds, sometimes as a legal-political strategy that leverages religious status for temporary protection, and sometimes as a public-formation tactic that seeks to remake civic discourse about belonging. As Randy Lippert and Sean Rehaag have noted, sanctuary is "a more international, institutionally-flexible, and perhaps above all, theoretically-rich set of practices."[2] Scholars must continue to interrogate this regional diversity in order to go beyond narratives that treat US 1980s activism as the archetypal movement, instead tracing genealogies of sanctuary practices that predate, intersect with, or run parallel to US developments.

That the 1980s movement was a transnational North American phenomenon is a well-known fact within scholarly literature. Nevertheless, close studies of the way sanctuary played out across borders—beyond a cursory knowledge of key players and actors south of the US-Mexico border—are scarcely known. Adam Waters and Mary Ward-Bucher prompted us to consider the roles that Latin Americans in Mexico and Central America played in this North American phenomenon. Central American refugees passed through the country, but not without the direction of clandestine networks in the country. What are the origins and development of the movement in Mexico? What were the roles of the country's Catholic church and relief agencies?

What sort of screening processes were in place for Central American refugees? In *Seeking Refuge*, Maria Cristina Garcia has provided an excellent overview of shifting Mexican policy as pressured by the Reagan administration, but we have yet to uncover the grassroots nature of the movement in these regions.[3] And what ways did *Evangélico* leaders and organizations in Central America and the United States weigh in on the question of sanctuary?

This call for further research on the transnational dimensions of sanctuary, however, should not imply that research on the US movement is remotely close to completion. This is true of both the 1980s movement and the New Sanctuary Movement (NSM). For example, only a few studies thus far have carefully examined the role of particular denominations.[4] A closer examination at the denominational level can shed light on the diversity of beliefs that upheld such robust sanctuary practices. Consider, for example, two of the central leaders of 1980s mobilization. John Fife, a Presbyterian pastor, and Jim Corbett, a Quaker, have enjoyed heightened visibility, more so than others in previous histories of sanctuary. Historians would do well to carefully consider the denominational specifics, inclusive of histories, theologies, and national support of traditions such as Unitarians, Presbyterians, and so on. Studies at the denominational level surprisingly remain largely absent in scholarly literature, and this dearth of information is even more acute if one considers the number of declared sanctuaries in the 1980s alone—a number that does not account for the broader base of supporters in local and regional coalitions. The following list, published in *Basta!* in the summer of 1987, indicates that the number of declared sanctuaries varied significantly, with some traditions proportionally lending stronger support than others.

TABLE C.1 Source: *Basta!*, Summer 1987.

Roman Catholic	64	Methodist	14
Quakers/Friends	57	Mennonite	14
Unitarian/Universalist	67	Brethren	13
Jewish	37	Lutheran	11
Presbyterian	26	Baptist	7
United Church of Christ	11	Episcopal	6

Source: *Basta!*, Summer 1987.

Moreover, to best understand the range of religious foundations of sanctuary, further studies on non-Christian traditions deserve closer attention. Rachel Ida Buff has modeled this in her chapter on the New Jewish Agenda, but far more research on Jewish sanctuary organizing is in order for both the 1980s movement and the NSM. Presently, our understanding of Indigenous (e.g., Seminole and Wampanoag nation) forms of sanctuary remains far from complete, as the few notable expressions fell outside of the movement's own sense of history.[5] While the majority of Christian and Jewish sanctuary advocates have cited the Hebrew Bible as a point of genesis for the concept of sanctuary, others, too, turned to their set of histories and scriptures. In the New Sanctuary Movement, Muslim and Hindu congregations also declared sanctuary, albeit with mixed results. The study of these other forms of sanctuary would also shed light on the interreligious aspects of sanctuary.

Further local studies of sanctuary, both at the congregational and the regional level, would greatly contribute to our understanding of the movement. Such studies possess the potential to analyze dynamics that might be unique or perhaps comparable from one site to the next. Sergio González has repeatedly made a call for regional studies in his analysis of sanctuary mobilizations in the Midwest, while Mary Ward-Bucher's recently completed study serves as a model for the close study of religious sanctuary in a metropolitan area. Ward-Bucher's research on the 1980s Sanctuary Movement in Philadelphia reveals the evolving understanding of sanctuary supporters and clearly demonstrates how Central American organizers led many of the efforts rather than being passive actors.[6] Chapters 1 and 7, for example, briefly touch on episodes of sanctuary organizing in New England. Beyond this volume, scholars have begun the important work of excavating hyperlocal iterations of faith-based immigrant activism. Among them is Carlos Ruiz Martinez, who has studied the Catholic Sisters from the order of the Adorers of the Blood of Christ. Their sanctuary efforts continued until 1996 in Ruma, Illinois—past the early 1990s, the oft-cited end of the first iteration of the movement.[7] Other hubs of sanctuary organizing in places such as Albany, the Midwest (beyond Chicago), the Pacific Northwest, and even Texas and Florida, merit further study based solely on our assessment of the materials available for study in archives. Moving forward, comparative, multisited studies that link parish records, migrants' testimonies, and legal outcomes, especially work that centers voices of those sheltered, will be crucial for understanding how sanctuary remains both adaptive and contested in an era of intensified border controls and shifting religious landscapes. Kristina Shull calls for continued scholarship on a central tactic of the movement: truth telling by centering the voices and testimonies of people speaking truth to the harms of US war, imperial violence, ecocide, and genocide perpetrated abroad. An important record of the movement was its effort to build alternate spaces of care and compile an archive of irrefutable knowledge that could counteract the prevailing narrative posited by the Reagan administration. Sanctuary, as activists consistently noted, means refuge, safety, freedom, a place of study and reflection, and all that they hold sacred. Historians must assess how this foundational strategy has informed other grassroots movements for peace, justice, and rights.

As historians, we are particularly keen on the idea that no social phenomenon emerges from a vacuum. Contingencies and conditions shape actions and reactions as expressed across new geographical and temporal contexts. Whereas chapter 1 draws explicit links between sanctuary for Vietnam War resisters and the movement for Central American refugees, it raises questions such as the following: What tradition did Vietnam War resisters draw upon? What "usable sacred histories" did they invoke? And how is such use of sanctuary and conscience in wartime an international phenomenon? Such questions prompted Susan Bibler Coutin to query what forms of sanctuary—whether or not invoked by Vietnam War resisters and their supporters—fall between the New Underground Railroad and the 1960s?

Furthermore, this volume's modest attempts to link 1980s efforts to the NSM broach another important avenue of historical inquiry. Chapters 8 and 9 provide excellent examples of how to study the 1980s Sanctuary Movement and the NSM in tandem, with Lindskoog offering insight into the macro-level transitions and Castillo-Ramos providing a view of this change in California. In articles and chapters about the NSM, it has become somewhat of a convention to at least briefly gesture towards the 1980s movement. To point out that the NSM is a resurrection of the 1980s movement and its key tactics of civil disobedience and taking undocumented immigrants into houses of worship for protection is a necessary historical move, but such overarching claims still call for close studies. This closer study could be conducted by rendering narratives of sanctuary through the perspectives of key players or at the congregational level, as demonstrated in chapter 1, which reveals differing philosophies of sanctuary offered for war resisters and refugees.

The philosophical and human-rights principles that sanctuary rests upon occasion us to point out the paucity of work in this area of the literature. The historical intellectual underpinnings of ideas such as civil disobedience, civil initiative, nonviolence, and solidarity are ripe areas of study. Take, for example, the voluminous writing of Jim Corbett on these related issues, both his published and his unpublished manuscripts. Chapter 3 by Adam Waters, for example, draws out the influence of liberation theology on movement leaders in the 1980s. Waters has similarly offered a reassessment of Jim Corbett's idea of civil initiative, tracing its development over the course of the 1980s.[8] The intellectual histories of refuge traditions can, for example, have profound meaning for the way denominations choose to offer support. In *The Church as Sanctuary*, historical theologian Leo Guardado offers a clear-eyed view on why the Catholic Church should reinscribe sanctuary provisions into its canon law.[9] These studies, whether anchored in historical theology, philosophy, or intellectual history, offer much to study about sanctuary, a tradition grounded in ideas of human rights.

Its wide and varied expressions notwithstanding, the term "sanctuary" as employed throughout this volume remains rather stable. It is a recognizable term and tradition invoked by congregations when other options for reprieve have been expended. Exceeding the term's use in the 1980s, as described by Grace Yukich in the context of the NSM, sanctuary operates as a moniker, identity, and strategy.[10] Such a growth in sanctuary's applicability and appropriation reminds us of the call issued by A. Naomi Paik, Jason Ruiz, and Rebecca M. Schreiber in their introduction to the 2019 special issue of the *Radical History Review* on the topic of "Radical Histories of Sanctuary." In it, they prompt historians to interrogate "sanctuary's expansive conceptual range."[11] Recent ethnographies, including that by Barbara Sostaita and volume contributor Gina Pérez, do exactly that while also expanding upon the way sanctuary and the sacred intermingle as categories in the lives of communities of care.[12]

But even in the 1980s, when it seemed so clear to many that sanctuary was based on religious principles of conscience, hospitality, and accompaniment, critics, as shown in chapter 6, attempted to portray it as merely political. Such attempts to paint sanctuary as political and not religious might have reflected a concern with the newly established Christian Right and its attempt to wrest control of religion in the public square and politics from the well-established but declining Protestant establishment. Who gets to lay claim to doing the work of public religion in America? And how does this limit or expand what is meant by "religion"? The Sanctuary Trial of 1985–1986 offers one such case to consider the ramifications of a government entity circumscribing the meaning of sanctuary and the very nature of what constitutes "religion" and "religious." The Sanctuary Trial never settled that question thanks to the presiding judge's granting of a pretrial motion *in limine* to prohibit mention of the defendants' religious motivations. But in order to convince the federal government to indict the sanctuary workers in the first place, government-hired spies infiltrated Bible studies and church services to record and collect intel. Similarly, with such persistent categories of the "religious" and "political" still at play, even into the present day, further studies on sanctuary ought to examine how the categories of "religious" and "secular" are troubled in phenomena such as sanctuary cities wherein clergy have played no small role in shaping local policy, not necessarily as private individuals but in their role as faith leaders.

Finally, perhaps the most challenging future direction we note concerns archival collections. Historians can only tell a story as complete as the sources made available to them. Because sanctuary relied heavily on media coverage to tell its story, the world of online and digital sources presents many possibilities for study as well as challenges in terms of retrieving materials. Whereas a considerable amount of material for the 1980s Sanctuary Movement has been formally collected in archives and special collections, there remain many regions, cities, and congregations that lack representation in these sites. Here, we commend the work of volume contributor Rady Roldán-Figueroa in leading a team of students and professors to recover 1980s sanctuary materials from basements and offices of houses of worship in New England, in an effort to permit greater access to these materials at Boston University.

Having examined materials from congregations in New England, Roldán-Figueroa notes that the role of arts and artist networks in the Sanctuary Movement demands attention from a multidisciplinary bench of scholars. He observes that New England provides an excellent example of how sanctuary activists tapped into a rich network of artists with a history of solidarity in the civil rights movement, the anti–Vietnam War movement, and the anti–nuclear proliferation movement. Singers and composers such as Carolyn McDade and Andrea Ayvazian crafted lyrics that inspired the movement and captured for posterity the conscience of a crucial time in American social protest movements. The author and puppeteer Wes Sanders lent his creative gifts and vision to establishing graphic connections between the Sanctuary Movement and the history of abolitionism in the United States.

Looking ahead, the past several decades of sanctuary organizing offer vital lessons for the future of faith-based immigrant activism. The movement's history shows the necessity of innovation—of adapting strategies to shifting political landscapes while holding fast to core commitments of solidarity and justice. Sanctuary has always been more than a shelter; it has been a site of *conscientización*, a process of raising collective consciousness and reshaping public opinion on immigration in ways that can outlast momentary shifts in voter sentiment. To carry that legacy forward, religious activism must not lose its political edge. Its power lies not only in providing direct relief to those facing detention and deportation but in advancing a deeper moral and structural transformation of the nation's immigration system itself. As one sanctuary organizer noted in 1987, sanctuary "can best be humanitarian if it is sufficiently political to end the war that creates death, misery and refugees."[13]

NOTES

1 Peter Mancina, "The Birth of a Sanctuary-City: A History of Governmental Sanctuary in San Francisco," in *Sanctuary Practices in International Perspectives: Migration, Citizenship, and Social Movements*, ed. Randy Lippert and Sean Rehaag (Routledge, 2012), 206–9. On the overlap of sanctuary from religious spaces to secular ones, see Loren Collingwood and Benjamin Gonzalez O'Brien, *Sanctuary Cities: The Politics of Refuge* (Oxford University Press, 2019); Melvin Delgado, *Sanctuary Cities, Communities, and Organizations* (Oxford University Press, 2018).

2 Randy K. Lippert and Sean Rehaag, "Introduction: Sanctuary Across Countries, Institutions, and Disciplines," in *Sanctuary Practices in International Perspectives: Migration, Citizenship, and Social Movements*, ed. Randy Lippert and Sean Rehaag (Routledge, 2012), 2–3. See also Randy K. Lippert, *Sanctuary, Sovereignty, Sacrifice: Canadian Sanctuary Incidents, Power, and Law* (UBC Press, 2005); Laura Madokoro, *Sanctuary in Pieces: Two Centuries of Flight, Fugitivity, and Resistance in a North American City* (McGill-Queen's University Press, 2024).

3 Maria Cristina Garcia, *Seeking Refuge: Central American Migration to Mexico, the United States, and Canada* (University of California Press, 2006), 44–83.

4 For one example of sanctuary studied at this level see Sergio M. González, "Catholics and the 1980s U.S. Sanctuary Movement," *U.S. Catholic Historian* 42, no. 2 (Spring 2024): 87–110.

5 Lloyd D. Barba, "'An Historic and Hallowed Principle in Religious Life': The Usable Sacred Histories of the 1980s Sanctuary Movement," *Journal of the American Academy of Religion* 93, no. 1 (March 2025): 32–33.

6 Sergio M. González, *Strangers No Longer: Latino Belonging and Faith in Twentieth-Century Wisconsin* (University of Illinois Press, 2024), 172–202; Sergio M. González, "Refugees, Religious Space, and Sanctuary in Wisconsin," in *Building Sustainable Worlds: Latinx Placemaking in the Midwest*, ed. Theresa Delgadillo, Ramón H. Rivera-Servera, Geraldo L. Cadava, and Claire F. Fox (University of

Illinois Press, 2022), 182–203; Mary Ward-Bucher, "Reconciling Liberation and Charity: Central American Leadership in the 1980s Philadelphia Sanctuary Movement" (PhD diss., Temple University, 2023).

7 Carlos Ruiz Martínez, "The Question of Sanctuary: The Adorers of the Blood of Christ and the U.S. Sanctuary Movement, 1983–1996," *U.S. Catholic Historian* 38, no. 4 (Fall 2020): 51–68.

8 Adam Waters, "Alternative Internationalisms: The Sanctuary Movement and Jim Corbett's Civil Initiative," *Diplomatic History* 46, no. 5 (November 2022): 984–1009.

9 Leo Guardado, *Church as Sanctuary: Reconstructing Refuge in an Age of Forced Displacement* (Orbis Books, 2023).

10 Grace Yukich, *One Family Under God: Immigration Politics and Progressive Religion in America* (Oxford University Press, 2013), 6.

11 A. Naomi Paik, Jason Ruiz, and Rebecca M. Schreiber, "Editor's Introduction: Sanctuary's Radical Networks," *Radical History Review* 135 (November 2019): 1–13, cited on 3.

12 Barbara Andrea Sostaita, *Sanctuary Everywhere: The Fugitive Sacred in the Sonoran Desert* (Duke University Press, 2024); Gina M. Pérez, *Sanctuary People: Faith-Based Organizing in a Latina/o Community* (NYU Press, 2024).

13 Malcolm Bell, "Unlocking the Political Handcuffs," *Basta!*, June 1987.

ABOUT THE CONTRIBUTORS

Lloyd D. Barba is Associate Professor of Religion and Core Faculty in Latinx and Latin American Studies at Amherst College. There he teaches courses on American religious history, Evangelicalism, immigration, and the Sanctuary Movement. He is the author of the award-winning book *Sowing the Sacred: Mexican Pentecostal Farmworkers in California* (2022), coeditor of *Oneness Pentecostalism: Race, Gender, and Culture* (2023), and editor of *Latin American and Latino Religions in North America: An Introduction* (2024). His research on sanctuary builds on his previous and ongoing scholarship on Latino immigration and the history of farm workers in California. His scholarship on sanctuary has appeared in numerous books and academic journals such as the *Journal of the American Academy of Religion* and *American Religion.* Along with Sergio González, he coauthored articles for media outlets such as *Time* and *Dissent Magazine.* Together, they also coauthored *Sanctuary in America: How Activists Defied the Government and Defended Immigrants–And What It Still Matters* (2026) and coauthored and cohosted the seven-episode limited podcast series *Sanctuary: On the Border Between Church and State*, produced by Axis Mundi Media. His forthcoming book on sanctuary is titled *A Refuge of Resistance: A History of the US Sanctuary Movement.* Barba received his PhD in American Culture from the University of Michigan and his BA in Religious Studies and History from the University of the Pacific.

Rachel Ida Buff is a writer, organizer, and working historian currently teaching at the University of Wisconsin–Milwaukee. She is the author of the bilingual book *A Is for Asylum Seeker: Words for People on the Move/A de Asilio: Palabras para Personas en Movimiento* and is currently working on a book tentatively entitled "The Gangster Buffs of Charleston, West Virginia: Jewish Safety in a 20th-Century Appalachian City."

TATYANA CASTILLO-RAMOS is a Postdoctoral Fellow in the Religion Department at Reed College. She earned her PhD in Religious Studies at Yale University with a specialization in American Religious History. Her work focuses on how friendship and militarization overlap and overlie each other in the creation of sacralized space at the binational Friendship Park. She has authored several articles and chapters on the Sanctuary Movement.

SUSAN BIBLER COUTIN is Professor in the Departments of Criminology, Law and Society, and Anthropology at the University of California–Irvine. She is author of *The Culture of Protest: Religious Activism and the U.S. Sanctuary Movement* (1993), *Legalizing Moves: Salvadoran Immigrants' Struggle for U.S. Residency* (2000), *Nations of Emigrants: Shifting Boundaries of Citizenship in El Salvador and the United States* (2007), and *Exiled Home: Salvadoran Transnational Youth in the Aftermath of Violence* (2016). She is coauthor with Barbara Yngvesson of *Documenting Impossible Realities: Ethnography, Memory, and the "As-If"* (2023) and coauthor with Jennifer Chacón and Stephen Lee of *Legal Phantoms: Executive Action and the Haunting Failures of Immigration Law* (2024). Her most recent book, *On the Record: Papers, Immigration, and Legal Advocacy*, was published in August 2025 and is available open-access.

SERGIO M. GONZÁLEZ is Associate Professor of History at Marquette University. He is a historian of twentieth-century US migration, labor, and religion, and his scholarship explores the intersections between faith and social movements as well as the development of Latino communities in the US Midwest. He is the author of *Mexicans in Wisconsin* (2017) and the coeditor of *Faith and Power: Latino Religious Politics Since 1945* (NYU Press, 2022) with Felipe Hinojosa and Maggie Elmore. His most recently published book, *Strangers No Longer: Latino Belonging and Faith in Twentieth-Century Wisconsin* (2024), explores the relationship among Latino communities, religion, and social movements in the twentieth-century Midwest. Along with Lloyd D. Barba, he coauthored articles for media outlets such as Time and Dissent Magazine. Together, they also coauthored *Sanctuary in America: How Activists Defied the Government and Defended Immigrants–And Why It Still Matters* (2026) and coauthored and cohosted the seven-episode limited podcast series *Sanctuary: On the Border Between Church and State*, produced by Axis Mundi

Media. González's current research examines the contentious battles over sanctuary movements in the late twentieth and early twenty-first centuries, exploring the pivotal role people of faith have played in developing contemporary social movements for immigrant and refugee justice as well as the opposing political movements that have risen to criminalize these forms of solidarity. Along with his academic scholarship, González is a committed public historian. He is engaged in several public humanities projects, including cowriting and cohosting *The Look Back*, a social studies show for middle school students on Wisconsin PBS, and serving as a founding member of the Wisconsin Latinx History Collective.

Katherine Holding is US Teaching Assistant through Fulbright Austria. A graduate of Amherst College, where she majored in History and Religion, she has conducted archival research on the Sanctuary Movement at Harvard University, Yale University, Swarthmore College, New York University, and MIT, and in Boston-area congregations.

Carl Lindskoog is Professor of History at Raritan Valley Community College and a member of the editorial board of the *Oxford Research Encyclopedia of Migration Studies*. He is the author of "Sanctuary Is Justice: Resilience and Ingenuity in the Sanctuary Movement Since 1986," in *Whose America? U.S. Immigration Policy Since 1980* (2023) and *Detain and Punish: Haitian Refugees and the Rise of the World's Largest Immigration Detention System* (2018).

Gina M. Pérez is a cultural anthropologist and Professor in the Comparative American Studies Department at Oberlin College. She is the author of two award-winning books—*The Near Northwest Side Story: Gender, Migration, and Puerto Rican Families* (2004) and *Citizen, Student, Soldier: Latina/o Youth, JROTC, and the American Dream* (NYU Press, 2015). She is also the coeditor of two anthologies: *Beyond el Barrio: Everyday Life in Latina/o America* (coedited with Frank Guridy and Adrian Burgos Jr., NYU Press, 2011) and *Ethnographic Refusals, Unruly Latinidades* (coedited with Alex Chávez, 2022). Her most recent book is titled *Sanctuary People: Faith-Based Organizing in Latina/o Communities* and focuses on responses by faith communities and secular activists from 2016 to 2020.

RADY ROLDÁN-FIGUEROA, ThD (Boston University), is Professor of the History of Christianity at Boston University School of Theology. An early modernist, he focuses the bulk of his research and writing on questions of European expansionism, global Christianity, and colonialism. The author of *The Ascetic Spirituality of Juan de Avila (1499–1569)* (2010) and *The Martyrs of Japan: Publication History and Catholic Missions in the Spanish World (Spain, New Spain, and the Philippines, 1597–1700)* (2021), he is also coeditor with David Orique of *The Transatlantic Las Casas: Historical Trajectories, Indigenous Cultures, Scholastic Thought, and Reception in History* (2023). In 2015, he began with Daryl Ireland the Sanctuary Project, a research initiative dedicated to documenting the history of the 1980s Sanctuary Movement in New England.

KRISTINA SHULL is Associate Professor of History at the University of North Carolina–Charlotte, specializing in race, empire, immigration enforcement, and climate migration in the modern United States and the world. She holds a PhD in History from UC–Irvine, a Master's in Humanities and Social Thought from New York University, and a BA in History from UCLA. Her 2022 book *Detention Empire: Reagan's War on Immigrants and the Seeds of Resistance*, explores the rise of migrant detention in the early 1980s as a form of counterinsurgency. Shull is also the creator of the digital history projects IMM Print, Climate Refugee Stories, and Climate Inequality CLT, and lead curator of the *Climates of Inequality: Charlotte* museum exhibit.

MARY WARD-BUCHER, an advocate for humanistic learning and community-engaged scholarship, is an academic affairs administrator and adjunct faculty member at Temple University College of Liberal Arts. In prior roles, she helped manage interfaith programming for the nonprofit Dialogue Institute as well as community-engaged learning programs at Temple University. She has also participated in leadership and service with several local and global advocacy and relief organizations.

ADAM WATERS is a PhD candidate in modern US and Latin American history at Yale University and an organizer with Local 33-UNITE HERE! Waters is the author of "Alternative Internationalisms: The Sanctuary Movement and Jim Corbett's Civil Initiative," published in *Diplomatic History* 46, no. 5 (November 2022).

INDEX